Madeira, The Island Vineyard

Cyprus and Paphos vales, the smiling Loves
Might leave with joy for fair Madeira's groves;
A shore so flowery, and so sweet an air,
Venus might build her dearest temple there.

From Camoens' Lusiad, 1569, Volume I Canto V

NOEL COSSART'S
MADEIRA
THE ISLAND VINEYARD

Original text by
Noël Cossart

New introductory and postscript material by
Emanuel Berk

Revised Second Edition
2011
The Rare Wine Co.
Sonoma, California

This is a revised second edition of *Madeira, The Island Vineyard*,
which was originally published by
Christie's Wine Publications, 1984.

The original material in this book was copyrighted to Noël
Cossart in 1984. The copyright for all material new to the
second edition belongs to Emanuel Berk © 2011.

This new edition is published by:

The Rare Wine Co.
21481 Eighth Street East
Sonoma, California 95476
www.rarewineco.com

ISBN 978-0-578-06647-9

This book is typeset in Weiss, designed in 1926 by Rudolf Weiss
for the Bauer foundry of Frankfurt, Germany,
and is printed on Huron Matte paper
Printing: Thomson-Shore, Inc.
Layout: Dorothy Scott
Indexing: Thérèse Shere
Proofreading: Denise LaVenter
Jacket Design: Russell Shaddox

Endpaper image: "Pátio da casa de vinhos 'Cossart, Gordon & Co,"
an undated, early 20th-century photograph by Perestrellos.
Collection of Museu Photographia Vicentes, Funchal, Madeira.

PREFACE

My late father's book, published in 1984, was out of print for many years, and since the demise of Christie's Wine Publications, it seemed destined to future oblivion. It is therefore with great pleasure and gratitude that I salute Mannie Berk for his energy and enthusiasm in re-publishing *Madeira, The Island Vineyard*—and making it available to a new generation of Madeira lovers.

Noël loved story telling. Consequently, I always felt that much of the allure of this book lay in its being more a succession of stories—or more correctly speaking histories, since they are factual—than a dossier of winemaking technology which has become more or less de rigueur now.

This is perhaps more in the style of previous generations of wine writers, such as P. Morton Shand, the author of four wine books early in the last century—and father of my late partner and director of Cossart, Gordon & Co. Ltd., Major Bruce Shand. It was Bruce who did so much to support and encourage the resumption of our trading in the U.K. in the late 1970's. Bruce also ensured that our Madeiras enjoyed an important place in the cellars of the colleges in Oxford and Cambridge Universities.

While the histories of the families and characters who once made and shipped Madeira are as romantic as the island is beautiful, this is not to suggest that winemaking in Madeira today has remained static and hidebound. The island's few remaining producers have kept abreast of modern developments, and they can be proud of the way they've balanced tradition against new technologies.

Similarly, there have been striking changes in the island itself. A new infrastructure of roads, tunnels, and dual-carriageways has reduced to one hour journeys that—when I was a child growing up on the island—took a whole day to complete. And the airport is able to handle a daunting volume of passengers to occupy the ever increasing number of hotels.

This is in stark contrast to the days when I and the island's other

British children were dispatched, aged eight, to the proscribed British boarding schools for our education. The only option then was a sea journey of three or four days on the Union Castle Steamers which stopped at Madeira en route to and from South Africa. An airport on the mountainous terrain of the island was inconceivable.

In the 1950s came an important leap forward with the advent of "Aquila Airways," whose unpressurized Sunderland Flying Boats were salvaged from the British Army Air Corps at the conclusion of World War II. The flying boats reduced the journey to anything between 7 and 24 hours, depending upon weather conditions. Sometimes shelter would have to be taken at Vigo, in northern Spain, Lisbon, Canary islands, or even north Africa.

But in the 1940s, there were no flying boats, and we had no choice but to travel by ship. Our "odysseys" would be "topped and tailed" by running the gauntlet of being met at Southampton Water by an unknown "universal aunt" and accompanied vigilantly on the school train to be delivered for the next, seemingly interminable months of incarceration. It was a toss-up as to whether these Mary Poppins-like figures, clad from head to foot in stiff navy blue felt, would turn out to be a Snow White or Cruella De Vil.

But very much more dramatic changes have been wrought on the island recently. In February of this year, 2010, catastrophic storms and mud slides resulted in over 40 deaths and colossal damage to houses, businesses, roads and vineyards. As I write this just two months after, the long-term repercussions are still unknown.

In my own family, my younger cousin, John de Bianchi Cossart, the last member of the family to be actively involved in the Madeira Trade, died tragically two years ago while celebrating his 63rd birthday. This makes me the only surviving bearer of the Cossart name to have been involved in the shipping of Madeira wine.

Producing a book is hard work, and the birth-pangs of the first publication were not trivial. My father had recently "retired" from Madeira to Suffolk, England—the reverse of the usual retirement route—and was tempted by more leisurely country pursuits. But Michael Broadbent M.W., then head of Christie's Wine Department and Christie's Wine Publications, succeeded in patiently coaxing and cajoling him to complete the book.

Looking back, I can not help but remark, with affection and admiration, that this was achieved with the same tenacity—not to mention an iron fist in a velvet glove—as when he encouraged and supported my struggle to attain the "Master of Wine" qualification in 1973, whilst working with him at Christie's. "That, and better, will do," he sometimes would say, an inspiration which still makes me feel privileged to have worked at his elbow. Without him and his team, the first edition of this book would not have seen daylight.

Equally, without Mannie, the second edition would not have come to fruition, and I am certain that my father would have been warmed and proud that his work is being revived in this manner. It is a further tribute to his beloved Madeira, "enduring and endearing."

David Cossart

Suffolk
Summer 2010

ACKNOWLEDGMENTS

Noël Cossart

I am deeply indebted to all those who have assisted me in my research. In particular I have to thank the following friends in Madeira: Eng. Francisco Perry Vidal, ex-agronomist head of the Estacão Agraria da Madeira, Eng. Rui Fontes, regional minister, agriculture and fisheries, Sr. João Carlos Abreu, regional minister, culture and tourism, David Pamment, managing director, Madeira Wine Co. Limitada, and his staff, Eng. João Teixeira and Dr. L. M. Ritto, respectively ex-technical and ex-financial directors of the Madeira Wine Co. Limitada, Dr. João Cabral do Nascimento of the Madeira District Archives, the late Dr. Fredrico de Freitas, Eng. Luiz Clode, Richard Blandy, William Leacock, Jeremy Zino, Peter Cossart, Anthony de B. Cossart-Miles, Mario Barbeito de Vasconcelos, and the late Solomão de Veiga Franca; and in England, Professor J. M. Ward of Earsham, Norfolk, Dr. C. F. Timberlake of Long Ashton Research Station, A. C. Simpson of IDV Technical Services, Pamela Vandyke Price, Mrs. South, Mrs. Roper, David Cossart MW, Dr. Dennis Babbage, President of Magdalene College Cambridge, and Professor Kendal Dixon, King's College Cambridge. Among those in the United States I am especially indebted to Mrs. Margaret Hill Collins, J. Malcolm Bell Jr. and Mills B. Lane of the Madeira Club of Savannah. Perestrellos Photographos and Photographia Vicente of Funchal have assisted with the illustrations. Many thanks are also due to F. Allan Cash Ltd., the Georgia Historical Society, Savannah, the Portuguese National Tourist Office and the Rainbird Publishing Company for supplying some of the photographs; also to the Telfair Academy of Arts and Science for permission to use the photographs of the Owens-Thomas House, Savannah, taken by Pollack and Daly Photography. The map on page 8 was drawn by Eygene Fleury. Anna Ward, Debbie Hamilton, Patricia Hood and Loveday Bolitho have been invaluable typing the manuscript. Finally, my best thanks to Christie's publications team: Michael Broadbent MW, Patrick Matthews, Rosemary Ward, Christopher Bradshaw, Alison Stanford and Naomi Good; and above all to Penelope Mansell-Jones MW, without whom this book would not have been possible.

Emanuel Berk

In the republication of *Madeira, The Island Vineyard*, my greatest debt is to the Cossart family: Noël's widow Pat Coates, his son David, his daughter Anna and his late nephew John Cossart. I suspect that I have not done as good a job as Noël did in keeping track of all the others who helped me, but from the Island of Madeira, I will mention particularly: Anthony Miles, Ricardo D. V. Freitas of Vinhos Barbeito, Luis D'Oliveira of Pereira D'Oliveira, Marianna Pinto of Barbeito, Adam Blandy, Francisco Albuquerque of the Madeira Wine Company, Dr. Helena Araújo of the Museum Vicentes, Ana Margarida Araújo Camacho of the Frederico de Freitas House-Museum, Dr. Paolo Rodrigues, former director of the IVBAM (Instituto do Vinho, do Bordado e do Artesanato da Madeira) and the late João Borges. In England, I must thank Alex Liddell, David Boobbyer, Ana Cossart Hall, John Avery, Patrick Grubb and Rupert and Anne Mullins, and in the United States, Gail Unzelman, John Skarstad of the University of California at Davis Library, Christine Nelson of the J.P. Morgan Library and David Hancock. Everyone at The Rare Wine Co., in both California and Connecticut, contributed to this book in one way or another, but I owe particular thanks to Jennifer Lieb, Janna Fuller, Paul Tortora, Denise LaVenter, Greg Dolgushkin and, of course my wife Jill, whose contributions range from the tangible to the incalculable.

CONTENTS

Preface

Acknowledgements

List of Illustrations

Introduction to the First Edition, *xvii*

Introduction to the Second Edition, *xxiii*

Foreword, *xxvii*

Noël Cossart, A Life in Wine, *xxxvii*

1. The Discovery of Madeira, *3*
2. The Madeira Islands, *15*
3. Birth of the Wine Trade, *31*
4. The Wine Merchants, *51*
5. The Market in India, *71*
6. Madeira in North America, *79*
7. Vines and Vineyards, *99*
8. Oidium, Phylloxera and Changing Markets, *115*
9. Wine Making, *127*
10. Types of Madeira, *141*
11. Vintage Madeiras, *153*
12. Soleras and Dated Soleras, *167*
13. William Neyle Habersham, *175*
14. Some Great Collections, *185*
15. Three Madeira Tastings, *191*

16   Getting the Most Out of Your Madeira, *195*

Appendices

I   Madeira Vintages, 1774-1956, *211*
II   Notes on Vintages, 1863 to 1981, *215*
III   Madeira at Auction, *219*
IV   Important Auctions of Madeira, *237*
V   Cossart, Gordon Principals, 1745 to 1990, *245*
VI   Madeira Wine Shippers, 1722-1880, *247*
VII   Shippers and Importers, 1984-2010, *253*
VIII   Early Settlers, *255*
IX   Municipal Districts, *263*
X   Quintas and Houses, *265*
XI   Robert Allston's Madeiras, *269*
XII   Elizabeth David and "The Napoleon Madeira," *273*
XIII   Madeira's Flying Boat Era, *279*
XIV   Roy Brady, *287*
XV   John Delaforce, *295*
XVI   The Habersham Sale, *299*
XVII   Habersham's "Hurricane," *303*

Glossary, *305*

Bibliography, *311*

Notes, *319*

Illustration Credits, *323*

Index

LIST OF ILLUSTRATIONS

Noël and David Cossart, *xvi*
Noël Cossart as a Child (three photos), *xxxviii*
Château Cossart, *xxxix*
Cossarts and Friends at Quinta do Monte, 1892, *xl*
Charles Blandy Cossart, *xlii*
The Cossart, Gordon Lodge, *xliii*
Noël Cossart as a Young Man (two photos), *xlv*
Graf Zeppelin I over Funchal, 1934, *xlvi*
Ellis Son & Vidler's Cellars, *liii*
Ellis Son & Vidler Silver Jubilee Madeira, *liv*
Cossart, Gordon 1984 Advertisement, *lv*
Program for 1984 Book Launching in Savannah, *lviii*
Alcaforado's *Discovery of Madeira*, *4*
Prince Henry the Navigator, *9*
Zarco's Statue in Funchal, *10*
Columbus' House, *14*
Looking Inland from near Faial, *16*
Agricultural Instruments, *19*
Levada near Santo da Serra, *21*
View from Cape Girão, *22*
Funchal, *27*
Banana Plantations near Funchal, *28*
Cabin Plan for the Madeira Packet Eclipse, *29*
Princess Maria Pia de Saboia's arrival in Madeira, *30*
Francis Newton, *31*
Thomas Murdoch, *31*
The Burying Ground by Henry Veitch, *38*

Funchal from the Bay by Andrew Picken, 1840, *39*
John Leacock's 1741 Indenture, *41*
Entrance to St. John's Vineyard, *45*
Henry Veitch's house, Jardim da Serra, *47*
Dr. Richard Hill's Quinta Achada, *52*
Charles John Cossart, *55*
Russell Manners Gordon, *55*
Peter Cossart, *56*
Quinta do Monte, *57*
John Blandy, *59*
Charles Ridpath Blandy, *60*
Henry P. Miles, *62*
Hugo Krohn, *63*
Carlo de Bianchi with Noël Cossart, *64*
The Cossarts at Quinta do Monte, 1888, *66*
The Madeira Wine Association's Lodge, 1925, *67*
H.M. Borges' Lodge, *69*
Christie's Auction, 1828, *72*
Cossart, Gordon Publicity, early 20th century, *74*
1763 New York Bill of Lading, *80*
Boston's Club Gastronomique Menu, *82*
United States Hotel, New York, Madeira bill, 1831, *85*
S. Weir Mitchell's A Madeira Party, *86*
The Madeira Club of Savannah, 1976, *90*
Wine Cellars in the Owens-Thomas House, *91*
Opening the Able Madeira, *93*
Grapes Await Pressing at Cossart, Gordon, *103*
Terraced Vineyards at Cama do Lobos, *105*
Câmara de Lobos, *118*
Bella Phelps' Embroidery Designs, *120*
Joseph and Elizabeth Phelps, *121*
Barrels at H.M. Borges, *124*
Loading Borges Barrels on Ship, *125*
Borracheiros in Funchal, *128*

A Lagar, *129*
Armazem de Calor, *133*
Leacock's Cooperage, *137*
Madeira Wine Association's Barrels, 1932, *142*
Cossart, Gordon Price List, 1895, *145*
Cossart, Gordon's Oxen, *149*
The Famous 1808 Solera Pipe, *152*
Winston Churchill Painting in Câmara de Lobos, 1950, *156*
Torre Bella Wine Label, *157*
The Palacio de Torre Bella, Funchal, *158*
Vintage and Solera Madeiras, Madeira Wine Company, *159*
Esquin & Co. Catalogue, 1968, *160*
Cossart, Gordon's 1846 Terrantez, *162*
A Typical Solera Store, *169*
Cossart, Gordon Solera, Bottled 1940, *170*
Noël Cossart's Father and Grandfather by Vizetelly, *173*
William Neyle Habersham's house, Savannah, Georgia, *177*
Shipping Manifest, *The Waccamaw*, 1836, *179*
Ward McAllister, *182*
Bill of Lading per *Two Sisters*, 1780, *183*
Michael Grabham, *185*
Sir Stephen Gaselee, *188*
Going to a Picnic in Madeira, *202*
Mountains from Pico Arieiro, *210*

Maps
Mid-19th Century Map of Madeira, *xxii*
The Medici Map (portion), 1351, *7*
Madeira's Geographical Position, *8*
Coronelli's Map of Madeira & the Canaries, c. 1690, *50*
Bowen's Map of Madeira, 1752, *50*
Map of Madeira, 1984, from the 1st Edition, *98*

Noël Cossart and his son David.

INTRODUCTION TO THE FIRST EDITION

The word "book" is derived from a combination of the old English *boc*, Danish *beuke* and German *buche*, all of which mean beech tree, possibly from the days before printing, when words were carved on beech bark. I am one of those who carve rather than take pen to paper; however, I have endeavored to write what I have learnt about the island I love and its wine. I know every part of Madeira, having explored it on foot, horseback, by boat and motor car; and, having spent over half a century in the Madeira wine trade, I think I probably know more about the wine than anyone else alive. There is no merit in this. It is simply because I have survived all those who knew more than I do.

I was born saturated in Madeira wine. On my father's side the family had been in the trade for five generations, spanning 180 years. On my mother's side the family grew vines and traded in Madeira wine for four generations. My father's mother was a Blandy and my sister married a Miles of Rutherford & Miles. Unlike other old Madeira families who started as wine shippers and then branched into other business, the Cossarts have always limited themselves to the wine trade, relying on it for their existence.

I have been most fortunate in that the archives of Cossart, Gordon & Co. have been preserved intact from the first letter of its founder, Francis Newton, written in 1748 to his brother in Virginia. These archives comprise 257 calf-bound volumes of "letters outward" up to 1889, written by partners and copied into books in fine copper-plate handwriting by wives and daughters. After 1889, letters were copied by letterpress. There are 208 account ledgers and 171 boxes packed with "letters inward," invoices, bills of lading and accounts, all neatly tied in bundles with red tape. I also inherited my great-grandfather's extensive library of books on Madeira and wine, to which my grandfather and my father and I have added. My library now consists of over

1,000 volumes, scrap-books, cuttings, maps and pamphlets referring to Madeira. I think I can safely say I have just about everything written about the island in all languages.

With such a wealth of information at my disposal I thought I should write about Madeira. I started collecting material in 1945 but did not get much further than that; there were more enjoyable things to do than writing, such as wine, women and song, not to mention *le sport*, balls, picnics and parties.

I had a burst of enthusiasm when the late Raymond Postgate, an eminent historian as well as a wine writer, came to Madeira to write a Christmas piece for *Lilliput*.

He encouraged me, and I wrote some history. I had written articles on Madeira for periodicals in the United States, Denmark, Germany and the United Kingdom, but a book is quite a different matter. In 1952, Mrs. Elizabeth Nicholas came out to Madeira to research for *Madeira and the Canaries*. She came to see me because she was having difficulty in obtaining historical information regarding the old English firms, so I placed the firm's archives and my library at her disposal. Although her book is about the island and not the wine, I am most grateful to Mrs. Nicholas because, as well as helping herself, she obtained material for me which I did not know existed. In thanking me from London, she wrote: "Finally—you may well think that I do not know enough about Madeira to write a book, to which I would reply that I know my limitations! But those who have lived longest in Madeira are not professional writers, and somehow, they never *do* get round to putting their knowledge on paper." Mrs. Nicholas's successful book stimulated me to continue my own writing. Then Rupert Croft-Cooke came to Funchal to gather material for his book on Madeira wine. I had been impressed by his writing; he was a professional, with a fine style, so knowing he would make a good job of it I gave Rupert my notes. He kindly presented a copy of *Madeira* to me at the launching in October 1961 inscribed on the fly leaf "For Noël Cossart who practically wrote it."

Soon after the publication of Rupert's book, an old friend, Douglas Sutherland, who was in charge of the Madeira advertising campaign, wrote to me suggesting he should come to the island to write a book on the wine, based on facts I could provide. I was about to agree to this when another friend arrived. This was Al Perkins, a New Yorker born and bred, who had spent his working life editing or writing for American magazines. Al and his wife Jane had retired to Bermuda but, finding it was dearer than New York, or even Florida, settled in Madeira. Al amused himself by writing magazine articles about the island, and finally suggested that we should collaborate on a book. Of course I jumped at his proposal and we started to write. But sadly Al died, and when I then turned to Douglas I found he was far too busy writing books about English gentlemen, their wives and mistresses, so I decided to tackle it myself.

I was still working at the time, and also doing a good deal of sailing, but the book progressed slowly and surely, until the manuscript was destroyed by fire in 1969. I was quite despondent: not only had I lost my manuscript, but reams of notes resulting from years of historical research. In January 1972 Michael and Daphne Broadbent came to Madeira. Michael waved a big stick at me, encouraging me to start up again. He is very persuasive and, I should imagine, a hard task master. He is of a generation which, in the Elysian days, when the Wine Trade Club flourished at 8 Lloyds Avenue, was known as "Harvey's bright boys."

Although by then I had retired, except for directorships of Cossart, Gordon & Co. Ltd., and the Madeira Wine Association Lda., I had obtained the Hertz franchise for Madeira, renting a fleet of 24 cars, which became a 14-hour a day pastime. All my old sailing companions had either died or left the island so I had to cruise single-handed, taking on students when I raced. These boys were fine dinghy sailors, but had jerky movements and were usually sea sick. Moreover, they could not navigate, which was dangerous should anything happen to me. At last I decided to sell my boat and my *quinta* and, finally, to retire and leave the island.

In 1976 my family and I moved to England, settling in Bungay, a charming market town on the Norfolk/Suffolk border, in some of the most picturesque countryside in England. That year was an important one in the history of Cossart, Gordon and Co. It was the year in which my son David took on an active role in London, shipping Madeira to England, the United States and Canada, and my nephew, Anthony Cossart-Miles, took over the management of the company's interests in Madeira; it also marked 51 years that I had been in the wine trade, both in London and Madeira. The object of coming to live in England was that it would be conducive to writing and, with nothing to distract me, I would finish my book in the long winter evenings. It took us some time to settle ourselves into our new house. When this was completed, however, to my surprise and joy I discovered the pleasures of English country sports and pastimes. Gardening, which never attracted me in Madeira, because one had gardeners, and flowers just happened, I now found to be a real challenge. Shooting, fishing and wild fowling are probably the best in England, so long winter evenings were spent on the marshes, or in a pub recalling the duck one never hit. My book remained in the inkpot although I did write articles for the *Journal of the International Wine & Food Society*, for *Christie's Wine Companion*, and the Madeira section of the new edition of André Simon's *Wines of the World*, edited by Serena Sutcliffe. I also collaborated with Phillip Allen in his *Atlantic Crossing Guide* for the Royal Cruising Club's Pilotage Foundation. On May 6, 1981, I met Patrick Matthews in Norwich and after an excellent lunch at the Hotel Nelson he formally commissioned me to write this book for Christie's Wine Publications.

I am old fashioned and conservative, so the opinions expressed in this book are personal and should be seen in that light; and if I mention the Cossart company, its wines and my family more than others, it is simply because I am better acquainted with them, and have had the good fortune to draw upon our unusually complete records.

Finally, I fervently hope that this record of the old and fascinating history of the island and its wines will stimulate readers to visit those shores and, above all, to enjoy the wine from the sunny slopes, thus assisting to restore to its former glory one of the very great classic wines of the world.

Noël Cossart
Bungay, Suffolk
Summer 1984

To Pat, David and Anna, with love

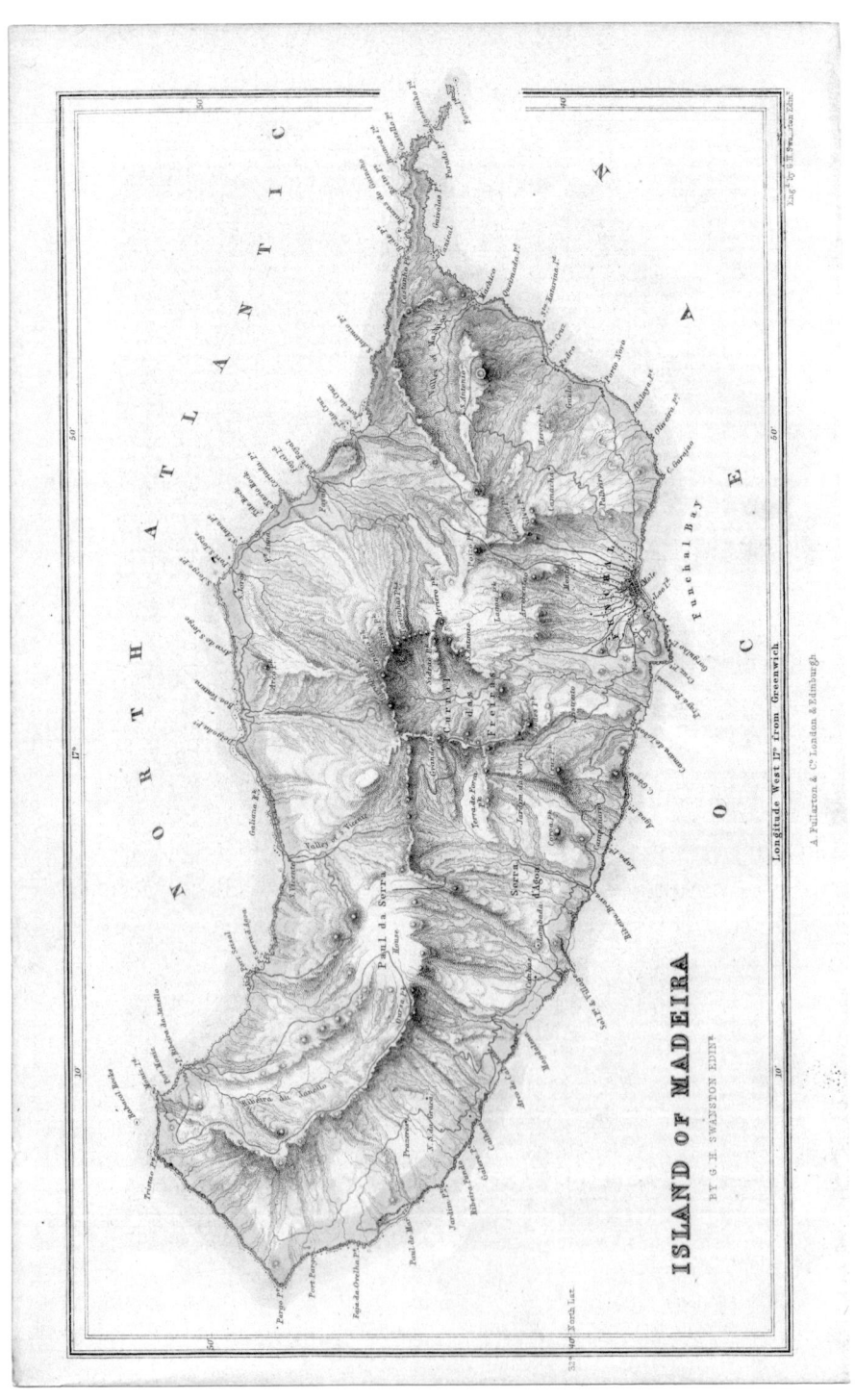

A mid-nineteenth century map of Madeira, published by A. Fullarton & Co., London & Edinburgh.

INTRODUCTION TO THE 2ND EDITION

The idea for this new edition of Noël Cossart's *Madeira, The Island Vineyard* originated in 2003—indirectly because of a phone call from Noël's nephew, the late John Cossart. John phoned to let me know that Noël's widow, Patricia Coates, was interested in selling the two dozen bottles of Madeira that Noël had left her when he died 16 years earlier. She cherished the bottles, but their sale would allow her to take her grandchildren on a long-delayed first trip to Madeira.

Each wine seemed to have a story attached to it. There were the last few bottles of the 1941 Bual Noël laid down for the birth of his son David. And there were the bottles of 1930 and 1934 "birth year" Torre Bella wines given to Noël by "Old Gordon's" great-grand-daughters, still unopened. (See Chapter 11.) Finally, there were the few remaining bottles of the 1926 Bual that his great-uncle laid down for Noël when he joined the wine trade.

The excitement with which I approached the purchase had far less to do with the wines' quality and rarity than their connection to Noël. I had long admired him, and had always regretted just missing the chance to meet him, as I joined the Madeira trade only six months after he died. The year was 1988, a time when Madeira's popularity was at a particularly low point. I was in London when I learned that Hedges & Butler, the former UK agent for Cossart, Gordon and Blandy's, was disposing of its stocks of old Madeiras. At that time, I was only on the fringe of the wine business as a writer and teacher, but with the financial help of a close friend, I managed to buy several hundred cases of irreplaceable old Madeira. Included were 50 or more cases *each* of Cossart's 1845 Centenary Bual and 1860 Sercial Soleras; Blandy's great 1907 vintage Bual; Blandy's 1864 Grand Cama de Lobos and 1863 Malmsey Soleras; and a few bottles each of Cossart's Bual 1895, Bastardo 1875 and Bual Solera 1815.

Later the same year, on my first of many trips to Madeira, I met

Noël's brother Peter, interviewing him at length about the wine and its history. This would be our only meeting; he died less than three years later. But I deeply regretted never meeting Noël. I had read his book through several times and considered it among the most important in the whole of Madeira literature. Of the several thousand British merchants who had made Madeira their life's work, only Noël had the sweeping perspective—as well as the time and patience—to put his story down on paper. But the book enjoyed nothing more than the single 1984 printing. By the 2000s, the only way to find a copy was through the second-hand book trade, and typically at quite a high price.

So I asked Pat Coates if she'd allow me to publish a new edition of *Madeira, The Island Vineyard*. She agreed enthusiastically. Christie's also graciously granted their permission.

My first instinct was to publish it more or less as it originally appeared, despite the fact that we know more about Madeira's history now, thanks to the scholarship of men like Alex Liddell, whose impeccably researched *Madeira* was published by Faber & Faber in 1998; David Hancock, who, over the past two decades, has done such important research on Madeira's trade, particularly with America, prior to 1815; and the Madeiran scholar, Alberto Vieira, who has compiled a great deal of material on his own island and its wines. Over the past fifteen years I, too, have done a great deal of research of my own—particularly with respect to the Madeira culture that once existed in America—but the value of my work is surely secondary to the work of these three men.

It was inevitable that, with all the new research coming to light, I would disagree with some of Noël's interpretations. Not only did Noël's writing predate much of this research, it was heavily based on Cossart family tradition and personal recollections that dated back a half century or more. He was not a scholar inclined to question Madeira lore, and he very much loved a good story. And so he insisted on the veracity of such legends as the 1792 "Napoleon" Madeira and Robert Machin's "discovery" of Madeira, both of which are perhaps more romance than history. He also never questioned the ancestry of William Neyle Habersham's Madeiras, despite the fact that the origins of many of them can easily be disproved by documents in the Georgia Historical Society in Savannah. (See Appendix XVII)

Furthermore, Noël viewed the history of the island and its wines through the prisms of Cossart, Gordon and the British trade. His knowledge of other firms was in large measure limited by his own experience, and his reliance on the Cossart, Gordon archives. Other houses, both British and Portuguese, may not have gotten the attention they deserved.

However, ultimately I decided to follow my original instincts and reissue the text of *Madeira, The Island Vineyard* as it had been published in 1984, with the addition of new introductory material, some new appendices, an updated record of Madeira auction sales and a few changes to the illustrations. Rather than updating and correcting his work, I decided that it should be left as originally published, so that another generation of Madeira lovers could enjoy the charm of Noël's words and benefit from the perspective of his place in history and his more than half a century in the Madeira trade. Any changes have to do with spelling, punctuation or currency, without altering the meaning or intent of Noël's writing.

Emanuel Berk

Guilford, Connecticut
Fall 2010

FOREWORD

Emanuel Berk

"I know no wine of its class that can beat Madeira when at its best.... In fact, I think Madeira and Burgundy carry combined intensity and complexity of vinous delights further than any other wines. There is possibly something of the unlawful about their rapture."
George Saintsbury, Notes on a Cellarbook, 1920.

Today, in the first decade of a new millennium, wine is enjoying unprecedented popularity. Its globalization—first promised two centuries ago—has at last been realized, with relative newcomers like the United States, Australia and Argentina breathing down the necks of such traditional wine powers as France, Italy and Spain. Far more people are drinking wine daily than ever before in history, and there is a growing sense of wine's inherent superiority over other alcoholic beverages for healthy living. Wine has transcended its traditional role as a mealtime beverage and symbol of sociability: it has become a cultural icon, with winemakers and consultants, wine writers, wine marketers and even wine collectors anointed as celebrities by the far-reaching electronic and print publishing industry that the beverage has spawned.

But for all of wine's unquestioned success in today's world, it is in danger of losing much of what makes it so special: its connection to a particular place and time. The advances of globalization have undoubtedly improved the overall quality of wine, by giving aspiring *vignerons* in virtually any temperate climate a shot at mimicking the quality and style of wines that have been famous for centuries. All it takes these days is a reasonably good site, deep pockets, the ear of an influential critic, and plenty of drive and ambition to create a "world class" wine.

But in this climate, wines of singular personality are becoming ever scarcer. By smoothing out the rough edges and removing or hiding flaws, modern winemaking tends to make wines more homogenous. Vintage variations become ever less important, as reverse osmosis, acidification, deacidification and roto-fermenters cover up the imperfections left by difficult summers. Irrigation, cultured yeasts, mechanical harvesters, sprays and expensive new French oak barrels compensate for an indifferent site.

Indeed, the technology exists today to produce wines of deep color, rich texture and powerfully opulent fruit in places where grapevines were non-existent a generation ago. Such wines win tastings, sway critics and fill cellars. But 100 years from now, will they be remembered? And will they add to our sense of history of the people, places and times that produced them?

A Singular Glory

Of all of the wines created over the past five hundred years, there is none that lays greater claim to being a wine of its time and place than Madeira, a highly improbable beverage forged by fire and heat. Its vines—nourished by the ashes of a primeval forest consumed by fire five centuries ago—are rooted in rock that exploded from the sea some 14 million years earlier. Only weeks after its birth, it is introduced to the tyranny of a world whose persistent, oppressive warmth would suffocate other wines but for Madeira is necessary to achieve perfection.

It is a wine of nearly magical complexity, whose powerful aromas can fill a house. Though a fortified wine like Port and Sherry, it has been made for centuries from its own range of ancient, enigmatic grape varieties, each with its own character and degree of sweetness. In fact, Madeira tastes little like Port or Sherry—as its palate is uniquely blessed by powerful acidity, which amplifies every flavor and dramatically frames the wine's honeyed richness, making it seem both less alcoholic and less sweet, and leaving the mouth refreshed. And it is arguably the world's longest-lived wine, with the greatest Madeiras postponing full maturity for a century or more, only to defy nature for another 50 to 100 years: gloriously rich, ambrosially textured, infinitely nuanced, yet majestically serene in their beauty.

Madeira's uniqueness among wines derives from a variety of factors. The island is itself volcanic, rising steeply from the sea, with vineyards planted on its slopes at elevations up to a half mile above sea level. Most of the common grape varieties are either unique to the island or of unknown origin. Grapes also don't ripen here as they do elsewhere in Europe, America or Australia. While recent increases in global temperatures have pushed potential alcohol levels for many varieties in Europe past 14 degrees, Madeira's Sercial achieves full physiological maturity—and the capability of producing all its classic nuances—at 10 degrees of potential alcohol. Even Malvasia, whose sugar levels tend to be the island's highest, is ripe at about 12 or 12.5 degrees. It is only with the addition of brandy that Madeira can achieve its classic form, combining substantial residual sugar with an alcohol degree of 19 to 21 percent.

But, of course, the element that contributes most to Madeira's individuality is the exposure to oxidation and warmth that molds its striking aromatic character. Such treatment, which would be abhorred in most other wine-producing areas, has its roots in history, from a time when Madeira was sent on long ocean voyages through the tropics, ultimately settling in hot climates like the Southern American colonies and the East and West Indies. The exposure to heat was found to improve the wine; so by the eighteenth century, Madeiras were often sent by sailing ship to the Indies and back to develop character. Such wines became known as *vinho da roda* or "wine of the round voyage." Other Madeiras passed through the Indies on their way to North America or England, earning the right to be sold as "shipped via India" or, in the event of a sojourn on one of the islands, "West India Madeira."

Inevitably, merchants sought ways to produce the same effects without the wine ever leaving Madeira. The simplest way, and a method used to this day for the finest wines, is *Canteiro*: aging the wine for years in a building exposed to the sun or in the attic of a shipper's wine lodge. But before ever using the *Canteiro* method, in the very late 1700s, producers anxious for quick results installed *estufas*, or "stoves," to heat wine to high temperatures, achieving in a few days what would have taken many months by ocean voyage. Of course, the results were hardly the same, and experiments ensued, reducing temperatures and extending the period of treatment to a few months. But so much bad wine was being turned out that there were three attempts (in 1802, 1803 and 1834) to ban estufas. Each time economics won out, and estufas have remained, evolving into sophisticated temperature-controlled heated tanks, reviled by purists, but economically necessary for the production of all but the best of today's Madeiras.

Six Hundred Years

For more than half a millennium, Madeira has been produced on a small Atlantic island, most of whose 306 square miles are too mountainous for any kind of agriculture. As a result, there have never been more than 3000 hectares of vineyards, all of them along the island's craggy coast. And because Madeira lies 365 miles from the nearest large land mass, Morocco, there has been no temptation to extend its vineyards beyond their traditional boundaries.

The first vineyards were planted here in the early 1400s, shortly after the arrival of the first European settlers. Vines—including the famed Malvasia Candida—were brought from Europe and the Mediterranean, and drainage channels called *levadas* were built, bringing water from the mountains to nourish the vines. The vineyards earned high praise from visiting Europeans, but for nearly two centuries, until the British began arriving at the end of the sixteenth century, there was little organized trade. The British made all the difference, organizing how the island's wine could profitably be made, promoted and distributed, establishing important markets throughout the British Empire, but especially in the North American colonies.

Madeira's position in the eastern Atlantic Ocean was crucial for the development of this trade, since the island lay at 32°45' north latitude and 17° west longitude, precisely in the path that ships took from Europe south and west. Whether they were journeying around the Cape of Good Hope, at the southern tip of Africa, on their way to India or China, or crossing the Atlantic to South America, the West Indies or North America, ships would stop at Madeira to trade with island merchants, frequently taking on wine as cargo. Because of the particularly large number of vessels destined for America, Madeira's wine made impressive inroads there, and came to dominate that market with special commercial privileges granted by the British Crown in the 1660s.

Thanks to the efforts of the British merchants who increasingly controlled the island's wine trade, Madeira became popular and admired throughout the British Empire. In fact, during the last quarter of the eighteenth century, Madeira was very possibly the most prestigious wine in the English-speaking world. Yet, it achieved its greatest renown in the British colonies that were to become the United States of America. As late as the second quarter of the eighteenth century, Madeira was a modest light, dry white wine, but by the time of the American Revolution, it had become a fortified wine of compelling character, and it was this wine that achieved a place in American popular culture unique in its history. Madeira was the ultimate luxury beverage, enjoyed almost to the exclusion of other wines by wealthy families, and its fame radiated throughout the world.

Madeira's enormous success attracted its share of imitators. Some, like Marsala which called itself Sicily Madeira, competed somewhat fairly, emulating the Madeira style but not hiding their geographic origins. Others were outright frauds: cheap concoctions from various parts of Europe that masqueraded as real Madeira. In fact, the imposters became so widespread that they seriously undermined Madeira's prestige in Britain, where many consumers came to assume that any wine labeled "Madeira" must be fake. While the United States' Minister to France in the 1780s, Thomas Jefferson had so little faith in the so-called "Madeiras" sold there that he had his Madeira sent from the States. And in the U.S. itself, the best way to be sure that a "Madeira" was real was to buy it *directly* from a reputable merchant on the island, a practice to which many connoisseurs adhered.

The Long Slide

After achieving such great success, Madeira began a long descent into oblivion. By the first two decades of the nineteenth century, it had lost its market leadership in Britain and India, but remained prized by serious connoisseurs, particularly in America, where it remained the wine that defined this young country and its top families. Even more than in the previous century, the United States' emerging upper class saw Madeira as not only America's wine, but *their* wine, inaccessible to the less affluent, and beyond the appreciation of those not born to refinement and privilege. Wines became known for the ships that brought them or the families that owned them. Madeira parties, for gentlemen only, were important social rituals in cities like Boston, New York, Philadelphia, Baltimore and Charleston. And in the decades after a new capital, Washington, was built, a conspicuous display of one's fine Madeira was used not only to demonstrate high social standing but to curry favor and build influence.

Madeira retained its powerful symbolic meaning in America throughout the remainder of the 1800s, but in the latter half of the century, events foretold its eventual demise. First, in 1851, a mildew epidemic ("oidium") struck the island's vineyards, reducing its production by 80% in one year and nearly 100% in four, and triggering a panicked exodus of many British merchants. Ten years later, just as the vineyards were recovering from oidium, the American Civil War not only eliminated the United States' Southern market, it made any transatlantic shipping treacherous. And a little more than a decade after that, the phylloxera vine epidemic put the nail in Madeira's commercial coffin not only by once again crippling production, but by convincing even more merchants to give up hope. It was a setback from which Madeira would never recover.

For the four decades following 1875, Madeira's trade with America virtually ceased, with an average of sixteen pipes shipped per year. The wine became hopelessly old-fashioned in a country where Madeira drinkers were increasingly old men—albeit powerful and influential ones—and Madeira's merchants expended very little effort to cultivate new customers. The loss of the American market was briefly made up for by Russia, which flourished until the October Revolution of 1917, and in a more enduring way by Germany, France and Scandinavia. Of all the important traditional markets for Madeira, only Great Britain remained, thanks, of course, to the fact that so many of the island's merchants were British and had well-established distribution there.

Madeira Today

Having once enjoyed a towering reputation among English-speaking wine drinkers, Madeira flirted with extinction in the early twentieth century, the victim not only of vine disease, but revolution, war, economics and fashion. In the decades after phylloxera arrived in 1872, all of the island's vineyards had to be replanted using American phylloxera-resistant rootstock on to which the classic varieties were grafted. Not only did farmers not bother to replant such classic grape varieties as Malvasia Candida, Terrantez and Bastardo, many skipped the grafting part altogether, leaving the American vines to produce their own grapes. To this day, "direct producers" like Isabella, Herbemont, Cunningham and Jacquet are common throughout the island, although the European Union is requiring that they be pulled up by 2013. The use of direct producers in making Madeira is now prohibited and can only be used to make table wine for local consumption. However, it is likely that juice of the likes of Isabela and Jacquet found its way into many of the Madeiras made in the first half of the twentieth century.

Owing to these and other factors, the vineyards available for the production of Madeira have declined dramatically. Though exact figures have never been kept, Madeira's vineyards may have occupied as many as 2500 hectares before phylloxera. Today, estimates of the amount of land devoted to vineyards vary from 300 to 420 hectares, divided among nearly 3000 individual farmers. To put this into perspective, these 300 hectares are less than the Rothschild family alone owns in the Médoc, and just two-tenths of one percent of the vineyards in all of Bordeaux.

The composition of the vineyards is also very different today. At the time of phylloxera, about two-thirds of the island's vineyards were planted to Verdelho, with the balance Sercial, Bual, Malvasia and small amounts of Terrantez, Bastardo and Moscatel. Verdelho had long been the island's workhorse variety—the backbone of the countless wines shipped over the centuries without the name of a grape variety. Perhaps because of this, and its abundance on the island, Verdelho had not been so highly regarded, and it was not until the twentieth century that it was accorded the same respect as, say, Sercial or Bual.

But Verdelho's heightened esteem has come at a price: its widespread disappearance in favor of an old, historically obscure variety: Tinta Negra Mole. Unlike the classic white varieties it has replaced, Tinta Negra Mole is a red grape of chameleon-like versatility, capable of producing the entire range of Madeira styles depending on where it is planted and how its juice is treated by the producer. Before phylloxera, Tinta Negra Mole was sparsely planted; today estimates of its use in the making of Madeira run as high as 90%.

A Shifting Landscape

As for the historically important varieties, most of Verdelho's great early vineyards on the south coast were long ago abandoned or replanted to Tinta Negra Mole or direct producers; today, Verdelho is mostly confined to the island's north side, particularly the area around São Vicente. Bual can be found in small amounts on the south side, while limited plantings of Sercial are on both sides of the island. Terrantez, which produced so many great wines in the eighteenth century, has now been relegated to a curiosity, with just a handful of vineyards producing fruit. Malvasia Candida—whose fifteenth-century origins make it arguably Madeira's most historic variety—is essentially extinct, as is Bastardo. Neither exists outside of a handful of experimental plantings. But in the meantime, a new form of Malvasia—Malvasia São Jorge—has proliferated on the north coast and is today the source of most of the wines labeled "Malvasia" or "Malmsey."

On the production side, there has been an astonishing consolidation over the past two centuries. In the early 1800s, scores of British, Portuguese and American merchants were in business on the island as wine exporters. In 1828, British merchants alone numbered at least 71. (See Appendix VI.) But the oidium epidemic of 1851-1852 took a heavy toll, reducing this number to fifteen by 1855. Numbers continued to dwindle, so that by the 1870s, there were only ten British wine merchants on the island, matched by twelve shippers of Portuguese nationality.

The twentieth century saw further contraction, largely due to the creation of the Madeira Wine Association which, between 1913 and 1940, absorbed some 28 independent firms, leaving few merchants to fend for themselves. Today, there are just eight companies registered as wine exporters: Vinhos Barbeito, Henriques & Henriques, Justinho Henriques, Pereira D'Oliveira, H. M. Borges, J. Faria & Filhos, P. E. Gonçalves and the Madeira Wine Company, as the Madeira Wine Association has been known since 1981.

But such numbers are deceptive. Thanks to concentrated resources and better vineyard management, the output of wine hasn't dropped nearly as much as one would think given the loss of vineyards and producers. While there's perhaps only one-tenth the vineyards today—and one-tenth the number of shippers—today's wine exports (30,000 to 40,000 hectoliters per year) compare favorably to what was shipped in the 1830s and 1840s, before oidium.

Yet, the future for Madeira is far from assured. The typical vineyard owner is in his 50s or 60s and possesses only about a tenth of a hectare (or a quarter acre) of vines. He was very possibly a sharecropper (*colono*) until Portugal's 1974 Revolution, when he was given the chance to buy the land he occupied. Unlike many of his brethren, he has resisted the temptation to switch to bananas, despite the fact that they can generate two or three times the income from the same amount of land. He has persevered as a grape-grower largely because growing grapes for one of the export companies is what he knows how to do.

But odds are that his children will not be interested in continuing his work. So, while the local government has enjoyed modest success in encouraging new vineyards, some say that for every hectare of new vines planted, five are lost, as vineyards give way to real estate development and other forms of agriculture. The situation has been particularly grim on the island's south side, where the finest wines of the 18th and 19th century were sourced. Today on Madeira's sun-bathed southern slopes, vineyards of historic varieties like Bual, Sercial, Terrantez, Verdelho and Malvasia Candida are a thing of the past, having largely succumbed to a century and a half of adversity. And with circumstances as they are today, there is little hope for their return.

There are few wines in the world with so colorful a history as Madeira—and none that has faced, and continues to face, such great challenges to its ongoing existence. But while those of us who love this heroic wine can do little more than hope for a profound change in its prospects, we can take comfort not only in the glorious old wines that have survived, but in Madeira's improbable, yet incredibly rich, history.

NOËL COSSART, A LIFE IN WINE

Emanuel Berk

Had it not been for the British, Madeira wine as we know it would not exist. They arrived on the island in the late 1600s and soon came to dominate Madeira's thriving wine trade, creating a beverage that was the most revered throughout the civilized world.

They continued to make and ship wine from the island for four centuries, withstanding disastrous vine epidemics, political upheavals, wars and economic collapses, until few Englishman remained. Finally, on February 27, 2008, the last resident British merchant still involved in the wine trade, John de Bianchi Cossart, chairman of Henriques & Henriques, passed away. And with John's passing, a profoundly rich and colorful tradition, spanning more than three centuries, ended.

John was born to what was once Madeira's most prominent British family. His great-great-grandfather Peter arrived in 1831 from Ireland to join his brother William as an employee of Madeira's largest wine shipper, Newton, Gordon, Murdoch & Scott. Within eight years Peter was the firm's managing partner, and by 1857, the company was a Cossart family business, Peter having bought out the last remaining non-Cossart partner. He soon renamed the firm Cossart, Gordon & Co., and for more than a century, one generation after another of Cossart men, based in both Madeira and London, made the Madeira trade their lives, building "Cossart" into the most recognized name for Madeira drinkers throughout the English-speaking world and beyond.

The last Cossart to run the family business was John's uncle, Noël, who was born on March 29, 1907, to Charles Blandy Cossart and Maria Anna de Bianchi. Noël was the oldest of three children: Margaret ("Margie") was born in 1910 and Peter (John's father) in 1919. As the oldest son, Noël was destined to one day take over the firm.

Noël joined Cossart, Gordon in 1925 at the age of eighteen.

The company had long been the island's biggest shipper, with sales towering above all others. Yet, the future of the entire Madeira wine trade was very much in doubt, and by the time he took control of the company's operations in 1936, conditions were even worse. Sales had been declining for more than a century, having nearly collapsed after the devastation of oidium in 1851 and phylloxera in 1872. By 1925, the majority of British merchants had given up the ghost, many leaving the island altogether. Most of the remaining firms banded together that year as the Madeira Wine Association (MWA) to improve their chances of survival.

As the island's largest shipper, Cossart, Gordon had the resources

Three photos of Noël Cossart as a child.

to remain independent, holding out until 1953, when Noël reluctantly joined the association, but only on the condition that he be allowed to handle the marketing of Cossart, Gordon-branded wines in the firm's most important English-speaking markets. Until the very end, he believed there was a future for the Cossarts in the Madeira trade. Even after most other British wine-producing families had left the business, Noël hung on. It was only after his death in November 1987, that his heirs finally, and reluctantly, agreed that there in fact was no future, selling their interest in the Madeira Wine Company, as the MWA had been renamed in 1981.

Beginnings

While writing a piece on Madeira for Britain's *Tatler* in 1985, the author Elizabeth David used "Wine for Empire Builders" for her working title. The article's main purpose was to review Noël Cossart's *Madeira, The Island Vineyard*, which had just been published by Christie's Publications in London. *Tatler's* editors rejected the title for the less intriguing "The Madeira Era," which is unfortunate, since the three nations that played the most important roles in Madeira's history did so as Empire Builders: Portugal, whose imperialists first settled Madeira in the 15th century; the British, for whom Madeira became such an important part of life in their American and East and West Indian colonies; and the United States, which in the early days of its expansion saw Madeira as the quintessentially American wine.

Yet, "Wine for Empire Builders" could easily apply to the Cossart Madeira dynasty as well. When William Cossart arrived in Madeira in 1809, the firm then known as Newton, Gordon & Murdoch had been in business for more than six decades, having been born when a Scot, Francis Newton, arrived from England in 1745. First employed as a bookkeeper for another wine shipper, Newton began trading in wine for his own account, and under his own name, in 1747. And in 1758, he entered into a partnership with Thomas Gordon.

Over the next four decades, the firm continued to evolve, changing its name every few years, and adding and subtracting partners. In 1775, it became Newton, Gordon & Johnston, and in 1791, Newton, Gordon & Murdoch. It grew into a leading source of Madeira throughout the British empire, shipping wine in barrel from the island to customers in places as exotic and remote as Penang,

Once the Funchal house of Henry Veitch, and later Château Cossart.

New Orleans, Dar-es-Salaam, Montréal, Bridgetown and Batavia.

By the mid-1800s, a London office became an integral part of its operations and remained so for nearly 150 years. The firm's first formal London office was opened in the 1840s, operating under the name of Webster, Gordon, Cossart and Co. In 1851, this name was changed for good to Cossart, Gordon and Co., and in 1861, the Madeira operation took that name as well, finally shedding the time-honored name of Newton.

Behind this change was Peter Cossart's acquiring a 100% interest in the firm in 1857 when his partner, Russell Manners Gordon, married the Countess Torre Bella, the largest landowner on the island. Gordon became the Count Torre Bella, but only on the condition that he relinquish his British citizenship (and ruling out any further ownership of the company he jointly owned with Peter Cossart).

Peter brought his five sons into the business, grooming Leland and Charles—the latter Noël's grandfather—to take over the Madeira end of the business on his death, while Webster, William and Henry ran the London office. The company's main business was the sale of wine—which it purchased and blended from hundreds of local growers—but it also traded in many other commodities, which it received as barter for the wine. Thus, wine shipped to the United

The Cossarts and friends at Quinta do Monte, 1892: from left to right, C. F. Raleigh Blandy, Charles J. Cossart, Leland Cossart, Harry Hinton and Charles Hinton.

States was paid for with cotton, rice, corn, indigo and tobacco, which it traded both locally and with other markets, and wood staves and iron hoops which it used for its own barrels.

By the end of the 19th century, with Webster Gordon Cossart and Noël's grandfather Charles in charge, the firm was also trading in other alcoholic beverages. Not only did it sell Port, Sherry, Tarragona, Marsala and Malaga under its label, it acted as an agent in London for producers in Bordeaux, Jerez, Burgundy, Champagne, Cognac and Scotland. As for the other commodities in which it had traditionally traded, these had been phased out of the portfolio, allowing the family to focus entirely on the beverage trade, and principally on Madeira.

A New Century

As the 19th century came to a close, the wine trade in Madeira was still reeling from the devastating effects of oidium and phylloxera that plagued the island's vineyards decades earlier. Exports had climbed back from the depths of the 1850s and 1870s, but they were still well below levels of a century earlier.

The early years of the 20th century brought little improvement, and the future looked bleak. Few shippers remained and even fewer believed they could survive on their own; and so in 1913 a consolidation process began with the merger of three companies—Wm. Hinton & Sons, Welsh & Cunha and Henriques & Câmara—creating the Madeira Wine Association Lda. (MWA). In the years following, the MWA's membership swelled, as shippers sought refuge from the shipping constraints of World War I, the weakening of the German market, the total loss of the Russian market and Prohibition in the United States.

The stream of companies joining the association climaxed in 1925. In that year, the association was reorganized as the Madeira Wine Association (1925) Lda. The shareholders of the new association included the original Madeira Wine Association, plus Blandy Bros. & Co., Leacock & Co., and Thomas Mullins. Mullins, who was widely liked and admired as Blandy's managing director, became the director of the new association, while John Ernest Blandy became chairman.

This made Blandy and its brand more important than it had ever been before. Historically, Cossart, Gordon had been by far the largest shipper of Madeira, larger than all the other British houses combined. However, with the pooling of wine stocks, the reconstituted MWA, with Blandy as its lead brand, began to rival Cossart, Gordon in size.

Personal Travails

Nineteen twenty-five was also a year of cataclysmic change for Noël Cossart. On June 7, 1925, at the family's Quinta dos Pinheiros, his father succumbed to complications from acute appendicitis. The attack was sudden, and an operation to save him was performed on the family's kitchen table (moved to his father's dressing room for that purpose). Charles Blandy Cossart did not survive the procedure.

*Noël's father
Charles Blandy Cossart.*

Noël was barely eighteen. He was good-looking, charming and, as the oldest boy, expected to one day take over the family business. However, he hadn't yet acquired the emotional maturity to pursue that calling. Depending on the version of the story told, at about the time of his father's death he had set sail for either Brazil or South Africa, in search of adventure as a cabin boy or to smooth things over after a "dalliance" with an older woman. Whatever the nature of the escapade, he was soon back on the island, where he joined Cossart, Gordon & Co. as a barrel-maker in preparation for the day when he would take over the firm.

His Uncle Arthur had been brought in to take over the business. A Colonel in the Royal Horse Artillery in India since 1905, Arthur was a year younger than Noël's father and a career army officer. He knew nothing about the wine business, yet he was entrusted with guiding Cossart, Gordon through one of its most difficult periods.

With Arthur's military bearing and his lack of knowledge of the wine business, it is understandable that he and Noël didn't get along. In fact, it is rumored that Noël left at some point in the late 1920s to work as a clerk for Graham Blandy, a relative by marriage, and well-liked by the Cossarts, but a rival nonetheless.

If he did go to work for Blandy, he didn't stay long; by 1928 he was rising within the ranks of Cossart, Gordon. He was sent off to London to learn the ropes at 75 Mark Lane, where the firm had both sales offices and cellars. Here he worked under his Great Uncle Henry Charles Cossart, the youngest of Peter Cossart's sons. While this was his first real training in the Madeira business, he got along with Uncle Henry little better than he did Uncle Arthur. In a 1981 article, Noël wrote: "My master was Uncle Henry, who knew wine inside out, and consumed quantities of it. He fought the International Exhibition Cooperative Wine Society when it started. He also had a habit of telling our important customers such as the Scandinavian Wine Monopolies what they should buy, not letting them buy what they wanted. It has taken me all my working life to erase his sins and cultivate these auspicious bodies."

In 1931, Noël returned to Madeira to work again directly under Arthur, while still living at home with his mother at the Quinta dos Pinheiros. His relationship with Arthur was no better, but at least his uncle's disinterest in the business allowed Noël to grow and expand his responsibilities. Noël was now a director of the company, and by 1935 he was in charge of production. "Production" for Cossart, Gordon at that time meant vinification, blending and shipping of wines still in barrel to Mark Lane for

The Cossart, Gordon lodge.

bottling and worldwide distribution. The London wine trade was then known for having some of the world's most skilled bottlers, and Cossart, Gordon's bottler, Jack, was one of the best.

In the meantime, Blandy grew in prominence in the marketplace, shipping most of their production in bottle directly from Madeira. The firm had clearly benefited from its consolidation with Leacock and others, and had gone from being a relatively small player in the 1800s to being one of the island's elite labels. Not only did they enjoy the marketing connections of more than a dozen different brands, the pooling of stocks gave them access to far more wine than in the past.

By 1940, the Madeira Wine Association's membership stood at twenty-eight. The 1934 addition of Power Drury and part of Lomelino enhanced not only the company's size, but its stature. It also meant that its conquest of the British shippers was almost complete. In fact, of all the British firms that pre-existed the Madeira Wine Association, the only holdouts were Cossart, Gordon and Rutherford & Miles, which by then had become independent allies, thanks in part to the 1933 marriage of Noël's sister Margie to Cecil Miles.

Coming of Age

In 1935, Noël's father's cousin, Sidney Gordon Cossart, took over the management of the London office, while Noël assumed responsibility for production in Madeira, with Sidney's brother Eustace to assist him. This was a prelude to Noël's taking over full responsibility for the Madeira operation from Uncle Arthur, which happened the following year.

Noël married in 1936 as well, to Kathleen Florence Gradidge of London, and the couple moved into the Quinta Bettencourt. With his marriage, Noël acquired a respectability that he previously lacked and opened up the possibility for Arthur to return to England, leaving the firm in Noël's hands. Arthur's decade in Madeira had been a strain for him—managing a company that was losing money in a business in which he had little interest. His wife, whom Cossart family members referred to as "Mother India," had moved back to England shortly after their arrival in 1925, undoubtedly bristling at the exclusiveness of the island's British community, as well as the social isolation of being so far from home.

With the departure of Arthur, Noël was now firmly in charge of

Cossart, Gordon & Co. Uncle Sidney still ran the London office, as he was to do until the early 1950s. The world was coming out of the Great Depression, but entering a still darker episode: the rise of Nazi Germany and World War II.

Even before Britain declared war on Germany on September 3rd, 1939, the conflict took its toll on Cossart, Gordon's future. In 1937, Noël's younger brother Peter returned to Madeira from school in Switzerland, ready to join the wine business. He would have been a huge asset to Cossart, Gordon in the decades ahead,

Two photos of Noël Cossart as a young man.

complementing Noël's strengths. He was far more serious in nature, a natural planner and a careful decision-maker—very different from the charming, more freewheeling Noël.

However, their mother worried that Cossart, Gordon, with its great size, would be too obvious a target in the event of war and didn't want both of her sons there. And so she insisted that Peter work elsewhere. Starting his own business was out of the question: he lacked both money and experience. However, in January, 1938, family friend João Henriques offered to take Peter into his firm, Henriques & Henriques, where Peter would serve ably for more than a half century.

Once Britain entered the war, Madeira shipments plummeted much as they had after oidium in the 1850s. To make matters worse, the London office at 75 Mark Lane was destroyed during a German

German air raid in 1941, forcing the company to move to the old Fenchurch Street Station Hotel. Noël undoubtedly achieved satisfaction working as a King's Courier, carrying diplomatic pouches between Madeira and Lisbon, and the 1941 birth of his son David not only made him a father, it gave him an heir for Cossart, Gordon. To commemorate David's birth, he laid down a pipe of 1941 Bual, which he later transferred to a pipe that had held the famous 1862 Terrantez.

An ominous view of Germany's Graf Zeppelin I passing over Funchal in 1934.

Otherwise, there was little to cheer about in the early years of the war. The main bright spot was the American market, where Cossart, Gordon's policy of shipping in barrel, not bottle, gave them a distinct advantage over its competitors. The manufacture of high-quality bottles in Portugal had ground to a halt and thus, as Noël later wrote, the United States government banned the importation of wine in bottle from Oporto and Madeira.

Helped by its strong American trade, sales rose between 1943 and 1947, when they peaked. Noël wrote in 1981: "After the war there was a fantastic run on our vintage and Solera wines. All our Soleras except 1808, 1815, 1822 and 1845 were exhausted and much of our vintage stock." Noël bemoaned the loss of this irreplaceable wine, but as he wrote: "I needed the money to renew our equipment, which was badly run down."

While Cossart, Gordon had achieved some success during and immediately after the war, the only other remaining independent British company, Miles, was not as fortunate. Consequently, in 1949, the same year that Noël became chairman and managing director of Cossart, Gordon & Co., Miles joined the Madeira Wine Association, leaving Noël very much on his own.

The 1950s

As Cossart, Gordon entered the second half of the twentieth century, Noël struggled to keep the firm solvent and independent. Uncle Sidney retired in 1951, leaving his brother Eustace in charge of the London office. Eustace had been left for dead three decades earlier on a World War I battlefield, and while recovered from his physical wounds, he was never the same emotionally. Over the decades, he bounced between London and Madeira, plugging holes for the company but never leading. He was, in short, not the man that Noël needed in London.

When he wasn't off selling in Europe or the United States, Noël was spending more time in England trying to keep the London office from descending into chaos. During his long absences from the island, his brother-in-law, Cecil Miles, acted on his behalf, but Noël soon realized that he could no longer run the Madeira end of the business. The inevitable had happened: in 1953, he decided to throw in the towel, joining the Madeira Wine Association.

It is believed that he sold the Cossart, Gordon brand and all of the wine stocks on the island for shares in the Madeira Wine Association totaling about 7%, plus an annual salary as director. He kept the wine stocks in London, including some very fine soleras still in wood, as well as exclusive rights to sell Cossart, Gordon products in the United Kingdom, United States and Canada.

Such an arrangement may have been attractive to Noël at the time, but over the long run it turned out not to be a good deal at all. No dividends were paid out to shareholders, the salary lacked an inflation clause, and by accepting such a small ownership position in the MWA, Noël inadvertently assured the eventual decline of the Cossart, Gordon brand in favor of Blandy and Leacock, whose families each owned one-third of the association.

Noël kept the London office going temporarily, finally deciding in 1956 to hand over the marketing of Cossart, Gordon in the

United Kingdom to Evans Marshall & Co. Noël believed that he would remain actively involved, and as part of the 20-year franchise agreement he became a director of Evans Marshall.

Here, too, things did not go as Noël expected. Shortly after the agreement, Evans Marshall joined Hedges & Butler in the large brewery group, Bass Charrington. Having been a leading London wine merchant for three centuries, Hedges & Butler brought a powerful marketing organization to the table, but there was one problem. They already represented Blandy Madeiras in the United Kingdom, and Hedges & Butler's managing director, Stanley Williams, was a "Blandy's man."

Once again, Noël found himself outflanked. The Cossart, Gordon brand was now destined to live in Blandy's shadow within the Bass organization, just as it would on the island. Furthermore, saddled with a twenty-year agreement with Evans Marshall, there was no clear way out.

Noël tried to make the best of it. He had been divorced from his first wife in 1953, but the next year in London he met Patricia Potter, a lovely woman twenty years his junior. They married in 1956, and Noël believed that the deal with Evans Marshall would permit them to remain in England, where he could promote the Cossart, Gordon brand on Evans Marshall's behalf. However, the Evans Marshall relationship soured, and though he continued to be employed by the firm as a marketing agent, in 1958 Noël and Pat returned to Madeira, with their one-year-old daughter Anna.

From his new base on the island, he promoted not only Cossart, Gordon for Evans Marshall, but also the company's other brands like Mähler-Besse Bordeaux and Lustau Sherries. However, Noël's stature in the Madeira world, particularly in Britain, continued to be lofty, and Evans Marshall took advantage of it. Over the next few years, Noël conducted several well-publicized and important Madeira tastings in England. The first such tasting in May 1959 was billed as the "Academy of Ancient Madeira Wines."

A two-day affair in Evans Marshall's cellars, it was attended by a number of prominent British merchants and writers, including André Simon, Ronald Avery, H. Warner Allen and Raymond Postgate. With soleras ranging in date from 1808 to 1845, and vintages from 1789 to 1898, it was undoubtedly one of the grandest Madeira tastings ever staged. It duly impressed Warner Allen, who wrote in 1961 in *A History of Wine*: "I was an old man when my senses were dumbfounded as if by a firework display by presentation to such a collection of glorious Madeiras as had never been seen before and will never again be seen … it was not until May 1959 that I had a unique opportunity of judging the supreme highlights to which the greatest of great vintage Madeiras could rise."

Allen continued: "There were thirteen ancestral vintage wines, venerable patriarchs, any one of them worth to the wine-lover a king's ransom, for an Honours Degree, Mr. Noël Cossart's expert palate gave six of them a First, and to that select company I ventured to add a fancy of my own Reserva Visconde Valle Paraiso Bual 1844, which I was lucky enough to taste at the moment when the bottle in which it had lived for 23 years was opened. Mr. Cossart faulted it for a bottle nose which wore off too quickly. These seven wines had an average age of 120 years, the youngest seventy-nine, the oldest a hundred and seventy."

Early the next year, Noël made a promotional junket to the United States, where he visited his importers in New York and Boston, while staying with his cousin Harry du Pont at Winterthur. By June he was back in England, where he participated in another historic Madeira tasting organized by Averys of Bristol. Although there were two rarities from Noël's grandfather's vineyards—1869 E.B.H. São Martinho Bual and 1865 Tinta Bianchi—the backbone of the June 21, 1960, tasting was a set of eight pre-1834 vintage Madeiras from the collection of the late Stephen Gaselee.

Apart from his occasional trips to England and the U.S., Noël was spending most of his time on the island, with his wife and daughter. When his mother died in 1960, he, Margie and Peter each received a one-third share of the family's Quinta dos Pinheiros, which had been given to their mother as a wedding present. Since none of the siblings was in a position to buy the others out, the property was sold. Noël used his share to purchase the Solar do Vale Formoso, just down the road from the much larger Quinta do Vale Formoso, which had been owned by his uncle Michael Grabham until his death in 1935.

With its 19th century grace and its peaceful walled garden, the Solar was a perfect Madeiran home for Noël and his family, but it was not the sort of house that was expected of a great wine shipper. In the past, even lower echelon merchants owned quintas, or estates, with large houses and beautifully landscaped grounds. The Solar was a far more modest dwelling with little land, and its small size undoubtedly raised eyebrows within the island's British community. But times had changed, and few of the shippers—and especially Noël Cossart—had the wealth they once had.

Noël also didn't have the same power and authority as in the past. He was given a small office at the Madeira Wine Association, but he was a minority director and had little to say on important questions, even the future of his own brand. He enjoyed the support of the association's longtime and respected managing director Horace Zino, but the adjustment from boss to employee was hard for him.

Towards the middle of the decade, he acquired the Hertz rental car agency for the island, but this did little to fill the void in his working life. He was still very sociable, loved entertaining his nieces and nephews, and enjoyed sailing off Madeira's rugged coastline, but wine had been his life for more than thirty years, and the Madeira Wine Association was more a source of frustration than satisfaction. The idea of writing his life story, and a history of Madeira as he knew it, began to take shape. In 1951, Elizabeth Nicolas, a travel writer from London had relied heavily on Noël in writing the Madeira portion of *Madeira and the Canaries* (Hamish Hamilton, 1953). Less than a decade later, the wine writer Rupert Croft-Cooke also mined Noël's vast knowledge in writing *Madeira* (Putnam, 1961).

Noël began thinking seriously that he, too, should write a book, and this notion was reinforced by two friends who were writers, Douglas Sutherland and Al Perkins, and for the next twenty years this became his highest professional aspiration. Noël wasn't temperamentally suited to writing continuously, and so he wrote in small pieces. The amount of progress he made during the 1960s is unknown today because, in 1969, a fire claimed his work up to that point.

A New Generation

For Noël, the early 1970s were much like the '60s. The Madeira Wine Association, controlled by the Blandys and Leacocks, continued to struggle, while his relationship with his UK marketing company, Evans Marshall, continued to be distant. He began writing again, urged on by Christie's Michael Broadbent who visited the island in 1972. Meanwhile, life in Madeira held little satisfaction for him.

In 1974, Portugal's fascist dictatorship was thrown out by a popular revolution. The implications for Madeira's wine growers and shippers were profound. The shippers had traditionally owned few vineyards, relying on thousands of tenant farmers each owning just a few vines. Historically, the farmers had no organization with which to demand high grape prices, but the dynamic of power had been changed by the revolution. The farmers were given the chance to buy the land they worked and were emboldened to seek higher grape prices. They also became far more contentious in their dealings with shippers, particularly the Madeira Wine Association.

The social upheaval created by the revolution also provoked labor tensions within the MWA. John Blandy and Edmund Leacock, who had been running the association, decided that the next generation would be better able to cope with this new reality, and so they retired, leaving behind a much younger three-man executive committee. Heading the committee was Blandy's chairman, Richard Blandy, joined by William Leacock and Anthony Miles.

These changes were momentous for the Blandy and Leacock families, yet they had little direct impact on Noël. Not only was he not actively involved in the association's management, he was to leave the island within months anyway. In 1975, his daughter Anna suffered a serious concussion in a fall in Germany, while Noël, nearing seventy, was beginning to experience neurological problems of his own. So, the Cossarts decided to move back to England where Anna and Noël could receive better medical treatment.

They found a house in the Suffolk town of Bungay, but they needed to sell their house on the island to buy it. In 1976, this was more easily said than done. The revolutionary junta forbade foreigners from buying or selling property, and the Cossarts were still British citizens. They advertised their house in the *Times* of London, finding potential buyers in a British couple looking to retire to Madeira. Although the Madeira house was more valuable, Noël and Pat agreed to an even swap, with the buyers purchasing the Bungay house on their behalf.

The return to England meant a fresh start. Noël and Anna regained their health and the twenty-year contract with Evans Marshall expired. This made it possible for the Cossarts again to market their own wines in the UK and US and for Noël's son David to finally join him in the family business, reviving Cossart, Gordon's

London office as the main marketing force behind the Cossart, Gordon brand.

The London office had been organized as a limited company in 1909 and had never been dissolved. In 1976, there were three shareholders: Noël and his two siblings, Margaret and Peter, with Noël having the majority of shares. Cossart, Gordon & Co. Ltd. was not only the legal owner of the Cossart, Gordon brand in England, it held the Cossart family's shares in the Madeira Wine Association.

David, who was now 35 years old, had been in the wine and spirits trade, with Gilbeys and Christie's, for more than a decade, and he was a Master of Wine. He brought to the enterprise not only his youth and energy, but also a knowledge of wine and the wine business. And he brought his relationship with Bruce Shand, a wealthy Englishman who had recently bought the old London wine merchant, Ellis Son & Vidler.

Bruce was the son of P. Morton Shand, a London architect and wine lover who had written four influential wine books in the late 1920s. Bruce was also socially well-connected with ties not only to the British aristocracy but to the Royal family; his daughter is the Duchess of Cornwall, the former Camilla Parker-Bowles. Bruce knew all the right people in the colleges at Oxford and Cambridge, who continued to be big buyers of Madeira and Port.

In 1973, David had joined Bruce at Ellis Son & Vidler as managing director. With the acquisition of the Cossart, Gordon brand in 1976, David became fully responsible for marketing Cossart, Gordon in the UK, while continuing to manage Ellis Son & Vidler.

To launch the Cossart, Gordon agency, Ellis Son & Vidler held a tasting of the brand's Madeiras on November 10th, 1976, at King's College, Cambridge. In addition to the undated blends like Good Company Sercial and Malmsey, and the Duo Centenary Celebration Very Old Bual, they showed the following vintages and soleras (prices are per bottle):

    1902 Verdelho Vintage £10.50
    1845 Cossart's Centenary Solera £6.00
    1822 Bual Solera £12.50 *London-Bottled 1964*
    1815 Bual Solera £15.00 *London-Bottled 1961*
    1808 Malmsey Solera £13.00 *London-Bottled 1961*
    1916 Malmsey Vintage £9.00
    1893 Malmsey Vintage £15.00

David and Noël collaborated on a second tasting on October 5th 1979 at 30 Pavilion Road, London. Billed as a "Tasting of Modern Vintages and Soleras," the name reflected the continued dissipation of the old wines. Only three soleras were shown—Malmsey 1808, Bual 1822 and Bual Centenary Solera 1845—and

An early photograph of Ellis Son & Vidler's cellars in Hastings, England. The cellars were carved out of chalk and maintained a constant temperature year round. This old nineteenth-century firm used the Hastings cellars not only for bottle storage but for bottling from cask, as was the custom in the English wine trade until the 1970s.

the vintage wines were more recent: Malmsey 1916, 1920 and 1954; Bual 1895; Verdelho 1934, and Sercial 1940.

With the appointment of Ellis Son & Vidler as Cossart, Gordon's UK agents, David Cossart and Bruce Shand were made directors of Cossart, Gordon & Co. Ltd. They joined Noël, his wife Pat and his nephew Anthony Miles, who had been so helpful to Noël during this period. In fact, Anthony played the same role that his father Cecil had a quarter century before: representing Noël's interests in the Madeira Wine Association during his absence from the island. David's entry into the business also allowed Noël to get back to writing and enjoying life.

"I retired for the third and last time," he wrote, "and my dream of a lifetime has become reality. David, the sixth generation of Cossarts, is at the head of the company." When he left Madeira for

Bungay, he hoped that he would find the time and peace of mind to finally write his book, but still he was distracted. Soon after his arrival, he purchased land with some friends which they used for shooting. Noël wasn't known as an early riser, but now he got up at the crack of dawn. He filled his days with hunting, fishing and gardening. Clearly, he was finding reserves of energy that had long lain fallow. This was a happy time for him.

Meanwhile, David energized the UK market, by strengthening ties to traditional Cossart, Gordon customers like the Wine Society. He also took advantage of Bruce Shand's connections, particularly within the colleges at Oxford and Cambridge, and he revitalized the American market through his appointment of Almaden as the brand's exclusive US agent and his regular promotional trips to the States.

The new structure worked far better than the arrangement with Evans Marshall, but by the mid-1980s, cracks began to appear, largely due to Bruce Shand's decision to sell Ellis Son & Vidler to Hugh Bidwell. Bruce had gradually lost interest in the business, and Bidwell, whose father had been a wine merchant with Sichel, was looking for a business platform from which to run for Lord Mayor of London (a position he was to win in 1989). A traditional wine merchant was just the ticket, and with the fortune Bidwell had made in the food business, money was not a problem.

But David soon became disenchanted with life at Ellis Son & Vidler under its new management. He was also becoming frustrated with his relationship with the Madeira Wine Company, as the MWA had been known since 1981. Under Richard Blandy's direction, the company was working to build a global marketing strategy for all its labels, and not having control over the marketing of one of its biggest brands, Cossart, Gordon, in two of its biggest markets, the UK and US, stood in the way. Yet, while David could tolerate tension with the Madeira Wine Company, he was far less happy working for Bidwell, and so he quit. He took the Cossart,

One of Ellis Son & Vidlers' last bottlings was in 1977, only a year after David Cossart joined the company, when four pipes of 1952 Cossart, Gordon vintage Bual were bottled in the Hastings cellars to commemorate the Silver Jubilee of Queen Elizabeth II's coronation.

DAVID COSSART HAS A BONE TO PICK WITH NAPOLEON.

The cellar of my Great Uncle Michael was an Aladdin's cave of near-legendary vintage Madeira.

Among them, shrouded in antiquity was a pipe of the 1792 vintage – the subject of a singularly dubious honour.

In 1815, it was 'liberated' by Napoleon as he passed en route for his last bitter exile upon the island of St. Helena.

During his rapacious military career, he had apparently lost the habit of paying for his acquisitions, and his account remained unsettled on his death in 1821.

Happily the pipe was unbroached and was repossessed by the British Consul, who returned it to Madeira.

It was finally bottled in 1840.

Today, our credit is a little tighter than in Napoleonic times.

Throughout Britain many wine merchants are currently offering their customers our fine Madeiras.

Please telephone or write for details of your nearest stockist.

FINE OLD MADEIRA WINES BY COSSART GORDON & CO. LTD. AS STOLEN BY EMPERORS.

57 Cambridge Street, London SW1V 4PS. Tel: 01-834 4101/3.
Cellars & Accounts: 12/13 Cliffe Cellars, South Street, Lewes, Sussex. Tel: 07916 77544.
USA Distributors: Charles Lefranc Cellars, 1530 Blossom Hill Road, San Jose, California 95118.

In the final months before taking Cossart, Gordon to Averys of Bristol, David Cossart ran this ad promoting his Madeiras in Decanter *Magazine (December, 1984)*

Gordon brand to Averys of Bristol, giving them the UK agency and agreeing to work for this old West Country house known for its fine Madeiras. But the regular commute to Bristol from London wore thin, as did being on the road selling after years of being a buyer. David remained with Averys for little more than a year.

The Final Sale

After Noël's death in 1987, the Cossart family had few options available to it. David had decided to leave the wine trade, and the only other family member capable of running the company was his cousin John Cossart, the son of Noël's brother Peter. However, John was obliged to succeed his father at Henriques & Henriques, which he did on the latter's death in January 1991.

To decide what to do, the family held two meetings, in 1989 and 1990, with Noël's widow Pat, David, John and Anthony Miles in attendance. Also at the first meeting was Sam Coulson, a chartered accountant with the firm of Barton & Mayhew, who had long been Noël's financial advisor. For years Coulson had urged Noël to sell his shares in the Madeira Wine Company, and now that Noel was gone, he continued to offer the same counsel to his family. At the first meeting the family rejected Coulson's advice, but the next time they met they decided to sell.

The buyer would be the Symington family of Oporto. The Symingtons —whose ancestors had been in the port business for over 300 years, and had achieved spectacular success in recent decades as the owners of Graham, Dow and several other port brands—had just become the second largest owner of the Madeira Wine Company by buying a block of shares from the Blandy family.

The Blandys' intention in selling shares was not to weaken their position in the company. In fact, their goal was the opposite: to create a new Madeira Wine Company, with just two partners, the Blandys and the Symingtons, forging an alliance built on more sophisticated production and marketing. While the Blandys knew Madeira, the Symingtons brought a much broader view of the world wine market, and had what Richard Blandy lacked, but always wanted: a global distribution network.

A decade before, the Blandys had secured a dominant position in the MWC by buying out the Leacock Family's one-third stake. Before selling to the Symingtons, the Blandys' share of the company stood at about 67%, with Cossart, Gordon & Co. Ltd. owning about 7%, the Miles family 5%, and a half dozen other families or companies with smaller shares. Their plan was to use part of their holdings to bring the Symingtons into the fold and then to encourage their new partners to buy out the remaining shareholders.

The Symingtons accepted Blandy's offer and in 1989 became a partner in the Madeira Wine Company. Over the next three years, Ian Symington succeeded in purchasing every share not owned by his family or the Blandys. He negotiated separately with each shareholder: Cossart, Gordon; Miles; Luis Gomes; João Freitas Martines; Power Drury; Lomelino; Abudarham, and the late Tom Mullins' Madeira Wine Antiga. Cossart, Gordon was the first owner to sell, and the Miles family the last.

This book

When he moved to England from Madeira in 1976, Noël Cossart expected that he would at last do the writing that he had promised himself and others. He started slowly; during the late 1970s, he produced little for his eventual book, but wrote two articles: "Madeira Wine" for *Christie's Wine Review* (1977) and "A Choice Malmsey Nose," for *Decanter*.

However, in 1981 things began to change. In that year, Noël had two pieces published: "Madeira Wine Past and Present" in *Wine & Food* and "Madeira Saga" in *The Christie's Wine Companion*. He also committed to write *Madeira, The Island Vineyard*, the outgrowth of a lunch meeting on May 6th 1981, with Patrick Matthews, the editor of the Christie's wine book series.

He completed his cherished book in early 1984 and it was published by Christie's in October of the same year. Christie's launched the book at three events. Two were virtually simultaneous, held the same evening, October 23, 1984, in Funchal, Madeira, and Savannah, Georgia. Noël personally attended the Funchal launching; he spoke in Portuguese for the benefit of the Portuguese government officials, and local and national press, in attendance. Later he was fêted at a dinner at Reid's Hotel.

In Savannah, Noël was represented by his son David, with Michael Broadbent representing Christie's, at a special dinner of the city's Madeira Club. The menu was classic for American Madeira lovers, featuring stone crab claws, she crab soup and lamb. The wines were also impressive: 1973 Bollinger R.D., Blandy's 1835 Sercial Solera, 1975 Lynch Bages, Blandy's 1864 Verdelho Solera, Cossart, Gordon 1941 C.D.G.C. Bual and Cossart, Gordon 1808 Malmsey Solera. Between the dinner and the availability for interviews of the very quotable Michael Broadbent, the event kept the Savannah newspapers' wine and food writers very busy over a 10-day period.

The third launching of the book was in London on November 6th, 1984. At this event Broadbent presented, on behalf of Christie's, a handsome calf-bound copy of *Madeira, The Island Vineyard*, inscribed "Noël, with congratulations and best wishes from the

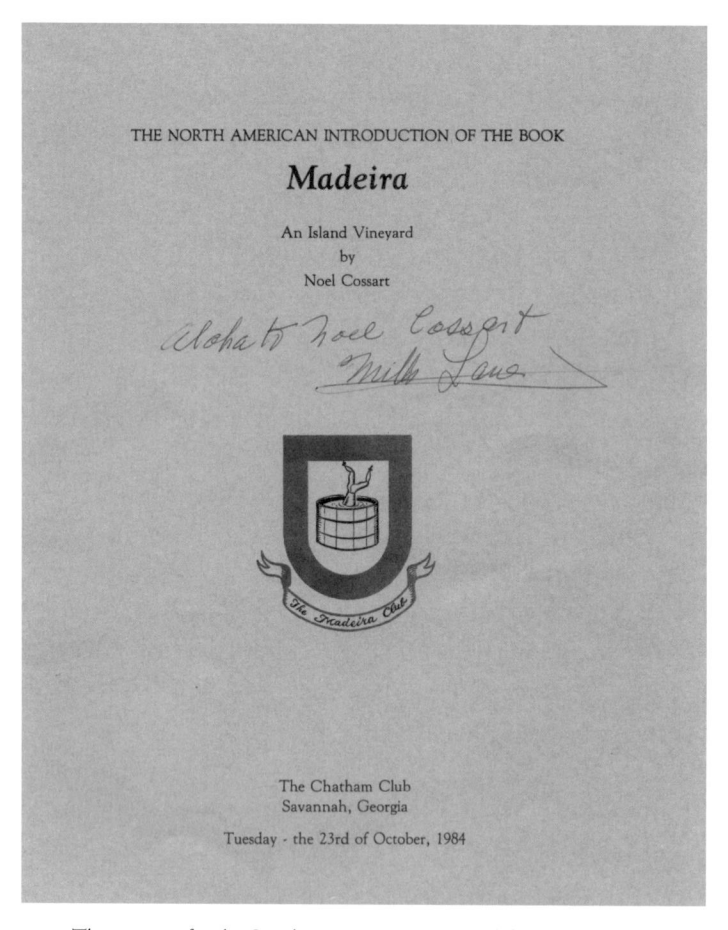

The program for the October 23, 1984, Savannah book launching.

Christie's wine publication team," and signed by Michael Broadbent, Rosemary Ward, Patrick Matthews and Penelope Mansell-Jones.

Noël's book quickly took its place as the most beloved book ever written on its subject, and the author became Madeira's preeminent storyteller. Overnight, Noël also assumed the role as Madeira's leading historian, and he quickly began receiving queries from other writers.

He heard first from John Delaforce, who had written a history of the British Factory House in Oporto, also published by Christie's, in 1979. On October 30th, 1984, just days after the book's publication, Delaforce wrote to Noël, correcting his brief history of Portuguese *feitorias* in Chapter 3. He went on to explore other subjects, including the possible existence of a British Factory building in Madeira as there was in Oporto. His letter and Noël's response can be found in Appendix XV.

In March 1985, food writer Elizabeth David wrote to Noël. She had become intrigued with the story of the cask of 1792 Madeira given to the exiled Emperor Napoleon during his voyage to St. Helena. Napoleon's ship stopped at Madeira and, according to legend, Madeira's British counsel Henry Veitch gave the emperor the wine. After Napoleon's death, as the story goes, Veitch took the unbroached barrel back and sold it to Charles Ridpath Blandy in 1822, who bottled the wine in 1840. Today, the few surviving bottles of Blandy's 1792 bottled 1840 represent the Holy Grail for many Madeira lovers.

There have always been those who believe the story and those who don't, but conclusive evidence for either point of view has never surfaced. Ms. David had discovered the contemporary journal of Baron Gourgaud, a friend of Napoleon's who accompanied him into exile. According to Ms. David, the journal describes the meeting with Veitch, and mentions some fresh peaches being brought on board the ship. She also says that there is no mention of a pipe of wine being loaded. Beyond what she found in Baron Gourgaud's diary, she also points out that Charles Blandy was only 12 years old (actually he was 10) when he supposedly bought the wine from Veitch.

Ms. David had planned to write an article about the wine for Britain's *Tatler* magazine. Instead, she wrote for *Tatler* about Noël's book, leaving the Napoleon story for another time, and another writer.[1] However, Ms. David's findings on the Napoleon Madeira are contained in two letters: a brief note written on February 26, 1985, to David Cossart, and a much longer letter written to Noël on March 6, 1985. Noël apparently wrote Ms. David twice, but only one letter, written March 25, 1985, survived as a carbon copy in Noël's files. The three letters can be found in Appendix XII.

Finally, just days after his first letter from Elizabeth David, Noël heard from Roy Brady in California, with whom he had enjoyed a vigorous correspondence during 1962 and 1963. Brady was the most prominent American Madeira connoisseur of his generation, and the author of a number of articles on the subject. His curiosity was a perfect match for Noël's knowledge, and their early letters are a fertile source of information on Madeira.

Noël's correspondence with Roy Brady in 1985 (see Appendix XIV) was brief, with only one letter written by each man. In his letter, Brady calls Madeira "the last great wine in the world," and compliments Noël on his book: "I am delighted with your book. I read it straight through as soon as it arrived and have been rereading parts constantly since then. It is fortunate that you managed to put *le sport* aside long enough to finish it. If only it had been available thirty years ago! My doubts would have been laid aside sooner and I would own a great deal more old Madeira than I do." Noël replied: "I am very glad you enjoyed it although its writing caused me to smoke some five million "gaspers" and to give them up after a stroke, heart failure and gout."

Noël's many complaints had in fact taken their toll, and he died on November 7, 1987. He had a long and difficult life, yet ultimately an important one. He spent most of his time on earth struggling to save not only a dying business, but a vanishing legacy, and that he would fail was perhaps inevitable. Virtually all the traditional markets for Madeira had all but disappeared, and with them the scores of companies who had made Madeira one of the world's most magical wines. Perhaps no single man, no matter how talented, could have saved Cossart, Gordon.

That a company of such noble history and valuable contributions as Cossart, Gordon could be dismembered and left as merely a "brand" is a tragedy. Yet, the tragedy would have been even greater if Noël Cossart, the last man to know the company in both good times and bad, had died without leaving behind his story.

Noël Cossart's

Madeira

The Island Vineyard

CHAPTER 1

THE DISCOVERY OF MADEIRA

The story of the discovery and rediscovery of the islands of Madeira is one of the most colourful and romantic in history. It is accurately documented in the original narrative of Franciso Alcaforado, a 15th-century squire of the household of the Infante Dom Henrique of Portugal, who sailed with João Gonçalves Zarco on all his voyages. In "Madeira Saga" in *Christie's Wine Companion* (1981), I stated that this 15th-century manuscript, written in the old Portuguese, had never been translated. I have, however, since discovered that it was published in Paris in 1671 under the title *Relation Historique de la Découverte de l'Isle de Madère*, and in London in 1675 as *The First Discovery of the Island of Madeira*. The history is continued by Dr. Gaspar Fructuoso in his 16th-century manuscript, *As Saudades da Terra*, an account of the islands of Madeira, Porto Santo, Desertas and Selvagens, which was edited with descriptive notes by Dr. Alvaro Azevedo and printed in Funchal in 1870.

In the reign of Edward III (1327-1377), "the father of England's commerce," there lived a young nobleman, Robert à Machin who traded with the ports of Genoa, Pisa and Venice, in his cog named *La Welyfare*. In 1346, Bristol supplied 24 cogs[2], *crageres, helebots, picards* and *balingeres* (ships of war) as well as 608 men for the service of the King. The men who manned these vessels were semi-mercantile, semi-marauders, with a dash of the adventurer, and their commanders became known as Merchant Venturers, who were formed into a corporation in 1564[3]. But it was not on this occasion a voyage of trade for which the tight little cog *La Welyfare* was used, nor in the service of His Highness the King. It was to carry off the daughter of one of Bristol's merchant princes[4].

> AN
> HISTORICAL
> RELATION
> OF THE
> DISCOVERY
> Of the ISLE of
> MADERA.
>
> After a tedious War, *England* enjoying a profound Peace, under the reign of her victorious Monarch, *Edward* the third. *London* her Metropolis (where then resided the King) surfeiting in Riches and Plenty, did allure the young Gentle men to participate of her pleasures: These, having now no imployment for their swords, did betake themselves to such Recreations as best suited

The first page of the 1675 edition of The First Discovery of the Island of Madeira, *by Francisco Alcaforado.*

Robert and Anna

Alcaforado tells how Robert à Machin fell desperately in love with Anna d'Arfet. In the manuscript he writes d'Arfet or de Arford, but since the story was passed to him by word of mouth, the lady's name may have been Anne of Dorset, Darbey or even Hertford. We know Robert's name was Machin because his banishment is registered in the Rolls of Parliament. Robert was a noble of inferior rank to Anna so they were not allowed to marry, the law of feudal England proclaiming that every man should marry within his rank. The couple therefore eloped in Robert's cog, manned by his servants, intending to reach the Mediterranean. They were overtaken by a north-easterly gale and driven into the Atlantic. After 13 days, running before the tempest, they found, and landed on, a thickly wooded deserted island. Anna died of exposure on arrival and Robert met his creator seven days later. Their crew buried the unfortunate couple, marking the grave with a rude wooden cross, and embarked in the cog, only to be captured by Moors and imprisoned by the King of Morocco.

Juan de Morales and Zarco

Among the crew's fellow captives was a renowned Spanish pilot and native of Seville, one Juan de Morales, who heard the reports of the land they had discovered. In 1416, on the death of Don Sancho, son of King Ferdinand of Aragon (who left his fortune for the ransom of Spanish Christians, captives of the Moors), Juan de Morales was among those repatriated. At the time Spain and Portugal were at war and the ship taking Morales home was captured by the Portuguese captain, João Gonçalves Zarco. Out of pity Zarco freed all his captives except for Morales, because he thought Morales's story of the Englishmen's discovery of land would interest his master, the Infante Dom Henrique of Portugal, better known as Prince Henry the Navigator.

Zarco discovers Porto Santo

> Glance southward through the haze, and mark
> That shadowy island floating dark
> Amid the seas serene.
> It seems some fair enchanted isle
> Like that which saw Miranda smile
> When Ariel sang unseen.[5]

In 1418 Zarco, together with Tristão Vaz Teixeyra, another squire, and a famous Genoese navigator, Bartolomeu Perestrello, were exploring the coast of Guinea on the instructions of Prince Henry, when a great storm blew them off the coast. After being battered by mountainous waves they were cast onto an island which, because it had given them shelter, they named Porto Santo.

From Porto Santo they could see a dense and dark cloud always hovering to the south-west which, Perestrello thought, or knew, as will be seen later, was land shrouded in mist. But the others thought it to be "vapours rising from the mouth of hell" and that if they approached it they would drop off the end of the world into the bottomless pit, to be eaten by the serpents and monsters which lived there. Zarco and Vaz returned to Sagres in the Algarve to report their find to the Prince, leaving Perestrello and some of the crew to occupy the island.

Rediscovery of Madeira

Knowing that the world was round, Prince Henry connected the "vapours rising from the mouth of hell" with an island he had been told of by Genoese masters of Portuguese ships during his crusading in the mid-14th century. He had of course since heard the report from Morales of the land Machin's crew had described. So he ordered Zarco and Vaz to return to Porto Santo with Morales as pilot, and thence sail into the cloud and find out what lay under it. They also took with them three transport vessels of settlers for Porto Santo. The expedition dutifully sailed into the cloud on July 1st 1420 and found there thickly wooded land which, when circumnavigated, they found to be a beautiful island, which they named for the first time, according to Zarco's log, Madeira – Island of Woods. Another island 18 miles to the south-east of Madeira was also discovered and called Ilha Deserta because it was so barren.

The group of islands was, however, known to the Moors when they invaded the Iberian peninsula in the early eighth century. They called them El Ghanam meaning small cattle, which implies herds of goats or sheep. The Medici Map in the Laurentian Library in Florence is a map of Africa, drawn in Genoa and dated 1351, which is about the time Machin died on Madeira. This map clearly marks the three islands, naming Porto Santo and Deserta and a third called Isola de Lolegname, Italian for Island of Woods. There is a marked resemblance in pronunciation between ghanam, meaning small cattle in Moorish, and *legname* meaning woods in Italian. My own theory is that Genoese commanders of Portuguese ships found El Ghanam to be thickly wooded and named it Legname: Zarco's "Madeira" is merely a Portuguese translation. Moreover, it is likely that Perestrello, as a Genoese in the service of

THE DISCOVERY OF MADEIRA

the Infante, knew of the Medici Map and so knew that the cloud was Legname/Madeira.

Prince Henry the Navigator

It may be asked why Madeira was only colonised in 1420 if it was known to Genoese masters of Portuguese ships as early as 1351.

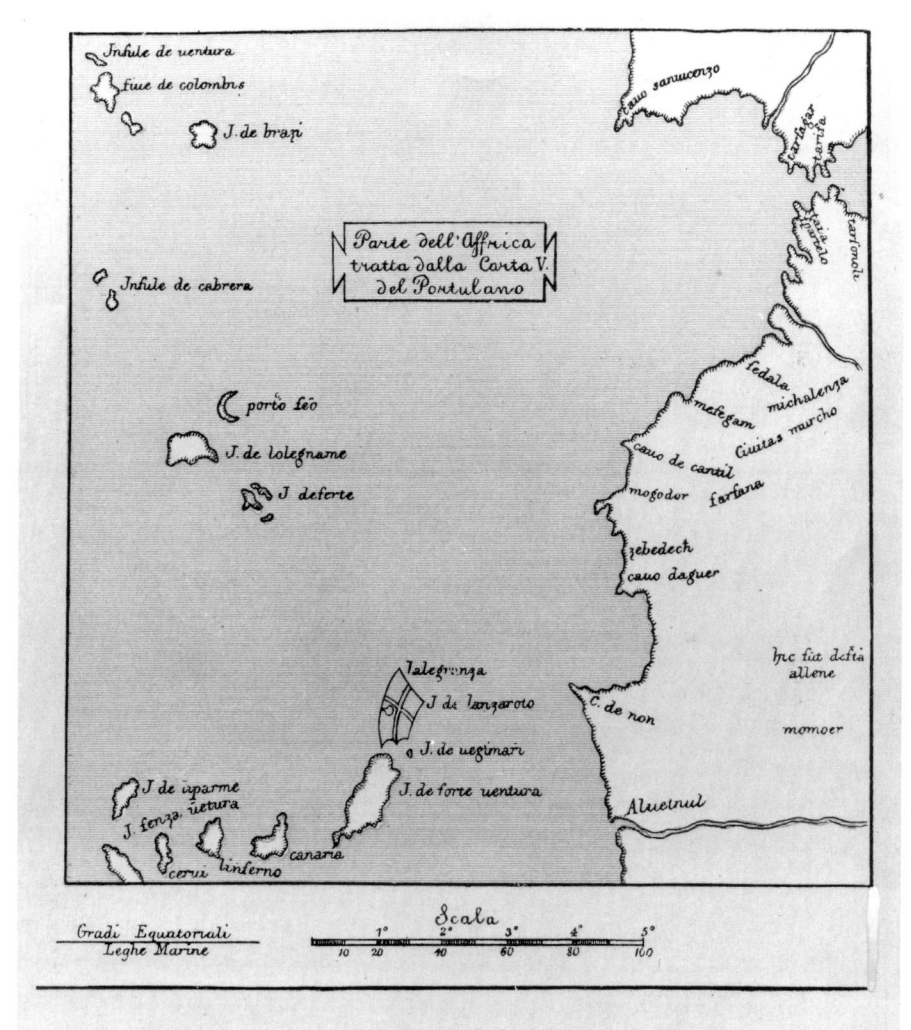

Portion of the Medici Map of Africa showing the Madeira islands.
The Medici Map, or Portulano Medicio, is of Genoese origin dated 1351. The original is in the Laurentian Library in Florence. Note that the islands of Porto Santo and Deserta are called by those names, Madeira is called "Isola de Lolegname."

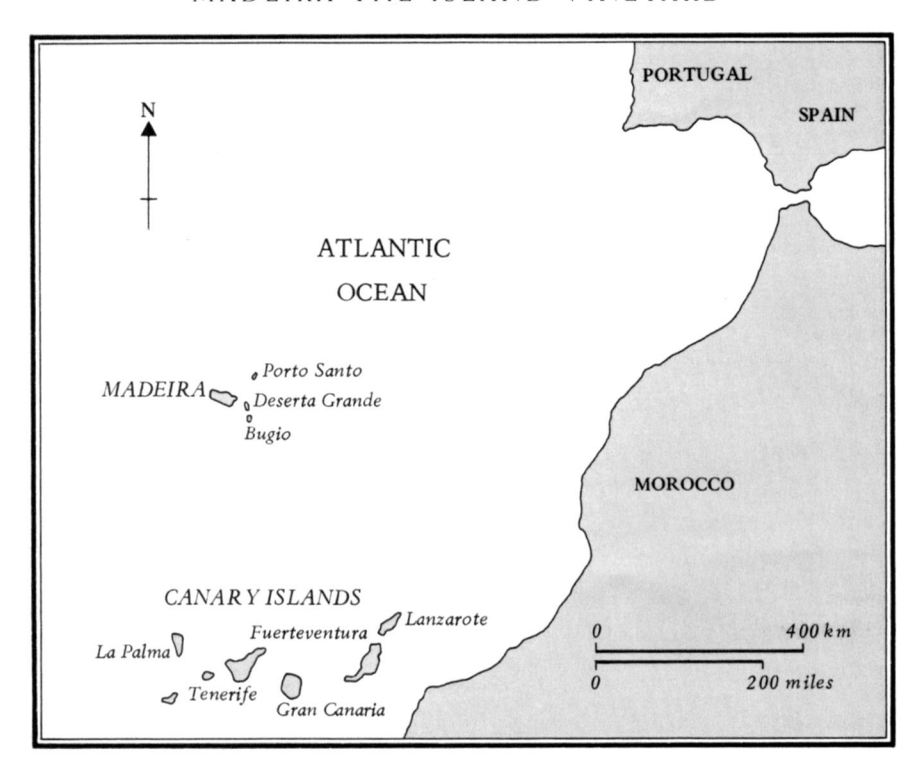

The answer is that Portugal was fully occupied ridding itself of Mahomedans. It was only when the Moorish invaders had been driven back to north Africa that the Infante Dom Henrique used his unemployed crusaders to go out and discover new lands "for the glory of God and the enrichment of Portugal."

Prince Henry was the most outstanding man of his time. He was the youngest son of the first united royal family in Europe, in which brothers did not fight each other or rebel against their father. He was a Plantagenet on his mother's side, born under the sign of Pisces on March 4th 1394. His father was King John I of Portugal and the Algarve, his mother Blanche of Lancaster, daughter of John of Gaunt. In his youth he acquired a love of travel, adventure and discovery, leading expeditions against the Moors. He conquered Ceuta in 1415 and was made governor a year later. Although he is called "The Navigator," Ceuta and Tangier were the limits of his travels. His great art was in teaching navigation and seamanship, organising expeditions and colonising the new lands. According to Azurara, after the conquest of Ceuta the Prince's renown became so high in Europe that he received separate invitations from Pope Martin V, Sigismund, Emperor of Germany, King John of Castile and King Henry V of England to take command of their armies. But he refused all four tempting invitations because he had set his heart upon discovery of unknown lands. *"Talent de bien fare"* was his adopted motto and he could not have chosen one more appropriate to his character.

On his return from Ceuta in 1418 he was appointed governor of the Algarve and took up residence on the promontory of Sagres in that province, surrounding himself with the leading navigators, explorers and astronomers of the day. The Infante Dom Henrique was granted, by royal decree, the exclusive right to send ships south of Cape Bojador, and a *quinta* (a fifth) of all profits to be obtained from those lands was reserved for him. Every year he equipped two or three expeditions, ordering them to round Cape Bojador and examine the African coast beyond. The captains received their orders with much trepidation. They knew black men lived in these dark parts, but white men could not be expected to survive in infested swamps and intense damp heat which turned men's skins black. Their *caravelas* were shallow, square-rigged craft which could not sail to windward, and they feared being unable to return to their homes because of the constant north-east wind. Failure followed failure and it was not until the *caravelas* were fitted with *patilhoes*[6] and lateen-rigged to enable them to go to windward that the Prince's wishes were fulfilled.

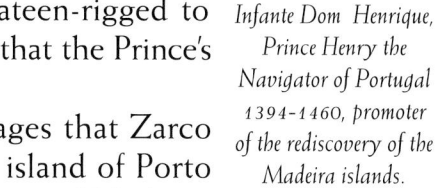

Infante Dom Henrique, Prince Henry the Navigator of Portugal 1394-1460, promoter of the rediscovery of the Madeira islands.

It was on one of these voyages that Zarco was blown off course onto the island of Porto Santo, which led to the rediscovery of Madeira. This discovery was Prince Henry's first successful enterprise, affording him a valuable weapon against his political enemies, who accused him of extravagance. These accusations were unjustified because his exploits were financed entirely from the revenue of the Order of Christ and St James and not from the public purse. This knightly order, of which the Prince became, in 1418, Grand Master, was founded in 1278 and incorporated the "soldiers of the temple," or Knights Templars, which had been formed in 1128 by Baldwin II, King of Jerusalem, to protect pilgrims. The Prince was deeply religious and a distinguished soldier, sailor and scholar. He died at Sagres in 1460.

Zarco as governor

Madeira was officially made a province of Portugal by order of the King in 1425 and donated to Prince Henry, who was not long in raising funds for fitting out a colonising expedition to his treasured islands. This expedition arrived in Madeira in 1425 headed by Zarco and Tristão Vaz Teixeyra. Three noble young bloods were commanded by the King to repair to Madeira and to marry Zarco's three daughters. Large grants of land were given to the newly wedded couples. Zarco became governor of the south side of Madeira and the Deserta Islands, and Vaz of the north, with a mountain range between them "in case they quarrelled," having left the sea. Zarco was the senior governor and occupied the position for 40 years.

Although his proper name was João Gonçalves, he was nicknamed "O Zarco" (The Squinter) because he had been wounded in one eye at Ceuta: When he was knighted and became hereditary captain of Madeira he adopted his nickname as a surname and became known as João Gonçalves Zarco. He was born at Santarem in 1395, the son of the overseer to King John's household. He was the first captain to introduce artillery on board ship, and a favourite of Prince Henry's, being a very brave and powerful man. The arms granted him by Prince Henry were confirmed by King Alfonso V in 1460. He had no sons and his descendants today are called Zarco da Câmara.

Shortly before he died, the inhabitants of Madeira were in great distress at the sight of three French pirate ships entering the bay of Funchal. Zarco ordered that he should be carried down to the beach where, carrying his mighty sword,[7] he mounted a grey horse with

Zarco's statue in the center of Funchal.

his men behind him. Although he had to be propped on his mount by two retainers on each side, such was his fame as a mighty warrior that the Frenchman went about and left Funchal in peace.

Zarco died when he was 80 (a great age in those times). He is buried in the old church adjoining the Santa Clara convent, which was built in 1492, the year of America's discovery.

Early Settlers

The first settlers consisted of scions of the noble families of Portugal, as well as Flemish, Genoese, German, Polish, French and British adventurers. The latter adopted Portuguese versions of their names; for instance, the son of Sir John Drummond, Master of Stobhall, became João Escocio, John the Scot. There are today two Portuguese branches of the family descended from him in Madeira, the Drummonds and Escocios.

Adam and Eve

The first children born in Madeira were twins who were named Adam and Eve. They were the offspring of Gonçallo Ayres Ferreira, a companion of Zarco on his first voyage who had subsequently taken his wife to the island in 1425. At first Madeira had only a few settlers, but in 1453 the new island attracted the attention of Europe's colonising countries and settlers from Spain, Italy and Holland began to arrive, as well as Moors and Negro slaves from Africa and the Canaries. A list of the early settlers is appended at the end of this book.

Vines from Crete

Prince Henry ordered plants of sugar cane from Sicily and vines from Crete to be brought to the islands and planted. The vines were of the sweet grapes originally from Monemvasia in the Peloponnese. The name became corrupted into *malmsey* in English, *malvasia* in Italian and Portuguese, and *malvoisie* in French. His plan was to capture for Portugal the trade in sugar and sweet wines hitherto enjoyed by the Genoese and Venetians, whilst not competing with produce grown on the mainland. The scheme succeeded, both vines and sugar flourishing in the favourable volcanic soil and mild climate of Madeira. The viticulture and viniculture were mostly in the hands of Jesuits. Alves da Mosto, a Venetian traveller who called at Madeira on his way to Africa in

1455, said the vines "produce more grapes than leaves, and the clusters were of extraordinary size."

Weaving

Weaving, brought from Holland with the second batch of settlers, became and still is, an industry; the hand looms used today are as primitive as those employed four centuries ago. The weavers use dyes made from wood, bark, roots and berries. Dogwood and copperas produce shades of purple and black; wild berries supply yellows, madder, red and brown. These are used for the dress fabrics worn by the country girls, whose full dress is not complete without an exquisitely embroidered bodice.

Seven years' fire

In the early days there were no villages in the interior. No roads had been built, because the forests were impenetrable, and the only way of getting from place to place was by sea. In order that the settlers should have cleared land to cultivate, Zarco deemed it necessary to denude portions of the island of the forests by setting fire to them. He sought permission from the Prince, who unfortunately agreed. The fire, once begun, burned for seven years. It is said that the wood ash greatly enriched the soil, which is undoubtedly true, but it also denuded the island of its magnificent trees, which attracted the moisture causing the "mouth of hell" effect.

Machico

When Zarco and Vaz first discovered Madeira, they found Anna's and Robert's grave under a pile of stones, marked by a wooden cross and bearing a message requesting any Christian who found it to build a chapel on the site in memory of the lovers. They called the place Machico after Machin and it became the first capital of Madeira. The chapel of Senhor dos Milagres (Lord of Miracles) was built and the cross placed inside it. The original building was partly destroyed by flood in 1803 and rebuilt by Robert Page.

Funchal

When Machico valley became too small to accommodate the first town, the settlers moved to the great protected bay of Funchal, which became Madeira's second capital and was raised to the rank of city in 1508. In this year the building of the cathedral was begun by King Manoel at his personal expense, and in 1514 the first bishop was appointed.

Invasion

In 1556 a calamity occurred. Payrot de Montluc, son of Marshal de Montluc, entered the bay of Funchal with his war fleet. They bombarded the cathedral, burnt residences, pillaged churches and robbed and murdered the inhabitants. Finally he carried off most of the male population to swell his depleted ranks.

Perestrello and his rabbits

Meanwhile, Bartolomeu Perestrello lost grace with his master. He had been a squire of Genoese origin in the household of Prince Henry's brother, the Infante Dom João, but, being a renowned seaman and navigator, he had been co-opted by Henry. When he was governor of Porto Santo he introduced rabbits onto the island, which ate everything. He was left on Porto Santo until his death but, in gratitude for his service to Portugal, the governorship became a family inheritance which lasted for many generations. Even when a descendant, Garcia Perestrello,[8] was beheaded for the murder of his mother, his son inherited the office.

Perestrello's daughter, Filipa Perestrello e Moniz, married a young Genoese map maker, Cristobal Colon (Christopher Columbus), who was later to discover America. Filipa inherited her father's log and maps and it was after studying these that Colon came to the conclusion that there was a short cut across the western ocean to Japan.

Christopher Columbus

In 1480 Columbus submitted his plan for crossing the ocean to the King of Portugal, but it was turned down by the council. It is quite certain that had Prince Henry been alive when the offer was made he would have backed it. Columbus hawked his theory round the courts of Europe for five years, until finally, in 1485, it was accepted by Isabella of Spain, who fell in love with the adventurer's flaming red mane and mountebank manner rather than his theories.

Columbus and his brother Bartolomeu lived in Lisbon and Madeira between 1470 and 1485. When in Madeira, Christopher lived in a palace[9] originally built by a Fleming, Jean d'Esmenaut (later Esmeraldo), which stood in a lane between Rua do Sabão and Rua do Esmeralda, now named Rua Cristovão Colombo.

*The house of Columbus, by H. Vanostrand, from the book
"A Winter in Madeira," New York, 1850.*

CHAPTER 2

THE MADEIRA ISLANDS

Queen Isabella once asked Columbus to give her some idea of the appearance of the island of Jamaica. The great explorer, taking a piece of paper, crushed it and opened it out. "This," he said, "will give your Royal Majesty a better notion than any I might be able to tell you." Such an apt demonstration could not be better used than to describe the geographical conformation of the island of Madeira, which rises abruptly from the ocean like a wall of vertical cliffs. The highest peaks are formed in a central group 1,860 metres above the sea. From these great peaks innumerable deeply furrowed ravines, with precipitous sides, radiate in all directions towards the coast, where the towns and villages nestle.

The Madeira islands are the summits of a vast mountain range, said to be the lost continent of Atlantis, running parallel to the African coast and thrown up by mighty volcanic upheavals countless centuries ago. Soundings in the north Atlantic have shown that the Madeiras rise from the midst of the ocean and their summits, if the water could be drained off, would tower more than six kilometres above the sea bed.

Formation

The islands are wholly volcanic and, with the exception of Porto Santo, are composed almost entirely of basalt, which may be seen in crystalline form arranged in vertical columns on the cliff faces. Between these strata of basalt are deposits of highly coloured red and yellow tufa which poured from the craters when the volcanoes, now extinct, ejected triturated material mixed with steam in the form of mud instead of lava. These deposits contain coral, shells and parts of plants.

Enterprising Portuguese navigators discovered and colonised

half the world in the 15th and 16th centuries, but the lands they found were never considered colonies: they were "provinces," as were Angola and Mozambique until their recent independence. Madeira is autonomous, with its own parliament and financial structure, but is still a province of Portugal. It is therefore politically in Europe, although geographically in Africa.

Looking inland from near Faial.

Position and dimensions

The name "Madeira" is shared by three other islands (or groups of islands) which together form the archipelago: Porto Santo, the Desertas and the Selvagens. The centre of Madeira is latitude 32 degrees and 45 minutes north and longitude 17 degrees west of Greenwich, 590 kilometres west of Casablanca and 978 kilometres south-west of Lisbon. Bermuda, Los Angeles, Savannah and Jerusalem are on the same parallel as Funchal, and in the southern hemisphere Buenos Aires, Valparaiso and Perth (Western Australia) are on the same latitude. The island covers an area of 741 square kilometres: at its widest, it is 57 kilometres from east to west and 23 from north to south.

Climate

A warm current flows past Madeira towards the south-south-west at the rate of 19 to 25 kilometres a day. The island has an average annual surface temperature of 21 degrees Centigrade and the trade wind blows regularly from the north-east for about 300 days in the year. The tide has a range of two metres and the depth of the sea round the island is between 3,000 and 6,000 metres. The mean annual temperature in Funchal, the capital, is 19 degrees Centigrade, with a daily range of two degrees out of doors. Summer temperatures rarely exceed 27 degrees Centigrade while winter temperatures seldom go below 16 degrees. In the lowlands the annual rainfall is about 75 centimetres (higher than in London), most of which falls between October and April. The rest of the year is practically rainless. There are occasional violent storms from the south-west in winter, which damage cultivation along the south coast but do not affect the deep sheltered valleys of the interior.

Sometimes an intense heat-wave known as the *leste* or sirocco blows from the south-east, lasting from one to nine days, during which temperatures of 40 degrees Centigrade or more are registered. The *leste* blows directly from the Sahara desert and brings with it a thick haze of suspended sand. These *leste* winds do enormous damage to the vines (especially as there is generally one in mid-August), covering the grapes with dust and destroying the natural ferments. Good vintage years are generally those when there has not been a *leste* in August.

Plant diseases

Many plant diseases have appeared from time to time. Of these the most important are the Mediterranean fly, the phylloxera, innumerable scale insects, and the Argentine ant. The latter arrived in the first half of the 19th century and by 1850 had overwhelmed the native ants.

The chief fungus pests are the canker of the chestnuts, oidium of the vine and gum disease of the citrus fruits. In spite of these pests and diseases the valuable economic plants seem to fight through successfully.

Agriculture

The extreme upper limit of cultivation is between 700 and 900 metres. Above that altitude there is a large area too rocky and exposed for tillage, but which is used to pasture sheep, goats and wild ponies and for afforestation with pine trees (*Pinus pinaster*). Terraces have been constructed on every mountainside, representing enormous expenditure of labour. In most cases retaining walls of huge basaltic blocks, six to ten metres high, are built with great neatness, no mortar being used, so that free drainage is assured. They are very rarely known to collapse, even after torrential rain. The soil used for filling these terraces, or poios as they are called, is tufa either scraped from the mountainside higher up, or collected and carted from the dry river bed below. Artificial manures are rarely seen except for guano used by the richer farmers.

Grape vines are planted on the terraces from sea level up to, and sometimes even above, 450 metres. Below 200 metres sugar cane and bananas are extensively cultivated, and in the eastern part of the island large crops of onions are grown for export. Custard apple, fig, loquat, and avocado pear trees are seen everywhere on the lowlands. At the higher altitudes of 450 to 900 metres, cabbages, maize, wheat and other cereals are grown. There are also extensive plantations of beans for export. Apples, pears and stone fruit are grown at these altitudes. The sweet potato, which features universally in the diet, flourishes at all levels.

Soil and implements

It is doubtful whether there is another place in the world where there are so many varied soils in such a small area. The names given to the principal soils are *saibro*, decomposed red tufa; *cascalho*, stony soil; *pedra mole*, an arenaceous soil of decomposed yellow tufa; and *massapes* (literally meaning thump-foot), clay resulting from the decomposition of dark tufas.

The implement used to cut up the soil for cultivation is a pickaxe or mattock, called an *enchada*, which has one short arm and a long handle. This type of implement was brought from the Algarve in 1440 by the first settlers and has been in use ever since. Because of the enormous variety of soils, no less than six different shapes of *enchada* have been developed in Madeira; and yet another type is used to cut up the limestone on Porto Santo. These *enchadas* range from the original *enchada de bico* which has a blade 25 centimetres long, the shoulders nearest the handle being 12 centimetres wide, sloping to a sharp point (for use on rough stony *cascalho*), to the *enchada de pá* which has a rather longer blade, increasing from the shoulders to a spade-shaped round cutting edge 20 centimetres wide (used on *massapes*). The blades are made of quarter-inch steel and weigh about two kilos. The handles are of tree heath (*Erieaeea arborea*), an exceedingly hard wood, and are usually one metre long (according to the height of the person wielding it), with a diameter of five centimetres. Every labourer has his own *enchada* made for him, fitted with the precision of a custom-made gun. The handles have been known to last for over a century.

Other agricultural implements peculiar to Madeira are the *fouee*, a toothed sickle used for cutting grass, and the *podão* which resembles a pruning hook. A rude wooden plough drawn by oxen is occasionally used on the flatter regions, but the size of the terraces on the steep hill sides makes the use of mechanical diggers almost impossible.

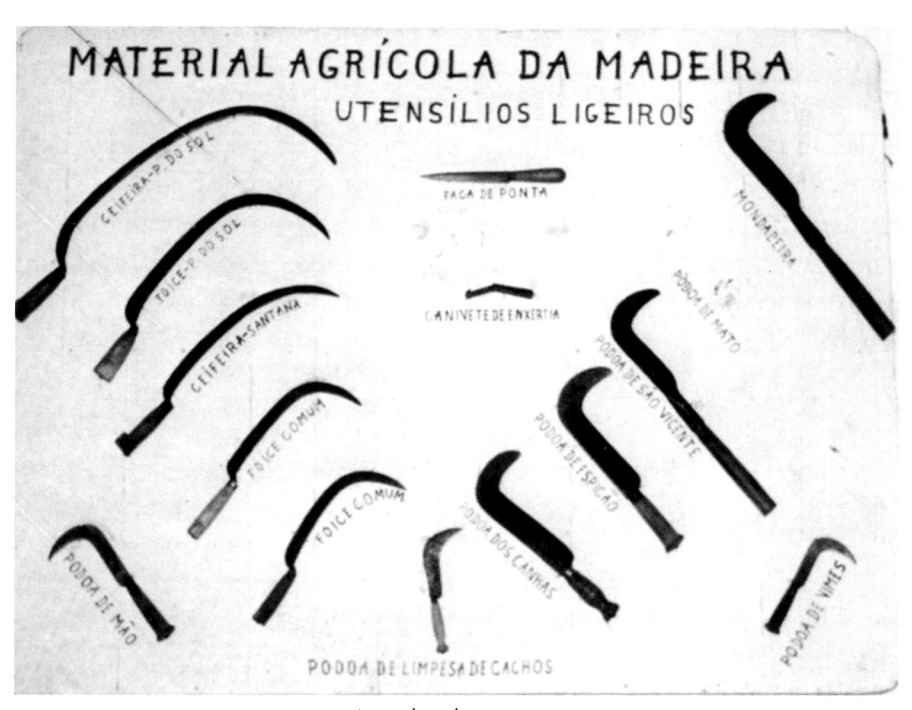

Agricultural instruments.

Irrigation

Madeira is a huge self-adjusting reservoir holding over 200,000 million litres of water. The wooded mountains attract moisture from miles around, which penetrates the light volcanic ash until it meets the solid basaltic floor. It is then forced upwards by its own weight until it gushes from mountain springs. These springs are tapped by a remarkable and intricate system of aqueducts (*levadas*) to irrigate the lowlands during the rainless months. These *levadas* penetrate into the moist valleys, intercepting every available spring, and distribute the water to the various properties to fill storage tanks. They were cut through the forests soon after the island was populated and are a feat of engineering. When Alfonso d'Albuquerque was in search of Prester John in Abyssinia in 1508 he took *levadeiros* (men expert in *levada* building) from Madeira with a view to damming the Nile.

The original *levadas*, built circa 1580, were solely for irrigation. At the beginning of this century there were some 200 *levadas* extending for about 1,000 kilometres. Most of these were in private hands, and although there was plenty of water, it was unfairly distributed, so that only two-thirds of the arable land was irrigated. In 1939 the Portuguese government instituted a combined irrigation-hydroelectric scheme which now assures regular distribution of water to every property, as well as generating electricity. The *levada* network comprises 2,150 kilometres of aqueducts flowing through 40 kilometres of tunnels. The new *levadas* are constructed where rainfall and springs are greatest, at around 1,000 metres altitude. Each *levada* is bordered by a path lined with mimosa, blue agapanthus, pink belladonna lilies and hydrangea hedges six feet high with blooms the size of soup plates.[10] The water is channelled to power stations at the edge of the upper limit of arable land, at about 600 metres. After passing through the power stations the water flows on to the irrigation zones where it is deviated from the main stream into each property.

Tenure of land

The land in Madeira is cultivated by *colonos*, or tenants, under a peculiar feudal system which, although it has been modified since the 1974 revolution, remains today very much the same as it was in the 15th century. In most cases the land is owned by *senhorios*, or landlords, descended from the first noble settlers to whom the crown gave large tracts of land. These *senhorios* let out the land to tenant farmers. If the tenant lives on the land he leases he is called a *caseiro* (from *casa* – the house that he lives in); otherwise he is called a *meyro* (from *meyo*, meaning half). The *caseiro* will generally pay, either in cash or kind, some sort of rent for the house he lives in or, if he has built a house himself on the *senhorio*'s land, he pays only ground rent in the form of either cash or a pig or several hens a year.

The *senhorio* usually owns nothing but the land, the tenant being owner of everything on it – trees, vines, walls, houses, etc. – to which the name *bemfeitorias* (improvements) is given. The tenants give one half of the main cereal crops, wine, willows, sugar cane, bananas and other fruit crops, to the landlord, who has a right to buy the tenant's half. The landlord has also the right to half the grass, but this is rarely collected. The landlord provides sulphur, copper sulphate, extra labour, stakes for vines, etc., but the tenant keeps the *verduras* – small crops such as potatoes, cabbages, lupins and beans. If the arrangement comes to an end, the landlord has to indemnify the tenant for everything he leaves on the land, provided it has been built or planted with the landlord's consent.

Levada near Santo da Serra.

Cattle and Sheep

These arrangements, however, seldom do come to an end, being carried on from father to son. The same sort of procedure applies to cattle and sheep. For instance, a calf is given by its owner (*dono*) to a *creador* who will raise it for him. The *creador* is entitled to two-thirds of the milk and manure, and the owner the remaining third. The milk co-operative insures the cow and collects the milk, accounting to the owner for his one-third share, from which the premium is deducted. When a calf is born, half its selling price belongs to the owner. When the cow itself is sold, the "seed money" (initial cost of the calf) is deducted and the balance divided in equal parts between the *dona* and *creador*.

This system works very well, so when my son was born and his godfather gave him £10, I bought a calf. By the time he went to prep school eight-and-a-half years later, he owned three cows and had £65 in the bank, all from one calf costing £10.

Cows are almost always kept in small shacks and manger fed, so much so that they will not crop grass when taken out for their usual Sunday afternoon walks. Due to this general lack of exercise they have to be manicured weekly. The object of keeping the animals in cow houses where beds of straw or bracken are laid for them, is, of course, to obtain the maximum manure so valuable for the crops. Writing about Madeira in the *Daily Mail*, Iris Ashley described how she visited a cow whose bed was made of camellias.

View from Cape Girão, the second highest cliff in the world.

Ornamental plants

In the lowlands, some of the chief ornamental plants which attract immediate attention are bougainvillea, *Brugmansia*, *Bignonia*, *Passiflora* (passion fruit), aloe, *Euphorbia*, wistaria, *Chorisia*, *Sterculia* and *Thunbergia*. Up to 300 metres and over are found hydrangea, *Clethra*, acacia, fuschia, *Ornithogalum*, ixia, *Watsonia*, *Vallota*, belladonna and camellia. In addition, pine and cypresses, tree heaths, innumerable ferns, the giant blackberry, buttercups and a quaint rosette-like flowering leek all flourish. In the last decade the growing of orchids and sub-tropical flowers for export has become a large industry.

Willows

In the damp valleys, willows are grown for wicker work, which has become one of the largest exports. The Madeira willow, a cross between *Salix alba* and *Salix fragilis*, produces very fine supple shoots, ideal for basket work. The tree is never allowed to grow up: the shoots are cut near the ground from January to March, and are kept in water until they start sprouting. Then they are peeled and dried. In 1850 Messrs. William Hinton and James Taylor imported craftsmen from England to teach the Portuguese at Camacha the art of basket making. The centre of the industry has remained at Camacha ever since. Madeira produces 900 to 1,000 tons of willows annually, which are exported as either bottle covers, baskets or furniture to England, America and South Africa.

Porto Santo

The second island, Porto Santo, is 74 kilometres north-east of Madeira, and is 12 kilometres long and seven wide. The island is formed entirely of limestone, which is not to be found in Madeira. It is very dry and arid, and the little water there tends to be brackish, but has medicinal properties and is bottled.

Porto Santo has a lovely protected bay with a yellow sandy beach 14 kilometres long. A full-sized international airport takes up most of the island, which is much flatter than the others. It rises to a peak 507 metres high, on which in 1418 a castle was built to defend the inhabitants from the raiding Moorish pirates. The island is inhabited by fishermen and in the summer months is invaded by tourists from Madeira who enjoy the beach and the fishing. Although the airport has taken much land, the Porto Santo vineyards produce some of the best wine.

The people of Porto Santo are nicknamed *profetas* after Fernando Nunes, a knight who was one of the early settlers. He was known as Fernando "The Brave" and, according to Fructuoso, he descended from the hills in 1533 ringing a bell and proclaiming he was Jesus Christ, sent by the Holy Ghost to save the people of Porto Santo from Satan. Fructuoso says he performed miracles, healing paralytics, so he became known as "The Prophet." It is recorded that "The Prophet" was preaching one day to the multitude who had "publicly confessed their many and abominable sins." During the sermon, he noticed the parish priest, Father Calaça, reading his prayer book so he called out "those who pray from books have the devil in their body," whereupon the crowd set upon the wretched priest and murdered him.

Desertas

The three Deserta Islands are uninhabited except for wild goats, cats, rabbits, birds and the Mediterranean monk seals (*Monachus albiventer*), which, since they are very tame, are killed by the fishermen. These islands, Deserta Grande (14 by 1.60 kilometres), Bugio and the flat Ilheu Chão, are 33 kilometres south-east of Madeira. They are the wildest islands in the Atlantic. To the north of Chão a curious needle rock rises from 150 metres deep to 50 metres above the sea; it is called Sail Rock because of its resemblance to a ship under full sail.

From 1420 these islands were owned by descendants of Zarco, Madeira's discoverer and first governor. Once there were eight houses and a chapel on Deserta Grande, the ruins of which may still be seen, with the remains of dew ponds, threshing floors and ovens that were used to burn *barilha* (ice plant) for making soda. Large and small cattle were pastured and wheat and barley grown, but the inhabitants left when the best grazing was eroded by a waterspout[11] in 1802. The *Orchilla* (lichen) which grows on the rocks was used in the preparation of dyes and exported for high prices, but it is valueless today. Owing to the lack of water the islands are virtually bare of vegetation and although there are a few blades of grass one wonders what even the goats find to eat. Fructuoso tells us that when the islands were discovered there were goats "which were taken with dogs," but it is difficult to imagine modern dogs hunting on the precipitous cliffs.

These wild goats are a rusty brown with black beards and markings down the back and shoulders. The male has beautifully curved horns which have a span of 55 to 65 centimetres. The Deserta rabbit, noticed by Darwin, shows great changes in shape, colour and size through continuous inter-breeding. The skull has remained the same size as that of the ordinary wild rabbit, but the body is about eight centimetres shorter. Their rust colour comes from the soil, which makes them almost red and, whereas other wild rabbits have blackish tips to the ears and upper part of the tail, the Deserta variety has lost these markings.

There is some broom and bracken and, in spring, masses of white poppy (*Papaver somniferum*). The giant Deserta carrot (*Monizia edulis*), growing to a height of 1.5 metres, is peculiar to the Desertas and Selvagen islands. The other plants peculiar to the Desertas are the *Echium nervosum* and the Bugio pink daisy (*Chrysanthemum hoematomma*). Another interesting inhabitant is the *Lycosa ingens*, a large black spider whose bite is supposed to be fatal. Fortunately, it keeps itself to one old threshing floor at the north of the main island.

I dwell a little on the subject of these wild islands because in 1894 my grandfather and Mr. Harry Hinton of Madeira bought them from the Marquez de Castello Melhor, who entitled himself "Eleventh Lord of the Desertas." By this time they had become valueless except for the excellent shooting and fishing they provide. I can look back on many happy days stalking wild goats and catching barracuda and tunny fish round the coast. Indeed many people came to the islands for this reason: our game book registers the names of such distinguished guests as Prince August d'Arenburg, Prince Sapieha, Duc d'Abruzzi, Duc de Leuchtenberg, Count Deym, Sir George Bullough and Admiral Fairfax. Major Weissman, governor-general of German East Africa, and Colonel J. C. Statham, RAMC, in their books on big game hunting both declared stalking on the Desertas to be the finest sport they had experienced. The Marquis de Vogué, of champagne fame, painted fine watercolours of the islands and that great sportsman Prince Albert of Monaco was so fond of the islands that he came regularly in his yacht *Hirondelle*. One year he brought a pair of Corsican *mouflon* to be put on the island, but in spite of much care, the goats destroyed them.

With much regret my brother, my sister, Mr. Hinton's stepson, Mr. George Welsh, and I myself sold the islands to the Portuguese National Trust in 1971 with the object that they, and the Selvagens, also privately owned, should become a marine biology observatory and bird sanctuary. The contract was signed on December 31st 1971 by Brigadier Antonio Braamcamp Sobral, then governor of Madeira, and ourselves.

The islands abound with every sort of land and sea bird, including the Atlantic herring gull, Cory's shearwater, Manx shearwater, Madeira little shearwater, Madeira petrel and the rare soft-plumaged petrel (*Petrodroma mollis*). A recent discovery by David Bannerman has shown that this rare bird, only to be found in

Madeira and the Australian islands, has two different breeding populations, one on Madeira and another on the Desertas. One population has a heavier bill than the other and they breed at different times. They are distinguished as *Petrodroma mollis madeirensis* and *Petrodroma mollis deserta*.

The shearwaters act as the eyes of the tuna fishermen. They flock over the bait which the tuna are following, showing the men where the fish are. The fishermen cannot afford modern sounding devices so they rely on the birds, but they are short-sightedly destroying the young birds for the down they produce. One of the main reasons we sold the islands was because we could not afford to protect the birds from the fishermen.

Selvagen islands

The uninhabited Selvagen islands, Great Piton and Little Piton, are also part of the Madeira group, although they are 280 kilometres south of Madeira and only 165 kilometres from Tenerife. Great Selvagen island (Wild island) is 2.5 by 2.2 kilometres and lies approximately 30 degrees north and 16 degrees west of Greenwich. The islands are used only by fishermen and used to be a rendezvous for diamond smugglers from Angola. It is said that great treasure from three Mexican treasure ships was buried on Selvagen island by Spanish pirates but, in spite of many searches, it has never been found.

Landing on Selvagen island is easy once inside the harbour, but the entrance is tricky because of submerged rocks. Two ornithologist friends of mine who were preparing to visit the islands were delighted to be offered a lift to be "dropped off" on the Selvagen Grande by the admiral commanding the Royal Yacht *Britannia*, which was in Funchal Roads on her way to the Caribbean to meet the Queen. When the yacht arrived off the island the admiral did not like the look of the entrance, so in mid-Atlantic he passed them by breeches buoy to the escort ship HMS *Naiad*, which dropped them off by helicopter.

The economy

The wonderful fertility of the island and the zeal of its inhabitants are shown by the fact that 400 square kilometres of tillable land support a population of over 254,000, in addition to which there is a considerable and varied tourist population, responsible for Madeira's largest source of income. Another major source is

Funchal

remittances, averaging some £45 million annually, from emigrants now living in Europe, Brazil, North America, Venezuela and South Africa. The bulk of this money is invested in property for the emigrants' retirement.

Until World War I, wine was the most important agricultural product exported. Today it represents only 11 per cent of total agricultural production and 16 per cent of total exports. Bananas are now more important, accounting for some 28 per cent of agricultural exports. These, however, are exported to the Portuguese mainland at preferential rates and it is expected that when Portugal joins the EEC, this export will diminish, and wine will again become the largest and most valuable export. Apart from wine and bananas, dairy produce, beans, tomatoes, fruit, orchids and sub-tropical flowers, embroidery and basket work are also exported.

The people

Of the total population, over 85,000 live in the capital town of Funchal. The Madeirians or, to use their correct name, Madeirense, are a most industrious people. We have seen in the first chapter that they are a mixed race, as is shown by their customs and language, which is different from the Portuguese spoken on the mainland. Many words derived from English are used in the Madeirense language. For instance in Madeira the word for potato is *semilha* whereas the Portuguese is *batata*. *Semilha* is derived from the word "Seed" because the British brought the first seed potatoes to the island.

In the early history of the islands, slaves were brought from Africa and sold in Madeira. There were some 2,700 of them in

Banana plantations near Funchal.

1552, and it was not until 1775 that slavery was abolished in Madeira by a decree of the Marquis of Pombal. The liberated negroes then intermarried with the natives of European descent. Furthermore, many of the Madeirense have a mixture of Moorish blood brought by pirates who infested the Mediterranean. When vanquished they settled in Madeira in large numbers. Thus may the dark complexion and peculiarities of race, costume, music and dances among some Madeirense be accounted for.

Pearl of the Atlantic

Until 1960 Madeira was a haven of rest in mid-Atlantic, where old wine and gracious living were enjoyed for little cost or effort. The wine seemed to absorb the character of the atmosphere in which it was produced. Madeira was the playground of the British upper class, and the *sportif* snorkling Parisian who came to escape the rigours of the northern winter. They arrived by the antiquated means of ocean liners bound for South Africa and South America, staying at the sophisticated hotels, or renting or buying houses. They settled down with the residents to benefit from the low cost of living, the near absence of taxation, and were attracted to the "Pearl of the Atlantic" by its beauty and the hospitality of its people.

Marshal Pilsudski of Poland and King Carl of Austria lived and died in Madeira, while ex-President Batista of Cuba settled with his considerable family on a whole floor of the famous Reid's Hotel. Among illustrious regular visitors to Reid's were Lord Birkenhead and family, George Bernard Shaw – who learnt to dance there – Lady Jellicoe, Sir Winston Churchill – who painted in Madeira – and Fanny and John Craddock, who wrote about the gracious living of Madeira, but were not so impressed after 1960.

The advent of air travel

In 1960 a radical change shattered the tranquillity of the happy-go-lucky residents: an airport was built on the island of Porto Santo, and later a small airstrip was constructed on the main island of Madeira. Whilst the peasant tilled his land with an ox and an ass harnessed

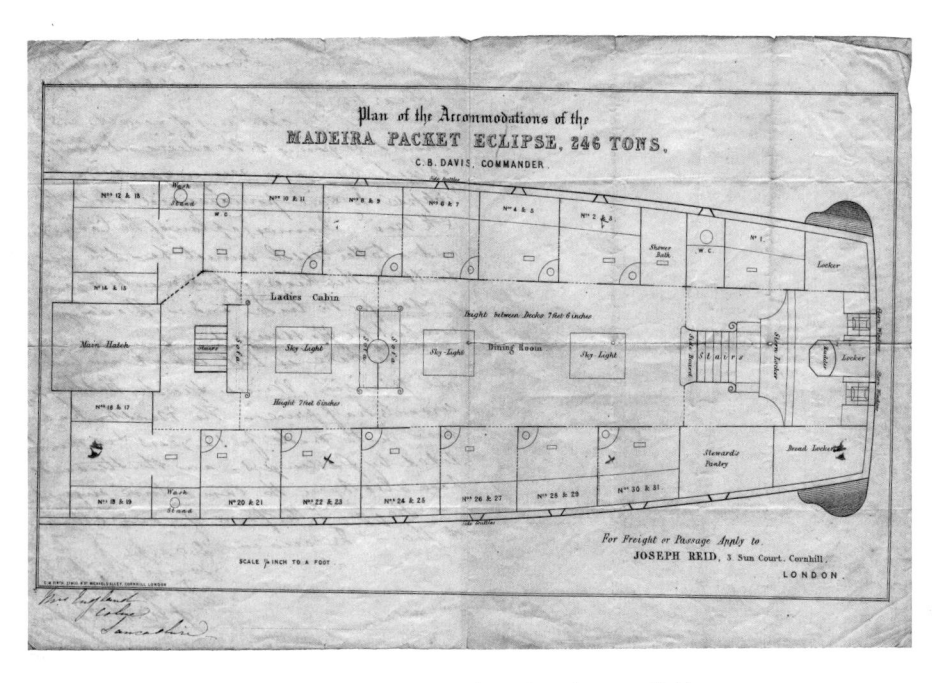

Cabin plan for the Madeira Packet Eclipse that travelled between England and Madeira in the nineteenth century.

to a wooden plough, bulldozers flattened mountains to make the airport on which jets first landed that autumn. The almost biblical peace was rudely disrupted, but Madeira was brought into the civilised world. For the first time one could read a London paper on the same day as it was published. Hotel accommodation immediately increased from 300 beds to 900 and tourists poured into the "Pearl of the Atlantic." Only the wine retained its gracious tranquillity.

Princess Maria Pia de Saboia was among the well-heeled visitors to travel to Madeira by flying boat in the 1950s.

CHAPTER 3

BIRTH OF THE WINE TRADE

Early records of viniculture in Madeira are scarce. The first reference to wine is of a levy imposed in 1485 to assist pay the council's expenses, and in the same year wine, together with a quantity of corn, was part of a parish priest's stipend. Paulo Perestrello da Câmara tells us that François I of France had "Malvasia" and "Seco" from Madeira during the wars with England. It has even been said that Malvasia was drunk when François met Henry VIII on The Field of the Cloth of Gold in 1520. Custom House records show Madeira was shipped to the Low Countries and France at 3,200 reis per pipe (approximately 14 English shillings) in 1566, and in his *History of Portugal* Rebelo da Silva says it was shipped to the New World in 1567. In the narrative of his voyage in 1588, Diego Lopes writes "Malvasia wine is the best in the universe, and is taken to India and many parts of the world."

Left, Francis Newton; right, Thomas Murdoch of Cumloden

Shakespeare and Madeira

There are no early records of Madeira being sent to England, although Shakespeare implies that it was a commonplace drink in London at the end of the 16th century. Mistress Quickly shrieked at Falstaff, "Yonder he comes: and that arrant-malmsey-nose knave, Bardolph." And elsewhere, "Jack," said Poins to the same noble knight, "how agrees the devil and thee about thy soul, that thou soldest him on Good Friday last for a cup of Madeira and a cold capon's leg?" These are some of Shakespeare's anachronisms, because Sir John Falstaff lived in the reign of King Henry IV (1399 to 1413), before Madeira was discovered. Prince Henry refers to "score a pint of bastard in the Half Moon," and "why then your brown bastard is your only drink?" in King Henry IV Part 1. Here Shakespeare was referring to Bastardo, wine from a vine which was not replanted in Madeira for a long time after phylloxera. The Madeira drunk in Shakespeare's day was a strong unfortified wine, and "Madeira Burgundy" was considered superior to and stronger than the wine from the French duchy. Although the Malmsey of that time was unfortified, and probably fermented right out, it was said to be "exceeding sweet."

The Castilian yoke

Phillip II of Castile seized the kingdom of Portugal in 1580. It remained under the Spanish yoke until the Portuguese revolted in 1640, restoring the kingdom by placing John, Duke of Braganza, on the throne. But it was not until the Spanish army was finally defeated at Villa Vicosa in 1665 that Portugal established its full independence and regained possession of the Madeiras.

The Spanish did not encourage the growth or export of wine during their occupation because it competed with their own, so there were virtually no exports from Madeira during this period. The growing of sugar cane, which had become well established, sugar being a valuable commodity of which Spain had none, was greatly encouraged and became a strong rival to the vine. However, when King John came to the throne he ordered his ships bound for Brazil to call at Madeira and take wine to his settlements: and this became the foundation of the Madeira wine trade.

BIRTH OF THE WINE TRADE

A royal wedding

It was the marriage on May 21st 1662 of Charles II of England to the *infanta* of Portugal (sister to King Alfonso VII) that gave real impetus to the Madeira wine trade. The King of Portugal was "not a little mad," he was, indeed, quite mad, so his kingdom was ruled by his sagacious mother, Dona Luisa de Braganza, assisted by the faithful old chancellor, Dom Francisco de Mello. The country's resources were depleted after 60 years of warring with Spain. Charles I of England had been approached for help but his subjects had cut off his head, so Dona Luisa was overjoyed to hear that the poor Stuart prince had returned home to become Charles II. She is known to have said, "The British are very like us, a seaboard race nurtured upon tradition and who like us cannot live beneath tyranny." Dona Luisa set about arranging a marriage, but there were difficulties. Charles was a heretic so a dispensation from the Pope was required. Hitherto the Vatican would not offend the Most Catholic King of Spain by recognising Portugal as a separate state so, as far as the Pope was concerned, the kings of Portugal remained dukes of Braganza. However, the cunning old Dom Francisco surmounted that difficulty by naming it the marriage of the Duke of Braganza's daughter to the king of England. But bargaining for the dowry was fierce. Charles was offered the strategic ports of Bombay and Tangier, together with Brazilian gold, in exchange for material help in the way of ships and soldiers. The alliance with Britain was so important that Dona Luisa held Madeira in reserve in case Charles wanted more than Bombay and Tangier.

Legend becomes fact

Dona Luisa realised that if Madeira were given away with the other two ports there would be an outcry from her subjects. If it were known, however, that the islands had been discovered by an Englishman this might soften the blow. There had been a rumour to this effect in the islands, but it had been dismissed as legend and Francisco Alcaforado's narrative had been suppressed. Alcaforado's story of Machin was therefore publicised by Dom Francisco de Mello, who said he had acquired the original manuscript, which he had guarded like a precious jewel. But Charles was satisfied with the territories he had been offered; moreover, he had fallen in love with Catherine after meeting her at Plymouth, so Madeira remained Portuguese.

Antonio Galvão in his *Treatise on the Discoveries of the World*, written in 1550, tells a similar story to that told by Alcaforado, but less detailed, and Richard Henry Major, FSA, FRSL, in his work, *The Life of Prince Henry of Portugal*, published in 1868, had beyond doubt proved that the legend of Robert Machin was fact. In addition, the late Rev. Samuel Lysons, M.A., of Gloucester, who did much research into the Machin family, has also found the story to be true.

Charles II's ordinance

In consideration of his protectionist policy, Charles issued an ordinance in 1665 banning the export of European goods to the "English Plantations overseas," but Madeira was excluded, thus granting Madeira shippers a virtual monopoly of trade in America and the Caribbean. The "Plantations" were, at the time, Jamaica, Barbados and the Leeward Islands, Virginia, New England, New York, Carolina and Bermuda – a vast and growing market. Drinking Madeira became a way of life in America and the West Indies.

S. Weir Mitchell in his book, *A Madeira Party*, called the wine an American discovery like tobacco, and Van Wyck Brooks in *The Flowering of New England* says that Madeira "softened the old rigidities" of Puritanism and made the residents in seaport towns in New England more human.

British West Indies

Christopher Jefferson of St. Kitts wrote: "there is no commoditie better in these parts than Madeira Wines. They are soe generally and soe plentifully drunk, being the only strong drink that is naturale here, except brandy and rum, which are too hott." He had visited Madeira in the spring of 1676 on his way to St Kitts, one of the most successful West Indies sugar plantations. The monotony of his voyage was relieved by many excitements, not the least of which was the delirious and fearful joy of being chased into Funchal Roads by a Turkish privateer, when he came within an ace of further emulation of Robinson Crusoe by untimely shipwreck – "The Master being unacquainted and coming too boldly near the shorr in a dangerous place." Master Jefferson, however, was denied this crowning felicity, and succeeded "with difficulties and not without well wetted in getting ashore" where, as may be gathered from the letter describing the adventure, he was received with the utmost hospitality and was promptly introduced to the "restorative and anti-rheumatic virtues of old Madeira." Jefferson also reported that

Madeira exported 2,000 pipes in 1648, but 30 years later 25,000 had been exported. This is clearly an exaggeration; 5,000 pipes would have been more accurate.

The first wine merchants

Attracted by trade with the American and West India settlements, British merchants started to set themselves up on the islands, and in 1680 there were some 30 wine shippers, seven or eight being Portuguese, ten British, and about ten of other European nationalities. By 1780 there were over 70 British houses in Madeira. Owing to the growing importance of foreign trade, consuls began to be appointed by several of the European powers. Mr. John Carter was the first British carrier consul to be appointed in 1658. He was by no means the first consul in Madeira, since Flanders and France had their consuls there in 1608 and 1626 respectively.

Lord Anson

Admiral Benbow, who had been given command of the West Indies fleet, called at Madeira in January 1695 with four men-of-war to take on wine for his crew and the West Indies garrison. With him was Edmund Halley in the pink,[12] Paramour, in which he explored the Atlantic with a view to constructing a chart of compass variations with Halleyan lines. In spite of Francis Newton finding plenty of rough wine in Madeira on his arrival in 1745, Commodore Lord Anson, who brought his fleet to anchor in Funchal Roads on Monday October 25th 1740, (his first port of call during the epic four-year journey round the world) noted in his journal:

> ... this Island of Madera (sic), where we are now arrived is famous through all our American settlements for its excellent wines, which seem to be designed by Providence for the refreshment of the inhabitants of the Torrid Zone. It is situated in a fine climate, in the latitude of 32.27 North; and in the longitude from London of, by our different reckonings from 18°½ to 19°½ West, though laid down in the charts in 17.[13] It is composed of one continued hill, of a considerable height, extending itself from East to West: the declivity of which, on the South-side, is cultivated and interspersed with vineyards; and in the midst of this slope

the Merchants have fixed their country seats, which help to form an agreeable prospect. There is but one considerable town in the whole Island, it is named Fonchiale, and is seated on the South part of the Island, at the bottom of a large bay. This is the only place of trade, and indeed the only place where it is possible for a boat to land. Fonchiale, towards the sea, is defended by a high wall with a battery of cannon, besides a castle on the Loo,[14] which is a rock standing in the water at a small distance from the shore. Even here the beach is covered with large stones, and a violent surf continually beats upon it; so that the Commodore did not care to venture the ships long boats to fetch the water off, as there was so much danger of their being lost; and therefore ordered the Captains of the squadron to employ Portuguese boats on that service.

Four years after this visit, Lord Anson, then in California, wrote in his journal:

> Since the first discovery of California, there have been various wandering missionaries who have visited it at different times, though to little purpose; but of late years the Jesuits, encouraged and supported by a large donation from the Marquis de Valero, a most munificent bigot, have fixed themselves upon the place, and have established a very considerable mission. Their principal settlement lies just within Cape St Lucas, where they have collected a great number of savages, and have endeavoured to inure them to agriculture and other mechanic arts. And their efforts have not been altogether ineffectual; for they have planted vines at their settlement with very good success, so that they already make a considerable quantity of wine, resembling in flavour the inferior sorts of Madera (sic), which begins to be esteemed in the neighbouring kingdom of Mexico.

Captain Cook

By the time Captain (then Lieutenant) Cook called at Madeira in 1768 on his first voyage to the south Pacific in *Endeavour*, the wine he took aboard was fortified. Owing to his dread of scurvy, Cook took with him 3,032 gallons of wine for his ship's company of 94 souls. This was a generous allowance, representing 200 bottles per man for the two-and-a-half-year journey. In this manner Cook achieved the conquest of scurvy, which in his day took a heavy toll of ships' crews.

Also on this occasion Sir Joseph Banks and his Swedish botanist, Dr. Solander, searched the island and found many botanical specimens. Captain Cook planted on the island trees and shrubs he had brought from England, including a tulip tree at James Murdoch's Quinta do Val. This tree flourished until it was blown down by a gale in 1963. It stood in a narrow lane not far from my house and, because the tree was considered a historic monument, while the tree remained the lane, which was bounded by high walls, could not be widened. Captain Cook returned on his second voyage with *Resolution* and *Adventure* in 1772.

In 1784 the 26-year-old captain of the frigate *Boreas* bought a quarter cask of Madeira for his locker and took four quarters for the governor of Dominica. He was on his way to "stir things up" in the West Indies, thus for the first time coming to the notice of the Admiralty as "somewhat assuming." His name was Horatio Nelson.

The British Factory

Wherever there was an English trading community, it was in those days usual to establish a chamber of commerce known as a "factory." This followed the experiences of the Portuguese, who had established defended trading posts called *feitorias* soon after they arrived in India in 1498, and later *feitorias* were started in west and east Africa: There were British factories in Lisbon, Oporto and Madeira. However, we do not know the exact date of the establishment of the Madeira Factory, the records previous to 1803 having been washed out to sea by the flood on October 9th 1803. From the archives of Cossart, Gordon & Co. and family papers my grandfather, the late C. J. Cossart, compiled a history of the establishment of the British chaplaincy and the Factory at Madeira. One of the papers is an account of a meeting on October 26th 1722 under the chairmanship of Consul William Rider, at which were present 11 factors. On January 31st 1754 the Factory committee consisted of William Nash, HM consul, Sam Sills, HM vice-consul, Francis Newton, John Catanach, William Murdoch, Richard Hill, Thomas Lamar, John Scott, John Pringle, Matthew Hiscox, Charles Chambers, James Gordon and John Searle.

The "new," early nineteenth-century burying ground depicted by Henry Veitch.

The factors were all-powerful, looking after the spiritual and physical needs of the British as well as their commercial interests. They built and financed, by means of a levy on shipments, the English church, a burial ground, a hospital and a capstan to pull up lighters on the beach and to load wine on to ships. Until 1761 non-catholics had to be buried at sea and it was only in that year that the Factory obtained permission from the Bishop of Funchal for "heretics" to be buried on shore. The Old Burial Ground (next to the present British cemetery), was therefore acquired and started to be used in 1767. There was a tradition handed down among the older British firms that one of the earlier partners in Gordon, Duff & Co. had such a horror of a watery grave that he begged his partners to bury him under his desk in the old Esmeraldo Palace. When some alterations were made to the house in 1885 a human skeleton was found under the patio.

The Factory House was a mansion at Ribeira de Santa Luzia which, when the Factory was wound up on December 31st 1838, became the counting house of Newton, Gordon, Cossart & Co. Eighteen-thirty-eight was therefore the last year of collective buying by British merchants in Madeira until it was resumed 88 years later by the Madeira Wine Association. The 1838 vintage was potentially large and of fine quality, so factors decided to buy heavily for their firms in September of that year. The vintage turned out as expected. Thomas Murdoch bought Bual and Peter Cossart preferred Verdelho, so between them they had considerable stock of both. It is said that the two partners had a wager as to which would eventually be the finest, but, alas, Murdoch died a year later.

The English Rooms

After the Factory was disbanded, the remaining factors formed an exclusive club in Funchal, situated on the sea front, called The English Rooms. These Rooms held the Factory library, which was added to periodically, as well as changing and rest rooms, a billiards room, card rooms, etc. The Rooms carried on the Factory's tradition of allowing only partners to be eligible for membership and there was a barrier by the front door where non-members had to remain until they were vouched for by a member. A room housing the Factory's enormous brass telescope was a unique feature. The walls were hung with charts of signal and code flags as well as silhouettes of ships, enabling members to identify shipping in the bay. As persons eligible for membership died out, the rules were changed to allow directors and managers to become members and the club moved to smaller premises in the centre of the town; it eventually closed through lack of membership.

Funchal from the Bay by Andrew Picken 1840.

The Factory's capstan for unloading ships, known as the *cabrestante*, was entrusted to the care of the senior member, Cossart, Gordon & Co., until the mole was built, when the loading and discharging of ships was taken over by the port authority. The original *cabrestante* was a simple affair operated by oxen which dragged lighters up the beach; it ended as a large operation with tugs and lighters occupying a considerable portion of the town beach.

The Bolton letters

William Bolton, a Warwickshire merchant, was one of the first to take advantage of the opportunity offered by Charles II's act. He returned to Madeira in 1695 with a commission to act for one Robert Haysham of London, and became a merchant banker and ship owner, importing wheat from Cornwall, timber from Pennsylvania, fish from Newfoundland, rice and maize from Carolina and Virginia, and all manner of manufactured goods from London. He exported wine to North America and to the East and West Indies. In 1926, André L. Simon, then agent for Pommery & Greno champagne in London, bought from a Mr. Halliday, a bookseller of Leicester, a collection of letters written by Bolton during the period 1695 to 1714 giving a complete account of the day-to-day affairs of a trader in Madeira at the time. A great debt is owed to André, not only by those interested in Madeira, but by all students of commercial history, for editing the letters from 1695 to 1701, adding an introduction and his own notes on Madeira, and publishing them in London in 1928. When André parted company with Pommery & Greno in 1932 he swore he would have nothing more to do with the wine trade. However, he was invited to Madeira in January 1933 and within three weeks he was again in the trade, helping to bring Madeira back into fashion – a daunting task at a time of acute depression.[15] Sadly, the venture was short lived, because the newly-formed Madeira Wine Association decided it could not afford to continue this promotion after the end of 1934. By this time the Wine and Food Society had been born, and had all of 500 members. This was the course André was to follow, and we in Madeira like to feel that his transition from trading in wine to promoting and writing about it came about during his stay in Madeira. André presented Bolton's unpublished letters from 1702 to 1714 to Graham Blandy, who published them in roneo form in aid of the English church in Funchal.

BIRTH OF THE WINE TRADE

John Leacock and Francis Newton

In the mid-18th century, two young men arrived in Madeira who were to found firms which are still trading today. Young John Leacock, son of a weaver, who had been educated at Christ's Hospital, London, became apprenticed to a firm of Madeira merchants, Messrs. Catanach & Murdoch, in 1741. He was only 15 years of age and after his apprenticeship expired on March 11th 1749 he was taken on by his employers as a clerk. In 1760 he started trading under his own name and from then on until 1981 the wine-shipping firm was owned and run by members of his family.

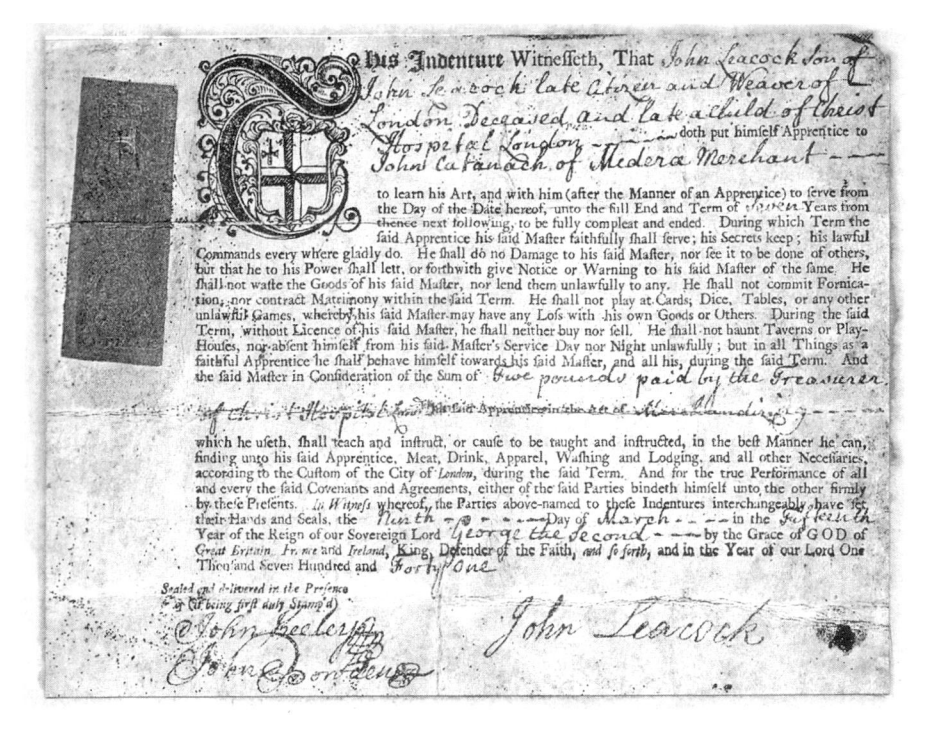

John Leacock's 1741 indenture to John Catanach.

On September 12th 1745 a young Scot sailed from Gravesend for Madeira. His name was Francis Newton and he was to found the firm which is today Cossart, Gordon & Co. His father had taken up arms under the Earl of Mar in 1715, and Francis and his brother, Andrew, had left Scotland. Andrew had gone to Virginia and Francis seems to have wandered about for some time until he arrived in Madeira. In our archives there is a letter from Francis in Madeira to his brother in Virginia saying, "Henderson and I set out for London and went directly to Flanders and got into the Life

Guards and continued there until they were broke [disbanded]." He went on to say that Henderson eventually found a job in St Kitts as overseer of a gentleman's estate, but Francis continues, "as for my own part, I was so lucky as to get into a Merchant's Counting House [in London] and after I was there three years was offered one hundred pounds but refused it to come to this island [Madeira] where I am in the quality of a book-keeper to Dom John [Dom João José da Câmara] one of the greatest men of estate of any in the island." In the same letter Francis tells how he was given £33 per annum, board, bed and washing, with liberty to trade for himself, which he was not long in developing. He asked Andrew to get him orders for wine. "I have in my power to sell as well and at as low prices, and if you will please to use all your interest to procure me consignments, or orders for wine, [you] may depend upon anything for their interests, as many Merchants would do, and all in my power to do them the strictest justice and to transact everything faithfully with which they are pleased to entrust me."

Francis's confidence

Newton was to remain for two years with Dom John during which time he was full of confidence, for he wrote to Andrew, "During this time I believe I will do a pretty deal of business and afterwards propose to set up for myself, as I have some particular Merchants in London my friends, who will assist me in all parts." He was referring to George Spence who, in 1748, became his London partner. Young Francis started in business for himself under the most difficult conditions. He was unfamiliar with the language, laws and customs of the island, and he had the ill will of its people, being a Protestant and in their eyes a heretic. "The only disadvantages one has here," he wrote to Andrew in 1748, "there are no recreations diversions or companions. The Portuguese are a very sullen, proud, deceitful people and in short there is no such thing as finding one to make a companion of, very few of them having good education unless the Priests and Collegeans whose ceremonies are so many and conversation so very narrow, being Roman Catholics, that their company is very disagreeable." However, being a dour Scot, he does not seem to have had a better opinion of his fellow Britons, adding "as for the English here, they are much worse, there is nothing but jealousy of one another's correspondents, everybody trying all he can to get another's that they scarcely speak to one another; if they do it is criticizing (sic) and telling stories. This shows how great lengths interest drives people."

In spite of obstacles, with indomitable courage and energy Francis fought through. His first object was to improve the product, which though plentiful was of inferior quality, being merely fermented grape juice which had received no treatment at all. By his efforts the wine improved. He built warehouses, installed elaborate appliances for the manufacture of high grade wine under hygienic conditions and employed skilled wine makers from Europe to handle the product.

Thanks to his brother Andrew's efforts, the North American and West Indies were Francis Newton's largest markets. Then, as a result of improved quality, officers and officials returning home after Independence brought the taste for Madeira drinking to the United Kingdom, where it rapidly gained favour and spread to Europe and India. It was not long before the price of the best wine increased from £20 to £45 per pipe.

Demand Exceeds Supply

Up to 1745, annual shipments averaged 7,000 pipes. By 1800 they had risen to 16,981. Newton, Gordon, Murdoch and Co. wrote to Francis Newton, who had gone to London on January 20th 1801, that "there are not one hundred pipes of old wine in the hands of the natives for sale. The exports of the year 1800 exceeding all previous exports, being upwards of seventeen thousand pipes, and, should the demand for our wine increase as much as it has done for some years, the island will not be able to supply the requisite quantity."

For some 15 years, however, shipments continued to average about 15,000 pipes and Francis was able to obtain enough fine wine to satisfy his orders.

Napoleonic Wars

Madeira was twice occupied by British troops during the Napoleonic Wars. The first occupation was on July 24th 1801 when the ship of the line Argo, with the frigate *Carrysfort* and the brigantine *Falcon* in attendance, escorted five troop transports carrying 3,500 officers and men of the 85th regiment and two companies of artillery, anchored in Funchal Bay. The fleet was commanded by Commodore Brown and the troops by Colonel Henry Clinton, who on arrival immediately came ashore to confer with His Britannic Majesty's consul, Mr. Joseph Pringle. After a short meeting, Colonel Clinton and Consul Pringle advised the governor Dom Jose Manoel da Câmara that the British forces intended to occupy the island to protect it against the hazards of war, invoking the ancient Anglo-Portuguese alliance. This exercise caused a diplomatic upheaval because the Portuguese authorities had not been advised of Britain's intentions; however, the governor was forced to acquiesce, in view of the might of the British forces. The occupation did not last long. The preliminaries to the peace of Amiens were signed on October 1st 1801 and Colonel Clinton and his troops left the island on January 25th 1802. The regiments had consumed a great deal of wine and the officers took a considerable quantity home with them.

Newton, Gordon, Murdoch & Co. were unaware that one of the greatest battles of the world was being fought at Trafalgar on October 21st 1805. The correspondence is strictly limited to trading until news of the victory reached Funchal on November 12th 1805. On that very day Thomas Murdoch wrote to Robert Lennox, Esq, in New York: "We have just heard that Lord Nelson with 27 sail of the line engaged the French and Spanish squadrons off Cadiz consisting of 33 sail and after a battle of four hours he took 17, sunk two, and one, the Admiral Graviana's ship, blew up. Lord Nelson lived only to sign the despatches; it is a complete victory and we hope may have a good effect on the politicks of the Continent where you will have heard that hostilities have commenced. The French Admiral Villeneuve and his second we hear are both prisoners. Graviana got into a frigate before his ship blew up and is thus escaped. The above statement is brought from Lisbon by two different vessels."

Murdoch goes on to complain, however, that no English newspapers had yet arrived to give particulars of the battle, although the action was fought three weeks earlier.

Second British occupation

The second occupation was during Napoleon's invasion of the Iberian peninsula. It did not cause any diplomatic confrontation, because it had been made quite clear to the Prince Regent of Portugal (who had removed his court to Brazil) that the British intention was merely to defend the island against a possible French attack. The

British fleet, under the command of Admiral Samuel Hood, arrived on the morning of December 24th 1807. It consisted of four ships of the line, four frigates and six transports. The land forces, commanded by Major-general William Carr Beresford, consisted of the 3rd and 11th regiments of infantry, each over 1,000 men strong, and two companies of artillery. The captain-general of the island at the time was Dom Pedro Fagundes Bacelar de Antunes e Menèzes, who received royal orders from Brazil that he was to hand over "the island of Madeira and its dependencies to the commanders of His Britannic Majesty's forces to be held and governed by them for the said Majesty with the same rights and privileges and jurisdiction as thitherto enjoyed by the Portuguese Crown."

The Union flag was flown over General Beresford's headquarters at the palace of São Lorenço and over all the forts on the island. In 1808, it was considered that half the garrison would be sufficient to protect the island. General Beresford then left for Lisbon, taking with him the Buffs and a company of artillery. Lieutenant-colonel Sir Alexander Gordon was left in command of a regiment of infantry and the remaining company of artillery. The British forces finally left for Lisbon in October 1814 and Dom Pedro Fagundes was reinstated as civil governor.

General Beresford was a remarkable soldier who had distinguished himself in Egypt and South Africa when he was still under 40. In 1806 he had captured Buenos Aires with only two regiments, and the fact that such a distinguished soldier was sent to

Entrance to St. John's vineyard at Pico São João, the property of William Leacock.

Madeira illustrates the importance the British government attached to the island.

The National Fund

The British factors paid 1,802 milreis for swords presented to General Beresford, and to Colonels Clinton, Gordon and Mead (Mead had been in command for a short time before Gordon). During the year of Clinton's occupation, in addition to money for their ordinary expenses, the factors, through the National Fund, raised 1,800 reis. This was largely composed of shippers' contributions of 500 reis per pipe on 11,661 pipes shipped on 183 British ships during the year. The factors, who also undertook the care of prisoners from Tenerife, paid for grapes to be given to the troops. In 1806 wine shippers Messrs. Colson, Smith & Robinson took the unprecedented step of refusing to pay contributions to the National Fund, maintaining that the consul and factors were not authorized to levy contributions. The firm also objected to some of the fund's disbursements. The factors, who had been making the levy for 85 years, were furious and, after a heated meeting on November 6th, Consul Pringle was asked to obtain an Order in Council, or even an Act of Parliament, to legalise the levy for the fund.

It seems that Mr. Pringle did not do what had been asked, and the dispute continued until General Beresford himself intervened, ordering Colson, Smith & Co., as it had become, not only to continue to pay the levy, but to pay the arrears. In 1808 both receipts and expenses forced the duty per pipe from 500 reis to 800 reis. On General Beresford's orders a new burial ground was bought and put into use next to the old one, and 400 milreis was paid to a military chaplain, the Reverend Cautley. There were also expenses for anchors lost by ships of war, seamen's funerals and presents of wine to the captains of men-of-war.

Consul Henry Veitch

In 1809 the much loved Henry Veitch, whose name became honoured in the annals of Madeira history, replaced Mr. Pringle as His Britannic Majesty's agent and consul-general. Owing to his great admiration of Napoleon, he was removed from the island in 1828, but he was so popular with both the Portuguese and British communities that the islanders begged Lord Palmerston to send him back. He was reinstated in 1831 and remained until his death in 1835. He was a man of substance, a good churchman and, according to a miniature in the possession of his great-grandson on his mother's side, the late Noël Coward, a very handsome one. He built the palatial town house[16] which was later known as "Château Cossart," as well as houses in the same Georgian style in most of the villages. He furnished each house with one or more girl friends and, in due course, all the villages where he had a residence were populated by fair-haired children whose descendants are distinguishable to this day. His favourite residence was Jardim da Serra. He is buried in the mausoleum he built himself on the hill behind the house, where he loved to sit gazing down his valley. Henry Veitch's cellar and Madeira parties were famous and it was a source of wonder where the cavalcade of gentlemen who rode up to the quinta were accommodated. It is known some of them slept on or under the dining table.

Effect of Napoloeonic Wars

As an instance of the effect of the French wars on the exports of Madeira, the following list will be of interest. It exhibits the rise and fall of prices of the Best London Particular as settled by the British Factory.

Henry Veitch's house at Jardim da Serra.

Cost in £ per pipe

1795 : £36	1811: £57	1817: £67
1797: £37	1812 : £60	1818 : £65
1798: £40	1813 : £63	1819: £60
1804 : £45	1814 : £70	1820 : £50
1808 : £50	1815 : £75	1826 : £46
1810 : £54	1816 : £77	

The price remained stationary at £46 until 1852, when it began to rise again, owing to the appearance of oidium, the scourge of all vineyards. Then, in 1865, it reached a minimum of £75 per pipe. As the vines recovered, the price for London Particular again fell off gradually to £50 per pipe. The above gives a fair average for the better qualities of Madeira, although, of course, special varieties of Madeira and fine old wines fetched far higher prices. During the first half of the 19th century Madeira continued to be exported to Europe and America in large quantities, and the East and West India men touching at the island spread the popularity of its wines among the regimental messes in different parts of the world, especially in India and the East.

The great extension of the export trade in Madeira wines during the early years of the last century, and their wide popularity among the people of many different races and climates, had demonstrated the importance of the industry, and led to a great increase in the amount of land on the island devoted to vine cultivation. In those years so much land was under the vine that nearly all breadstuffs had to be imported.

Royal Cellarman

In the archives of Cossart, Gordon & Co. from 1813 to 1865 there is considerable correspondence between Mr. James Christie, from St James's Palace, and our partner, Thomas Murdoch, which shows the popularity of Madeira at the time. James Christie was no relation of the James Christie who auctioned Madeira in his first sale on December 5th 1766. He was cellarman to the Prince Regent from 1813 and then Gentleman of Wine and Beer Cellars in the Lord Steward's department from 1821 to 1856 when he retired "in consequence of infirmity." He had an office and rooms at St James's Palace, and ordered Madeira not only for the royal cellar but also for the nobility in England and Ireland. His orders were always for best quality Madeira in "cased hogsheads." Mr. Christie presents his compliments to Mr. Thomas Murdoch and begs he will desire his House in Madeira to send one Hogshead, cased, of fine "London Particular" as before to Sir Matthew Tierney Bart. in Bruton Street, and two hogsheads of the same description also *cased* for his brother Edward Tierney Esq., of Dublin. Should no opportunity offer of a vessel direct to that port perhaps the wine had better come here . . ." This was a typical order, but when Madeira became scarce, Mr. Christie literally begged Murdoch to supply wine of whatever quality or price, for the royal cellar and his friends, which illustrates that Madeira was very much in demand.

MADEIRA THE ISLAND VINEYARD

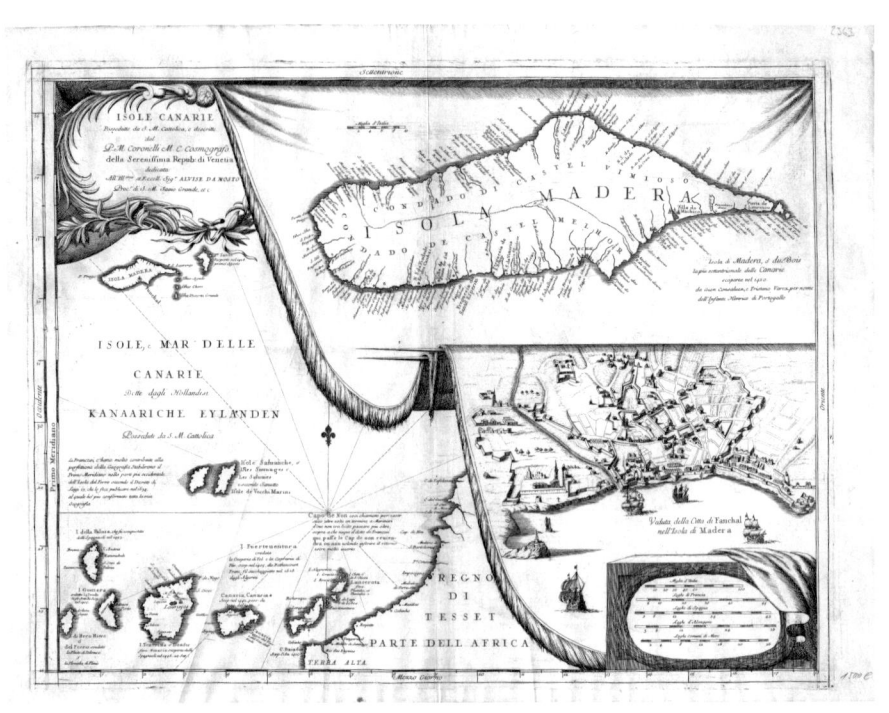

Coronelli's Map of Madeira and the Canary Islands, circa 1690.

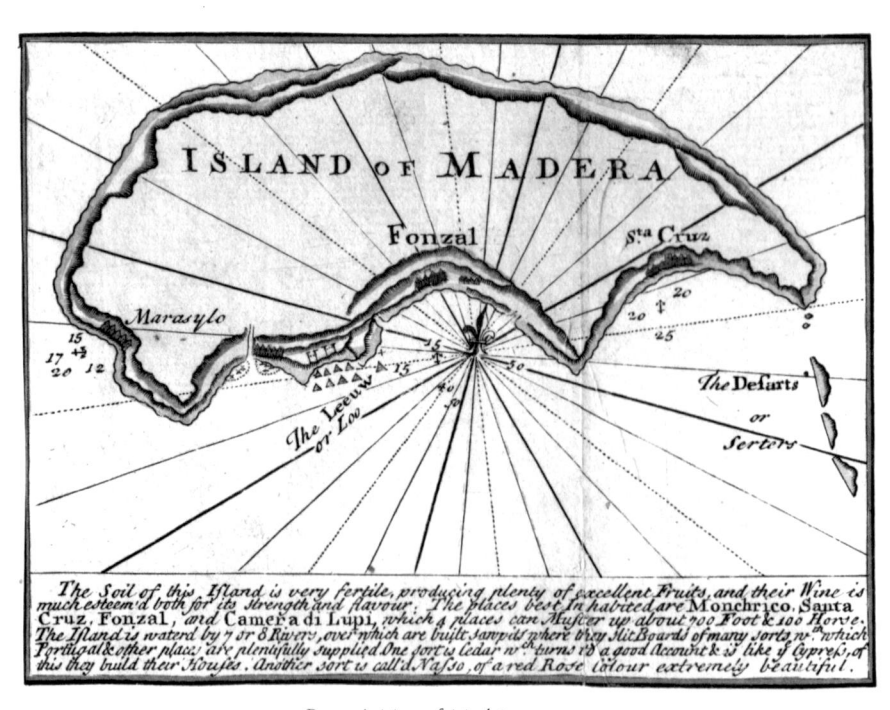

Bowen's Map of Madeira, 1752.

CHAPTER 4

THE WINE MERCHANTS

Dr. Richard Hill, Lamar, Hill, Bissett & Co.

Among the early Madeira shippers Dr. Richard Hill is listed in 1754 as the only shipper of his time who did not come from the British Isles (see Appendix VI). He is mentioned by Francis Newton in a letter addressed to his London partner written in 1748 as "Mr. Hill who came from America and has numbers of ships from New York, Philadelphia, Maryland, etc." According to Mrs. Louise Whitney Griswold (a descendant of Dr. Hill whom I met on a liner returning from New York to Madeira) the doctor came to the island in 1739 to escape his creditors and later returned a very rich man. His office was at 28 Rua do Esmeraldo and he lived with his wife Deborah and their large family at Quinta da Achada, where until recently John Blandy Sr. lived. It seems he had the largest share, after Newton, of the American business. At first he traded as Ricardo Hill, then as Lamar, Hill, Bissett & Co. When he returned home he acted as the Philadelphia partner.

Dr. Hill was planning to return to Philadelphia when he was about to buy the São Martinho vineyard. "The planting can be done without me as well as with, Richard Bissett being quite fond of the purchase and of making the proper improvements; the place now gives but three pipes of wine a year." The vineyard was large by Madeira standards and I calculate that Dr. Hill was expecting to vintage some six tons of grapes per hectare after his improvements, whereas the average today is from 10 to 15 tons, which shows the advance in viticultural technology in the last century and a half. Dr. Hill was a most prosperous Madeira merchant, competing with Francis Newton and causing him "much worry." Newton was therefore delighted when Hill returned home, enabling him to take on Dr. Hill's business in New York, Philadelphia and Maryland, the latter being particularly extensive.

Dr. Richard Hill's Quinta Achada.

Shortridge Lawton and Welsh & Cunha

Among the older Bntish firms whose names are used today are Shortridge Lawton & Co. and Welsh & Cunha established in 1757 and 1794 respectively. John Shortridge was the first president of the Associacão Comercial (Chamber of Commerce) of Madeira from 1835-1839 and was responsible for protecting the interests of shippers in respect of the Portuguese government. Welsh & Cunha (now Welsh Brothers) had a substantial share of the imperial Russian market and were suppliers, by appointment, to the late King Gustav of Sweden. Both these names are now brands owned by the Madeira Wine Company.

Newton & Gordon

Francis Newton was joined by his younger brother, Thomas, from 1758 to 1763. Meanwhile, his London partner, George Spence, had come to Madeira and to Newton's disgust had that same year joined his rival, John Leacock. Also in 1758 another Scot joined the firm in Madeira; he was Thomas Gordon of Balmaghie. Whilst he was "merchant at Madeira," Thomas Gordon was granted the freedom of the Scottish burghs of Dumfries, Kirkcudbright, Glasgow, New Galloway and Dundee, a rare honour for one resident abroad. Thomas's nephew, William, was a partner from 1798 until his death in 1809, and his son, also William, became a partner in 1840.

THE WINE MERCHANTS

Newton, Gordon & Murdoch

In 1791 the name of Thomas Murdoch was added to the title of the firm. Thomas was a Murdoch of Cumloden, cousin of James and George Murdoch, who were members of the old established Madeira firm of Catanach & Murdoch. Thomas was one of the "poor Murdochs" so the two sides of the family never spoke or acknowledged each other. It therefore seems incredible that they lived on a small island, doing business together for some fifty years.

Thomas Gordon's son, James David Webster Gordon, joined Newton, Gordon, Murdoch & Co. in 1802 and his grandson, Russell Manners, became a partner in Newton, Gordon, Cossart & Co. in 1850. Newton, Gordon & Murdoch were now shipping "half the growth of the island" and it is recorded that Newton's brother procured orders for him in America.

Johnston and Scott

In the meantime, other Scotsmen had become partners: William Johnston in 1775 and Robert Scott in 1805. From 1775 to 1791 the firm was Newton, Gordon & Johnston and from 1805 to 1834 Newton, Gordon, Murdoch & Scott.

Francis Newton retired to live in London in 1800 and was given by his partners "five pipes of Best London Particular Madeira per annum" to keep him comfortable in his old age. This was equal to 2,700 bottles a year, which lasted him until he died in 1805.

Newton, Gordon, Cossart & Co.

The Scots domination of the firm was finally broken when my great-great-uncle, William Cossart, joined the firm. He had been in Newton, Gordon, Murdoch & Co., acting for them in Ireland and London until he sailed for Madeira in 1802. He was captured by the French on the way, finally arriving in Madeira at the end of 1808. In 1831 William was joined in Madeira by his nephew, Peter, my great grandfather, who came from Dublin. The title of the firm then became Newton, Gordon, Cossart & Co., although Newton had died and the only partners were now Gordons and Cossarts. The name remained the same until 1861, when it became Cossart, Gordon & Co.

The firm has always maintained its British nationality with a branch in London since 1748, and in 1909, because the family had grown so large, the firm was registered as a limited company. At this stage many other British firms had become Portuguese limited companies.

Cossart, Gordon & Co

The Wine Trade Annual of 1881 published an article entitled "Old Maderia" (sic) the preamble to which read as follows:

> It is an interesting task to dive into the historical past and to discover the initial circumstances which have led to the founding of many of our most notable commercial houses. Adherence to a religious faith or loyalty to an unfortunate cause have given us not a few instances where the most worthy scion of a good family has had to seek pastures new, carrying with him his knowledge, experience, enterprise, and capital, with a result, like wind carrying the seed, that it is often more fruitful on new soil. . . Many a metropolitan business and industry can trace its beginning to the Huguenots of France, of whom the Cossarts are one of the oldest families. . .
>
> Many of those of the best blood of Scotland had to retrieve their fortunes in foreign lands during the earlier part of the last century, and it was the participation of the Gordons in the Stuart cause that led to a member of that family seeking refuge in the island of Maderia (sic), and to the founding of the well-known firm of Cossart, Gordon & Co., in the year 1745. That year is memorable. . . [for] the end of the war in Scotland [which]meant the beginning of an era of peace and plenty in Madeira, and the firm referred to have ever since contributed largely to the well-being of the island. . .

At the end of the 19th century, during the administration of Webster Gordon Cossart (my great-uncle), and Charles John Cossart (my grandfather), the firm expanded considerably, branching out into its own port, Sherry, Tarragona, Marsala and Malaga, besides representing in London Clossmann (Bordeaux), B. Vergara Jerez de la Frontera), Morin Père & Fils (Cote d'Or), Duhr-Conrad-Fehres (Trèves), J. Champion et Cie (Rheims), B. Léon Croizet (Cognac) and Duncan McCallum & Co. (Glasgow). This business continued until the outbreak of hostilities in World War II and has not been resumed; the firm now specialises in Madeira only.

THE WINE MERCHANTS

At left, Charles John Cossart, 1853-1919, and at right, Russell Manners Gordon, the Visconda de Torre Bella, photographed in 1896, ten years before his death in 1906.

The last Gordon

Russell Manners Gordon, Webster Gordon's son, left the firm in 1857 when he married Dona Filomena Gabriela Correia Brandão Henriques de Noronha, Viscountess Torre Bella in her own right. The King of Portugal offered Russell the title of Count Torre Bella on condition that he took Portuguese nationality, which he accepted, thus, with his wife's properties, becoming the largest landowner and vineyard proprietor on the island. In spite of having adopted Portuguese nationality, he called his son James Murray Kenmure Gordon. The statutes of the partnership demanded that partners had to be of British nationality, so Russell had to retire, but the firm has continued to absorb the products of the vineyards, which are still owned by Russell Manners Gordon's two great-grand-daughters, now living in Scotland and London.

Peter Cossart

When Russell Manners Gordon resigned, his only partner, Peter Cossart, bought his interest in Cossart, Gordon & Co., and it became the property of Peter and his five sons, Leland, William Carlton, Webster Gordon, Charles John and Henry. Peter was the son of John Cossart, of the Ballast Office, Dublin. He joined the firm at the age of 25 after his education at Trinity College, Dublin. He married Jane Edwards, daughter of Thomas Edwards, a Madeira wine shipper. On the death of his father-in-law he took over the firm of T. Edwards, established in 1810, and also their subsidiary firm, Selbey & Co., which is still trading in Denmark. In a letter to a connection in America Peter describes his good fortune, writing that he has a "fine house with deer in the park, pheasants in the woods and trout in the stream." He adds that he has also "five fine sons who are well educated and can ride, shoot and handle a rod as well as dance and play bat and ball games." This house was Quinta Gordon at the Mount, which he had bought from Russell Manners and named Quinta Cossart. It is a lovely Georgian mansion situated in a park in which he built a trout stream. The pheasants, deer and trout were all imported from England.

Peter Cossart, 1807-1870.

Peter's sons

Peter's sons Leland and Charles took over the firm after their father's death and Webster, William and Henry were in charge of the London business. Leland was the salesman and although he lived in Madeira he travelled extensively, being very popular at various courts of Europe.

It was in the old house, now known as Quinta do Monte, that Charles Hapsburg, former Emperor of Austria, lived and died during his exile in Madeira. He arrived at Funchal in HMS *Cardiff* in November 1921 with the Empress Zita (who was of Portuguese origin) and stayed at Reid's Hotel annexe, Vila Vitoria. In February 1922 when their children arrived, they moved to Quinta do Monte, where Charles died on April 1st 1922. His mortal remains were buried in the parish church at Monte.

Quinta do Monte, photographed in 1922.

J. & W. Phelps

Joseph Phelps succeeded his father as head of the firm of J. & W. Phelps, wine shippers established in Madeira in 1786. The family came from Dursley in Gloucestershire and Joseph was born in Madeira, the seventh son of his father, who had emigrated to the island in 1784. He married Elizabeth Dickson in 1819 and had a large family of seven daughters and four sons.[17] The Phelps family, who owned extensive vine-growing estates all over the island, were not only large in numbers, but were very large physically. It was said that the family ox-carts carried "a ton of Phelps" to church on Sunday mornings. It was also said that when Joseph's youngest daughter Bella got into her bath the water came out, and it was once recorded that "Bella was found with the [hip] bath firmly fixed around her like the shell of a snail, and she was only liberated by the concentrated action of the entire family."

Phelps & Page

In 1804 Robert Page joined the firm, which continued trading as Phelps & Page until Joseph and his family returned to England and settled in Clapham Common towards the end of the 19th century. Both the Page and Phelps families were great public benefactors. Robert Page, who left the island in 1840, repaired at his own expense most of the roads and bridges damaged by the great flood of 1803. He built the bridge over the Ribeira dos Frades at Câmara de Lobos, opening roads and paths across the mountains, and building rest houses at various points in the interior. He contributed six beds and 100 blankets to the hospital, improved the municipal theatre, and constructed public fountains all over Funchal. He was twice decorated by John VI of Portugal with the Knighthood of the Tower and Sword, later becoming Commander. Robert Page is best known for rebuilding, again at his own expense, the Milagres chapel originally built over Machin's tomb at Machico, to which he presented a magnificent oil painting now in the Museum of Sacred Art in Funchal.

Joseph Phelps, who was no less of a benefactor to the island, was an academic. The family lived above the counting house of Phelps & Page in Rua do Carmo. The square out of which the street leads is now called Largo do Phelps. The family country house was Quinta da Paz. In 1819 Joseph founded the Lancastrian school for educating the children of the poor, named after Joseph Lancaster, a young Quaker who began teaching poor children in England in 1796. The school was for boys only but it was so successful that later Mrs. Phelps and Mrs. Blackburn started one for girls. In 1821 Joseph founded the Funchal Association for Mutual Education for the children of the middle classes.

During the early part of the last century the Madeira hills were almost entirely denuded of trees. Mrs. Elizabeth Phelps realised that reafforestation was essential to the well-being of the islanders. The island was becoming exceedingly dry without the trees necessary to attract rainfall. She frequently sent to England for suitable trees, seedlings and seeds and when she organised their customary enormous picnic parties, each of the guests would be given a seedling tree and required to plant it at the spot. To this day one finds on the hills circles of fine European oaks, chestnuts and beeches which are known as "Mrs. Phelps' picnics." It was she who introduced to the island the pine (*Pinus maritimus*) which covers the higher regions, as well as eucalyptus, mimosa and many other trees and plants, including the hibiscus.

John Blandy & Sons

A young quartermaster came to Madeira in 1807 with General Beresford's forces. He was 23 years old and had been born near Dorchester. His name was John Blandy. He showed great interest in wine all the time he was serving and in 1810 he went to England to marry Janet Burden at St Andrew's Church, Holborn. He returned to Madeira in 1811 and started to deal in wine in his own name, thus founding John Blandy & Sons, now Blandy Brothers & Co. Ltd.

John Blandy, 1782-1855.

John Blandy made the first butter at his *quinta* at Santo Antonio da Serra in 1850, which he marketed at Mr. Payne's grocer's shop in Funchal. His grandson, John Burden, became a public benefactor, giving land to build the sea wall, now Estrada da Pontinha, and land at Rua do Teatro where there is now a public garden. When in 1882 the bourbon sugar cane started to fail he imported other types of cane from Mauritius. These were later replaced by Mr. Harry Hinton with the present yuba cane.

John's son, Charles Ridpath Blandy, was born in the year the firm was established and carried on the business after him. His grandson, John Burden, succeeded Charles and the firm expanded into coaling, shipping and banking. During the disastrous oidium plague of 1852, Charles had the foresight to buy up a great proportion of the stocks of old wine on the island and these wines formed the basis of the stocks held by the firm. In 1874, his daughter, Anna Mary, married my grandfather, forming the happy alliance between the two houses which still exists.

In those days merchants lived in the counting houses and the Blandy family house and wine store was in Rua de São Francisco where the Madeira Wine Company is today. However, with the expansion of the firm it moved to the present offices on the sea front, although the wine department remained at Rua de São Francisco. John's son, John Ernest, followed him. By that time the firm's interests had grown so large both in Madeira and the Canaries that members of the family ceased to take a direct interest in wine.

Charles Ridpath Blandy, 1812-1879.

Blandy's Madeiras Lda.

Blandy's Madeiras Lda. was formed in 1926 under the very able direction of Thomas L. Mullins, who was later to create the Madeira Wine Association. John Ernest lived at Quinta Santa Luzia and his magnificent country seat at Quinta do Palheiro, the gardens of which are famous. On the death of Ernest his two sons took over the parent company, Blandy Brothers & Co. Lda., in Madeira. The late Graham Blandy and his brother, John, their sisters, my sister and I were brought up together. Now only John and myself are left and, like myself, John is retired. Adam, who is Graham's son, is head of the firm in Madeira and Richard, John's son, is chairman of the Madeira Wine Company and looks after wine interests and the famous Reid's Hotel, which is also owned by the company.

Leacock's

After Murdoch's death in 1757, John Leacock married Murdoch's widowed daughter, Mrs. Durban. The following year he was joined in partnership first by George Spence, Francis Newton's former London partner (and later by his son, John Russel Spence) and in 1759 Michael Nowlan joined the firm.

The Leacocks had two sons, John (Jackie) and William. In 1791 the name of the firm was changed from Nowlan & Leacock to John, John & William Leacock. Jackie ran the Madeira house and William moved to London. After the death of their father in 1799, the firm continued as Leacock & Company, with William in charge.

Thomas Slapp Leacock (see Chapter 8), a grandson of the first John Leacock, was head of the firm in 1877 when Vizetelly visited his São João vineyard at the time of phylloxera. He was succeeded by his son, John Milburn Leacock who died in 1915, when the firm was taken over by Edmund Leacock.[18] In 1925 Leacock's (with Blandy's and Viuva Abudarham & Filhos) joined the Madeira Wine Association.

The Leacock family no longer has any interest in the Madeira Wine Company, but the name remains as a brand.

Rutherford, Drury and H.P. Miles

James Rutherford, the only surviving partner of Rutherford & Grant which was established in Madeira in 1814, was joined by Dr. Dru Drury, and traded under the title of Rutherford & Drury. After several changes, in 1878 the partnership was dissolved and James Rutherford continued trading as Rutherford, Browne & Miles. A few years later Henry Price Miles, the partner who in 1872 had started brewing in Madeira, took over the stocks of the old firm and undertook, in the name of Rutherford & Miles of Madeira, to supply from the lodges of H. P. Miles & Co. all Madeiras required by Rutherford & Co. of London. When Henry P. Miles died in 1929 his sons, Henry and Charles, and their sons carried on the business until they joined the Madeira Wine Association in 1951. The wine interests of H. P. Miles & Co. are now looked after by Anthony Cossart-Miles, Henry P. Miles's great-grandson and my nephew. Anthony is also a director of Cossart, Gordon & Co., Rutherford & Co., and the Madeira Wine Company. Rutherford & Miles have a considerable trade in Madeira, not only with the United Kingdom but worldwide. The wine is shipped by the Madeira Wine Company. The late Jack Rutherford, senior partner of the London company, Rutherford, Osborne & Perkin, was not only one of the greatest Madeira experts but, in his day, one of the finest wine salesmen in Great Britain. His son, David, is a director of the London company now owned by Martini Rossi Ltd.

Henry P. Miles

Krohn Brothers & Co.

The firm was founded in 1858 by John and Nicholas Krohn. The Krohn family had lived in Russia for two generations although they originated in Denmark, but by the time they came to Madeira they were British. One of the family had been food-taster to the Czar and the imperial arms of Russia were featured on their labels. John and Nicholas married Elizabeth and Wilhelmina, the daughters of William Grant of Rutherford & Grant.

The firm was the last to use the *estufa do sol* to mature its wines, which were of the very finest quality.

At the turn of the century Krohn Brothers were second only to Cossart, Gordon & Co. in importance. Unfortunately they relied entirely on Russia and Germany so when these great markets collapsed in the First World War, William and Hugo Krohn went out of business. Of their children, Ronald, Ester and Helen settled in South Africa, Edmund joined the Royal Flying Corps and was killed in 1918 and only Raleigh stayed in Madeira to become manager of the Madeira Wine Association. Raleigh had no surviving children and there are no longer any Krohns living in Madeira.[19] This is extraordinary because in 1900 it was the largest family, numbering 24 adults, not including children. Indeed, Funchal was known as Krohnstadt among the British residents.

Hugo Krohn, 1875-1960, in a photograph taken in 1899.

Hugo Krohn was the only foreign wine merchant to visit Petrograd during the war. His voyage was reported in the *Wine & Spirit Record* on July 8th 1915. He certainly recommended "no other merchant to go while the war was on unless it is a *must* because they would certainly only be disappointed and find that they could not even amuse themselves." Mr. Krohn left London on March 3rd 1915, taking 40 hours to cross the North Sea from Newcastle to Bergen. He visited Norway and Sweden, where he was not impressed with the restrictive drink laws: "One can buy not less than a litre of spirit, and not more than five litres each month. One has a little book in which merchants register all purchases. This essential book may be confiscated by doctors and magistrates."

He went to Finland and then to Russia. In both countries the sale of vodka had been stopped and wine was difficult to obtain. Surplus potatoes were being distilled into methylated spirit at 96 per cent alcohol (vodka is 40 per cent). There were stills on all the large farms and the peasants told him: "We can get drunk for 13 kopeks for three days," (a kopek was worth about a farthing). He was told that the distilling of vodka would be allowed but only under government supervision, otherwise the peasants would be drinking poison. Hugo Krohn returned to Madeira very disappointed, with only a small order book. The 900 million litres of wine produced in Russia was insufficient for the demand. Foreign wines would have been welcomed, especially port and Madeira, but merchants had no money with which to buy them.

It is sad that the Krohn family has disappeared from the island and the great name of Krohn Brothers is now merely one of the Madeira Wine Company's minor brands. Krohn Brothers included among their distinguished clients the Czars, Czarevich and the King of Bavaria.

Carlo de Bianchi, with his great-grandson, Noël, in 1911.

Power, Drury & Co.

Dr. Dru Drury's son, Henry, started trading in Madeira under the name of Henry Dru Drury & Co. and on his death in 1888 his partner, Charles O. L. Power, who had come to Madeira in 1878, carried on as Power, Drury & Co. His son, Charles le P. Power, followed on until he died and the company joined the Madeira Wine Association. Charles Power Sr. who lived at Quinta Deão, known as "The Deanery," was a great horticulturist and introduced many species of rare flowering trees and shrubs from all parts of the world. And no one knew Madeira better than Charles Power Jr. He walked all over the island and published *Power's Guide to Madeira*. Although rather dated, it is in my opinion the best book about the island.

Lomelino

In 1820 a Portuguese gentleman and vineyard owner, Tarquinio Torquato da Câmara Lomelino, took over the old established shipping firm of Robert Leal and started shipping in his own name. My great-grandfather, Carlo de Bianchi, a ship owner of Genoese origin, was married to his sister, Anna, and on Tarquinio's death he inherited the Lomelino business. Carlo was a magnificent judge of wine and collected a stock of old-bottled wine which remains unrivalled today. The firm supplied HM the King of Sweden, and also the late kings of Italy and Portugal. Old Carlo, whom I remember well as a child, was an amusing character. He lived on his estates in the Machico Valley and directed his business in Funchal by remote control, which in the days of no telephone or motor transport was quite a feat. He had an army of messengers mounted on nags who galloped backwards and forwards between the wine store in Funchal where his two grandsons worked, and the quinta. Carlo said one could only live either at Machico or in Paris, where he spent six months of the year. To look after his soul and health, he retained a resident chaplain and doctor, but their raison d'être was to play chess with him. My mother's parents went to Paris one year leaving her with her grandparents. When they returned old Carlo would not give her back so she was brought up in his household at Machico. Thus she learnt a great deal about wine, acquired his magnificent palate and after she married my father she directed all the blending at Cossarts. She was also a partner in Lomelino, with her two brothers, Antonio and Gabriel Bianchi. When Lomelino joined the Madeira Wine Association, Antonio was its first technical director and had one of the finest palates in the island.

In 1976 I was asked by Michael Broadbent what the initials "C de B" stencilled on some bottles of old Madeira represented. The wine was the property of a member of the Blandy family, and the initials those of Carlo de Bianchi, from whose cellar the wine had come. The title of Barone de Bianchi had become extinct in the family but Carlo's godfather, Maximilian, Emperor of Mexico, revived the title and gave it to him "and to all his progeny male or female." Carlo never used it because he said it was an Italian title given to him by an Austrian who had become a Mexican, so he doubted Maximilian's ability to grant it.

Quinta do Monte, 1888. Mildred Blandy Cossart, Leland Cossart, Anna Mary Cossart, Jane Cossart and C. J. Cossart.

William Hinton & Sons

William Hinton and Sons is an old established British company which through acquisitions held the monopoly for sugar milling in the island, as well as large sugar interests in Angola. The firm was founded by William Hinton, the son of a Wiltshire landowner who had come out to Madeira in 1838 for health reasons and married the daughter of Robert Wallas, a wine shipper who also owned a steam driven flour mill. After they were married, they returned to England but finding that his immediate family was too numerous (13 in all), he sold up and returned to Madeira to start up a sugar mill. This was developed into a great sugar empire by his son Harry, who over the years, and, until it was prohibited, supplied the Madeira shippers with cane brandy to fortify their wines.

THE WINE MERCHANTS

The old Madeira Wine Association

Harry Hinton took no interest in wine until 1913 when he joined forces with Welsh & Cunha (now Welsh Brothers) and Henriques & Câmara. The new company was called Madeira Wine Association Lda. Many other firms joined during the lean years that followed, including Donaldsons, and locally the company became known as "the shippers' cemetery." Krohn Brothers, the second largest shipper at the time, vigorously opposed the union, especially the title, but after the collapse of the Russian market, they too joined the Association.

The Madeira Wine Association's lodge in 1925.

In 1925 Blandy and Leacock amalgamated their wine interests with a Portuguese-Jewish firm, Viuva Abudarham & Filhos, established in 1825. They also joined the Madeira Wine Association. John Ernest Blandy, grandfather of the present chairman, Richard Blandy, was the new company's first chairman, and Thomas L. Mullins, who had looked after Blandy's wines, became managing director. Subsequently, many of the most famous exporters became members, for example, Luiz Gomes da Conceição & Filhos, established in 1868, Miles Madeiras Lda. (Rutherford & Miles), F. F. Ferraz & Cia, established in 1880, T. T. da Câmara Lomelino, established in 1820, and many other famous names. The Association was most ably organised by the doyen of the Madeira trade, Tom Mullins, a great palate and technician as well as a brilliant planner and accountant. The spirit of the union was to maintain the individuality of the associates and their styles of wine, selling it through individual channels, but at the same time, reducing overheads by buying collectively and by bringing the hitherto separate establishments under one roof and management.

Cossart, Gordon & Co. Ltd. became a partner in 1953,[20] 27 years after the formation of the *new* Madeira Wine Association, and 207 years after its own foundation in the island. At the same time, the Madeira assets of the London company were put into a Portuguese company, Cossart, Gordon & Co. Lda., which now supplies all the London company's requirements through the Madeira Wine Company.

The Madeira Wine Company

On December 31st 1981, the Madeira Wine Association Lda. changed its title to Madeira Wine Co. Limitada. However the company continues to trade in the famous names of its partners and brands.

The Madeira Wine Company calculates its average permanent stock to be in the region of 10,000 pipes. It ships about 50 per cent of the island's exports and incorporates seven firms, including all the British ones. It is by no means a monopoly for it has as competitors several important independent Portuguese firms.

Henriques & Henriques

The firm was founded in 1850 by João Joaquim Gonçalves Henriques, a landowner and a member of an old family living at Belem, Câmara de Lobos, who owned some of the finest vineyards on the island. He was succeeded by his sons João Joaquim and Francisco Eduardo (known as "the young gentlemen of Belem"), who in 1913 formed the present company.

The firm was reconstituted and took in several other houses: Casa dos Vinhos da Madeira Lda., Belem's Madeira Lda., Carma Vinhos Lda., and A. E. Henriques Sucrs. Lda.

In 1925, the company, with offices and cellars in Funchal in addition to the cellars at Belem, entered the export business. The firm soon became regular suppliers to the Scandinavian wine monopolies and, after the Second World War, the largest shippers to the Canadian Liquor Boards. The surviving brother, João Joaquim Henriques, died in 1968 at the age of 90. The present partners of the firm are Albert N. Jardim, my brother, Peter Cossart, and Carlos M. Nunes Pereira.

Henriques & Henriques still own the family vineyards at Câmara de Lobos and all their wines are produced from their own grapes.

A.E. Henriques Sucrs. Lda.

João Joaquim Gonçalves Henriques had a third son, Antonio Eduardo, who founded an independent firm to which he gave his name. Soon after his death Antonio Eduardo Henriques Suers Lda. was taken over by Henriques & Henriques.

Justinho Henriques Filhos Lda. and Companhia Vinicola da Madeira Lda.

A cousin of the three brothers founded yet a third firm in 1870, Justinho Henriques, which later shipped a great deal of Madeira to the United States of America. Whilst they are run as separate entities, this company and Companhia Vinicola da Madeira (which also dates back to 1870) are today under common ownership.

H.M. Borges Sucrs. Lda.

H. M. Borges was founded in 1877 by Henrique de Menèzes Borges, who was still at the head of the firm when he died in 1916. The firm had a good market in the United Kingdom, which faded during the war. Their most important markets were the United States of America, Scandinavia and Italy.

The company is still run by the family today, and is famous for its old vintage wines. These were collected by Mr. Henrique Borges and bottles of Terrantez stencilled with the initials, H. M. B., are found today.

The H.M. Borges lodge on Rua de 31 Janeiro, Funchal.

Veiga França (Vinhos) Lda.

The firm was established in 1944 and is run by the family of the same name who also own substantial vineyards in the Câmara de Lobos region.

At Estreito, they have an interesting museum of agriculture (see page 19) which was started by Mr. Solomão da Veiga França.

Until recently his son, Mr. Jorge da Veiga França, was the president of the wine section of the Funchal Chamber of Commerce.

Vinhos Barbeito (Madeira) Lda.

One of the most recent firms to be established is Vinhos Barbeito Lda., founded in 1946. The firm has the most modern lodges in Funchal (close to Reid's Hotel) and has lost no time in becoming one of the leading shippers, and the only one with a market in Japan.

The proprietor, Mario Barbeito Vasconcelos, has a great library of books on Madeira and is a historian of note. He is also a world authority on Columbus and, in conjunction with the explorer's descendant, Admiral Cristobal Colon, Duque de Veragua, is at present organising the Columbus Museum on Porto Santo.

CHAPTER 5

THE MARKET IN INDIA

Oh, East is East, and West is West, and never the twain shall meet, Till Earth and Sky stand presently at God's great Judgment Seat ...
The Ballad of East and West, Kipling, 1899

The Portuguese navigator Vasco da Gama left Lisbon on July 8th 1497 and, having sailed round the Cape of Good Hope, reached Calicut in India on May 20th 1498. In the same year, a Venetian pilot, Giovanni Cabotto, better known as John Cabot, discovered Labrador on the North American coast and a Florentine merchant, Amerigo Vespucci, sailed along the south coast of North America. There is evidence that Vasco da Gama took with him to India Malvasia wine from the new island in the Atlantic which had been populated only half a century earlier.

Trading Posts

Soon after, Pedro Alvares Cabral brought Portuguese settlers to India and established fortified trading posts which were called *feitorias*. The first was at Cochin and subsequently the brothers Francisco and Alfonso d'Albuquerque established others at Goa, Calicut and Quilon. Pedro Alvares Cabral was the grandson of Zarco, who had rediscovered Madeira. His father, Diogo Cabral, was one of the three noblemen sent by Alfonso, King of Portugal, to marry Zarco's three daughters. Diogo had married Brites, the second daughter. All this was before the Mogul empire and a century before the first charter granted to the Company of London Merchants which led to the incorporation of the East India Company. The British then founded "factories" based on the *feitorias*.

Beverage Madeira

The Portuguese continued to take Madeira to India, not only for consumption on the long voyages, but also for the officials who manned the *feitorias*. In these early days, the only Madeiras one hears of are "Malvasia" and "Seco." Malvasia has been described as rich and potent (even though it was not yet fortified) and, as the name implies, Seco was dry and not as popular. One presumes the latter was made from the *gouveiro* grape, later known as *verdelho*.

At that time Madeira was an unfortified beverage wine. Although there was plenty of the same sort of wine produced in the Douro and Lisbon regions of Portugal, that from Madeira seems to have been preferred even before the days of fortification because, we are told, it was hardy, retained its qualities despite extremes of temperature, and improved with age. It seems that in the 15th and early 16th centuries Madeira was considered sturdier and less likely to turn into vinegar than other wines. Nonetheless there must have been a point at which it turned acid, otherwise shippers early in the 18th century would not have added "a bucket or two of brandy per pipe" to preserve it (see Chapter 9). However because this was a gradual process, we do not know exactly when Madeira became a fortified wine, but it was after the wines of the Douro and Jerez. By the middle of the 18th century fortification was general practice. At roughly the same time it was found that port could not tolerate and did not improve with heat treatment, whereas heat became an important part of the maturing process of Madeira.

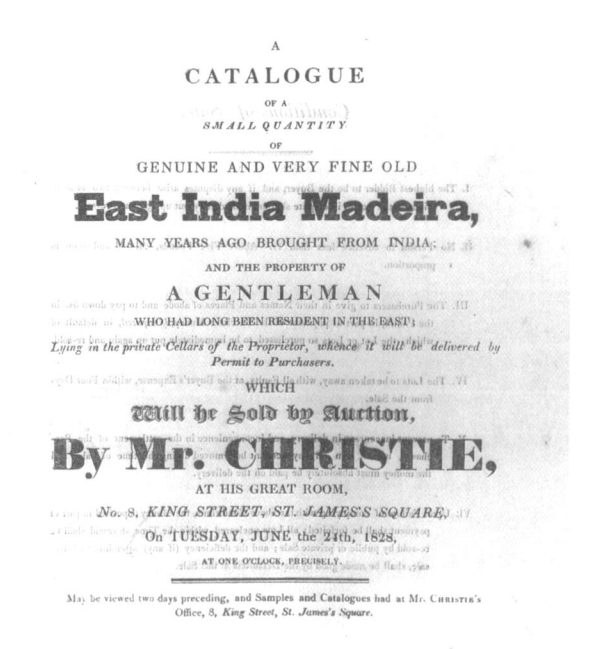

<blockquote>
A
CATALOGUE
OF A
SMALL QUANTITY
OF
GENUINE AND VERY FINE OLD
East India Madeira,
MANY YEARS AGO BROUGHT FROM INDIA,
AND THE PROPERTY OF
A GENTLEMAN
WHO HAD LONG BEEN RESIDENT IN THE EAST;
Lying in the private Cellars of the Proprietor, whence it will be delivered by Permit to Purchasers.
WHICH
Will be Sold by Auction,
By Mr. CHRISTIE,
AT HIS GREAT ROOM,
No. 8, *KING STREET, ST. JAMES'S SQUARE,*
On TUESDAY, JUNE the 24th, 1828,
AT ONE O'CLOCK, PRECISELY.
May be viewed two days preceding, and Samples and Catalogues had at Mr. Christie's Office, 8, *King Street, St. James's Square.*
</blockquote>

A Christie's broadside for an 1828 auction of East India Madeiras.

THE MARKET IN INDIA

The Dutch East India Company

The Dutch, who formed the first United India Company, and then the British learned the merits of Madeira drinking from the first Portuguese settlers, and it became the traditional wine in which regimental messes and clubs drank the health of the monarch. This tradition was maintained until India's independence. One would have thought that in a hot climate the lighter Madeiras, as drunk in the southern American states, would be the most popular but, strangely, the heavier after-dinner Madeiras constituted the bulk of the wine shipped, especially Bual and Bual types, which became known as "Bull" by the troops. The use of heavier Madeiras may possibly be explained by the fact that planters used to drink a Bamboo cocktail, half gin and half "Bull," with ice, so it may have served both as an aperitif and an after-dinner drink. They say today that only alcoholics and diplomats are able to obtain wine or spirits in India. Madeira is still shipped there, but only in small quantities, presumably for diplomatic consumption. Sadly the closure of the India market is a loss which has not been replaced.

Growth of shipments

Although vessels of the British East India Company were calling regularly at Funchal in 1680 and taking on wine for use on the voyage, one hears little at this time of Madeira actually being consigned to India. In 1710, however, William Bolton mentions he had sent 40 pipes to India, and by 1805 the island shipped no less than 6,260 pipes, specifically for consumption in India. This represented 47 per cent of the total exports. In 1797 Cossart, Gordon made a single shipment of 300 pipes to one importer. On October 14th 1799 a convoy of 96 ships bound for Bombay loaded 3,041 pipes. This consignment, averaging 2,915 gallons per ship, may seem a lot of wine, but when one considers that Captain James Cook loaded 3,032 gallons for the crew's consumption on his ship 31 years earlier, the amount seems modest. Cossart, Gordon's order book for Bombay in the year 1800 reads as follows:

Dec. 6th 1799	500 pipes for Law, Bruce & Co.
Mar. 19th 1800	300 pipes for David Scott & Co.
Aug. 2nd 1800	250 pipes for Forbes, Smith & Co.
	1,050 pipes equal to 96,600 gallons

Another large order in a letter from William Simons, East India House, London, dated July 28th 1809 reads as follows: "Three hundred and thirty pipes of India Market Madeira Wine. One hundred and twenty pipes best London Market Madeira. For account of the East India Company and to be shipt on board their ships of the season 1809/1810." India Market Madeira was paler and lighter than London Market, of superior quality and equal to London Particular, but with the same sweetness of 2.5 degrees Baumé. Newton, Gordon, Murdoch & Co. were the largest shippers at that time, being responsible for one-third of the island's wine exports. There also were some 69 other houses, so the above figures will give readers an idea of the amount of business transacted in Madeira in the early 19th century.

LIST OF MESSES, CLUBS, &c.,
Which have been supplied with
COSSART, GORDON & Co.'s MADEIRAS.

Royal Artillery Mess, Meerut.	14th Regiment Bengal N.I.	25th Regiment Bombay N.I.
Royal Artillery Mess, Mount, Madras.	17th ,, ,, ,,	26th ,, ,, ,,
Royal Artillery Mess, Secunderabad.	18th ,, ,, ,,	7th ,, Bengal Light Cavalry.
Royal Artillery Mess, Bangalore.	19th ,, ,, ,,	14th ,, ,, ,,
Royal Artillery Mess, Kirkee.	22nd ,, ,, ,,	8th Bareilly Native Infantry.
Royal Artillery Mess, Meean Meer.	24th ,, ,, ,,	2nd Regiment Punjab N.I.
Royal Artillery Mess, Dum Dum.	25th ,, ,, ,,	3rd ,, ,, ,,
Royal Artillery Mess, Kamptee.	26th ,, ,, ,,	4th ,, ,, ,,
Royal Artillery Mess, Peshawur.	29th ,, ,, ,,	6th ,, ,, ,,
Royal Artillery Mess, Rawal Pindee.	30th ,, ,, ,,	25th ,, ,, ,,
Royal Artillery Mess, Umballa.	31st ,, ,, ,,	3rd Ghoorkha Regiment.
Royal Artillery Mess, Morar.	33rd ,, ,, ,,	5th ,, ,, ,,
Royal Artillery Mess, Ahmedabad.	34th ,, ,, ,,	1st Sikh Infantry.
Royal Artillery Mess, Trimulgherry.	37th ,, ,, ,,	2nd ,, ,,
Royal Artillery Mess, Colaba.	38th ,, ,, ,,	2nd Regiment Central India Horse.
Royal Artillery Mess, Lucknow.	41st ,, ,, ,,	Nagpoor Irregular Cavalry.
Royal Artillery Mess, Hyzabad.	43rd ,, ,, ,,	5th Infantry Hyderabad Contingent.
Royal Artillery Mess, Quetta.	44th ,, ,, ,,	Hyderabad Contingent Messes.
Royal Artillery Mess, Jhansi.	45th ,, ,, ,,	Gwaloir Contingent Mess.
Royal Artillery Mess, Singapore.	46th ,, ,, ,,	Lingospoor Mess.
Royal Artillery Mess, Calcutta.	52nd ,, ,, ,,	Jaulnah Mess.
Royal Artillery Mess, Mhow.	53rd ,, ,, ,,	Aurungabad Mess.
Royal Artillery Mess, Bhamo.	54th ,, ,, ,,	Hingolee Mess.
Royal Artillery Mess, Mooltan.	57th ,, ,, ,,	Bolarum Mess
Royal Artillery Mess, Ceylon.	59th ,, ,, ,,	Secunderabad Mess.
Royal Artillery Mess, Aden.	61st ,, ,, ,,	Ellichpoor Mess.
8th Mountain Battery, Rawal Pindee.	66th ,, ,, ,,	Ceylon Rifles.
9th Mountain Battery, Jalapahar.	67th ,, ,, ,,	Sappers and Miners.
Royal Engineers' Mess, Roorkee.	71st ,, ,, ,,	Himilaya Club.
Royal Engineers' Mess, N.W. Province.	74th ,, ,, ,,	Secunderabad Club.
Royal Engineers' Mess, Ceylon.	101st ,, ,, Fusiliers.	Madras Club.
23rd Pioneers, Umballa.	4th Regiment Madras N.I.	Western India Club.
2nd Dragoon Guards.	5th ,, ,, ,,	Byculla Club.
7th Dragoon Guards.	9th ,, ,, ,,	Naini Tal Club.
4th Hussars.	19th ,, ,, ,,	United Service Club, Simla.
7th Hussars.	25th ,, ,, ,,	Bengal United Service Club, Calcutta.
10th Hussars.	28th ,, ,, ,,	Wheler Club.
Northumberland Fusiliers.	29th ,, ,, ,,	Umballa Club.
24th Regiment.	30th ,, ,, ,,	Ootacamund Club.
58th Regiment.	33rd ,, ,, ,,	Meerut Club.
66th Regiment.	34th ,, ,, ,,	Lahore Club.
67th Regiment.	39th ,, ,, ,,	Amraoti Club.
97th Regiment.	42nd ,, ,, ,,	Murree Club.
1st Battalion The Buffs.	44th ,, ,, ,,	Agra Club.
1st Battalion Middlesex.	50th ,, ,, ,,	Mangalore Club.
2nd Battalion Middlesex.	52nd ,, ,, ,,	Punjab Club.
1st Battalion East Surrey.	1st Madras Pioneers.	Rawal Pindee Club.
1st Gloucester Regiment.	2nd Madras Lancers.	Quetta Club.
2nd Battalion S. Wales Borderers.	3rd Madras Lancers.	Pegu Club, Rangoon.
5th (Royal Irish) Lancers.	2nd Regiment Madras Light Cavalry.	Rangoon Gymnkhana Club.
10th Bengal Lancers.	3rd ,, ,, ,, ,,	Upper Burma Club.
11th Bengal Lancers.	5th ,, ,, ,, ,,	Hong Kong Club (China).
1st Regiment Bengal N.I.	6th ,, ,, ,, ,,	Union Club (Malta).
3rd ,, ,, ,,	7th ,, ,, ,, ,,	Australian Club (Sydney).
5th ,, ,, ,,	31st ,, ,, ,, Infantry.	Hawkes Bay Club (Napier, N.Z.).
8th ,, ,, ,,	Marine Battalion, Bombay.	Wellington Club (Wellington, N.Z.).
9th ,, ,, ,,	1st Regiment Bombay Light Horse.	2nd West India Regiment (Jamaica), and
11th ,, ,, ,,	7th ,, ,, N.I.	Sierra Leone.
13th ,, ,, ,,	22nd ,, ,, ,,	

Information from Cossart, Gordon publicity of the early 20th century.

THE MARKET IN INDIA

East India Madeira

Apart from wine for ships' stores and for consumption in India, whenever possible a considerable amount was loaded for maturing on the round voyage. This was shipped in specially reinforced hogsheads and scantling pipes holding one-and-a-half pipes each, for stowage in the bilges under other cargo. Obviously these casks must sometimes have been awash with bilge water. Anyone who has sailed in a ship will have experienced the foul, filthy smell of bilge water and will wonder why the wine in these casks did not become tainted. Yet I have never tasted an old *vinho da roda* that had an odour of bilge water. Or perhaps this is what gave old East India Madeira its lovely mellow aroma: possibly even bilge water eventually mellows.

Prices at auction

Madeira which had been in the East or West Indies sold for high prices in London, as will be seen from Christie's catalogues. In October 1783 a "Pipe of Madeira 5 years in West Indies" sold for £83 16s 0d, whereas the same pipe shipped from Madeira would, at the most, have cost £40 in London. On December 22nd 1796 "London Particular Madeira (vintage 1791) which has been in the East Indies a considerable time and now to be tasted at the Company's Warehouse at Adelphi Wharf," sold for £10 16s 8d per chest of 50 bottles. In January 1804 Christie's held a "sale of wine of Daniel Seaton late governor of Surat in the East Indies." It included "East India Madeira purchased in India, has been round by Bombay and sent Home for the Governor's own private use" at 100s per dozen.

The sale of wines from Brook's Club, "sold in consequence of a dissolution of partnership" on July 18th 1815, included 3,000 bottles of East and West India Madeira, bottled from 1812 to 1814, which sold for 80s to 90s per dozen; and on June 26th 1820, amongst the stock of a wine merchant, John Grant "*Curious* East India Madeira" fetched 127s per dozen. One can put these prices into perspective by comparison with Sercial at 25s per dozen and Old Madeira at 60s per dozen in the sale, in 1828, of wines of the Rt. Hon. George Canning, deceased, "lying in the cellar of Downing Street."

Clubs and officers messes

The importance of the market in India itself can be judged by the list of the numerous messes and clubs supplied by Cossart, Gordon & Co. (see page 74).

Contemporary price lists read: "These Madeiras have been specially selected for the requirements and tastes of Indian residents, and, we flatter ourselves, with success, judging from the quantities we ship there." The circular goes on: "We would draw the particular attention of Messes to the fact that these wines may be ordered in 1/4 pipes (equal to 11 dozen), which, on account of their small size, need not be bottled, but *if pitched on end*, the wine can be drawn off to the last half-gallon perfectly bright, thus saving a great expense in bottles and corks." This circular should have added "also improving the Madeira."

Gunner Madeira

My late uncle, Colonel Arthur Blandy Cossart, DSO, who served with the Royal Horse Artillery in India from 1905 to 1925, remembered bottling Madeira for his mess when a subaltern. It seems to have been part of the subalterns' duty and, after bottling in the heat, they became quite drunk. A letter addressed to me on June 7th 1982 by Brigadier C. R. Templer, DSO (first cousin of Field-marshal Sir Gerald Templer), enquiring about a pipe of Gunner Madeira, reads as follows:

> In 1924 when serving as a subaltern in the Royal Artillery in Meerut, United Provinces, India, I helped the Mess Secretary to bottle off a pipe of Madeira, bottles were then sent to other Gunner Messes in India.
>
> The story of this wine was told to me as follows: In the last century a ship on which Mr. Cossart (or Mr. Gordon) was sailing was wrecked and his life was saved by a Gunner Officer then stationed at Meerut, India.
>
> In recognition of this act, your firm promised to send to the Gunner Mess at Meerut, a free pipe of Madeira annually. This custom I have heard continued until the granting of Independence to India.
>
> I would like to write this story in our Regimental Magazine "Gunner", and would be most grateful if, from your records, you could confirm and possibly add to the tale.

The story, which is unique, is that William Cossart Jr., was travelling in India on business in 1857. By chance he happened to be staying in Meerut on Sunday May 10th when the 3rd Bengal Light Cavalry mutinied while the British troops were attending evening church. The mutineers, joined by the sepoys of the Bengal

Native Infantry, swept through the cantonment, attacking and killing any unarmed civilians they found. William Cossart was fortunate to be saved from certain death by an officer serving with a field battery. The gunners of the Bengal army also saved from the mutineers many pipes of Cossart's Madeira. The family and other partners were so impressed and indebted that they gave the gunner mess at Meerut "a pipe of best London Particular Madeira each year for as long as the Mess or the Firm will last;" in other words in perpetuity. Thus the Bual in the pipe became known as Gunner Madeira. Its value then was £40 (the equivalent today of £1,500) and a pipe was delivered every year until 1936 when the firm sent the mess the sum of £40 annually in lieu. This payment continued long after India's independence in 1947. I discovered in 1950 that no one had woken up to the fact that India had become independent and, because the mess had been disbanded, the money was no longer due.

Brigadier Templer estimates that the action of the gunner officer benefited his mess by over £10,000 spread over nearly 100 years. A pipe yields 44-45 dozen bottles, more than the requirement of the Meerut mess, so Gunner Madeira was sent to other artillery messes all over India and much of it was brought home. In 1972, another gunner contacted me from India because he had obtained some of the wine through the Army and Navy Stores in 1971 and found it so delicious he wanted some more. Now called Medium Rich Bual, the wine is still a favourite of clubs and messes in the United Kingdom.

Correspondence between Madeira and India is nearly as great as that between Madeira and America, which from the years 1800 to 1900 is second only to that with London. In the Cossart archives there is a letter dated 1808 from Kishrngar (Bengal) to Madeira which, according to Robson Lowe, Christie's philatelic experts, is the earliest letter known from this state, the next known being 1855. There are also orders from Prince of Wales Island (Penang) from Sir Edward Stanley, the recorder, who told us that in 1810 the penal settlement accounted for 90 per cent of the population. In China Madeira was traded for Canton's ginseng.

Africa

There was also a special Madeira for Africa. The settlers in Angola and Mozambique found the quinine they had to take was more palatable with Malmsey, so a special Malmsey laced with quinine called vinho quinado was developed. This cocktail became so popular that, even now, the settlers who returned to Portugal drink it as an aperitif. When quinine is mixed with wine or any other liquid it goes cloudy, but Count Canavial, a most ingenious wine chemist, discovered a manner of keeping it bright and Cossart's bought his patent.

Brazil

Madeira's popularity in Brazil is another proof of its lasting qualities before fortification. Cabral who, as already mentioned, brought the first settlers to India, was returning there from Lisbon when he strayed off course and landed on the coast of Brazil, which he called Land of the Holy Cross. Portuguese settlements were soon established there and in 1530 the King of Portugal divided the settlements into captaincies and again, because it was hardier, the wine of Madeira was given preference over the wines from the mainland. In 1643 John IV, by royal decree, ordered all his ships bound for Brazil to call at Madeira to load wine for his captaincies. The French seized Portugal in 1807 and the following year the court and royal family established themselves in Brazil, thus giving impetus to the Madeira trade, which was booming by 1815 when Portugal and Brazil became united. By the time the court was in Brazil, Madeira had become a fortified wine of a very different character from that drunk in the captaincies, but this does not seem to have made any difference to its popularity, which was increased by the many migrants from the island.

CHAPTER 6

MADEIRA IN NORTH AMERICA

In the days when Madeira was unfortified it was consumed in large quantities in colonial America and the West Indies, in the way port was drunk after fox-hunting in England. The largest shipments, however, occurred after fortification, between 1788 and 1828, when Madeira was drunk after dinner but with no great ceremony and still in large quantities. Between these dates the price rose from £20 a pipe for the best qualities to £45 and the new colonies in north America were taking a quarter of the wine produced on the island.

In the 19th century it was drunk and appreciated in fine glass in small quantities, great stress being put on the difference between the various wines, as is shown in Dr. S. Weir Mitchell's book.

Madeira parties

Langdon Mitchell describes parties at his father's house in Philadelphia from 1880 onward; subsequently he gave the parties at his own house in New York, where he had 26 demijohns of his father's old Madeiras, all of different sorts. Madeira parties, Mitchell tells us, which usually began at 5 pm and lasted two or three hours, were normally composed of eight men at table. Five or six different Madeiras were circulated clockwise in old decanters on silver coasters. While the wine was tasted and discussed, biscuits and nuts were eaten. After the first three wines had been tasted, fine Havana cigars were allowed. Madeira is the only wine whose strict devotees allow smoking. This is a controversial matter, with which non-smokers disagree. Personally, I have been smoking for some 60 years and I find a cigarette tickles up and revives my now rather jaded palate.

Madeira wine played such an important part in the American way of life that it was used to toast the Declaration of Independence. Thomas Jefferson used it in July 1792 to toast the decision to locate the US Capitol in Washington, DC, and George Washington's inauguration in April 1789 at Fraunces Tavern was toasted with Madeira wine. Francis Scott Key composing the "Star-spangled Banner," and Betsy Ross sewing the American flag, drank Madeira in 1777. Malcolm Bell Jr., a member of The Liberty National Bank & Trust Company of Savannah, read a paper on the "Romantic Wines of Madeira" to members of the Madeira Club of Savannah on April 24th 1953, which was published in *The Georgia Historical Quarterly* of December 1954. In this paper he says, "George Washington drank a pint [of Madeira] at dinner daily, Gilbert Stuart who mixed claret with his paints had a taste for the best Madeiras which he poured from a half gallon ewer, throwing off tumblers like cider in haying time." He also tells us that Benjamin Franklin, Thomas Jefferson and Chief Justice Marshall were connoisseurs of Madeira. The latter was famous for his boisterous lawyer's parties at which Madeira was always drunk, and which kept the Virginia wine merchants prosperous. Daniel Webster called on a friend and stayed put until he had polished off a dozen bottles of the famous Butler 16 Madeira (see page 87).

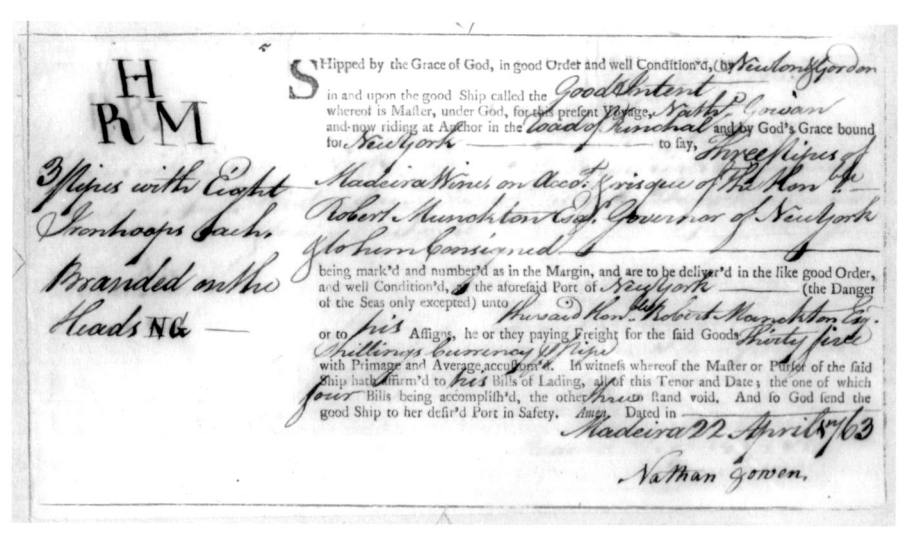

Bill of lading for wine shipped to the Hon. Robert Monckton, Governor of New York, 1763.

From Cossart, Gordon's letter books of the years following 1812 one observes that the writers were anxious to do business with Madeira, even if it was necessary to fly the Portuguese flag to avoid the British blockade of American ports. Many of the letters[21] written from other towns went via Philadelphia, whence a constant stream of vessels sailed for Madeira with cargoes of grain and flour, returning with wine. This illegal export of American currency flourished and the merchants in Madeira were authorised to sell the cargo, and even the vessels, and pay their unnamed friends in London the proceeds for safe-keeping.

Barter Madeira

Many choice wines were returned from the East Indies, but a considerable proportion of them were acid and lacked the full flavour of those sent to the West Indies. This was not due to the climate, but to the original quality of the wine, coupled with the conditions under which it was shipped. A part of the cargoes, matured for the London market by transportation to East India and back, was purchased by unscrupulous and often inexperienced British speculators, who thought the voyage would turn any quality of Madeira into nectar. The wine was purchased at long credit or bartered for other goods, so that the best qualities were not always bought. These wines acquired in the island the contemptuous description of Truck or Barter Madeira. West India Madeira, on the other hand, was usually selected and bought either by discerning American merchants or by colonists for their own consumption. Today both East and West India Madeiras and their types are equally fine, all Truck and Barter Madeira having been eliminated long ago.

In the 18th century most of the best production was known as American Madeira. When Madeira became fashionable in England some American Madeira was sent to London where it sold for high prices and was recommended by doctors, who, according to Croft's *A Treatise on the Wines of Portugal*, "put invalids and wine merchants on writing their correspondents in Madeira, to send over their very best sorts." Early this century, to avoid Truck or Barter wines, *bona fide* London shippers offered East and West India Madeira quoted in pipes and half pipes of 92 and 46 gallons respectively "in Bond landing gauge after respective voyages."[22] The ship and date of landing were generally declared. It was accepted that two gallons per pipe were lost on voyage. Cossart, Gordon's offers generally read: "EAST & WEST INDIA MADEIRA. We have by long experience found that Madeiras shipped to acquire these respective peculiarities on the sea-voyage must, of necessity, be of the finest quality to repay the heavy expense incurred on them. We therefore quote only one quality of each, in which we have full confidence, and which will meet the requirements of every one desiring high-class old Madeiras." As an example, in 1879 the firm offered "Finest Old, full flavoured Cama de Lobos East India ex *Star of Bengal*, Calcutta, November, 1877" at £90 per pipe and "Finest old, very choice and delicate Reserve West India, ex *Agatha*, Jamaica, August, 1878" at £85 per pipe. It will be noticed that whereas the East India was full-flavoured the West India was delicate, being directed at the American market. Because West India was favoured it was quickly consumed, so it is bottles of East India that are now more often found in the United States.

A Boston tasting

Messrs. S. S. Pierce held a tasting of bottle-aged Madeiras on March 1st 1936 at 59 Marlborough Street, Boston. There were no vintages and all the Cossart wines had been bottled in Boston. Madeiras shown were Sercial bottled 1908, Bual bottled 1910 and 1920, Malmsey bottled 1920; also three Old East India Madeiras, Verdelho bottled 1915, Reserve bottled 1920 and Cama de Lobos bottled 1915. All the wines were approximately of the same age. I was not present at the tasting for it took place in the year I took over our Madeira house, but the late Russell Codman of Boston, a Madeira connoisseur and director of that famous house, very kindly gave me his notes. It seems he preferred the Old East Indias which, he said, had a "pre-phylloxera flavour."

The Codmans and other members of Boston's wine and food elite belonged to the city's Club Gastronomique. This menu from a 1935 club dinner features two Madeiras belonging to members.

Both Mr. and Mrs. Norman Pierce and Mr. and Mrs. Russell Codman used to visit me regularly in Madeira on buying missions. I greatly appreciated their experience, knowledge and choice of wines. On Mr. Codman's death, Mrs. Codman carried on the good work.

In colonial days it was not the habit to name Madeira after grape varieties, as it was in the United Kingdom. One rarely finds the names Sercial, Bual or Malmsey, because the wine shipped was mostly Cama de Lobos and/or São Martinho, both known in America as South Side. The Madeiras were generally given their names by the importers and often called after the ships which brought them or the merchants or families who imported them. There was, for instance a Jenny Lind 1849 which featured on the Gibson House Hotel wine list in 1856 at $2.50 per bottle. These names were, to say the least, non-descriptive. Who today would know what was in a bottle labelled Jenny Lind? However, the American public knew their Madeira so well that Sercial or Bual might have been marked on the bottle.

Madeira was also named after places it had travelled to, such as India, East India or West India. There was a famous Japan Madeira brought home by Commodore Perry in the Susquehanna for Mr. Kennedy, secretary for the Navy in 1852. In his book on Madeira, Mr. Charles Bellows says that in 1895, a quarter-century after Mr. Kennedy's death, 207 bottles of Japan Madeira were found in his former residence, which were sold for $2.60 per bottle. During my time with Cossart, Gordon before the war we used to ship Old South Side in wood for Bellows & Co. by Royal Mail and Blue Star steamers en route to Buenos Aires. The wine was then brought up the coast and bottled in New York. I understand this was known as Argentine Madeira. Some of the ships that carried the famous wines of the time were: *The Widow, The Rapid, Catherine Banks, Wanderer, Favourite, Bethune, Southern Cross, Juno, Comet, Hurricane, Mentor, Mary Elizabeth, Rebel, Adelaide, Earthquake, Meredith, Three Deacons, Bramin* and *Constitution*.

'Bramin' – and non-drinkers

The late Judge William W. Douglas, describing a Madeira party given in Providence, Rhode Island, in 1907, mentions that Madeiras from the brig *Bramin*'s voyages of 1825 and 1827 were among the 20 wines served. The judge adds that the last of the Bramin Madeiras were bought by a well-known temperance ex-governor of Vermont for "medical purposes." The latter does not seem strange to me. I had a great-aunt who would not touch a drop of liquor, but regularly drank a glass of Malmsey at 11 am with a biscuit and another at 4 pm with cake. When I was in New York I saw a well-known wine merchant bottling one-eighth bottles of Madeira with "tear-off tops." I enquired whether they were for airliners but was told they were for chemists to sell to non-drinking old ladies to carry in their handbags. I actually saw an old dear having a swig at one of these little bottles whilst waiting for a train. It is curious how teetotallers do not seem to consider enjoying the medicinal qualities of Madeira to be against their principles. When I was a small boy I attended bible classes given by a Miss Watney, daughter of Dr. Watney, a member of the brewing family. When he retired to Madeira he devoted his time and considerable fortune to spreading the gospel and preaching temperance, but neither he nor his family was averse to a glass of Madeira as a restorative.

'Constitution'

All the ships which gave their names to Madeiras were merchant men with the exception of the famous frigate *Constitution*, 2,200 tons, after which the 1802 Madeira was named. *Constitution* was one of six frigates built under the American Naval Act of 1794 as escorts to merchant ships which were being harrassed by the Bey of Algier's pirates. Two unsuccessful attempts were made to launch her with a baptism of water, but she was finally launched on October 21st 1797, when Madeira was used as the baptismal wine.

'Red Jacket'

Another famous ship connected with Madeira was *Red Jacket* named after the Red Indian Chief whose resplendent figurehead she bore. This great American clipper made history in her transatlantic race with *Lightning*, which left Boston on February 18th 1854. *Red Jacket* sailed from New York the following day but both ships arrived at Liverpool on March 4th. Both "flyers" reached speeds of 18 knots and *Red Jacket* logged a total of 2,020 nautical miles in six days, a feat surpassed only by *Cutty Sark*. When her working life was over *Red Jacket* was sold to Messrs. Blandy Brothers of Madeira[23] where she ended her days in their service, rather ignominiously as a coal hulk in Funchal Roads. A quantity of Red Jacket Madeira was sold and bottled in New York in 1883; it had crossed the Atlantic several times in the famous ship.

MADEIRA IN NORTH AMERICA

The "Liberty" incident

I have mentioned Judge William Douglas's reference to a Madeira party held at Providence. These Madeira parties, at which 20 or more different wines were drunk, were common in the colonial and early federal days. However, the 1765 Stamp Act led to a Madeira party of a very different kind. The colonists resented taxation, and in this matter Madeira played an important part. It was common practice for customs officers to allow only part of a cargo to be entered in the Custom House books, the remainder to be landed free of duty. But the commissioners decided to put an end to this practice when, in 1768, Mr. Hancock's sloop Liberty arrived at Boston laden with Madeira wine. The captain, as usual, proposed that half the cargo should be landed free. His proposal was refused, but Mr. Hancock proceeded to discharge his Madeira, whereupon the commissioner arrested the sloop. The crowd ashore, on hearing they were not to have cheap Madeira, became violent, assaulting the customs officers, smashing the inspector-general's windows and making a public bonfire of his boat. The commissioner and customs officers had to take refuge in Castle William. In the later Boston Tea Party tea was thrown into the sea, but at this party the crowd had the cheap Madeira, and possibly some free of duty.

The necessities of life at New York's United States Hotel in 1831 were food, washing of clothes, sundries, Champaigne (sic) and Madeira.

'Juno'

Mr. Charles Bellows, the noted New York wine merchant and connoisseur who died in 1934 at the age of 85, found six casks of Madeira lying in Water Street in one of the old houses near Peck Slip. They had been brought to New York by the ship *Juno* in 1821 and, in spite of having lain unattended, were in perfect condition.

Family names

In Charles Bellows' unpretentious but valuable little book *Articles on Madeira* (published privately in 1900) he declares that almost every family of repute in New York, as in every other town, had its annual pipe of Madeira. The best known New York family names given to Madeiras are, Remsen, Coffin, Howland, Aspinwall, Griswold, Lenox, Bradly, Martin, Townsend, Fearing, Goelet, Buchanan, Gebhard and Travers. In recent years some very large, low, squat bottles bearing the initials D.L. have been found – even empty they are worth preserving. They were handblown for a respected New York merchant, Dominic Lynch, who imported vintage Madeira in pipes and bottled it in balthazars containing two American gallons (seven-and-half litres). The date of the vintage and his initials were embossed on the side of the bottle. I had one of these balthazars in my collection of old bottles in Madeira which was unfortunately destroyed by fire.

In Philadelphia, Cadwalader, Butler and Mitchell are family names associated with famous Madeiras. Dr. S. Weir Mitchell, pioneer American neurologist, was born in Philadelphia in 1829 and lived until 1914. A great authority on wine, in 1895 he published a calf-bound volume entitled *A Madeira Party* in which he tells how Colonel Lambert Cadwalader, busy fighting the Revolution, wrote to Jasper Yates in 1776 asking him to be "kind enough to let the two quarter casks of Madeira painted green, be deposited in some place under lock and key ... I value them more than silver and gold in these times of misfortune and distress." These green-painted casks had been shipped by Newton & Gordon. John L.

The title page of S. Weir Mitchell's A Madeira Party.

Cadwalader No. 8 Bual was famous and described as magnificent when tasted in New York in its 99th year and again in Connecticut, at 101 years of age. Butler Madeiras, well-known in the States, belonged to Major Pierce Butler, the Georgian planter, who became closely identified with Philadelphia. Major Butler, who married the fascinating Victorian actress, Fanny Kemble, owned the famous Butler 16 (vintage 1716) which kept Daniel Webster busy.

In Charlestown, where a Madeira Club once thrived, famous family-name Madeiras were Middleton, Huger, Ravenel, Pinckney, Gadsden, Laurens and Two Bottle Rutledge. Mr. Bellows maintained that Charlestown was on a favourable latitude for the improvement of Madeiras. In Baltimore, T. W. Walters & Co. were famous Madeira merchants; and, in Virginia, the Carters and Fitzhughs were also well known for their wines.

Georgia

Georgia and Virginia were Newton's great markets and, in fact, extensive markets for the island in general from very early times. Most of the old colonies, Georgia in particular, had an affinity with Madeira. The Georgia founders had viticulture in mind from the beginning and, at a meeting of the trustees in London in October 1732, the sum of £75 was voted for this purpose to be advanced to William Houston, who was sailing for Jamaica. His orders were "while the said ship lies at Madeira [loading wine] he designs to inform himself of the manner of cultivating the vineyards and making the wines there, and to carry with him to Jamaica, cuttings of their best sorts of vines and seeds, roots, or cuttings of any other useful plants he shall meet with on that Island, which are wanting in our American Colonies." On November 9th 1732 William Houston, writing from Madeira to Mr. Oglethorpe in London, told him that he had sent two tubs of "Cuttings of Malmsey and Other Vines. Mr. St. Julian at Charles Town for the use in the Colony of Georgia." The *york Madeira* vine was developed from these cuttings in America, and later imported into the island, after phylloxera. The species, which was by then known as the American *Vitis labrusca*, very surprisingly did not flourish in the soil in which it had originally grown. Neither did the vines do well in Georgia, and no wine to speak of was produced. We hear that a gentleman made a pipe of wine in Sapelo, to which he added 10 to 15 gallons of brandy, being a believer in fortified wines; however "had he gathered his grapes punctually, [he] might have made three pipes."

Although the climate of Georgia was not favourable to viticulture it certainly seems to have suited Madeira wine, and a thriving barter business grew up by exchanging Georgian produce for wine. For instance, oak staves for building casks were much in demand in the island and these were therefore shipped to Madeira from Savannah.

Madeira drinking became an institution during the colonial and early federal days. The years of oidium did not materially affect shipments, for there was wine left over on the island. It was only after 1861, when the effects of the disease had been coupled with those of the Civil War, that shipments were reduced to three figures. However, the planters, who were the best customers for Madeira, would take as much as they could obtain. It is said that they buried it for safety. There is no record of cargoes of wine being lost by action in the Civil War, but Charles Blandy lost a cargo of oak staves he was importing in the barque *Lauretta*, which was sunk by the Confederate ship *Alabama* in 1862. He lodged a protest with the British consul, but having received no satisfaction a year later, he wrote to the Hon. Jefferson Davis, president of the Confederate States, claiming £1,840 16s 3d. He might have saved his time. Jefferson Davis was occupied with more important matters and Blandy received no compensation. Business revived but was severely curtailed during and immediately after phylloxera, improving again until Prohibition finally put an end to the wine trade in the United States. It is only in the last 50 years that it has picked up once more.

Savannah

In 1780 Newton, Gordon & Co. effected a single shipment of 500 pipes to Savannah, and another, later the same year, per *Two Sisters*, of 200 pipes, 12 boxes of lemons and some onions, for John Shoolbred, Esq. Unfortunately not only the wine, lemons and onions were shipped by Newton, Gordon: in 1761 the manifest of the *Fame* included "by the Grace of God in good Order and well conditioned a Negro Man named York." Slaves, who were brought from the coast of Africa in exchange for wine, were listed in the firm's inventories, together with a valuation for oxen, mules and horses. When they became "old and ailing" they were written off.

Mr. Malcolm Bell recalls that the early Georgia newspapers, journals, records and letters all abound with Madeira items. The first issue of *Georgia Gazette*, published on April 7th 1763, listed among current Savannah prices Madeira wine at £30 per pipe.

Through the years advertisements for "Madeira Wine of First Quality" and "Old Particular Madeira" were numerous. A merchant, William Price, would sell among other things "Best London Particular Madeira Wine," and would take in exchange rice, tobacco, beaver fur or deerskin. Also a rich wine known as Thompson's Auction, from an undecipherable vintage year, was sold at $25 a bottle. Savannah was, and is, a great Madeira city, still maintaining a Madeira Club, which is described later in the chapter.

Until Delmonico's of New York obtained the Carolina Jockey Club's stock of Madeira, those from the collection of the late Mr. DeRenne of Savannah were the restaurant's pride and joy. These stocks included a Reserve so named because it was ordered in 1812 and held in Funchal until after the war to avoid the blockade. Harry Emerson Wildes tells us about another Savannahian, mad Anthony Wayne, who fought the British in the "sands and swamps" and flirted with the Georgia girls, and how "always he read with Madeira or rum punch by his side; he gave more attention to the bottle and bowl than to the book." Some of the other Savannah names associated with Madeira were Oglethorpe, Telfair, Anderson, Gordon, Scheley, Chrisholm, Wilder, Jackson and, of course, Habersham (see Chapter 13 and Appendices XVI and XVII).

The Madeira Club of Savannah

The repressive legislation during Prohibition in the United States forced its people to imbibe for effect, rather than to savour their wine, and a nation of hard liquor drinkers emerged. Madeira drinking receded into the dim past, except for an *élite* who, when Prohibition was lifted, returned to the traditional wine which had been identified with gracious living for more than 200 years.

One such notable *élite* are the members of the Madeira Club of Savannah, a lively and intellectual group who eat good food and, above all drink good wine and talk in a discerning manner, recapturing some of the flavour of gracious living that Madeira symbolises. Although the club itself owns no Madeira, individually its members possess the finest collections in the world. These gentlemen meet monthly at a member's house while another member reads a paper on any subject he thinks will be of interest to the rest. Subject matter is intended to provoke discussion. The reading is preceded by a sumptuous meal and, to revive an old custom, a fine Madeira is served before and after the food in order to stimulate warm and intelligent criticism of the paper to be read.

It was at one of these gatherings in April 1953 that Malcolm Bell read his paper, the "Romantic Wines of Madeira" already mentioned. He and Mills Lane, the president, with whom I correspond regarding old Madeiras, are among the great connoisseurs of the wine. To my regret, I have been unable to accept their kind invitation to visit them. The Club's coat of arms shows the unfortunate Duke of Clarence's legs protruding from a butt of Malmsey, from which he is having his last and very final swig.

Members of the Madeira Club in dress of the period, on the occasion of their bicentennial dinner at the Owens-Thomas House on November 11th, 1976.

On November 11th 1976 the Club held its bicentennial dinner, when members were attired in the dress of that period. By coincidence, the date was *dia de São Martinho*, the day of St Martin, official end of the Madeira vintage and therefore most bucolically celebrated on the island, especially in that district. A loving-cup was drunk, but instead of the usual spiced sack a choice vintage Madeira filled the cup. Mr. Darrell F. Corti of Sacramento, California, a connoisseur, read his paper on "Vintage Madeiras." The wines served were Cama de Lobos Solera 1792 from the cellars of Mr. Haywood S. Hansell Jr., Terrantez 1870 from Mr. Thomas H. Gignilliat, Rutherford's Bual Solera 1814 from Mr. Mills B. Lane and Blandy's Malmsey Solera 1863, also from Mr. Gignilliat. Clay pipes accompanied the *demi-tasse*, and J. Bally's 1929 Rhum.

On this occasion the dinner was held at the Owens-Thomas House, originally the Richard Richardson House, one of the most beautiful and important houses in all America. Designed by William Jay for the first president of the Savannah branch of the Bank of the United States, its plans were drawn up in London, before Jay reached Savannah in 1817 from Bath. The cellars of this elegant house are full of old bottles and other Madeira relics, including a rare vintage barrel which was strapped on the back of a mule. Another notable occasion was *une soirée printanière* held at the Chatham Club, Savannah, on April 29th 1980 to welcome Captain William Kinsey and Michael Broadbent of Christie's.

The wine cellars in the Owens-Thomas house.

As a present from me to Mills Lane, Michael had taken a bottle of Malmsey 1808, which I consider the best. Fortunately Madeira is the one wine least likely to be affected by the journey in Michael's briefcase from London to Savannah via Miami, Houston, Mexico City and the Pacific coast. In addition to Captain Bill Kinsey's contribution of Able Madeira there were Blandy's Malmsey Solera 1792, bottled 1957 on the occasion of HM the Queen's state visit to Portugal, the magnificent H.M. Borges vintage 1846 Terrantez, Cossart's Boal Solera 1815, bottled in 1959, and Justinho Henriques' Malmsey Solera 1880.

According to Michael, whose palate is one of if not the best in London, these were some of the finest old Madeiras he had ever tasted. The Sercial vintage 1864, with which the meal opened, seems to have taken top marks. Michael wrote in his tasting notes: "A beautiful, intense yet delicate bouquet which reminds me of an old, refined, Grande Champagne vintage cognac." The Terrantez, described as a classic, took second place: "Deepish, very rich--looking amber, with a slightly orange-tinge; a fabulous bouquet, rich, most pronounced; medium-sweet entry leading to a very dry finish." In third place came the Waterloo Bual, "Curiously paler than the Sercial, but with a delicate, flowery nose; a light, elegant style of Bual." Michael's notes confirm my theory that it is a grand but tired old war horse, yet with enough life to be classed third by an auspicious gathering. Our itinerant expert wrote of the famous Malmsey Solera 1792: "A sweet, gentle, harmonious wine on nose and palate, soft yet intense, beautifully balanced and the hallmark of a great Madeira with an exceptionally excellent finish." I am not surprised that this great wine did not take the first place because, in my opinion, it is not a wine to be drunk after dinner with other wines when concentration is fraying. It is rather a *vinho de lenço*, a few drops of which should be sniffed from the palm of the hand, to be savoured from the glass in a peaceful environment. The Malmsey Solera 1880, which in my opinion was the best Malmsey after 1808, was from a special bottling totalling 700 bottles. The bottle sampled was No. A-135 and should have been equal to the other soleras. It was served last, being the sweetest, but Michael said it was not in the same class.

'Able'

I have mentioned briefly but not explained the "mystery wine" from the deep presented at the dinner by Captain William Kinsey. In January 1976 Bill Kinsey was searching for a lost shrimp net on the ocean floor with what he calls his "ear" when he located the uncharted wreck of a ship lying on the Atlantic shelf off the coast of Georgia, within sight of Savannah harbour. Upon further investigation he found the wreck to be an oak brig or barque of British construction. The vessel was approximately 100 feet long with a beam of 30 feet, and her anchor and chain, of British type, dated her from the early 1830s. Around 1840, when entering Savannah harbour the ship had struck a shoal and broken in two. The bow had remained on the shoal in about five fathoms, whilst the stern half had dropped into deeper water. So far the name of the ship is unknown but, for the purpose of identification, has been labelled *Able*. However, Bill Kinsey has found numerous bottles which have been identified by Alexander McNally, of Heublein's, as Scotch whisky, burgundy and Madeira. Mills Lane obtained several bottles of Able Madeira and very kindly gave me one. This particular bottle, recovered from the wreck in January 1980, was round and squat, of black free-blown glass, circa 1790, and held 35 centilitres; the cork had been protected by a wax seal. When bottles from wrecks are spilled onto the ocean bed they become covered by thick salt mud so that they are sealed in an airless condition. The salt and crustations help to protect the cork so that the wine should remain in the same condition as when it was submerged; because it cannot breathe it does not age as wines which are kept on shore and exposed to air.

Noël and David Cossart opening a bottle of Able Madeira, and a close-up of the bottle, recovered after more than a century on the sea bed.

Michael Broadbent had tasted the contents of one of the larger bottles of Able Madeira at the Savannah dinner in April 1980 and found the nose subdued but surprisingly sound, old, with a very faint *Muscat* grapiness. It was still sweet. This and its preservation clearly indicated that it had been a fortified wine but lacking the acidity normally expected of old Madeira, which led Michael to think it might not be Madeira, but Tarragona or possibly Rota Tent. According to his tasting notes the wine had lost quite a bit of colour but had a ruddy glow, with a faint redness which, he thought, ruled out old Madeira.

My son and I opened my bottle at noon one Sunday in September 1982. The level of wine was high, and the cork was sound, but covered on the outside with a dark, almost black, stain. We also found the dark amber wine to have a reddish tinge around the sides of the glass reminiscent of a young Tinta Madeira. The nose was sound and old, with a very faint *Muscatel* fragrance, which ruled out the *Tinta* grape. On the palate it was clearly an old fortified wine, rich, with a hint of *Muscatel*. My son declared it to be port or possibly Tarragona and I was, at first, inclined to agree with him. I thought that if it was Madeira it was an undeveloped Tinta, but I was puzzled by the lack of acidity and the hint of *Muscatel*. We returned to the examination after lunch, about two hours later. By this time the wine had opened out considerably, and the redness had practically disappeared. I am fairly sure that my bottle contained Muscatel Madeira made from the black grape of the sort known on the island as *Muscatel lliquoroso*, or, in English, *Muscat liqueur*. This would explain the small bottle and the redness of the contents.

All the wine found in the wreck was in bottle, which leads me to believe it was intended for the ship's stores rather than cargo, which would have been in bulk.

The 1814 Pipe

Perhaps this would be an appropriate place to mention the famous 1814 Pipe, another interesting Madeira which had been submerged for a number of years. This was a pipe of old Madeira which had lain under the sea in the hull of a ship wrecked at the mouth of the Scheldt in 1779. The wine was brought to the surface in 1814, and when Louis XVIII heard of the discovery he ordered his ambassador in Antwerp to acquire "the precious treasure." A portion of the 1814 Pipe passed into the cellar of Baron de Raguse, and at the sale of the effects of the late Duchesse de Raguse in Paris in 1858 the remaining bottles were sold. This wine had lain under the sea in wood, as opposed to the Able Madeira, which was in glass. The pipe had been protected by submarine crustations, so when Louis XVIII bottled the wine there was no ullage from evaporation. Being unable to breathe, the wine would not have developed as much as wine kept in wood on the surface for 36 years. However, it must have been very fine, for Baron de Rothschild chose to pay "their weight in gold" for the 44 bottles remaining in 1858.

Allowing Madeira to breathe

It is absolutely essential that, in order to develop, Madeira should be allowed to breathe. In *A Wine Primer* (Michael Joseph, London 1946), André Simon says that Madeira was understood in America as it has never been understood elsewhere. He goes on to tell how the Americans discovered that it was quite different from other wines because it needed more air to breathe, to enable it to live and expand. The Americans of course kept their Madeira in demijohns, not in cool cellars but in their lofts, under the roof where it would have plenty of air, and would feel the alternatives of summer heat and winter frosts. When the wine was "ripe" it was syphoned from the demijohn and passed through cheese cloth into decanters where it was given yet more air, before it passed to the "red-brick" noses and the palates of the tribunal of old connoisseurs for judgement. André writes in his typical flowery prose: "Madeira in those days, when men had both taste and time, was never inflicted by the humiliation of the straight-jacket – that is, a black bottle – nor the impure contact of a soft spongy cork, as was the fate and still is of Madeira in other lands." Today, although we still have the taste for it, we have neither the time, space nor wealth to keep our Madeiras in demijohns as did the American connoisseurs, but put it straight into bottles for drinking. Although not ideal, the black bottle and soft spongy cork are a good alternative to demijohns, providing that the bottles are kept standing and the wine is allowed a period in which to breathe when the cork is drawn.

Fictitious dates

After the last war, the American government lifted restrictions on bottled wine from Portugal and the market was flooded with Madeira bearing fictitious dates. There was nothing wrong with the wine, except that it was not what it claimed to be. This would not have been possible today because of the Madeira Wine Institute's quality control and United States label regulations. Where dates are concerned, the latter require age certificates sworn before an American consul. This caused reliable shippers, who could sell all their fine Madeira in markets not requiring tiresome formalities, to send it to London and Bristol, where many American buyers had to obtain their fine Madeiras.

One American writer said that bottles bearing seductive vintages were no rarity on the American market. The years 1860, 1870, 1880, 1890 and 1900 were so favoured that it seemed some quirk of the Madeira climate had persuaded the vines to adopt a decennial habit of bearing. After sampling these vintages he decided they were not the sort of Madeiras Saintsbury had regretted. "One could imitate them rather well with a mixture of alcohol and molasses generously flavoured with vinegar and scorched pop-corn." I have never tasted a Madeira, however horrible, faintly resembling this mixture, but it sounds far more palatable than some of the cocktails I have tasted in New York. The writer's reference to Saintsbury's regret was prompted by the eminent professor's remark, "Sir, I drink no memories," in connection with really fine Madeira having become only a memory due to the oidium in 1852.

One Chicago merchant managed to obtain and sell over 400 cases of 1874 Madeira in 1949/1950. This amounted to nearly nine pipes in two years, an impossible quantity because in that year production was reduced by phylloxera. This sort of fraud was not entirely due to unscrupulous islanders. The lower class of American merchants felt they should stock Madeira, but could not sell it unless it had a date tag, which they expected from the shipper, although they were not prepared to pay more than $10 per case fob. The reputable shippers merely laughed at these offers but, tempted by the almighty dollar, the mushroom firms accepted, and ran themselves into the ground, bringing disrepute to the Madeira trade in general. At about this time the firm S. S. Pierce were listing Cossart Terrantez 1846 at $11.75 per bottle, and Blandy's famous Solera 1792 at $27.50 per bottle in Boston and New York. They were able to sell all they could obtain.

Roy P. Brady

In April 1960, I was introduced by Warner Everett to Roy P. Brady, a connoisseur and a Madeira enthusiast from California. He had become very depressed because he had been badly swindled by fascinating dates on bottles. He told me that, as far as he was concerned, fine Madeira had become a mere "literary wine." He remembered with nostalgia the warmth, on a cold night, of Cossart's Crown Bual No. 93 and Crown Sercial No. 104, with its orange label bearing a picture of a pipe on a bullock-drawn sledge. He could have obtained these anywhere in the United States but, once bitten twice shy, he had passed them by. He cheered up considerably when I told him the orange label was still the same wine and told him where to look for fine Madeira. The secret of knowledge is knowing where to find it, and having missed the opportunity of some Blackburn Rainwater and Malmsey from Fred Burka's shop in Washington, my friend bought some of the Terrantez 1846 from S. S. Pierce of Boston in 1960, and never looked back, gradually building up a cellar of fine Madeiras. Two years later he wrote an article for *The Journal of the Wine & Food Society* describing his rediscovery of fine Madeira and displaying his remarkable scholarship.

One seldom comes across old Rainwater, although it is less rare in America than in England. Mr. Brady's reference to Blackburn Rainwater is interesting. G. & R. Blackburn were an oidium casualty. The Rainwater and Malmsey had come from an estate in Baltimore where it had been put in five-gallon demijohns in 1832, so it was a very old wine when Mr. Brady first came across this. When he returned, having discovered fine Madeira still existed, it had all gone. He said the vintage dates had been lost and only Blackburn and the name of the wine were decipherable. Rainwater would not have had a date but it is possible that this may have been some of Mr. Kennedy's original Japan Madeira. Roy Brady ends his interesting article: "The only mystery that remains is the very fact of their sale. Why were they sold and who, exactly, owned them? Those sold in New York bore Blandy labels, those in Boston Cossart, Gordon, and those in Bristol, Avery labels . . . Perhaps the best that can be said about the appearance of such grand wines in our market comes from Mr. Noël Cossart who recently wrote, 'I suppose the real answer is that none of us are as rich as we were. Although these precious wines are very scarce on the market partners and directors have taken care that they have enough to keep them comfortable in their old age.'"

du Pont Madeira

One of the most perfect Madeiras that I have ever tasted was a Cama de Lobos 1836 offered to me by Harry du Pont, when I stayed with him at Winterthur in March 1960. It had come from a pipe sent to one of the many du Ponts by my grandfather around 1885 and had been bottled in Wilmington at some unknown date. At that time Harry possessed a quantity of this lovely rich yet delicate and fragrant wine. The du Ponts and Cossarts, both being Huguenot families from Rouen, are connected by marriage from the distant days before the St. Bartholemew Day massacre. Eleuthère Irénée du Pont started making gunpowder on the Brandywine river in 1802, and in the same year William Cossart sailed from Dublin to make wine in Madeira. There is a station on the Wilmington and Northern Railway in Pennsylvania bearing the Cossart name. The du Pont who built the railway named the stations after members of his and "allied families" and I understand that Madeira wine was used to baptise the first train to run on this railroad. Cossart is the next station to Granogue where Irénée du Pont Jr., the present head of the family, lives. The last train passed this track on March 31st 1976.

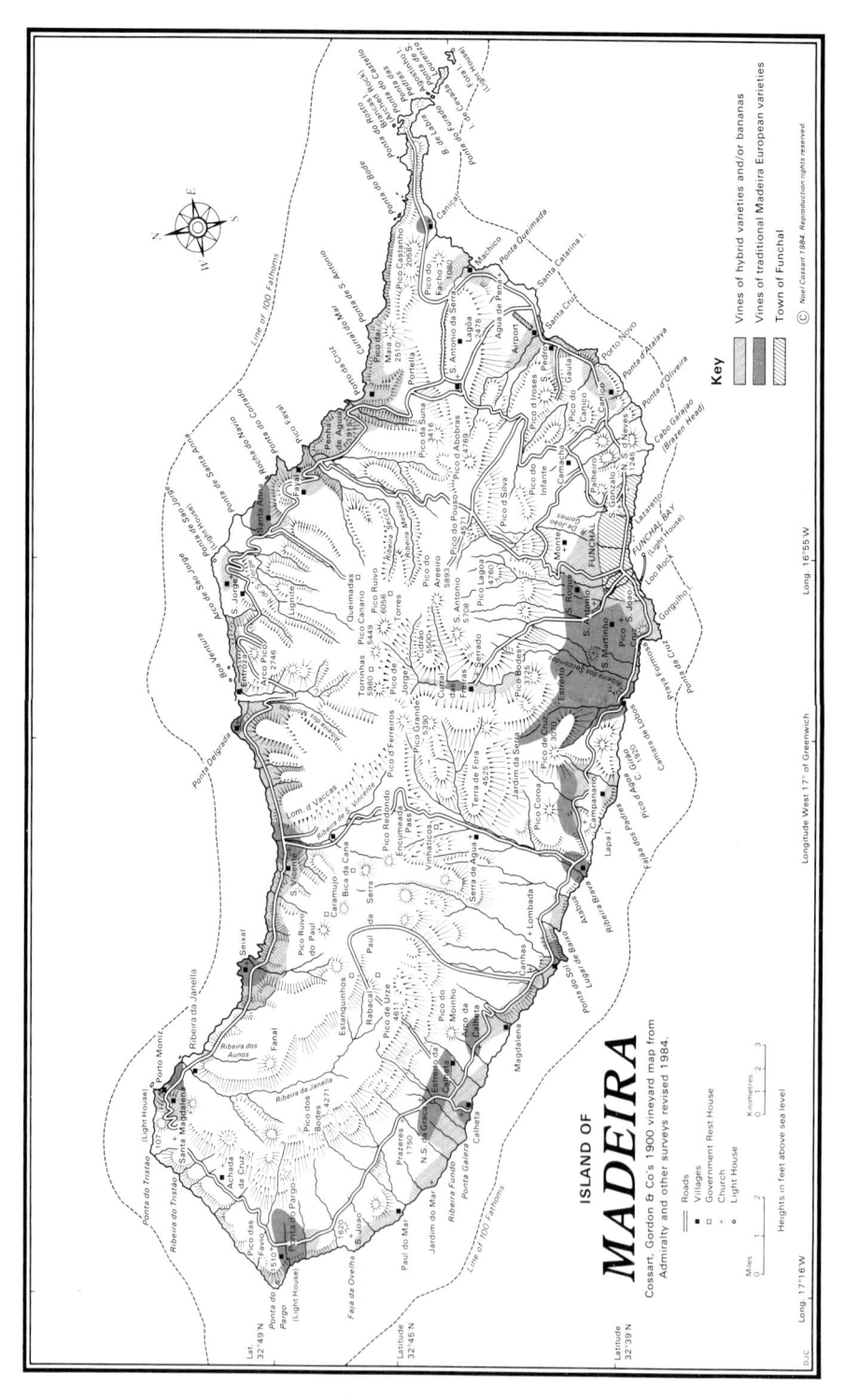

Map of Madeira, 1984, from the 1st Edition.

CHAPTER 7
VINES AND VINEYARDS

Noble varieties (castas nobres)
Sercial (white)
Bual (white)
Verdelho (white)
Malvasia Candida (*Malmsey*, white)
Terrantez (white)
Bastardo (black)

Good varieties (castas boas)
Tinta Negra Mole (black)
Malvasia Roxa (black)
Verdelho Tinto (black)
Moscatel (white)

Authorised species (castas autorizadas)
Rio Grande (a form of *Boal*, white)
Boal do Porto Santo (a grape with very little acidity, white)
Tinta da Madeira (black)
Complexa (a new form of *Tinta Negra Mole*, black)
Triunfo (a variety from mainland Portugal, black)

The principal vine, which accounts for 50 to 60 per cent of total production, is the prolific *Tinta Negra Mole*. It is classified among the *castas boas* or good varieties and is a splendid Madeira in its own right. I believe it should be promoted to the *nobre* class as was the *Verdelho* early this century. It is also unique in its ability to acquire the characteristics of the different *castas nobres* according to the height at which it is grown, therefore becoming a most useful basis for blends representing the noble varieties.

The variety of *Tinta* grown today was developed from crosses involving the Burgundy variety of *Pinot Noir* and the *Grenache* and has been grown on the island since at least the beginning of the 19th century. It is just possible that the wine known in the 18th century as "Madeira Burgundy," "Tent" or "Tinto" was produced from early varieties of *Tinta* but it is more likely to have been a mixture of *Malvasia Babosa* and wine from the *Mole Preta* vine which was the forerunner of the present *Tinta* and which was also referred to as *Tinta*.

The leaf of the *Tinta Negra Mole* has seven lobes, decreasing in size, and the sinews are very deep and rounded; the centre lobe is sub-divided into two and the leaf is yellowish green turning to russet. The grapes, which are small, soft and black, with greenish pulp, grow in small or medium-sized bunches. They are very sweet. The wine has a distinctly reddish hue when young, maturing to tawny with age: Practically all blends have, or used to have, Tinta as their base. If the wine is to be used for colouring, the husks are allowed to remain in the must during fermentation, imparting a deep colour to the wine. It also has an attractive astringent aftertaste. The grapes *Negra*, *Maroto* and *Castelão* are varieties of *Tinta* grown on Madeira. There are insufficient quantities of the different varieties to warrant separate pressings, so these grapes are all pressed together. The *Tinta Molar* is a firmer and sweeter variety grown on the island of Porto Santo.

Verdelho

Next in order of importance is the *Verdelho*, or *Gouveiro*, which is similar to the *Verdia* of Italy and the *Pedro Ximenez* of Spain. Until early this century the *Verdelho* was the principal wine-making grape in the islands, but being less prolific it has now given way to *Tinta*. The leaf has seven lobes, the sinews of which are not strongly marked; it is a smooth dark green, and the two lowest lobes are indistinct. The grape is very small, hard and oval and has a golden hue. It is a sweet, full-flavoured fruit grown in small bunches. This grape was also once known as *Vidonia*.

Malvasia

It is *Malvasia Candida*, a corruption of Candia, whence it came, which produces the famous rich Malmsey or Malvoisie wine. The vine is a shy grower, requiring sheltered sunny positions at sea level so that the grapes may ripen until they are almost raisins. It is also prone to mildew. The leaf has four very deep and rounded sinews with two others less distinct; each dentation has a small yellow tip. The back of the leaf is as smooth as the upper surface, but is of a deep yellowish green. The grapes, which are small, round and very soft, ripen late to a rich golden colour and are born on large long bunches. They are very sweet and fragrant. True Malmsey has a peculiar bouquet imparted to the wine by the skins and some leaves[24] remaining in the must during fermentation and, although rich, it has a dry finish.

There are other varieties similar to *Malvasia Candida*: the *Malvasia Babosa* (lazy malmsey), with firmer and less sweet grapes, and *Malvasião*, which has rosé grapes. *Malvasia Babosa* was introduced to Madeira by Simon Accioli, a Genoese nobleman, in 1515 and is thought to be the French *Malvoisie*. These different types of *Malmsey* are usually all pressed together.

Between 1748 and 1800, Francis Newton was frequently writing to his London partners: "Malmsey is in short supply. . .," or "Malmseys are few. . .." On one occasion he wrote, "There are no Malmseys this year" and "There are not 100 pipes of Malmsey on this Island." He refers to Malmsey as being something special and apart from other wines: "The Malmseys will be rich and good, and the [other] wines we believe will be the same" and "Vidonias and [other] wines are plentiful this year but Malmseys are short."

Bual

Boal or *Cachudo* (in English *Bual*, referred to as *Boyal* by John Leacock) is a hardy vine, but not very prolific. The leaf is hairy on both sides, small and compact, with four of the sinews deep and sharp, the two lower indistinct, and the indentations irregular and sharp. The grapes are hard, round and straw coloured, and grow in tightly packed, medium-sized bunches. These grapes are very full-flavoured and sweet, but it is not a common vine and the wine it produces always commands a high price.

Sercial

Sercial or *Cerçal* was thought to be similar to the German *Riesling*, which, like its cousins in the Rhine valley, grows at high altitudes. It is fairly prolific, but rather a shy bearer, and only grows in certain places. The leaf has four round lobes and very strong nerves which, by their projection, form a wrinkled appearance. The grapes are round, soft and white and, like the *Malvasia*, ripen very late. The fruit is rather tasteless but fragrant. The wine, which is rough and unpleasant on the palate when young, requires some seven to eight years to mature, but when old it is considered one of the finest Madeiras. Locally the vine is called *Esgana*, *Esganinho* or *Esganiso*, from the verb *esganar* meaning to choke, because it is so astringent when young that it chokes one to swallow. My great-grandfather, Carlo de Bianchi, had some bottles of very old Sercial from his properties. These bottles had a handwritten label, *Esganacão* (dog choker), but the wine in them was dry, soft and mellow.

Terrantez and bastardo

There are also two traditional vines which were not replanted after phylloxera: *Terrantez* and *Bastardo* or *Bastardinho* (bastard or little bastard). Both have large, oval and firm bunches with very sweet and fragrant grapes, ripening to a rich golden colour. They both produce rich wine with an almost bitter aftertaste acquired from the skins, stalks and even leaves which should be left in the fermenting must. There is also a black variety of the *Terrantez*. These two wines were considered very special and were much sought after. There is a verse in old Portuguese which urges one not to eat or give away *Terrantez* grapes, because God made them for wine making.

Moscatel and other vines

There are three different sorts of *Muscatel* – *Muscatel de Quintal*, *Muscatel de Santa Maria* and *Muscatel de Setúbal*. However, because the *Muscatels* are so valuable as table grapes, very little wine has been made from them since 1909. In any case Muscatel is not a typical Madeira, being very sweet, about 4 degrees to 4.5 degrees Baume with a very low acid content.[25] The notable *Muscatel* vintages today are 1900, 1903 and 1909. I had all these in London in the 1950s and 1960s, but because they were not typical Madeiras I found them difficult to sell. The vintages 1900 and 1909 were *Muscatel lliquoroso* which had been *abafado* when fortified and was stronger than other Madeira. The 1909 vintage of *Muscatel*, incidentally, had the merit of being made from the first grapes to be brought from Câmara de Lobos to Funchal by motorised transport.

Other vines are *Listrão*, which has large round, hard very sweet white grapes, *Carãa de Moça* (maiden's face), whose grapes are round, hard and shiny green (I do not think many maidens would appreciate this description of their faces), and *Malaga* (now called *Alicante*). *Feral* and *Barrete de Padre* (padre's hat) have large, round, hard purple grapes with green pulp.

Newly harvested grapes awaiting pressing at Cossart, Gordon.

American root stocks

After the vines had been destroyed by phylloxera (see Chapter 8), American root stocks were imported which were highly resistant to the disease. These roots (*bacelos* in Portuguese, but known locally as *cavalos*, or horses), were to be grafted with *enchertos* (scions) of traditional Madeira vines. The first American stocks were imported in 1873 by Thomas Slapp Leacock and consisted of *Vitis riparia, rupestris, solanis, taylor* and *clinton*. In 1885 Sr. Almeida e Brito, the entomologist appointed by the government to deal with the phylloxera crisis, imported *rupestris monticola, vialla, elvira, othello* and *cinerea*. However, most of the *cavalos* were not suitable for the low lime content of the soil, or would not accept the cuttings of the island varieties, and of these only the *rupestris monticola* is robust enough to be grown today. It thrives at high altitudes and is especially suitable for taking grafts of Sercial. It is called locally *silvado*, meaning bramble. The chief stocks now used are therefore *riparia x rupestris, rupestris monticola, rupestris martin, cordifolia x rupestris* as well as *riparia berlandieri*. These vines can produce only small and very sour grapes, which is why they are used solely for root stocks.

Hybrids

Among the phylloxera-resistant stocks were vines of the *Vitis labrusca* variety known as the American fox grape, namely *Isabella, Black Pearle, Gaston Bazile* and *York Madeira*. The latter had been taken from Madeira to Georgia in 1732 to be planted in that settlement. There were also hybrid vines thought to be crosses of *Vitis aestivalis* (similar to *Vitis labrusca*) with *Vitis vinifera* (the European varieties), *Cunningham, Herbemont* and white and purple *Jacquet*. Most of these American vines have disappeared except for *Isabella, Jacquet, Herbemont* and *Cunningham*. The white variety of *Jacquet* is very similar in appearance to the *Vitis vinifera* vine, *Terrantez*.

These imported varieties were well established by the late 19th century. They are prolific, hardy and, because of their resistance to phylloxera, do not require grafting. *Herbemont* is of no use for making wine. *Isabella* is a good table grape but the wine has a *moisi*[26] brackenish flavour which, however, appears to be attractive to the Madeirense. It is therefore used to make *vinho americana*, an unfortified table wine for local consumption. The purple *Jacquet* produces a strong full wine which was used in the production of cooking Madeiras, and to bolster up thin wines in blending. *Canica*, as the *Cunningham* is called, produces pale, light wine known locally as a poor man's Verdelho and was used in the blending of Rainwater. These wines were also undoubtedly used in blending Madeiras when they were at their peak of fashion. It was said that wines from hybrids and *labrusca* varieties did not age well, but in 1967 I tasted a straight *Jacquet*, vintaged in 1907, the year I was born, and bottled in 1926, the year I joined the wine trade. It was a typical old Madeira, although rather a heavy peasant wine.

The EEC

As we have seen, wines from hybrids or straight *labrusca* vines were used for blending into Madeiras and in the making of "industrial wine" for the French and West German markets, Indeed, since the phylloxera two-thirds of the production has been from these vines, but since the early 1970s the position has changed and many improvements have been made, partly because of Portugal's impending entry into the EEC.

The European Economic Community which, together with America, accounts for some 75 per cent of Madeira's markets, has condemned the use of these grapes in the making of quality wines because they contain malvisa[27] (known locally as *malvina*). European wines are therefore routinely screened for this component. In theory it can be detected by paper chromatography, although I am not convinced that this analytical method could be used to discover the origin of grapes in a specialised wine such as Madeira, which has been *estufado* (see Chapter 9).

The EEC does not like any *labrusca* vines or hybrids because of their high yield and resistance to disease. They claim, with some justification that the flavour is poor and their extensive use would depress the quality of European wines. Yet, in some circumstances, for example in Madeira, hybrid grapes are perfect for the climatic conditions and some of the wine is useful for bringing body to *Vitis vinifera* wines or, conversely, thinning wine with too much.[28] It is, however, now illegal for the Madeira exporters to buy wines made from American hybrid grapes, which can only be locally consumed as table wine.

In no way do I condone the use of any wines which are not derived from *Vitis vinifera*, but personally I consider that the EEC's ban is purely political. There are too many vine varieties in Europe, so the less fine varieties, which tend to be the most prolific and disease resistant, must be excluded.

A terraced hillside in Cama do Lobos.

Labrusca in the USA

The story that hybrids of *labrusca* are harmful to the liver is based upon some German research which has since been refuted in America and elsewhere. Nevertheless the story persists. If it were true then a large part of the population in the northeastern states of the USA should be similarly afflicted, since they consume large quantities of wine, juice, jellies, etc made from *Vitis labrusca*. Some books quote *seibel* or *Vitis labrusca* as containing the toxic component malvisa. It is in fact one of the pigments or anthocyanins which occur naturally in such grapes, namely malvidin 3,5-diglucoside. In the EEC the ban has nothing to do with toxicity and, in fact, a large US company marketing grape pigments derived from the *concord* grape (a *Vitis labrusca*), has done extensive toxicological investigations to satisfy the Federal Department of Alcohol, Firearms and Tobacco that its product is safe for human consumption; its use has accordingly been approved.

Among others, in his book *An Account of the island of Madeira*, published in London in 1812, Dr. N.C. Pitta, who practiced medicine in Madeira in the late 18th century, notes that disorders of the liver were a common complaint among the Madeirense. This could not, however, have been due to drinking wines from *labrusca*[29] vines because these were not introduced until the mid-19th century. It has since been proved that the liver disorders are not caused by wine drinking, and indeed at about this time literally thousands of books and pamphlets were written by doctors in all European languages, recommending the climate of Madeira for invalids and the wine as a cure for most ailments, including liver disorders.

The soil

The vine is partial to stony or rocky ground and the best soil for it in Madeira is decomposed red tufa, or *saibro*, with an admixture of stones. In this environment, vines have been known to last from 50 to 100 years and the wine produced is of the highest quality. The next most suitable habitat is the stony soil known as *cascalho*. The quality of the wine produced here is as good, but the life of the vine is not as long. There are two other main types of soil: arenaceous decomposed yellow tufa (*pedra mole*), and clay or *massapes* from decomposed dark tufa. Here the vines produce greater quantities of grapes, and the wine is consequently weaker in body and the plants exhausted at an earlier stage.

Planting

A great deal of labour goes into the preparation of the ground before planting, for the life of the vine and the quality of the wine largely depend upon it. The vines are planted in trenches, the depth varying from two to two-and-a-half metres, according to the type of soil. The object of cutting so deep is to allow the roots to penetrate downwards through the freshly dug earth and therefore prevent them from being dried by the sun or long periods of drought. Lumps of *pedra mole* and basalt are put at the bottom of each trench to keep the earth loose and prevent the roots from reaching the hard soil below. The trenches are then filled at an angle to one-third of their depth. The vines are planted two-and-a-half to three metres apart, never lower than two-thirds of the open depth, thus making a trough into which irrigation water will run when the vineyard is flooded from the *levada*.

The land is usually prepared during the spring and early summer and planted in October so that the plants benefit from the winter rains and are established by the spring.

Grape yield

One hectare of well-cultivated land with the best soil should, in an average year, produce from 15 to 20 tons of grapes, whereas in well-cultivated medium-quality soil only 10 to 15 tons may be expected. Ground of either best or medium quality in bad hands will not produce more than five or six tons. One ton of grapes is calculated to produce 85 litres of *vinho claro* after fermentation. Vines bear six to seven years after grafting and are in full production in the eighth year. After 12 to 13 years' production they are usually on the decline, although vines have been known to bear at 60 years old and more. A *Cunningham* vine, planted when my house was built in 1858, is a good example. When I left the island in 1976 it covered 20 square metres of trellis; its trunk had a diameter of 15 centimetres and it was three metres high. Although of course it was only used for shade, in the normal vintage of 1960 it produced 240 kilos of grapes and in a bad vintage 17 years later it yielded 215 kilos.

Corredors

The original vines were planted with a chestnut tree as a "tutor" or stake and the vine allowed to grow over the tree. In the north of the island, it is still possible to see this method in use today. The more modern practice, however, is to train the vines on trellises called *corredors* which usually slope from 30 centimetres at the front of the terrace up to two or two-and-a-half metres at the rear of the terrace. The *corredor* is usually made of pine laths supported by chestnut stakes, but the richer proprietors now use iron supports with wire frames. Although these will undoubtedly last longer, it seems that the vine actually prefers contact with wood rather than metal. The main branch of the vine is bent onto the *corredor* and the shoots are tied with banana bark,[30] which being very much stronger makes an excellent substitute for raffia. When the leaves have fallen off the vines, the appearance of their framework, as seen from the hills above, is of nets spread on the ground. In autumn, when the leaves are yellow and russet, it is a beautiful sight to look down from the church at Estreito de Câmara de Lobos, over the *corredors* and to the sea beyond. These *corredors* are similar to the *pedamenta* and *juga* (poles and frames) upon which the ancient Romans trained their vines.

A new method of training called *espalmado* has recently been adopted by the government and the Madeira Wine Company, with a view to growing more vines per hectare and therefore facilitating cultivation. The vines are planted in rows growing upright, espaliered on wires. The merits of this method have still to be proved.

Pruning and grafting

Pruning, grafting and tying are usually carried out in February or March. Wise viticulturalists choose to prune when the moon is waning. The moon has a great effect on all life and plants. If a plant is cut with an ascending moon, when the sap is rising, it bleeds profusely, whereas if it is cut when the moon is waning, it will hardly lose any sap. I have lost vines (and many rose bushes) by pruning with a waxing moon. It is also advisable to graft in February and March with the waning moon. The plant will not bleed from the wound, which will have begun to heal by the time the sap rises with the waxing moon, and a strong scion will develop.

The buds form 60 days after pruning; the leaves open and the flower appears in April. When the bunches start to form, dusting with sulphur is immediately carried out and, depending on the weather, continues until the grapes are picked.

Fertilisers

The use of chemical fertilisers is generally frowned upon. *Guano* is sometimes used, but the peasants say that once it is dug in it must be continued, which is hard on the pocket; so cow dung and the grace of God are preferred. As soon as the leaves fall, dwarf beans or edible lupins are planted under the vines, which are later dug into the soil as fertiliser. Dwarf beans are the most popular because two or three shipments can be sent to the Covent Garden market before the Channel Islands start shipping. With land on the island being so scarce, this sub-crop is very important financially.

Diseases and pests

Phylloxera is usually latent in the soil but with modern sprays and plenty of water at the right time it has ceased to be a menace. The most troublesome fungus pest is *mangara* (the mildew, oidium) which attacks the vine all the year round especially in overcast damp weather, of which there is plenty in May and June at an altitude of over 150 metres, particularly on the north and south sides of the island. The vines have to be constantly sprayed with Bordeaux mixture, and sulphur dusted.

Lapa which is a *Coccidae (Aspidiotus hederae)* is a pest, manifesting itself by red scales on the stems and under the leaves. It is not fatal but retards the vine. It is kept under control by spraying the underside of the leaves with Bordeaux mixture. The mild equable climate of Madeira is splendid for growing vines but pests thrive equally. At Porto Santo, in vineyards close to the sea, there is a small snail *(Littorina striata)* known locally as *caramujo de dama*, which is very troublesome. It settles on the stalk when the bunch is forming, eventually becoming completely covered by the grapes. It does no harm to either the vine or the grapes, but when the bunches are crushed the wine has a salty musty flavour. These *caramujo de dama* are kept under control by leaving ducks to roam the vineyard; they enjoy eating the snails before the bunch is formed, but do not eat the grapes. Lizards *(Lacerta dugesii)* and birds eat great quantities of grapes when they are ripe. The common London sparrow *(Passer domesticus)* will eat twice as many grapes as a blackbird. These little pests have been imported quite recently by an Englishman and have become a menace. Lizards are poisoned and birds scared away by various methods, but it takes a lot to scare the cocky little sparrow.

The vineyards

The classic vineyards, producing the finest wine, are in the parishes of Câmara de Lobos, São Martinho, São Pedro, São João, the lower parts of São Antonio, Estreito de Câmara de Lobos, Campanario and São Roque. The upper parts of the last four parishes produce only second rate wine, except for the part of the Estreito called Jardim da Serra where fine Sercial is produced at Dr. Alberto de Arujo's *quinta*. When I was a junior in the stores of Cossart, Gordon I used to look forward to the visit of Dr. Alberto's father, who would arrive with great pomp and ceremony accompanied by bearers carrying baskets of samples of their grapes on their shoulders. Unfortunately, the vineyards known as "Environs of Funchal" namely, São Roque, São João, São Pedro, São Antonio and, to some extent, São Martinho have now been curtailed by the growth of the city. Mr. Leacock and Dr. Marcelino Pereira, however, still produce some fine wines at their properties in São João and São Martinho.

In the lower parts of Câmara de Lobos[31] known as Vila, Ponta do Sol, and Magdalena, there has been a marked decrease in the area of European grafted vines planted, and an increase in banana plantations. On the other hand, at Estreito and Campanario there has been an increase; the latter produces *Negra Mole* and is famous for its fine Bual. The best Malvasia used to come from Fajã dos Padres, the vineyard which is almost on the beach under the great Cabo Girão cliff and only accessible by sea. The grapes there were baked to raisins before they were picked and produced about 20 pipes[32] of the most exquisite Malmsey. The vineyard is said to have been planted soon after the island was discovered, and remained in the same family until some time during the last war. On the death of the last member, the precious vines were uprooted and bananas planted.

At Ribeira da Janella in the parish of Porto Moniz, fine Verdelho is produced, and at São Vicente in the highlands on the north coast there is a considerable increase in the production of *Negra Mole*. At Achadas da Cruz, in the parish of Ponta do Pargo, and at Seixal various varieties are grown. Seixal produces fine *Sercial* grapes. Other vineyards at Paul do Mar, Fajã da Ouvelha, Ponta Delgada (where the government intends to set up experimental stations), Boa Ventura, Arco de São Jorge, Fayal, Fajã do Mar and Porto da Cruz produce mostly American hybrid grapes.

Reorganisation

By the early 20th century, direct-producer (ungrafted) vines had become well established, accounting for the majority of wine produced. Normal vintages yielded between 11 and 12 million litres – of which only 20 per cent were from grafted European vines. The remainder, which because of its origin could not be sold in the EEC, was being burned (distilled) or consumed locally in the form of *vinho seco*. This was a rough, unfortified wine which had become the main drink of the population since the production of grog or *aguardente*, distilled from sugar cane, had been limited by government decree.

During the early 1960s and 1970s, shippers had not been able to acquire sufficient wine for their export requirements because of the banana growing taking over from vineyards and the high local consumption of *vinho seco* in spite of their efforts to encourage drinking of superior Lisbon wine. They realised, therefore, that the island's viticulture had to be drastically reorganised if exports, which averaged four million litres annually, were to continue. Madeira growers consist of thousands of small tenant farmers seeking a living out of minute terraced vineyards. Naturally they were loath to uproot their prolific ungrafted vines, the wine from which they could easily sell to local vendedeiros (shopkeepers) who, in exchange, supplied them with the necessities of life.

Although wine from hybrid and *labrusca* vines will continue either to be consumed locally as table wine or distilled, EEC regulations have reduced the exports of Madeira for industrial purposes in France and West Germany by one-third. Madeira is undoubtedly the best wine for use in the kitchen because its flavour and character will come through more positively than those of other wines. So far its use has been possible because of the small quantities required, but with ever-increasing prices it will no longer be economic. I hope that these industrial Madeiras will disappear because the island and its production are so small that it cannot afford to make, or even be associated with, cooking wine.

Government intervention

Fortunately, anticipating entry to the EEC, the Portuguese government intervened by initiating in 1972 an aided replanting programme, ably directed by Engenheiro Francisco Perry Vidal, chief agronomist to Madeira's "county council." This programme was designed to aid and encourage growers to replant their vineyards with the classic varieties. Experimental stations, run by oenological experts, were set up at Ribeira Brava, Ponta do Pargo, Câmara de Lobos and Estreito da Calheta, some of which are now in full production. Stations at Seixal, São Vicente, Ponta Delgada and São Jorge are nearing full production. Over 25 hectares are now covered and production of the noble varieties (see p 72) has risen from 1.5 million litres in 1973 to 3.7 million in 1980. The following charts (from the Madeira Wine Company) show the number of plants of new improved root stock distributed free, and of grafts of noble varieties registered:

Year	Plants of stock distributed	Free grafting effected
1973	77,700	63,683
1974	88,000	106,745
1975	110,000	84,324
1976	120,000	109,620
1977	130,000	109,000
1978	127,000	99,000
1979	109,000	102,000
1980	143,110	122,083
1981	125,213	109,753
1982	103,196	108,400
1983	123,300	110,950

Apart from the above distribution and free technical advice, the programme offers smallholders more tangible incentives, such as a grant of five escudos per square metre from which the direct producers are removed, with a further grant of four escudos per annum per square metre for four years to compensate for loss of production due to replanting. Preferential rates are offered for the hire of machinery used in any replanting operations, these rates being one-third of current rental rates.

Besides this conversion, new vineyards are also being planted. The Madeira Wine Company has acquired a modern vineyard at Achada do Gramacho on the north side of the island, which comprises 22,260 square metres of best quality land, on which 7,406 vines of traditional Madeira varieties are flourishing, having produced 25 tons of grapes in 1982. It is estimated that the vineyard will be in full production on a lucrative basis by 1986. Although its full production will account for less than five per cent of the company's requirements, it is a valuable contribution towards the effort being made to produce high quality grapes and to restore the traditional varieties. Apart from reviving these traditional vines, experiments are being made with Vitis vinifera introduced from the Portuguese mainland, namely *Triunfo, Portalegre Mindelo, Deleciosa, Rio Grande* and *Complexa*. These experiments seem to be satisfactory.

To illustrate the effect of this reorganisation one has to compare exports with production. In 1974, when the effects of the government's programme were being felt, production of good and noble vines amounted to 1,734,187 litres against exports of 4,094,723 litres. By 1977 production had increased to 2,745,106 litres and exports 4,566,990 litres. In 1980 production reached 3,770,259 litres, and exports had been reduced to 3,521,442 litres. The dramatic decrease of shipments by 25 per cent in 1980 is due to the steady increase in prices paid for must at the vintage in the last ten years, which were as follows:

Vintage	*Description*	*Price paid per kilogram of Negra Mole (grapes yielding 10° Baumé)*
1974	Normal	Esc 11.20
1975	Small	Esc 10.88
1976	Small	Esc 12.00
1977	Normal	Esc 17.00
1978	Subnormal	Esc 24.00
1979	Normal	Esc 35.00
1980	Normal	Esc 40.00
1981	Normal	Esc 44.00
1982	Subnormal	Esc 44.00
1983	Very subnormal	Esc 54.20

Over the last ten years grape prices at the vintage have increased by almost 500 per cent, and inflation at approximately 25 per cent per annum has added considerably to the cost of stocking and maturing wine for the long periods required.

Madeira is now over twice as expensive to produce as port. However, although continuing high inflation and fluctuations in the value of the escudo have to be taken into account, the trend is for prices to stabilise at current levels. Total island sales continue at depressed levels owing to world recession. Exports of 2.8 million litres in 1982 were the lowest since 1957. However, shippers are heartened by the demand for quality wines and the increase in production of fine Madeiras. They have been able to build up reserves of fine medium and old wine and are well placed to meet any future market improvement.

Madeira Wine Institute

All matters to do with viniculture and viticulture are regulated by an official body, the Instituto do Vinho da Madeira (IVM), ably headed by Dr. Palma. This organisation, which was formed in 1979, is responsible for drafting legislation bringing the theory and practice of viticulture and viniculture into line with accepted standards of the EEC. The first legislation has been produced and a representative committee of exporters has examined and drafted legislation in connection with labelling to conform with EEC and USA requirements. The draft was presented to the Institute in 1983 for final approval. This is an important achievement, which is considerably in advance of most other demarcated wine regions in Portugal. The Institute has an up-to-date laboratory and is organising an official tasting panel, but shippers complain that they have been regrettably slow in starting.[33]

Postscript

I may be old fashioned but I feel that too much importance is attached nowadays to the chemistry of wine. I have reservations about official palates and official panels. Apart from the excellent panels employed by the Scandinavian wine monopolies, the only satisfactory one I have worked on was that of the original Madeira Wine Association's four experienced tasters, who brought in a fifth off the street as a tie-breaker.

CHAPTER 8

OIDIUM, PHYLLOXERA AND CHANGING MARKETS

The wine-growing industry of the islands flourished until 1851, when *Oidium tuckeri*, the first of two major disasters, struck the vines. Oidium was first detected in England in 1847 and rapidly spread to France. In February 1851 a French botanist brought a collection of plants to Madeira, among which were some vines infected with oidium. The disease is a mildew which attacks the green parts of the vine, causing white patches on the leaves, which then turn to grey. If not checked the fungus sends out minute suckers into the vine itself and destroys it. By 1852 the disease, known locally as *mangara*, had spread all over the island.

Madeira, which relied entirely on the vine for its commerce, was not prepared for such a calamity. Sugar cane, bananas and other fruit could not make up for the loss of the main crop, so the devastation of the vines resulted in acute economic crisis. The average production of must during the years 1849-1851 was 50 million hectolitres, falling to eight million hectolitres in 1852 and to three million in 1853. In 1854 only 600 hectolitres were produced – a fall of 98 per cent.

It was not until July 1853 that the government, fully occupied with oidium in the port wine district, appointed an eminent agriculturalist, Sr. João Andrade Côrvo, as commissioner to deal with the calamity. But by this time it was too late, since 90 per cent of the vines had already been destroyed. Robert White, author of *Madeira – Its Climate and Scenery*, wrote: "The wine of Madeira which has acquired a worldwide celebrity, will soon be no more than a thing of the past." On February 5th 1855 the *Illustrated London News* produced a drawing of Madeira together with the full story of the "wine famine," for in spite of emigration to Brazil, America, Canada and the Cape, acute famine raged. The British colony appealed to its government and a subscription was opened by the Lord Mayor of London to send a ship laden with food, clothes, blankets, etc to the island.

On November 22nd 1852, to help alleviate unemployment, the Portuguese government ordered the building of new roads and the repair of old and, as a result, the present "New Road" linking Funchal and Câmara de Lobos was built, employing 300 men for 12 months. Little did they know then that most of the wine exported in future would travel by the Estrada Monumental, as it is now called.

Almost all of the old-established British shippers left Madeira for Spain. The 70 British houses trading in 1850 were reduced to 15 by 1855, and it was their courage, endurance and persistence that kept the Madeira wine trade going. These shippers were fully recompensed for their tenacity because, to carry them over the period of wine famine, they were able to buy large stocks of old wine from those who abandoned the island.

João Vicente da Silva

It was a Madeira grower, João Vicente da Silva, working in conjunction with Baron de Ornelas, a relative who had lived and experimented in France, who finally discovered the beneficial effect of sulphur dusting. This method is still used today and, from the time the buds begin to swell until the grapes are picked, the vines are regularly dusted with sulphur powder. By 1861 the vines had recovered and 2,500 hectares were once again covered by vineyards. It is estimated that the area covered today is approximately 3,500 hectares.

Phylloxera vastatrix

The second scourge which struck the island's economy through its vines was the dreaded vine louse, *Phylloxera vastatrix*, which also came from America. In 1860 it had appeared in Europe and quickly spread to every vine-growing country in the world, efficiently and methodically bringing havoc and devastation to the vineyards. These lice, which incorporate the worst characteristics of the *Coccidae* and *Aphides*, have two different forms, one attacking the root and the other the leaf. Moreover, each louse breeds between 25 to 30 million individuals each breeding season. In Europe the louse has a winter hibernation, but in the warmth of Madeira it breeds all year round, adding considerably to the devastation.

The phylloxera reached Madeira in 1872. The first districts to be struck were the driest regions of Funchal and Câmara de Lobos.

It is thought that the louse was brought to the island direct from America on plants of the *Vitis labrusca isabella*, which was imported in 1840 because of its resistance to mildew. Surprisingly the island of Porto Santo was only mildly affected by phylloxera, and then not until 20 years after its appearance on Madeira. This was unexpected because the island is very dry, and the water there is brackish, but the soil, unlike Madeira's, is limestone.

The Madeira growers appealed to the Lisbon government for help many times, but they too were preoccupied with the ravages of phylloxera on the mainland of Portugal, where it had appeared four years earlier. Only in 1883 when, as with the oidium, it was too late, were the petitions granted and in June of that year Sr. Almeida e Brito was appointed inspector and started an anti-phylloxera campaign. In his report published in 1883, he suggested that phylloxera already existed in Madeira in 1865 but that because of the very dry summer of 1872 and the consequent lack of water to the roots it became manifest only in that year.

Thomas Slapp Leacock

Thomas Slapp Leacock, great-grandfather of William Leacock, the present head of Leacock & Co., was one of the leading entomologists of that day. It was he who identified the phylloxera and it is entirely due to his efforts to combat the disease that today we have left any of the traditional grape varieties; for he was able to save them at his St John's vineyard at Alto do Pico de São João (where he produced the St John Madeira so popular in Scandinavia). In 1873, a year after its appearance, Thomas Slapp Leacock was, with some success, treating the roots of his vines with resin and essence of turpentine. Later he used tar and managed to stamp out the root form of the disease. In conjunction with Almeida e Brito, Thomas Slapp used a sulphate of copper spray (now known as Bordeaux mixture) to combat the aerial form and, in his own vineyards, the disease was under control by February 1883.

Thomas Slapp bequeathed the results of his research to Cambridge University.

In larger vineyards, however, the root form is harder to control since the roots cannot all be treated and, as a result, disinfecting the soil has become widespread. Water, which penetrates to the root and washes away the lice, is also a great help and, fortunately, Madeira now has plenty of water with which to irrigate vineyards that in 1873 had none.

MADEIRA THE ISLAND VINEYARD

Henry Vizetelly, author of *Facts about Port and Madeira*, visited the island in the autumn of 1877, the worst year of the phylloxera. He described Mr. Leacock's vineyard, which had been attacked by the louse: "The owner by watchful care and judicious treatment including the application to the principal roots of the vine of a kind of varnish which in this instance seems to have provided a specific, has succeeded in restoring most of the diseased vines to a comparatively healthy condition." He also mentions looking from "the breezy heights" down the valley to the village of Câmara de Lobos, which once "yielded one of the finest and most robust of Madeira growths." His companion, Russell Manners Gordon, who owned most of the vineyards, told him that "a year or two ago vines sloped down from the summit of the peak on all its sides and occupied every cultivated spot in the rear of the village." But phylloxera had devastated the vines, and the famous wine-growing district, which once produced 3,000 pipes of the best quality wine, in 1877 produced only 100. Vizetelly found signs of former prosperity but, wherever a fair supply of the necessary water could be obtained, vines which had died were being replaced with sugar cane.

Câmara de Lobos

Restocking

To restock the vineyard, American root stocks of the types *Vitis labrusca, riparia* and *rupestris* were imported. These vines are quite different from the European vines, which are all of the type *Vitis vinifera*. The American vines had allegedly become immune to the disease, but this is not strictly correct. In a report issued in August 1883 from the president of the State Viticultural Commission of California, he said that the presence of phylloxera had been discovered in ten counties in the state of California, and suggested that a more comprehensive investigation would reveal phylloxera in every wine-growing county of the state. He added that experiments made by the Board of Commissioners had proved conclusively that with the correct application of carbon bisulphate at the proper season, and by the addition of the necessary fertiliser, phylloxera could not only be checked in its ravages, but totally exterminated at the insignificant cost of less than 40 dollars an acre. It seems therefore that the American stock was not actually immune but highly resistant to phylloxera, and the treatment of the soil and vine were eliminating the disease.

Restocking the vineyards was a slow, arduous and costly undertaking, interrupted by the Portuguese government, which then prohibited the importation of American vines since it was from America that the louse had originated. However, shippers' and growers' efforts, assisted by Sr. Almeida e Brito, the inspector, prevailed and the government was made to realise that importing American stock was the only way to revive the economy of the island. In 1883 the ban on importing vines from America was lifted. Of the 15 British shippers left before the phylloxera only 10, and 12 of the other nationalities, remained and it is due to these gallant gentlemen that we owe the recovery of the island's wine trade. The American vines took many years to become established before they could be grafted with the traditional vines. Once grafted, the vines took a further seven to eight years to reach full production. It was not therefore until the beginning of this century that the vineyards of Madeira had fully recovered from the ravages of phylloxera, and by this time the island had lost its principal markets.

A new industry

Perhaps I could mention here a new industry which arose out of the chaos caused by oidium and which was to become one of the island's largest sources of revenue. The men were unemployed because they had no vines to tend and the islanders were at that time in a state of great poverty. However, an enterprising British lady, Miss Elizabeth Phelps, had noticed that the women and girls were very able with their hands. Elizabeth Phelps (known to her friends as Bella) started a school for the women on the Phelps estates, in which they were taught to work embroideries from original designs drawn by Bella Phelps herself. This led to the island schools generally producing the most exquisite work which became known as "Madeira fine art embroidery."

In the early days the embroideries were sold privately, but later on as their popularity increased they were entrusted to agents in London, Messrs. Robert and Frank Wilkinson, who handled the embroidery on a commercial basis for the benefit of the native workers, and established themselves in Madeira in 1862. At this time there were 1,029 women employed, using 15 kilos of thread per day, and producing a revenue of some £22,000 for the island. Later, the exports spread to the United States and many American firms established themselves in Madeira to ship its fine embroideries.

Embroidery has always been and still is a cottage industry. All that is exported is the work, the linen, thread and designs being imported. Embroidery merchants in Funchal send out the linen with the designs stamped on it for the women to work in the villages. Factories in the town wash, iron and finish the work.

Some of Bella Phelps' original designs for Madeira embroidery: top, a v-shaped piece for the bodice of a baby's long gown, in white; below, part of a length for edging or founcing (carried out in pale blue thread).

VINES AND VINEYARDS

The lean years

For the few shippers remaining in Funchal, the years following the oidium and phylloxera were lean ones. Oidium lasted from 1852 to 1862 and phylloxera from 1872 to 1885, but the vines did not reach full production until around 1900. Annual total shipments averaged some 12 to 14,000 pipes up to 1820, falling to 8 to 10,000 pipes between 1821 and 1825. By 1851 the figure was 7,500 pipes. From 1852 to 1862 shipments averaged about 1,500 pipes, until the effects of oidium were really felt from 1862 to 1869, when an average of only 800 pipes were exported. Shippers had stocks to tide them over the phylloxera years, so from 1870 shipments rose to over 1,000 pipes and in the year phylloxera started until 1882 an average of 2,500 pipes were exported. From 1882 shipments rose to 5,000 pipes, stabilising at 6,000 by 1896.

Oidium reduced the vintages drastically but did not kill the vines, whereas phylloxera wiped them out. Before phylloxera, an area of 2,500 hectares was covered by vineyards, producing an average of 16,000 pipes per annum, but in 1883 the area was reduced to only 500 hectares which produced under 3,500 pipes of wine.

It is therefore not easy to draw a firm line between post- and pre-oidium and -phylloxera vintages. Strictly speaking, pre-oidium should be vintages prior to 1852 and pre-phylloxera those before 1872. However, during the oidium troubles there were three small but fine vintages and in the phylloxera four notable vintages were produced, namely 1872, 1874, 1883 and the unique 1880 Malmsey. I would say that today one would consider Malmsey 1880 a pre-phylloxera vintage, whereas Malmsey 1893 would be in the post-phylloxera class.

Joseph Phelps (1791-1876) and his wife, Elizabeth, whose daughter Elizabeth (Bella), introduced the embroidery industry to Madeira.

Shipments to Britain

During the years from 1909 to 1913 the island resumed an average total shipment of 7,000 pipes annually. As production and export decreased, the price, for instance, of London Particular rose from

£25 to £75 per pipe. The fall in popularity of Madeira in the United Kingdom has been erroneously attributed to the very man who made it fashionable, George IV, who is said to have switched from Madeira to Sherry. However, as Vizetelly says: "This can scarcely have been the case, since it was not until the 'First Gentleman of Europe' had been interred in the Royal Vault at Windsor that any great falling off in the importation of Madeira occurred. . ." It was undoubtedly the difficulty in obtaining supplies of Madeira, caused first by the oidium and then by the phylloxera, that created the loss of interest. The East India market was also affected by the dissolution of the East India Company, which imported the wine to its possessions; and the opening of the Suez Canal offered a more favourable route to the east, so that shipping ceased to call at Funchal to take on wine.

The taste for Madeira was undoubtedly brought to the United Kingdom by colonists returning home after the American War of Independence. Madeira drinking had, however, been commonplace in England for a century before it became really fashionable in the early 1800s when as in America "Madeira parties" were held in private houses. At dinner Verdelho and Rainwater were drunk with the soup, Verdelho or Bual with cheese and Bual or Malmsey with dessert. Afterwards there was a choice of either Madeira or port. If port was served, a glass of astringent Sercial was often offered after the port. After the 1820s Sercial became better known, and was taken before dinner or at lunchtime, eventually being drunk as an appetiser when these became popular. At this time Madeira was as popular in Britain as port.[34]

Sadly the high prices following phylloxera changed all this and forced consumers to fall back on Sherry and Marsala, which Spanish shippers managed to maintain at one-quarter of the price of Madeira, and Madeira is now, unfortunately, the least known of the three classic fortified wines. Old Madeira has always been, and still is, a connoisseur's wine but there is, however, a marked increase in consumption of ordinary Madeiras among discerning drinkers.

Return to normal

When shipments returned to normal earlier this century Britain imported only 11 per cent of the total shipped, whereas Germany and France were taking 40 and 25 per cent respectively. Russia was importing 12 per cent, about the same as England, but the quality supplied to the English and American markets was far superior to that sent anywhere else. The Russian quota was entirely for the court and nobility, highly priced but not of such high quality because shippers had to allow for commissions to stewards and courtiers.

British interests threatened

In 1902 there was a severe threat to British business in Madeira, which, if it had materialised, would have been the end of our interests in the islands. On July 23rd 1905, the Paris edition of the *New York Herald* reported: "German Company Plans to Make Madeira Up-to-Date Resort." A German syndicate, Madeira Actien Gesellschaft, chaired by Prince Frederick Karl Hohenlohe, planned, with the support of the Portuguese government, to take over all business interests in the island. The Portuguese government, tempted by the promise that the MAG would build sanatoria and hospitals, treating 40 tuberculosis patients annually free of charge, was known to support the scheme. The company was given considerable concessions of land and allowed to import all building material free of duty and, in fact, built the present hospital and sanatorium at the Mount. It was soon appreciated, however, that the Madeira Actien Gesellschaft was an extension of the Kaiser's expansionist policy. British interests were to be expropriated and, instead of hospitals, hotels and tourist complexes were to be built. Pictures of the sanatorium and a sketch of the "proposed Strand Hotel" were published in the *New York Herald*. The British press vigorously took up the matter and there were questions in the House of Commons. The *Evening Standard* of November 14th 1905 reported that, "The Kaiser has realised that there are no plums in Madeira cake as there are in the Sultana," when the Portuguese government cancelled the concessions as suddenly as they had been granted. In 1914 Portugal joined the Allies, and all German interests, including the assets of the Madeira Actien Gesellschaft, were confiscated by the government.

Markets lost and regained

During the First World War shipments were not greatly affected and production was small, averaging six million litres, 1917 producing only 2.8 million. There were nine British and four Portuguese shippers, not counting a number of small firms whose total exports amounted to less than four per cent of the island's shipments. Funchal was shelled by German submarines twice and a British cable ship and French merchantman were sunk in Funchal Roads. The target was obviously the Western Telegraph station, which was the main junction of the submarine cable from Europe to South Africa. After the war, Madeira lost two of its most important markets, Russia and the USA. The Russian proletariat considered drinking Madeira to be an unnecessary luxury of the bourgeoisie so it came to an abrupt end.

Prohibition

According to Jewish tradition Satan buried a lion, a lamb, a pig and an ape under the first vine Noah planted when he "began to be an husbandman, and he planted a vineyard" (Genesis 9:20). This was to teach Noah that man, in time, reveals the characteristics of all four, according to the amount of wine consumed. Satan's prophecy extended to all mankind, but the US government seems to have taken the prophecy to be directed at the American public, causing the notorious Eighteenth Amendment of January 16th 1919. Prohibition came into force a year later, closing for 14 years Madeira's oldest and finest market. The Eighth Amendment and

Barrels being prepared at H.M. Borges for shipment to Oslo, Norway.

the Volstead Act not only affected Madeira, but also ruined the California wine industry, whose promising products were becoming known and respected in Europe. However, Madeira's shippers have always been resourceful in finding markets to replace those which have failed them.

Scandinavia

The shippers turned their attentions to Scandinavia, \and exports to those countries increased rapidly. For example, in 1913 Sweden and Denmark had imported just over 100 pipes, but in 1936 the two countries were importing over 5,500 pipes per annum, amply making up for the loss. Norway, Sweden, Denmark and Finland continue to be Madeira's best markets for fine wine.

In Sweden, Norway and Finland, the importing of wines and spirits is controlled by state wine monopolies, which are the only importers and distributors. Denmark, on the other hand, has always been a free market for very fine wines, except for a period in the 1920s when a price war raged. This was the result of a new sort of wine merchant who had sprung up in Madeira. These were capitalists

Borges' barrels for Oslo being loaded onboard ship.

who bought heavily at the vintage, looked after the wines and supplied them to the shippers as and when they were needed. They were known as *partidistas*, and became useful to shippers, saving them from immobilising their capital in a wine which had to be kept for a long period before it could be sold. Many small shipping firms mushroomed, relying entirely on the *partidistas* who, in some cases, were not too scrupulous about supplying rather inferior wine. This led to a price war in Denmark, a new and developing market. The new shippers limited themselves merely to exchanging wine for money, with resulting bankruptcies. The old-established shippers weathered the storm, and Denmark, with Norway and Sweden, are now prestige markets for Madeira. In Sweden Madeira became so popular that the State Wine & Spirit Monopoly opened its own depot in Funchal. It acquired must at the vintage and treated and shipped its own bulk wine, as well as buying from the established shippers.

CHAPTER 9

WINE MAKING

The vintage in Madeira is the longest in the world. The traditional commencement date[35] is August 15th, the day of Our Lady of the Mount, the patron saint of Madeira. Grapes, however, do not ripen to accommodate either tradition or saints and in fact are seldom harvested before August 20th.

The first pickings are of *Malvasia Babosa*, *Tinta* and *Verdelho*, grown from sea level to about 200 metres, proceeding up the mountainside with *Boal* and *Tinta* at a higher level until the *Sercial* is picked at about 700 metres above sea level in October or early November. At the same time *Muscatel*, which grows at sea level, is harvested. The last grapes to be picked are the very small amounts of *Malvasia Candida, Terrantez* and *Bastardo*. Vintaging is a social affair. Families join in the picking festivities, which involve much eating, drinking and fun as well as hard work. Women, children and old people fill 50-kilo vintage baskets for the men to carry to the nearest wine press, although nowadays plastic containers are more often used. They are identified by a shipper's colour or mark and are left on the roadside for collection by lorry. The grapes are then transported to the lodges in Funchal.

In the old days when shippers bought *mosto* (must or grape juice) payment was made for the goatskin containing 45 litres in the south, and 50 litres in the north to compensate the buyer for extra transport expenses. Early in the 20th century, the goatskin as a measure was substituted by the vintage barrel, which held the same amount as the skin but was easier to make to size. However the goatskin (or *borracho*) is still used to transport *mosto* or wine on the steep mountain paths. To add to this complication of the measure being larger in the north, land was measured in *alqueires* of ground, and vineyards were said to produce so many goatskins per *alqueire* for the purpose of advance payments. An *alqueire* of ground contains 15,625 square *palmos* (hands). Strictly speaking the *palmo* is equal to eight-and-a-half English inches, but it varies from place to place. For instance, at Câmara de Lobos five *palmos* correspond to 43 inches, at Santana a *palmo* is nine inches, and at Machico it is eight inches. I have known completely illiterate peasants working out complicated conversions of *palmos, alqueires,* litres and goatskins in their heads more quickly than I could with paper and pencil (this was before the days of calculators). Now shippers buy grapes instead of must, which has the advantage of enabling the grapes for each pressing to be selected, thus ensuring that the odd bunch of a different variety has not crept into the baskets.

Borracheiros in Funchal with their goatskins full of wine.

In the parish of São Martinho some grapes are always left to be picked on November 11th, the feast of Saint Martin, who was Bishop of Tours and is the patron of wine growers and drunkards. The Madeirense considers that God gave wine to man to enjoy, so, once a year, on the day of Saint Martin, every self-respecting person takes advantage. With much feasting and revelry they become roaring drunk to show their appreciation of the Lord's bounty. It is believed that just for this day the good Lord closes his eyes to excesses.

WINE MAKING

Pressing in lagares

The traditional wine presses or *lagares* are rectangular wooden troughs about two metres by two-and-a-half metres by one metre deep, raised above the ground so that the butts, into which the *mosto* runs when the grapes are trodden, can stand before them. There is room for four men to work and in the centre is a huge hinged crossbeam balanced by a stone which weighs over a ton. The first treading or *impesa* starts the *mosto* flowing along a gutter through a strainer into the open butt. With the retreading (*repisa*), the *mosto* gushes out of the *lagar*. When the workers have extracted all they can with their bare feet, the stalks, skins and remaining pulp are raked up into the centre of the trough and bound by a thick rope. With a screw like an old fashioned letterpress the crossbeam is then brought down on to the coil until the stone is suspended. This squeezes out more juice, called *vinho da corda* (wine of the rope). After the *vinho da corda* has been run out of the *lagar*, the remaining *marc* (grape skins and residue) is soaked in water which is strained off to make *agua pé* (foot water), a refreshing drink for the workers, which will be drinkable until about Christmas. The *marc* is then fed to pigs or dug in as manure.

A lagar, showing the vara, tina and a vintage barrel on the tina.

Treading grapes is very hard and thirsty work. In 1941, with a little help, I trod 500 kilograms of grapes to make a pipe of Bual to put down for my son; I did not, however, repeat the process for my daughter 16 years later.

Lagar workers operate in shifts, always with the traditional musicians to accompany the songs on a *machete*, a small guitar which was taken by Madeira emigrants to Honolulu, where it became known as the ukulele. The men are knee deep in grapes, and with the *impesa* the *machete* beats a slow laborious rhythm. The song is slow and solemn, mostly improvised verses about fellow workers or the vineyard proprietor, ending with the refrain which means:

> If you want a man to sing
> Give him a good offering,
> Give him *poncha* or *aguardente*,
> For the sake of Charity.

Traditionally only men work in the *lagar*, but girls join in the singing. In *How to Prepare Nectar*, Major J. Reis Gomes writes: "As sportsmen do not eat their game, so *lagar-workers* rarely drink wine." They prefer the stronger *aguardente* (sugar-cane brandy) or *poncha*, made by mixing the brandy with water, sugar and lemon juice. When it comes to the lighter *repisa*, and the refreshment has done its work, the *machete* beats a barbaric dance, the singing becomes louder and lewder and the treaders, their skin, shirts and shorts stained with juice and their sweating faces wild, work themselves up in a frenzied hysterical dance.

Major Gomes describes their faces as "terrifying and grotesque, of sanguinary bacchanals." They are not drunk with alcohol, but with the joy of a new vintage which may produce the nectar of nectars. (It was in this atmosphere that I was showing a pressing in progress to a young lady journalist on the staff of the *Daily Mail*, when a swarthy treader offered her, with a flourish, a horn full of grape juice from the *lagar*. Although she turned noticeably green, she valiantly quaffed it.) The human foot presses the grapes more cleanly and with fewer broken pips and crushed stalks than any modern machinery. I know to my cost that if one treads too hard it hurts; it is amazing how a grape pip can hurt, so one goes gently, not breaking the pips and damaging the jelly under the grape skin, which gives the wine its flavour.

Mechanical presses

Unfortunately the treading of grapes is giving way to modern sophisticated mechanical presses, which are known locally as "French presses," wherever they come from. There are three stages. When the grapes leave the reception hopper they are conveyed by an Archimedian screw to the *esmadador* or de-stalker. This removes the stalks and pulps the grapes. Then the pulp is pumped into a light press, *esgotador*, which extracts about 90 per cent of the finest quality must. Finally a heavy press, *prensa*, crushes out the remainder. The latter is equal to the *vinho da corda* of the old *lagar* and is of inferior quality. Co-operatives have been set up in all wine districts where the grapes are either trodden or pressed mechanically. The presses are certainly faster and, they say, more hygienic than the *lagar*, but in my opinion they are not as efficient as the human foot. Moreover, the must coming into contact with metal cannot be avoided. Apart from their technical merits, the new presses are not as romantic or conducive to a good party as is the old *lagar*. Wine is susceptible to atmosphere, so why should it not start its long life with singing and dancing to launch it on its way finally to be drunk, one hopes, with joy. Over every *lagar* or press one finds a pair of horns and an empty bottle hanging neck downwards. This is to drive away the dreaded "evil eye." The Madeirense is very superstitious and thinks that a neighbour or stranger may cast his jealous eye on the pressings with evil intent. The reasoning is that neither the horns nor the empty bottles are desirable so the evil eye goes somewhere else.

In the old days the must was brought to shippers' lodges by *borrachieros* (goatskin carriers) or in vintage barrels strapped to the back of mules, or in pipes on bullock sledges. Motor transport was first used in 1909 when wine was brought to Funchal from Câmara de Lobos on the New Road.[36] The vehicle was Cossart, Gordon's chain drive "horseman" lorry. It achieved the fantastic speed of eight metres per second, leaving oxen and mules standing. The single-cylinder engine was later installed in a fishing boat, and finished life working a wine pump.

Today shippers buy grapes instead of must, paying for them per degree of specific gravity (potential alcohol) per kilogram. They are weighed and graded before pressing. Only grapes from the environs of Funchal used to be pressed in the lodges of the town; all the rest were pressed on the spot by the various co-operatives, under supervision of the shippers. It is however now becoming common for the shippers to transport all their grapes to the lodges in Funchal and elsewhere. Grapes of different species and from different altitudes and regions are pressed and fermented separately.

Fermentation

With *Sercial* and *Verdelho*, the juice is normally taken off the skins before fermentation, but in the case of other varieties, both skins and juice go into the fermentation tanks. Fermentation often starts soon after pressing, depending on the temperature. In hot weather the casks are wrapped in wet hessian to prevent fermentation starting during transport. Many shippers have depots around the island where the must is fermented, and the *vinho claro* is then brought into the lodges in Funchal. Fermentation is aerobic and generally takes place in concrete tanks, except in the case of the finer growths which are fermented in new shipping casks. This has the added advantage of thoroughly seasoning new casks, which is otherwise an expensive process.[37] Fermentation takes from two to four weeks, depending on the air temperature. In Madeira the question of the temperature being too low does not arise; the problem is rather one of keeping the fermentation vessels cooled. And there is no malolactic fermentation as the wine is either fortified or heated in *estufas* before this fermentation is able to take place. The whole process of fermentation is under the strict control of the Madeira Wine Institute, whose inspectors are always present.

Sweetening

The grape sugar in the must is traditionally fermented right out to obtain the maximum degree of alcohol and the sweetening is then added in the form of *vinho surdo*. This is unfermented juice of the same quality and of high specific gravity, to which alcohol has been added.

Latterly, however, some shippers have adopted the method of sweetening by making *vinho abafado* (smothered wine). Fermentation is halted by adding grape alcohol to the wine at the required degree Baumé, thus conserving part of the natural grape sugar and producing a lighter Madeira. It is not general practice yet because it is an expensive method in terms of both alcohol and labour.[38] Like time, fermentation waits for no man, and alcohol may have to be added at any time, day or night. An official of the Madeira Wine Institute must be in attendance when alcohol is added, and they do

WINE MAKING

not appreciate turning out at night. The merits of this system have still to be proved.

With the Bual I put down in 1941, fermentation was arrested at three-and-a--half degrees Baumé. It is now lighter and more elegant than another Bual of the same year and Baumé degree from the same vineyard at Campanario. Only time will tell which will accept age more gracefully. I personally think that, with age, wine whose fermentation has been arrested will lose vinosity and richness sooner than that sweetened with *surdo*.

Fortification

Malmsey will be fortified very early on, possibly after only a few hours' fermentation, in order to retain the richness which it requires, whereas Verdelho and Sercial are fermented dry and Bual would be fortified when rather more than half the available sugar had been fermented out. It follows that a sweet wine requires much more grape alcohol to stop fermentation than an almost dry Sercial which has been left to ferment out and produced much more of its own alcohol. In most cases, fortification takes the strength of the wine up to between 14 and 18 per cent of alcohol by volume.

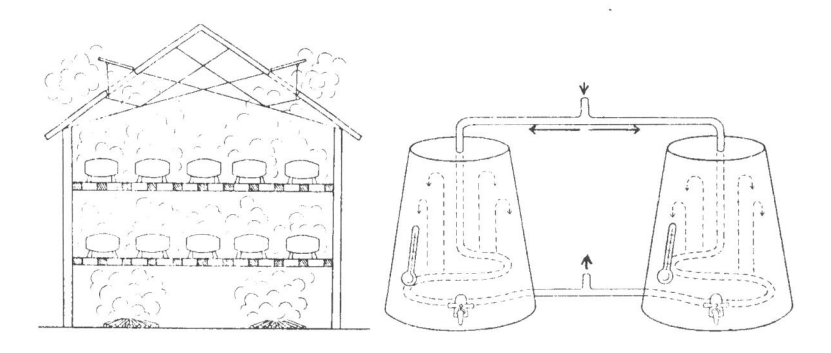

Left, primitive armazem de calor. The modern armazem is identical with the exception that heat is produced by waer radiators instead of open fires. Right, modern estufa.

After fermentation the *vinho claro* is racked off the *bras* (lees). Accountants allow ten per cent for fermentation ullage, but in practice it is more likely to be 12 to 15 per cent. At this point a selection is made. If the wine is destined as a reserve, for replenishing soleras or for observation for a potential vintage Madeira, it is fortified to 17 per cent of alcohol by volume before it goes into the *estufa*. If it is to be an ordinary Madeira it is *estufado* without being fortified (except of course, that some alcohol may already have been added to arrest fermentation). The reason for not fortifying ordinary Madeiras before the *estufa* process is that it is expensive. There is a loss of alcohol of two degrees Gay Lussac during heating which, added to the normal volume loss of ten per cent, is considerable, but the wine which is fortified before going into the *estufa* is much superior and warrants the extra cost.

Ocean voyages

Very early on it was discovered that Madeira wine greatly benefited from a long sea voyage. It was not considered mature unless it had crossed the tropics twice, so wines were sent to the East and West Indies for the sole purpose of maturing (see Chapter 5).[39] Mr. Malcolm Bell Jr. wrote in his paper published in the *Georgia Historical Quarterly* in 1954: "Merchants in Madeira truly began to deliver a full measure of romance with each pipe. The pipe contained nothing more than Madeira wine when they left the island, but after mellowing in the heat of the hold of a sturdy sailing ship, rolling and pitching over thousands of miles of distant seas, they gained something of the character of the ship itself. When the big pipes were skidded and eased ashore it was not Madeira wine alone that was restrained by oaken staves, but rare wonderful Hurricane from the ship *Hurricane* – a new Madeira for men of the day to taste and compare with Wanderer, Bramin, Rapid, Three Deacons, Southern Cross, Comet and all the other Madeiras named after ships." This wine was called *vinho da roda* (wine of the round voyage). A wine which was matured on the island by the age-old process of time is *vinho canteiro*, meaning matured on a scantle (trestle).

As late as 1907 Cossart, Gordon & Co. advertised: "We are holding in London upward of 1,000 pipes of finest Madeira for shipment to India and back for the express purpose of benefiting from the sea voyage." However, *vinho da roda* became very expensive. Normal ullage on voyage was calculated at five per cent and pilfering could bring it up to as much as 15 per cent. The pipes were therefore cased in an outer cask made of pine wood with shavings stuffed between the cask and cover – for sailors are great "sippers." In my younger days when I was working as a cooper, we used to break down returned pipes so as to build them up again into hogsheads. Some of the staves looked like ladders inside where hoops had been knocked aside and pegs driven in to stop up the holes after Jack Tar had claimed his swig.

Early estufas

At home resourceful Madeira merchants set about simulating a long sea voyage through the tropics. An enterprising abbot built a glass house, or hot house, which gave its name, *estufa*, to the present method. The wine placed in it was roused by monks sitting astride the pipes stirring with "green wands made of laurel saplings, inserted through the bungs." One presumes these wands gave a taste of laurel to the wine. The sun warmed the wine during the day and the night temperature then had a counter effect.

In 1794 Sr. Pantaleão Fernandes warmed his wine in an *armazem de calor* (hot store) heated by flues to 70 to 80 degrees Centigrade and stirred in the same way. *Armazems de calor*, although much improved, are used today. In 1889, Count Canavial invented a method of passing wine through a coil starting at *bain-marie* and increasing to 70 degrees Centigrade, the wine then falling into casks where it was kept at 50 degrees Centigrade for several weeks. This method caused oxidation and although the Count claimed the "toasted" taste came out by the use of active charcoal the process was put aside in favour of the more gentle method of *armazem de calor*.

There was much abuse of the *estufa* system and it was forbidden by the captain-general of the island on August 23rd 1802; but the ban was short-lived and it was lifted by royal decree on May 7th 1803. Abuse and fraud continued by heating to 70 to 80 degrees Centigrade, until the use of *estufas* was again declared illegal in June 1834. However, the influential Sr. Paulo Perestrello da Câmara strongly defended the merits of *estufas* and a royal decree dated February 20th 1835 once again made them legal. The preamble to this decree blamed the system for "discrediting the good name of Madeira wine which had hitherto enjoyed great favour." This decree regulated for the first time the temperatures to be used, and the general use of the system to what it is materially today.

The knowledge that wine improves in the heat of a ship's hold was not new. Pliny and, later, Cervantes referred to it. The ancient Romans treated their wine by heat, placing it in *amphorae* in their *fumerium* or drying kiln, whilst, in the Middle Ages, Leonardo da Vinci aged his wine in shallow pans by playing the violin to it, thus causing vibration to set up minute ripples which motivated the wine. This was rather a long process, but ingenious, and one wonders whether today's pop music would have a more rapid effect.

Estufas today

The modern *estufas* are of two kinds. The *armazem de calor* is a store heated by hot water pipes to a maximum air temperature of 50 degrees Centigrade, in which the wine is placed in scantling pipes in tiers. A hole of about one inch diameter is bored into the bung of each cask to allow for expansion and for the escape of vapours. The casks need frequent coopering because of the heat, and are usually inspected once or twice in the day and once at night. These hot stores are undoubtedly the best method of *estufagem* and are used for the fine wines, and to finish off wines from the *cubas de calor*, or hot vats. The latter are concrete vats with epoxy-resin or ceramic linings which hold from 20,000 to 40,000 litres. They are heated by a stainless steel coil at the bottom of the vat: the heating wine moves away and upwards from the coil, causing circulation, which is aided either by a propeller or by pumping air through the wine. Each vat has a thermometer taking the reading at the centre of the vat. By law the temperature must be 45 degrees Centigrade, with a tolerance of five degrees each way, so in fact the wine may be heated from 40 degrees to a maximum of 50 degrees Centigrade. There are very heavy penalties if the maximum is exceeded. There is a minimum time of three months for *estufagem* but no maximum, most shippers preferring the lower temperatures and longer periods (up to six months) to avoid the wine becoming "toasted." *Estufas* and their thermometers are sealed by an official of the Madeira Wine Institute.

Cooling the wine

When the wine has finished its *estufagem* it cannot be drawn off until it is cool because, if it comes into contact with air at temperatures higher than 20 degrees Centigrade, problems may result and the wine may become hazy,[40] or oxidise to an undesirable degree. It is now called *vinho estufado*. If the wine was not fortified before *estufagem*, this is done as soon as it is cool and the alcohol content raised to 17 per cent by volume.

The period of cooling an unfortified wine after *estufagem* is probably the most dangerous in the life of the Madeira, because if great care is not taken the wine not only over oxidises, but volatile acids may develop in the form of acetic acid.[41] Madeira has high constituents of fixed acids, and a permissible high degree of acetic acid, the greatest enemy of the wine maker: so during cooling the wine has to be carefully watched, daily or even hourly. The modern practice of cooling by refrigeration, however, appears to be quite beneficial.[42]

Leacock's cooperage, where barrels were made and repaired.

Estagio

After *estufagem* the wine needs a rest to recover from the shock. This resting period of from 12 to 18 months or longer, depending on the wine, is called the period of *estagio*. The wine is either filtered or fined with bentonite or gelatine and put away in oak scantling pipes in a cool store for its *estagio*.

Passagem

After *estagio*, the wine is fined and undergoes a brisk racking called *passagem*. It is usually pumped so that) it falls from a height into a trough in order to pass air through the wine. It is then stored in casks on the solera system, to be drawn on for blending, or to be observed as a potential vintage Madeira. The special growths and fine wines are by now 28 months old and the lower qualities 18 months.

Madeira as a fortified wine

Madeira was an unfortified beverage wine until the mid-18th century, although before this time one hears of "Madeira Burgundy,"

"Tent," "Tinto" and "Tintoreto" from the *tinta* grape. During Queen Anne's reign, owing to disturbed conditions around Gibraltar, ships bound for North America and the Caribbean (both leading markets for Madeira) ceased to call at Funchal and stockpiling resulted. Moreover, the shortage of storage capacity became acute. Merchants had financed and encouraged the building and planting of vineyards on the steep mountain sides, and therefore felt morally obliged to continue to buy the wine produced. Looking to the future, they wanted to maintain production, and the only thing they could do was to distil their surplus wines into brandy, with which to fortify and preserve stocks. At the time there was much controversy over this practice, but it became a necessity and finally general practice to blend "a bucket or two of brandy" into each pipe of Madeira. Assuming the buckets were of two gallons, this would bring the strength of the wine to approximately 15 per cent alcohol by volume.

A Portuguese wine book on vine agriculture published in 1720 recommends the addition of three gallons of brandy per pipe to improve the wine. The author was certainly referring to "old gallons" equal to three-and-three-quarter litres (an imperial gallon is four-and-a-half litres), but one does not know the quantity of wine to which it was added. He may have been referring to the Port pipe of 138 old gallons or the Madeira pipe of 110 old gallons; however, the amount roughly tallies with the "buckets" used by Francis Newton in 1753. The disparity between the gallonage of the Port and Madeira pipes exists because the shipper paid the freight, so, to compensate himself, the Madeira shipper gave less wine, Madeira being further away from Europe.

William Bolton mentions the making of brandy in Madeira in 1704 by Messrs. Durrell & Morgan, a firm which he later joined. It was made only "to try an experiment, and I fear will not answer the charge," he writes. Durrell & Morgan write in the same year: "We have shipped 10 pipes of Brandy which we were making when Mr. Bolton left [for London] . . . [it is] supposed to arrive at the goodness of French: they are a trial, we consigned them to Mr. Bolton by reason he knows the nature of them." The brandy must have been very rough in those days. In 1705 Durrell & Morgan supplied some quarter casks to a man-of-war, but a competitor did not seem to have much opinion of Durrell's product nor the palates of merchant seamen. He wrote to his London house: "It is only suitable for the lower deck of merchantmen, and not for the

Quarter Deck."

There seems to have been an improvement in distilling methods, and in 1756 a Mr. Burgess wrote from London to Michael Nowlan, an associate of John Leacock: "I am advised here to carryover a Small Distillery to rectify Brandy & some Gentlemen here that are knowing in the Wine Trade assure me that if a couple of gallons of fine clear Brandy was put into each pipe of our best Wines twill improve them greatly. I believe that some of the Houses in Madeira use this method. . . I observe that their Madeiras drunk here in gentlemen's houses are fine pale amber colour nothing tending to a reddish." Mr. Burgess was referring to the wines of Cossart, Gordon's founder, Francis Newton, who at first had objected to the adding of brandy to his wines. He wrote: "My wines lie tranquil and peaceful in my stores and are fresh and full flavoured unlike the ones laced with Brandy," but he was forced to use brandy to preserve his "tranquil wines." The first mention that the fortification of Madeiras was general practice in the island is in a letter from Francis Newton to his partner George Spence in London dated October 27th 1753: "I really impute the complaints I have had of wines to my not putting a bucket or two of brandy in each pipe as other houses do."

When peace returned, more ships than ever called at Madeira to load a new wine, stronger and of different character, "not tending to the reddish," which gained an enthusiastic reception. The only complaint was from Francis Newton's brother, Andrew, in Virginia, that the men who hitherto had drunk two bottles every day now made do with only one.

With the improvement of distilling techniques a highly refined spirit was used and when there were small vintages shippers imported it from Oporto. A decree of January 11th 1822 forbade the import of spirit or, rather, aguardente (alcohol rectified to 72 degrees Gay Lussac) and forced shippers to use alcohol distilled from sugar cane, when there were insufficient lees and wine to "burn," on the island. Our vintage 1828 was alcolisado, with cane alcohol and the 1836 with wine spirit, but no difference could be noted 100 years later; in fact, the former was more vinous than the latter. There was further legislation in 1928, which did not materially change the position except that shippers could not distil their own lees; they all had to be handled by an official distillery.

Again in August 1973 a decree law obliged all alcohol to be purchased from the Junta Nacional do Vinho (the forerunner of the

Instituto do Vinho da Madeira), which, when there was insufficient produced on the island, imported it from Portugal. This was at the time when Europe was being flooded with synthetic alcohol, which caused chaos to the port trade, and, to a much lesser extent, in Madeira. It will be appreciated that owing to the limited production of wine, Madeira has suffered much legislation and counter legislation regarding fortification since the haphazard "bucket or two of brandy" was added to each pipe, and the matter was taken out of shippers' hands.

The position is now greatly improved, all spirit being supplied by the Madeira Wine Institute, which imports it from mainland Portugal where it is bought by the government. Portugal is unable to satisfy the requirements and much alcohol is therefore imported from France and a number of eastern bloc countries. This is fine grape alcohol, highly rectified to 95-97 per cent alcohol by volume and well conditioned, which was not always the case previously. By law it must be the product of the distillation of wine, wine lees or pomace. Application of spirit is controlled by the Institute by means of a current account of shippers' stocks and their strengths.

Ordinary Madeiras are stored at 17 per cent by volume, and fine Madeiras at 19 per cent, being increased to 18 and 22 per cent respectively some time before bottling or shipment in wood.[43] The average amount of natural alcohol produced in a normal vintage when the must has been fermented right out is around ten per cent by volume, with the exception of Sercial, which is about eight per cent. These wines require 8.5 per cent, and the Sercial about 11 per cent of added alcohol to produce the storage strength of 17 per cent by volume. There is, of course, contraction, so ten litres of spirit added to 100 litres of wine will not produce 110 litres, but just over 100 litres.

Summary of wine making

After fermentation (which may have been arrested by the addition of alcohol), the *vinho claro* is sweetened and then goes through *estufa*, either in *armazem de calor* or *cuba de calor*. Fine Madeiras are fortified before *estufa* and ordinary Madeiras after estufa. Once fortified, the wine is called *vinho generoso*. After *estufa*, it is cooled and then fortified (if this has not already been done) and filtered or fined before being put away for a period of rest *(estagio)*. Then it is racked again *(passagem)* before storage on the solera system. The solera system and blending are dealt with in more detail in the next chapter.

CHAPTER 10

TYPES OF MADEIRA

When the *vinho generoso* has completed the *estagio* and treatment described in the previous chapter it will pass into stock *lotes*. These are parcels of wine of all the different kinds from the special growths down to ordinary Madeiras and range from pale to very dark, from dry to very rich and are of various ages from 18 months to 20 years.

The stock *lotes* will in turn be used to replenish by blending the shipping *lotes* of those brands whose names are familiar to the customer. Included in the stock *lotes* are reserve *lotes* which are used to top up soleras, and special growths – Sercial, Verdelho, Bual, Malmsey, Terrantez and Bastardo – which are being kept under observation as potential vintage Madeiras. The reserve *lotes* must of course match the *lotes* to be topped up: Malmsey can only be topped up with Malmsey and so on. Should these not live up to expectations they will be demoted and returned to the finer stock *lotes*.

The Madeira shipper has to look many years ahead. It requires considerable experience to choose a wine to be reserved as a potential vintage. Some Madeiras develop fast from their third to their sixth year and then remain static. Others such as Sercial develop very slowly, only opening out in their seventh or eighth year. For instance, Jardim da Serra Sercial vintaged in 1950 was only declared suitable as a vintage in 1981. It is now in bottle and was put on the market in 1983. It has all the characteristics required of a noble Sercial and enough body to carry it a long way, although it is still rather rough.

Storage

The storage of shipping *lotes* is most important because the *lote* will take much of its character from the cask in which it is stored. Some of the storage casks are over a century old and the same *lote* has been stored in them ever since they were made. In fact, the cask will make the *lote*. The only wood really suitable for storing Madeira is American white oak, which is imported from the United States. The flavour of Baltic oak and chestnut is too strong. Trees are not growing as tall as they used to so it is becoming increasingly difficult to obtain wood long enough to build large casks and vats. Cossart, Gordon had, in their old wine store, some 35,000-litre vats which were made of Madeira eucalyptus. They were built in 1906 and took a year to season after being boiled out with caustic soda. The Madeira Wine Association had some made in 1925 of Brazilian satin wood. They received the same treatment and are satisfactory storage vessels. There is nothing, however, like American white oak.

The most practical size of cask for maturation is, in my experience, the 650-litre scantling pipe and, for other wines, butts of 2,000 to 2,500 litres. They are easy to handle and, when necessary, coopers can take off the heading boards in order to clean and scrape off the tartaric crystals which form on the inside. Larger vats are much more difficult to clean. Usually there is a trap-door and the men actually get inside. Even though vats have been left empty for a long time, men can become intoxicated just from the fumes without having tasted any wine.

Barrels in the Madeira Wine Association's lodge, 1932.

In Portuguese, the places where wine is treated, matured and stored are called *adegas*; the English call them stores in Madeira and lodges in Oporto. Vizetelly, writing in 1877, refers to the Madeira wine stores and the Vila Nova wine lodges, but Croft-Cooke, 84 years later, referred to Madeira wine lodges. They are both now correct. The Madeira name "stores" has become a casualty of tourism: they are now known as lodges.

The art of blending

With the exception of special growths and vintages, all Madeiras are blended. Even soleras are blended by the topping-up process. The blender is an artist: his palate is five dimensional and \ever changing, and the character he gives to his blend is like his signature. When I was working I could tell who had produced a blend just by tasting it. As with people, some wines will never "marry." Even if happily married, they may fall apart if one brings in a third; or they may live contentedly in a *ménage à trois*.

I once devoted over 2,500 hours over a period of five years to perfecting a blend of old Madeiras, and I would still be working on it now if an old and experienced blender, whose judgement I respected, had not told me to stop. I was young then and he made me realise that one can never reach absolute perfection.

It all started because there was a tradition that Sercial, Bual and Malmsey would not mix. Having at the time some remains of soleras, all about 60 years old, I set about to disprove the theory. I found that a mixture of one-third of each would fall apart, but I also found that a little Sercial would come through and give the blend the character I wanted. My object was to create a full and rich Madeira but with a dry finish, similar to that of Terrantez. I worked on this basis, tasting every day, until I obtained the type required, which would stay together for some time. A small *lote* was made up and a hogshead sent to our London cellars, where it arrived still "married." But when it was sent to Newcastle-on-Tyne it fell completely apart. In fact, one could draw off the Sercial from the top, the Bual in the middle and the Malmsey at the bottom of the hogshead.

I started afresh and after much work I obtained a lighter wine, without so much character as the first but at least one that stayed together after being submitted to drastic changes in temperature. However, I went on adjusting and tuning, endeavouring to get the dry finish, and this is where my friend stepped in and told me to stop. A hogshead was sent to Bergen and to my relief and joy it held together. The bulk *lote* was made up and, after a suitable rest, it was bottled in 1945 to celebrate Cossart, Gordon & Co.'s 200th birthday. It was first named Jubilee Solera, and later Good Company Solera, but André Simon christened it *ménage à trois*.

I was complimented on the blend by many good palates, including André and Ronald Avery, who preferred it to our Terrantez 1898. Sir (then Mr.) Winston Churchill was ecstatic about it, and the late King of Denmark, to whom I presented a case, graciously complimented me. Only a limited amount was made because I had not the component parts to make more, so the original *lote* has disappeared. Its successor is our Duo-centenary Celebration, 1745-1945, which is based on the original Good Company. It is now a blend of old Buals, rather lighter than the original and without the Sercial influence. I understand that today it is considered in the trade a standard for Fine Old Bual.

When making up blends, environment and physical condition have a great influence on one's palate and judgement. If one is feeling well and happy wine tastes good, but if one feels rotten it tastes rotten; consequently good wine in bad company is not as good as bad wine in good company. "Good Company" has now been adopted as the house name for Cossart, Gordon's range of Sercial, Bual and Malmsey types.

Refrigeration

When a *lote* has been made up it requires some time to settle down and allow its components to get together. Some shippers submit their wines to refrigeration to prevent "throwing" of deposit later. They are kept at seven degrees below zero for about 30 days in order to precipitate their tartrates, at which temperature they are filtered. I have my reservations regarding this treatment. It may be suitable for ordinary Madeiras, but I do not think that any wine can age if it has its tartrates removed and that is why this method is not used for vintages or reserves. However, refrigeration has been found to be beneficial to Madeira after *estufagem*.

Shipping and bottling

Landing age before bottling is also very important. Before the war we always gave our Madeiras six months' landing age in London and Denmark. Today, because of the high cost of duty, warehousing and other overheads, this is out of the question, but the wines are allowed to stand for at least a month before bottling. Personally I feel that Madeira bottled at its destination, after a voyage in wood (or even in metal containers), is superior to island bottlings shipped in glass. I have recently been able to demonstrate this by examining London and island bottlings of the same soleras shipped at the same time; the London bottlings were far superior. At one time Cossart, Gordon used to bottle all their wine for America in London; now it is island bottled.

COSSART, GORDON & Co.

MADEIRAS (2s. 6d. Duty) in Bottle.

MADEIRAS.		CANTEIROS.	
Good (Dry)	17/	Rich	17/
„ (Rich)	17/	Rich, Medium	18/
„ (Very Rich)	17/	Rich, Old	20/
Pale Delicate, dry	18/		
Dark Rich	18/	**RAINWATERS.**	
London Market (Finest)	20/	Very Pale	22/
Selected Ditto, delicate, dry	21/	Very Pale Dry	24/
Superior Old (Finest)	22/	Very Pale Rich	26/
Choice Old, Dark Rich	24/		
"Verdelho," Finest Selected	24/	**BUALS.**	
"London Particular" (Finest)	26/	Finest Young	32/
"Palhetinho," very pale	28/	„ Old	38/
Reserve	30/	Crown Bual	43/
Old Reserve	32/		
Pale Reserve	34/	**MALMSEYS.**	
"Sao Martinho," choice old	36/	Finest Young	32/
"Cama de Lobos," very Old Rich	41/	„ Old	38/
Crown Madeira	50/	Crown Malmsey	43/
OLD SOLERAS.		**SERCIALS.**	
		Finest Young	32/
1868	55/	„ Old	38/
1862	65/	Crown Sercial	43/
1851	78/		
1844	90/	**VERY OLD BOTTLED MADEIRAS.**	
1836	100/	1862	84/
1822	110/	1851	90/
1815	120/	1850	96/
		1842	150/
OLD EAST INDIA.		1836	200/
60/ & 70/		1828	240/

Per Dozen (Duty Paid) in Cellars in London.

Terms—6 months' Credit, or 2½ per Cent. discount for Cash.

LONDON HOUSE,
75, MARK LANE, E.C.

Cossart Gordon price list 1895.

Early Madeira names

The first classification of Madeiras was for wines auctioned on the London docks in the 1760s. The names given to the lots were, in ascending order: Common Madeira (dry or rich), London Market, London Particular and East or West India. London Particular was the best of the Madeiras that had not been to the Indies and back. The name became so well known that Dickens even used it to describe fog. It was not long before another name was added, that of American Madeira, later called Rainwater (see below). Shippers in Madeira were so encouraged by trade with America in light wines that they introduced them to the London market. There is no doubt that Madeira drinking was brought to London from America, the fashion being set by the "First Gentleman."[44] It is curious that these original names for Madeira have disappeared in the United Kingdom but are still in use in Scandinavia.

Rainwater or American Madeira

Rainwater is a blend originally prepared for the southern colonial American market. It is a soft light pale Madeira, ranging from Pale Dry at one degree Baumé to Pale Rich at 2.5 degrees. It should be remembered that wines taste richer in warmer climates than in cold, so Rainwater drunk in London at 2.5 degrees would be medium rich, whereas in the southern states it would be considered a rich wine. Today Rainwater should be served chilled. Originally the basis of the blend was Verdelho and, after the phylloxera, some wine from the *cunningham* vine was used. Today the basis is Tinta Negra Mole, although all still contain some Verdelho. In Portugese it is called *palhete* or *palhetinho* from the word *palha* meaning straw, an apt description for its straw or light golden colour. After Malmsey, Rainwater has become the most popular Madeira in the United Kingdom and United States.

Naming Rainwater

There has been much speculation regarding its name, originally attributed to Mr. William Neyle Habersham of Savannah. After a considerable amount of research I have come to the conclusion that the name was started by the brothers Francis and Andrew Newton. In the early days Madeira was floated out to ships in half-empty pipes by men swimming and pushing the casks. They were taken on board by the booms, topped up and the empty pipes floated ashore in the same way. In the mid-18th century, Francis was about to make a shipment of "Verdia"[45] to his brother Andrew in Virginia. The pipes were left on the beach over night and by mistake they were unbunged. It rained and some rainwater seeped into the shipment which, however, still went forward. Andrew particularly liked the style, which he described as "Soft as Rain Water and the colour of rain water which has run over a straw thatched roof into a butt,"[46] and asked his brother to send him more of the "pale soft wine" although he was unaware that part of it was water. Francis, being a cunning Scot, made up a blend which he privately called RWM (Rainwater Madeira), one of the components being AP (*agua pura*). The name Rainwater started to appear in price lists at the end of the 18th century. It was then, as now, the same strength as all other Madeiras. The name was never patented, so it has become generic, like Bual, Malmsey etc.

Later Madeira names

For over a century before the outbreak of World War II, Madeira was offered for sale under the headings "Madeiras," "Rainwaters," "Special Growths," "East" and "West India," "Soleras" and "Vintages." A specimen of a typical early 20th century price list from Cossart, Gordon & Co. is illustrated on page 145. The wines under the heading "Madeiras" would mostly be dry, rich and very rich blends, styled on the three special growths Sercial, Bual and Malmsey. Today Verdelho is classified as a special growth but it was then listed as a Madeira. At the time this list was published the base wine of all blends was Verdelho, but today it is Tinta. *Canteiro* is wine not matured by the *estufa* system and is merely a type, like East and West India. Rainwater has already been described and soleras and vintages will be described later.

District names

Classified under "Madeiras" are wines bearing the names of districts, such as "Cama de Lobos" (or "Câmara de Lobos"), "Campanario," "São Martinho," "Quinta da Paz" and "St John" (or "São João"). The latter is very popular in Scandinavia, where it is said there is never a funeral without St John being drunk. It is a dark, heavy rich Madeira, originally from Leacock's São João vineyard, but it has now become a type. Cama de Lobos and Campanario are both rich Bual-type wines, very fragrant, with Malmsey noses. São Martinho is lighter and drier. Joseph Phelps owned Quinta da Paz until the middle of last century, and his firm shipped its light medium-rich wine. When Joseph Phelps left the island the *quinta* passed to the Bianchi family and the wine was shipped by Lomelino. Quinta da Paz became so popular that other wine had to be bought in from the surrounding district, so it became much heavier and richer. The name "South Side" is sometimes found in the USA: it is the same as Cama de Lobos. Madeiras labelled by the names of districts are from mixed grapes, mostly *tinta*. However, outside Scandinavia, the use of these names is disappearing.

Comparable prices

Early this century Madeira was more expensive than either port or Sherry, and prices did not alter materially until 1939. At present a Madeira comparable to London Market would be £45 per dozen, duty paid and delivered, to London Particular £48 and to Crown Madeira £102, whereas a wine of the age and quality of Solera 1815 would cost around £50 per bottle, when available.

Varietal names

Between the two world wars production of the classic grape varieties decreased and the practice of using their names on labels to describe types developed. For instance a pale dry blend would be labelled Sercial and a dark rich blend Malmsey. During the Second World War the UK import controls had allowed shippers only one type of wine at the same price. Cossart, Gordon chose their Fine Rich, a Bual-type wine of the same quality as London Market and now known as Good Company Bual. Prior to World War II there were large shipments to the United States of America and to Scandinavia, but grape varietal names were not used in these markets.[47] In fact, shipments to the USA were so great that Portuguese bottle factories could not keep up with demand, producing such poor glass that imports were prohibited by the US government. Cockburn and Cossart, sharing the same agent, Munson G. Shaw Co., who bottled in New York, were the only shippers sending wine from Portugal to America after Prohibition.

Immediately after the war the advertising campaign for port and Madeira sponsored by the Portuguese government increased the awareness of styles. Madeira was represented by a bucolic uncle telling his nephew that Sercial was dry, Verdelho medium dry, Bual medium sweet and Malmsey sweet, under the title "things my uncle taught me." Port was represented by an equally bucolic Major Tawny leering from the pages of glossy magazines at Miss Ruby. I do not know who thought up these advertisements, but the campaign was a success, possibly more so for Madeira than port, because the Madeira shippers spent their allocation on public relations rather than on direct advertising.

At first my company did not agree with the practice of using the names of special growths (grape names) on blends, but in the

TYPES OF MADEIRA

end we had to go along with the rest. My father's cousin, Sidney Cossart, who was in the London house at the time, would spit with fury when he saw a comparatively modestly-priced Madeira labelled Malmsey.

Cossart Gordon's prized oxen.

Labelling today

Nowadays, Madeira is mostly labelled under the names of the classic grapes from which it is produced or the type it represents. These are defined as follows:

Sercial

Pale, light-bodied, dry or extra dry, 0.5 degrees to 1.5 degrees Baumé. True Sercial has a nutty nose and with age becomes mellow and medium dark, the mellowness rather covering its dryness.

Verdelho

Golden, darkening with age. Medium dry, 1.5 degrees to 2.5 degrees Baumé. Medium-bodied, light and elegant, with a dry finish. When old becomes dry on the palate, retaining its fullness.

Bual

Medium to dark, full-bodied and very fragrant. Rich and fruity, 2.5 degrees to 3.5 degrees Baumé and well-balanced. Bual was a great favourite in officers' messes and clubs in India, being lighter than Malmsey or port. Bual mellows quickly with age and is eminently suitable for laying down.

Malmsey

Medium dark to dark. Full-bodied, very fruity, luscious and fragrant. Very rich, 3.5 degrees to 6.2 degrees Baumé. Some blended Malmseys reach eight degrees which may seem too rich, almost "sweet," but is comparatively normal when tasted in the winter, in, say, the north of Norway. Candida Malmsey is more fragrant and has more body than the Babosa variety but there is very little left. The last vintages made of *Malvasia Candida* that I know of are 1916 and 1920. Both varieties mellow quickly with age, and tend to become drier and more elegant. There are also what are called Malvasia Seca, such as the 1880, some of which has become as dry as Verdelho, yet retaining the delightful Malmsey nose.

The Madeira Wine Institute allows the use of the names of the classic grapes on types as a temporary measure only. This practice has led Madeira shippers into a great deal of trouble in connection with Portugal's forthcoming entry to the EEC, which demands that if a grape name is used on a label the wine must contain a minimum of 85 per cent of that grape. Personally I feel that the sooner we return to the old Fine Dry and Fine Rich labels the better because the practice is misleading. There are many fine Madeiras based on Sercial, Verdelho, Bual and Malmsey on the market, but these names mean nothing to the uninitiated, whereas descriptive labels such as Pale, Dark, Dry, Rich, Delicate Choice are more appropriate and honest.

Styles and legislation

The legislation governing the labelling of Madeira has undergone and is undergoing complete modification to comply with EEC and USA laws and practices. At present it is explained as follows:

Vintage Wine

Vintage wine may be made only from wine of the noble varieties and from a single year. It must remain in cask for a minimum of 20 years and be kept in bottle for two years before sale. Thus a Sercial

1950 will have been in cask for at least 20 years following completion of *estufagem*, been in bottle for a further two years before being released for sale and will be made from 100 per cent *sercial* grapes picked in 1950.

Extra Reserve or Over 15 years old

This will be a blended wine, the minimum age of the youngest component being 15 years old. If the grape species is stated on the label, ie *bual, sercial*, etc, the wine must contain at least 85 per cent of that grape variety.

Special Reserve, Old Reserve or Over ten years old

This will be a blended wine, the minimum age of the youngest component being ten years old. If the grape species is stated on the label, ie *bual, sercial*, etc, the wine must contain at least 85 per cent of that grape variety.

Reserve or Over five years old

This will be a blended wine, the age of the youngest component being five years old, following the completion of *estufagem*. This is the youngest category which may use the name of the grape species on the label. As with the other styles, it must contain at least 85 per cent of the grape variety specified.

Finest, Choice, Selected, etc

This category may only use the name "Madeira" with one of the above words coupled with a description, ie dry, medium sweet, etc and/or a trade name. The minimum age must be three years. Wine of this type would be made almost entirely from *Tinta Negra Mole* or an authorised variety.

Rainwater

Rainwater, which is a soft style of Verdelho, must be at least three years old and may not use the name of any grape species. A term such as medium dry may be used on the label.[48]

Soleras

Soleras are dated wines augmented by fractional blending. They generally carry the date the solera was begun and it is permitted to draw off no more than ten per cent of wine per year. This quantity of wine must be replaced by old wine of a quality approved by the Madeira Wine Institute until such time, as the original quantity of wine would no longer exist, *i.e.* ten years. These regulations are currently under review and only a very few shippers are maintaining or maturing solera wines.

The famous 1808 Solera pipe. The barrel is a good deal older than 1808.

CHAPTER 11

VINTAGE MADEIRAS

Madeira is the only wine akin to the wines of the Sorrentine hills, drunk by the ancient Romans, loved by Horace and described by Martial as *immortale*. It is mostly made from the same *verdia* or *verdelho* grape, grown in light volcanic soil, on "corridors" identical to the Roman *juga*, and matured by heat in *estufas* similar to the ancient *apothecae* used by the Romans. Madeira is certainly among the *firmissima vina*, which was Martial's description of the old Falernian wines, whilst in the 15th century Cadamosto said Madeira wine was *assai bunissimi*.

Longevity of Madeira

The extraordinary durability of Madeira wine is attributed, as I have explained earlier, to the semi-pasteurisation it receives during *estufagem*, or to the shipment to the East or West Indies before the invention of *estufas*. However, most of, if not all, the ancient vintages known to us today were not *estufado* or *vinho de roda*; they are *canteiro* wines, or at best matured by being submitted to the influence of the sun's rays in an *estufa do sol*. Vizetelly tells us he saw this method in practice when he visited Krohn Brothers' Carmo wine stores in 1877. Personally, I think it is more likely that Madeira's long life is as much due to the volcanic soil in which the vines grow, as to the trouble and time taken to bring the wine to the degree of perfection it demands. Rupert Croft-Cooke writes in his book on Madeira that "there must be an age beyond which Madeira is undrinkable but it is a remarkably great age."

We know today the lovely old pre-phylloxera vintages which have survived, but there must have been many vintages which perished young by not having enough stamina, becoming absorbed by the current wines for immediate drinking of that day, so that only the chosen survived. As a modern example, on a visit to the island in May 1982 I found that out of a total of 69 reserved *lotes* from 1950 to 1976, which the Madeira Wine Company had under observation as potential vintage wines, 48 had been discarded because they were not up to the high standard required. The discarded *lotes*, ranging from 2,000 to 20,000 litres each, representing 70 per cent of the total, were returned to ordinary stock *lote* reserves. If a Madeira has no solid base it is impossible to expect it to retain its virility to ripe old age, whereas robust wine from a *casta nobre*, with body and depth to live on when young, should retain its qualities unimpaired in extremes of climate for centuries, requiring no great attention except dry, cool cellarage and recorking every 20 years.

Preservation of old wines

We are fortunate that the old shippers and growers reserved their best vintages as a "nest egg" or an investment against emergencies. They just kept them in wood, locked away, rarely drinking them except for a wedding or an anniversary, selling them only when they were hard up. There was certainly a loss from evaporation, calculated at two per cent per annum but, on the other hand, this ullage was far surpassed by the gain in quality. Nowadays, these old wines are kept in 20-litre glass demijohns before final bottling, to avoid ullage. In 1949, I bought a pipe and a hogshead of Terrantez, vintaged in 1862, from Sr. Tomaz, the owner of the Golden Gate Hotel, who had acquired it from Mr. W. A. Reid, founder of Reid's Hotel. This Terrantez pipe, which had come from a much larger *lote*, had been kept in the same pipe for 87 years. When I transferred the wine to glass I then used the pipe to mature the 1941 Bual I had put down for David when he was born.

When I retired to England and moved my household effects from the island to Bungay on the Norfolk/Suffolk border, I brought with me the last few remaining bottles from this pipe, together with other valuable old Madeira, including the remains of a pipe of Bual vintaged in 1926 which my great-uncle put down for me when I joined the wine trade. For want of better accommodation I kept these bottles in the garage until they could be removed to the firm's cellars at Hastings. The garage was broken into and 22 bottles stolen, among them some of the Terrantez. The thieves were caught and turned out to be ten boys from 10 to 15 years of age. They had taken the wine for a lark. Not liking it because it was not sweet enough they smashed the bottles. I would gladly have given them lemonade or any sticky sweet drink if they had left my precious old wine alone.

In the context of casting pearls before swine, this pathetic story is surpassed only by the one told by Rupert Croft-Cooke regarding Sir Walter Calverley Trevelyan, the naturalist, who died in 1879. His cellar contained wonderful old Madeira from 1803, the year of the great flood in Funchal which washed away part of the British consulate with all the records of the British Factory. This Madeira was considered to be of "the finest quality in the world." It was a great shock to wine lovers to find that Sir Walter's cellar with all its treasures had been bequeathed "to be applied to scientific purposes" to the "eminent anti-alcoholist," physician to the London Temperance Hospital, Doctor (afterwards Sir) Benjamin Ward Richardson.

Napoleon Madeira

The 1792 vintage Madeira is probably the most famous and controversial vintage existing today. The year was a particularly fine vintage and it became famous because Napoleon took a pipe with him to St Helena when he passed the island in HMS *Northumberland* on August 7th 1815. Nobody was allowed on board except HM consul-general, Henry Veitch, who consented to do some shopping for England's embarrassing guest. Mr. Veitch courteously addressed Napoleon as "Your Majesty," instead of "General" as he had been instructed by Whitehall,[49] and persuaded him to take a pipe of 1792 as well as the fresh fruit and books which he had been requested to buy. Napoleon thanked Mr. Veitch by giving him some *louis d' or*, which were subsequently built into the foundations of the British church in Funchal. The 1792 vintage had been picked out as likely to become very fine with age. But Napoleon suffered from a gastric complaint and was not allowed to drink it.

When the ex-emperor died in 1820 the pipe was still intact and the curious thing about it was that nobody had paid for the wine. That is to say Mr. Veitch had paid the merchant who put the pipe on board HMS Northumberland in 1815, but he had never been able to get the money refunded. So he claimed the pipe as his own, and arranged for its return to Funchal, where it arrived in 1822 and was sold to Charles Blandy. The wine was considered hardly ready for drinking when it reached the island so it was only bottled by Charles's son, John Blandy, in 1840.[50] The year 1792 was not only a very fine vintage but also a very large one, so the Napoleon pipe was stretched considerably, all 1792 wine purporting to be from the same pipe. It seems that Charles Blandy had acquired most of the vintage and used it as the basis for Blandy's famous 1792 Solera. However, there are still bottles of the original straight vintage to be found. The wine is so concentrated that it is more interesting than agreeable.

A bottle of the 1840 bottling was opened at Reid's Hotel at a dinner given by the British community to Sir Winston Churchill on the occasion of his visit in 1950. Sir Winston insisted on serving each guest in turn himself, asking: "Do you realize that when this wine was vintaged Marie Antoinette was alive?"

Winston Churchill painting in Câmara de Lobos during his 1950 visit to Madeira.

Waterloo Madeira

The 1815 vintage has been immortalised by the famous battle of that year, but in fact it was not one of the best vintages. This is not to say that examples of the straight vintage 1815 to be found today are not very fine. I have recently been able to compare a specimen of Cossart's Bual vintage 1815 with Berry Bros' 1816 (as supplied to the royal cellars in 1907) and Bual 1820. I found the latter two wines noble and full of vigour, whereas the former is a very fine wine but lacks vigour. Eighteen-twenty-two was a far superior vintage to any of the above-mentioned. The wine was very sound from birth and specimens to be found are splendid although without the romantic background. Bual and Verdelho are especially good as they have more body to live on. I have tasted a Sercial 1822 which had a lovely nose but was a bit thin on the palate; I have never heard of Malmsey 1822, although it must have been made in this good year. Possibly it was so good that it was all drunk, but this is unlikely, because our ancestors were very thrifty, insisting on continuity. If there had been an outstanding Malmsey in 1822 which was in danger of becoming extinct, it would have been made into a solera, but I have never heard of this either.

Torre Bella vintages

The Casa Torre Bella vineyards at Torre, Câmara de Lobos, have produced more fine vintages than any other on the island but the name will not be found on labels except perhaps on the bottles of Russell Manners Gordon, who became a member of that house by marriage. His very considerable collection was sold at Christie's on March 16th 1864. One of the bottles from this collection, a Cama de Lobos,[51] vintage 1789, made in the year of the French revolution,

TORRE BELLA

Madeira

The Torre Bella wines sold at Christie's in 1988 had this front label.

The Palacio de Torre Bella, on the rua dos Ferreiros in Funchal until demolished in the late 1930s or early 1940s.

was again sold at Christie's in London on September 29th 1977, this time for £175. This wine is known in the firm as "Old Gordon's Madeira." There is a very marked characteristic of all wines made by the Torre Bella family which seems to have been prevalent during four generations. The wines, which are mostly from the Câmara de Lobos and Arco da Calheta vineyards, are full, rich, well-balanced wines with a very attractive acid finish. The vineyards are still producing fine modern vintages. Two of the best are Casa Torre Bella Bual 1930 and Sercial 1934 both made by the family and labelled with their coronet-mounted label. A bottle of each was given to me by "Old Gordon's" great-grand-daughters, the 1930 by Mrs. Ann Ogilvy Farlie, who now lives in Scotland (it was first served on her 21st birthday at which I was present), and the 1934 by Mrs. Susan Gale Seldon, who lives in London. The wines had been laid down at birth for Ann and Susan by their father, my old friend and companion, Dermot Bolger.

Henriques Verdelho 1858

Another particularly fine vineyard is that of Ribeiro Real which lies in the valley dividing Estreito de Cama de Lobos from Campanario and belongs to Henriques & Henriques. In the 1970s they shipped some of their Ribeiro Real, Verdelho vintage 1858, to New York. The bottles were sold with the words Henriques & Henriques embossed in the glass on the shoulder and the labels were all numbered and signed by one of the firm's partners.

Vintage and solera Madeiras in the Madeira Wine Company's Frasqueira. Note the bottles are upright.

My friend Dr. Louis C. Skinner Jr., who lives in Florida, acquired a quantity of this wine and was puzzled to find that the main label covered a little old label with the initials V. L. and the dates of rebottling or recorking. I was able to inform him that they were the initials of Virginia Lomelino, Mr. Henriques's mother, from whom he had inherited the *lote* in wood.

Blandy's Bual 1869

Also in the 1970s Blandy's were able to offer through their American agents, Foreign Brands Inc, Bual vintage 1869, a most beautiful Madeira. Each label was signed by a director, testifying the authenticity of the date. This vintage came from the properties

MADEIRA THE ISLAND VINEYARD

at São Martinho of Sr. João Pereira de Oliveira, a great landowner in that district well-known for the skilful manner in which he treated and matured his wine. From the same stable at that time Cossart, Gordon offered Buals vintage 1870 and 1882, Sercial 1884, Malmsey 1885 and an exquisite Verdelho 1900 bottled in 1957.

The Bianchi family wines

Apart from the above-mentioned from São Martinho there is a Bual 1869, older in bottle and bearing the initials E. B. H., some of which appeared for sale at Christie's in 1976. At a famous tasting of Madeiras held at Avery's cellars in June 1960, this Madeira, then

MADEIRA AND VINTAGE MADEIRA

Whether old vintage Madeiras or younger blends, Madeiras are never completely dry, nor are they absolutely sweet. They have an unusual dry-sweet finish. This makes Madeiras ideal companions when served with soups, at the end of a meal, or any time during the day with biscuits.

Here are some excellent examples of superb blends of old and younger Madeiras:

	Bottles	Case
SERCIAL, Avery - The driest	$4.20	$45.36
RAINWATER SACK, Avery - Medium	4.20	45.36
VERDELHO, Avery - somewhat sweeter, but still on the dry side.	4.20	45.36
FINEST BUAL, Avery,-Fairly full, dark-colored, very rich dessert wine.	4.20	45.36
BRISTOL PARTICULAR, Avery,-A fine reserve of a Sercial with considerable age. Fairly dark in color and, although not as dry as a dry Sherry, it is quite crisp and reasonably light. Very rare flavors and there is no cloying sweetness.	5.39	58.21
DUKE OF MALMSEY, Avery,- A noble wine with a very full color but not too heavy in body. Attractive old Madeira bouquet and reasonably rich.	4.59	49.57
CAMA DE LOBOS, Solera 1864, Avery,-Deep, rich golden color. Dry and crisp for Madeira. Very attractive.	5.39	58.21

Pure vintage Madeiras live forever. They are magnificent but so scarce that soon they will be memories except for a few bottles in private cellars. Of the wines listed below, only very small quantities are available. Some of them might already be sold out by the time this price list comes off the press.

```
    1862 MALMSEY
    1846 CAMPANARIO
    1868 MALMSEY
    1863 BUAL-VERDELHO       $19.00 per bottle
  x 1868 BUAL                205.20 per case
  x 1893 VERDELHO LU.        (assortments permitted)
    1885 SERCIAL
    1893 MALMSEY
    1892 SERCIAL
    1902 VERDELHO
```

(x) Only one bottle per customer of these two wines.

Avery's Madeiras featured in the 1968 catalogue of Esquin & Co., San Francisco.

offered by Avery's at 70s a bottle, received the highest accolade, surpassed only by Terrantez 1862. This E. B. H. Bual, together with Tinta Bianchi 1865, were from Carlo de Bianchi's vineyards at Câmara de Lobos and were inherited by his grand-daughter, Dona Eugenia Bianchi Henriques, *née* Bianchi, whose initials appear on the bottles.

Lomelino Bual 1874

In the same Christie sale a bottle of T. T. da Câmara Lomelino Bual 1874 from the same vineyard, but which had come from the Blandy cellars, was sold for £82. This Bual was vintaged during the phylloxera and rebottled in 1900 by Lomelino. It was recorked in 1975 in the Blandy cellars. The bottle sold in 1976 was uncapsuled and the label merely stated "T. T. da Câmara Lomelino, C. de B. Bual 1874." The initials of course stood for Carlo de Bianchi. It was one of the old man's favourite wines, which he drank in the morning *para matar o bicho*, to kill the serpent which tore at his entrails. This was one of his terms which disgusted me as a child, so great-grandfather Bianchi was always known to have a frog in his tummy.

Family connections

In 1957 I was requested by Ronald Avery and his associate, Mr. Gunyon, to collect historical data about his old Madeiras. It was during this research that I realised how intermarried the Madeira families were, and how their vintages had interchanged. Christie's sale in 1977 included some bottles of Sercial 1864, from the same collection as the Bastardo 1870. These had been bought by Sir Stephen Gaselee from Dona Eugenia Bianchi Henriques, who had inherited them from her grandfather, Barone Carlo de Bianchi. In 1960, Avery's had some Sercial 1860 from the same vineyard, but which they had bought from T. T. da Câmara Lomelino. It was put into demijohns in 1939 and bottled by Lomelino in 1957. Ronald called this "Sercial Frasqueira Particular Avery"[52] and listed it at 50s per bottle.

Carlo de Bianchi was married to Dona Anna Leal and was senior partner in Tarquinio Torquato da Câmara Lomelino, founded by his father-in-law, Robert Leal, in 1820. His son, my maternal grandfather Ferdinando Bianchi, married Dona Maria Anna Lomelino. Their two sons Gabriel and Antonio carried on the firm and were succeeded by Antonio's son Ferdinando, who became managing director of the Madeira Wine Association. Dona Eugenia

Bianchi also had a famous Sercial from the Bianchi vineyards vintaged in 1864 and marketed by Cossart, Gordon.

There is another branch of the Bianchi family, descended from Giovanni de Bianchi, which own vineyards at Porto Moniz. Giovanni's son became Visconde Val Pariso, and produced noted vintages, namely Reserva Velha Visconde Val Pariso Bual 1844 and Reserva Velhissima Verdelho 1846, both magnificent wines. I bought them in cask from the viscount's son, Dr. John Bianchi, my cousin, when he was Portuguese ambassador in Washington, and bottled them in 1936.

Terrantez vintages

The variety is certainly an old one in the island. As early as 1720 an English traveller, Mr. Atkins, who called at Funchal managed to obtain two pipes of Terrantez in exchange for two used suits of clothes and three second-hand wigs. Articles of clothing were certainly in great demand in those times, but one wonders whether Mr. Atkins got confused and exchanged his clothes for two gallons and not two pipes.

Unfortunately, the *terrantez* vines are unprolific and prone to disease, so they were not regrafted after phylloxera. The wines have therefore always been rare and considered a great delicacy. Terrantez wine is an individual taste: the Romans called this sort of wine *dolce-piccante*, sweet and bitter. It is, in fact, fruity, rich, very

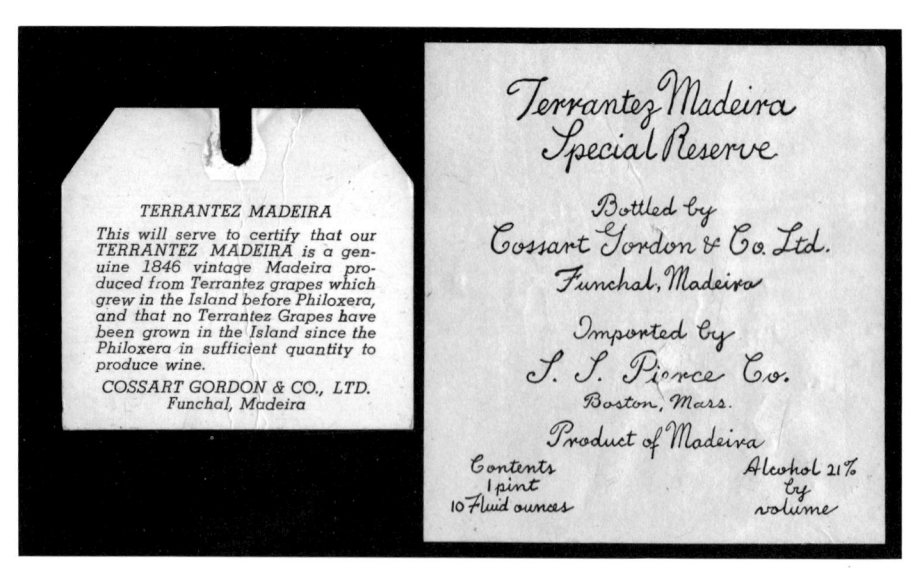

Label and neck tag for Cossart Gordon's 1846 Terrantez sold by S.S. Pierce, Boston, in the 1950s or 1960s.

VINTAGE MADEIRAS

fragrant and elegant, with a dry, almost bitter aftertaste; its great charm is in its sparkling freshness.

The oldest Terrantez I have tasted is the 1789 vintage which I offered at the "Academy of Ancient Madeira Wines" in London on May 5th and 6th 1959 (see Chapter 15). This magnificent wine, from the Torre Bella vineyards, had been kept in its original pipes for 133 years until it was bottled in Madeira in 1928, and recorked for the voyage to London in 1959. Fortunately, it had not been sent to London before the war, as intended, or we would have lost it in the blitz in 1941. This Terrantez is a splendid example of its kind.

I also know the 1842, another fine vintage, of which some, old in bottle, was auctioned at Sotheby's in June 1982. One of the finest specimens of Terrantez, however, is the 1846 vintage, bottled in 1906, which was also shown at the "Academy" in 1959. Three bottles of this were sold at Christie's in 1977. They had passed from Harry Hinton, the great sugar magnate, to the Bishop of Gibraltar, whose diocese included Madeira. There is also a fine Terrantez of the 1870 vintage.

My favourite, and which in my opinion surpasses all others, is the Terrantez 1862, which was also shown in 1959. I have tasted this vintage from various sources, but that shown at the "Academy" came from the vineyards of Dr. João Alexandrino dos Santos, who was connected with the Bianchi family. It was aged in wood until 1905 when it was placed in glass demijohns, and bottled in 1936, the year we acquired it. I ceded a quantity to my friend, the late Ronald Avery, in 1960, which he then listed at 70s a bottle. Four bottles of this fine Terrantez from the Avery lot fetched from £52 to £62 each at Christie's in 1977, which in my opinion is surprisingly low considering that in the same auction, the 1846, which I think is less good, reached £80 per bottle. A bottle of H. M. Borges Terrantez was sold more recently at Christie's for £94. Regrettably, this lovely Terrantez is now becoming rare.

In a sale at Sotheby's in June 1982 there was some 1895 Terrantez, old in bottle. This is a post-phylloxera vintage which I do not know but, since the vine was scarce before phylloxera and was not replanted afterwards, I feel it must be a mixture. We showed a similar Madeira labelled Terrantez 1898 at an Evans, Marshall tasting.[53] I had bought the wine as such from a reliable grower and we bottled it in 1952. At the tasting we explained that because of the scarcity of Terrantez in the 1890s, this wine either must have been a good deal older than the date it bore or possibly had been blended with some 1898 vintage Verdelho. Unfortunately, we had insufficient records to verify this, and invited comments. The wine attracted more discussion than many other finer Madeiras. André Simon pronounced it to be "a noble winsome bastard." Mr. F. G. Cox, for many years wine buyer of Harvey's, described it has having "Good nose, full in colour, body and fruit, dry soft end." My own notes said "Prominent fine nose, rich and fruity, lacks typical bitter finish." It was a particularly fine old Madeira but the end was too soft for Terrantez. In fact, had it been labelled Verdelho the description would have fitted perfectly.

Avery's 1898

Avery's showed Terrantez 1898 at their tasting on June 21st 1960, where it had a good reception. It was priced then at 52s 6d per bottle, whereas Malvasia 1880 (Frasqueira Particular Avery), which I consider a far superior Madeira, was priced at 55s per bottle.

Bastardo Vintages

The use of the diminutive in colloquial Portuguese implies endearment and there were those old fashioned enough to consider that *bastardinho*, the dimunitive of *bastardo*, was more genteel. Personally I fail to see that a little bastard is more lovable than a big one, both being love children. However, one does find wine from the *bastardo* grape labelled Bastardinho.

The *bastardo* vines, like *terrantez*, are shy bearers and vulnerable to pests, so were allowed to languish after the phylloxera. They are also being replanted but production on the island is only eight to ten pipes per annum. Even before 1872 production was so small that there was insufficient to press separately and *bastardo* was pressed with other grapes and marketed under the names of districts such as Câmara de Lobos. Straight vintages of this lovely Madeira are therefore rarely found.

The wine seems to have been known in England in Shakespeare's day and referred to as "Bastard." The wine is dark, rich and heavy, with a fruity freshness. Vizetelly says it combines richness with a peculiar freshness of flavour, and he describes a Bastardo of 15 to 20 years of age as "powerful yet refined in flavour."

Cossart, Gordon's Solera 1844 was based on that great Bastardo vintage, and there are some lovely pre-phylloxera straight vintages to be found today, in spite of their rarity. Some bottles of 1870 fetched £75 each at Christie's auction of Finest and Rarest Wines on September 29th 1977. These bottles had an interesting history. They originated from the cellars of Padre Henriques, vicar of Estreito de Câmara de Lobos. As already mentioned, the Henriques family owned extensive vineyards in the parish, and the vicar had amassed a great collection of old wine from his properties, enriched by gifts from his flock. He sold a considerable quantity of Bastardo 1870 to Sir Stephen Gaselee and, when Gaselee died in 1943, Ronald Avery acquired the Bastardo with other wines of the collection. It was from Avery's that the vendor, an "American connoisseur" had obtained the wine sold at Christie's.

Until recently, Cossart, Gordon offered two vintage Bastardos of the years 1875 and 1876, two of the worst years of the phylloxera. It is curious, considering the shortage of the variety and the years, that the original Cossart *lotes* amounted to 10 and 12 pipes respectively, very large quantities for such a rare Madeira. The grapes came from and were pressed at Quinta do Salão, the Doria family vineyards at Câmara de Lobos. Some of the 1876 was bottled in the *quinta* only two years after it was vintaged, and the rest was put into 20-litre demijohns in 1926 by my grandfather and bottled by myself in Madeira in 1950. Only 106 dozen of the original 990 dozen remained when it came to the London house in 1953. There is none left now, except for private stocks. When I retired I enjoyed some of the 1876 exactly 100 years after it was vintaged, wonderfully robust, powerful wine, with great character and fragrance. There was no comparison with the *quinta* bottling; the later bottling was far superior and more mature.

Cossart and Blandy vintages

When I first joined Cossart, Gordon & Co., I was engaged in the cooperage, so I was not supposed to take an interest in wine. Coopers have the reputation of being heavy drinkers, and are only allowed into the wine store under supervision in order to repair leaking casks. In any case I was much too busy in the cooperage, so it was only two years later, in 1928, that I started to take an interest in wine.

At that time the Cossart vintages were Sercial 1842, Verdelho 1850 and 1858, Bual 1851, Malmsey 1862 and 1880, and Câmara de Lobos 1867. Blandy's had declared Sercial 1864, 1885, 1898; Verdelho 1893, 1898; Bual 1869, 1870, 1882, 1891; Malmsey 1880 and 1885. For many years, Blandy's had specialised in the bottled trade whereas Cossarts had chosen to deal almost exclusively in bulk. Our Madeira house was purely a depot, all wine being shipped to London in wood where it was bottled for worldwide distribution. When I retired and left Madeira fifty years later the Cossart vintages were Sercial 1892, 1910, 1915, 1940; Verdelho 1875, 1900, 1902, 1907, 1934; Bual 1895, 1915, 1920, 1934; Malmsey 1880, 1893, 1916, 1920, 1954. Blandy's were Sercial 1885; Verdelho 1900, 1917; Bual 1907, 1911; Malmsey 1880, 1901; Campanario 1846; São Martinho 1897. At the time of writing, Cossart, Gordon offer vintages Sercial 1910, 1940; Verdelho 1934; Bual 1895, 1915, 1920, 1934; Malmsey 1916, 1954.

CHAPTER 12

SOLERAS AND DATED SOLERAS

It is not correct to say that Madeira is matured by the solera system as Sherry is in Spain. Rather it is made and matured on the *lote* system as explained in Chapter 10, but there have, however, always been the so-called soleras such as Blandy's Gran Cama de Lobos and Cossart's Crown Madeira, bottled from *lotes* of old wine which are kept in special casks and replenished with a suitable blend from time to time. Special growths are also matured on the solera system, the "Fine" qualities passing on to the "Finest" and then on to the "Crown" qualities. See specimen price list on page 145.

Dated soleras

What are generally referred to as Madeira soleras today are, in fact, the dated soleras which started after oidium in 1851 and more especially after phylloxera in 1872. Although at the time shippers found themselves with good stocks of very old vintage wine, they could not necessarily afford to reserve these valuable old *lotes* as vintage Madeiras. Some shippers were short of younger wines and were consequently forced to blend their old wines into their medium *lotes* to enable shipping to continue. Others who did have sufficient stocks were able to put aside their old wines to keep as straight vintages, turning the rest into soleras. It is accordingly due to the latter that today we are able to enjoy these selected magnificent pre-oidium and phylloxera vintages in solera form.

This is how dated soleras work. The date indicates the year in which the original wine was actually vintaged. This is called the *vinho madre* or *matriz* (mother wine). When the decision is made to turn a vintage wine into a solera, as it becomes ullaged, the *matriz* is topped up from a back-up *lote* of old wine of the same style, and in turn the back-up is replenished with a blend to suit the style. Usually the solera is topped up either when ten per cent down or annually, whichever occurs first, but the figure varies from ten per cent to 25 per cent. As an example, the Malmsey vintaged in 1808 was a vintage until 1873, when it was founded as a solera and has been topped up ever since. The soleras are kept in the same casks that held the vintages to assure maintenance of character and style.

Origin of name

Solera is a system rather than a type of wine. The word is both Spanish and old Portuguese, written *soleira* in the latter, but corrupted by the British wine trade to the Spanish way of writing. Both words are pronounced in the same way. It is sometimes thought to have been derived from the word *sol* meaning sun, but the fact is it is derived from the Latin *solum* the sole (of the foot). The casks are arranged in tiers with the wine ready for shipment in the bottom tier and the back-up wine above. The *solera* is drawn from the casks nearest the ground. *Soleira* stems from *solo*, the Portugese word for ground, and it also means lintel of a door, or threshold, implying something fundamental and basic, that is that the casks never pass the threshold after they have originally been stored. There have been protests from Spain regarding the use of solera in connection with Madeira, but these were dropped on the grounds of usage.

Correcting soleras

The beauty of these magnificent old wines is that one can correct any faults they may develop whilst maintaining their standard type and character. I had experience of this directly after the last war. Due to very little movement our soleras had improved enormously, but had become heavy and atrophied, especially the Buals. I decided they needed new blood. I may say that it took a lot of courage to perform what seemed sacrilege. However, after tasting I added to the 1868, which at the time averaged some 60 years, ten per cent of ten-year-old wine. After a *passagem*, which is not usual with soleras, it opened out and was splendid, so, after this, all Cossart's soleras were treated in the same manner.

Blandy's Solera 1792

The most famous of all soleras is probably the Blandy 1792. In his book *Facts about Port and Madeira*, published in 1880, Henry Vizetelly describes visiting Blandy's wine stores, where 5,000 pipes of old wine had been accumulated by Charles Blandy after oidium.

SOLERAS AND DATED SOLERAS

Vizetelly describes Blandy's wine stores as being a veritable vinous museum. He says he tasted a solera founded in 1792. This is not strictly correct. The wine was vintaged in 1792 and bought by Charles Blandy in 1822, who turned part of the *lote* into a solera after oidium in 1853. This was one of the few early soleras and is one of the finest ever founded. It was based on the fine Cama de Lobos vintage 1792, which was connected with Napoleon and has already been described. During the state visit of Her Majesty Queen Elizabeth II and the Duke of Edinburgh to Portugal in 1957 the remainder of this rarity was drawn from the casks and bottled. Some of the wine was presented by the Madeira shippers to Her Majesty.

The wine list of the Blackstone Hotel, Chicago, dated January 20th 1913 offered "Crown Royal Solera 1792 the Oldest Wine in Madeira" at $10 per bottle. The same list describes "Grand Old Solera 1830" and Cossart's "Solera 1815" as "Extra Choice" and "Big Generous Wine," respectively.

A Suffolk wine merchant who specialises in old and curious wines told me recently that he had obtained a considerable amount of 1792 rare old solera from a farmer who had inherited it and had been drinking it with soda water.

A typical Solera store.

The Cossart soleras

I do not know how long other shippers kept up their soleras on the original system. Both Blandy and Leacock have fine soleras and Krohn Brothers were renowned for theirs. Cossart, Gordon's were started by my great-grandfather Peter and grandfather Charles. They were kept up by my father and myself, and attending to our old pre-phylloxera soleras became a family ritual.

They were all kept in their original scantling pipes in a separate store at our Serrado property, and maintained strictly on the old principle of being topped up annually or when ten per cent ullaged. Malmsey Solera 1808, the original *madre* of which had come from the Jesuit vineyard at Fajã dos Padres, was from grapes of the *Malvasia Candida* variety. It became a solera in 1873 and was discontinued in 1955 because we could not find suitable Malmsey to top it up. Bual Solera 1815 was our Waterloo Madeira, and rather a tricky wine because the original Bual had not been really robust enough; however, we nursed it along and the stocks available today are very fine. Bual Solera 1822 was the best, having originated from a solid Bual from Campanario; it became a solera after the phylloxera. Verdelho Solera 1836 became a solera after the oidium and was a fine old wine, light and elegant. Bual Solera 1845 was our centenary wine and became a solera in 1875. It is the basis of

A Cossart, Gordon Solera shipped across the Equator twice before being bottled in 1940.

our Duo-centenary Bual and was splendid from the day it was vintaged. Our two youngest soleras were Cama de Lobos 1862 and 1868, real robust full Madeiras, founded in 1874.

There was one other solera, which was given up around 1949. It was curious because, although it was described as Cama de Lobos Solera 1844, the *madre* was a Bastardo vintaged at Câmara de Lobos in 1844 and to my knowledge is the only solera which had this variety as a base. Bastardo is a rich luscious wine with a charming but distinctly bitter aftertaste like Terrantez and, to a lesser extent, Verdelho. These *dolce-piccante* wines are very difficult to achieve by blending. As supplies of Bastardo became increasingly hard to obtain for topping up, the solera was replenished with other wines such as Bual and Verdelho until it lost its character and was terminated. There are some bottles of this lovely Madeira still about.

The age of the Cossart soleras in 1953 ranged from the youngest at 50 years old to the oldest at 80 years. I was able to obtain these figures by setting a rather chatty young accountant the task, which kept him quiet and produced some useful information. Being a blender I had no sympathy with accountants, especially cost accountants who pulled my artistic work to pieces for practical purposes. When I was young I was irascible: I once accused an accountant and a solicitor who were on our board of being "parasites." I have heard no more from the solicitor, but from the accountant I received Christmas cards from "your parasite."

When Cossart, Gordon joined the Madeira Wine Association in 1953 our soleras in wood were moved to their stores at Rua São Francisco, and the bottled stock was shipped to London. The wines in wood were no longer topped up, but shipped whilst stocks lasted. The reason for this may seem sacrilege, but will be appreciated when it is known that the Association had, at the time, 14 member firms as well as over 80 brands (of firms which had gone out of business). Each of these had from 100 to 150 labels, including 10 to 15 soleras each, so the Association's soleras had to be streamlined. Cossart's in London have only limited stocks of soleras – 1808, 1815, 1822 and 1845.

Soleras in the United Kingdom

I would say that there are more old soleras in bottle in London and Bristol, and in Oxford and Cambridge colleges, than there are in the island. Many merchants are still able to offer fine old soleras, among them Avery's of Bristol and Berry Bros. of St James's.

However, because of the running down of these lovely wines, as well as inflation, prices have risen astronomically. For example, in 1982 Berry Bros. offered Verdelho Solera 1851, bottled by themselves in 1973, at £20.70 per bottle, whereas in their 1971 list the same solera bottled in 1969 was being offered at £2.25 per bottle. In 1970 this company also offered our famous Bual Solera 1845, bottled in 1969, at 45s per bottle. Waterloo Solera 1815, bottled in 1964, was offered at 50s per bottle, whereas in 1957 this same solera, bottled in 1951, cost 40s per bottle. The great Malmsey Solera 1808, bottled in 1959, was offered at 40s per bottle in 1963, and Verdelho Solera 1862 was only 28s per bottle in 1954.

Today more than ever, London salerooms are the great outlet for old Madeira soleras. As prices go up, so are more of the remaining old bottles tempted out of cellars and on to the market.

Madeira's dated soleras are an endangered species and will soon become a thing of the past, leaving an even greater gap between straight vintages and ordinary Madeiras. The cause of this lamentable situation was the great demand immediately after the war and in the 1950s when British and American importers bought heavily. Shippers in Madeira could not obtain enough old wine with which to replenish their soleras, and consequently they were run down. Cossart, Gordon shipped as much stock to London and Boston as was practicable without completely eliminating their soleras. Then, in 1956, when Evans Marshall & Co. became Cossart's agents in London, John Baker, the managing director, brought over a great deal more, the origin of our present stock.

Disreputable soleras

Before the war, when Funchal was a busy port, dated soleras had fallen into disrepute as a result of bottles being sold on liners and cruise ships by bum-boatmen, together with bananas, embroidery, canaries and wicker work. This business was out of the jurisdiction of the Junta Nacional do Vinho. The bottles bore fantastic dates, but the wine inside was made in backyards only a year before it was sold. One would have thought that buying old wine from bum-boats was asking for trouble, but passengers frequently succumbed and were sadly disappointed when they opened their bottles. At that time all liners from Europe to South Africa and South America called at Funchal, as well as many cruise vessels. An average of eight ships per day throughout the year called at the port of Funchal, so the adverse publicity was enormous. In spite of this, *bona fide* London and American merchants bought heavily.

London bottlings

I have previously mentioned the superiority of London bottling, with which my friends in the island will not agree. Madeira is very insular, and its residents cannot imagine anything away from it being better. Most soleras had an advantage over vintages in that they were London-bottled. Most of ours were bottled by Evans, Marshall's cellarmaster, the late Harry Long, whom I consider to be the greatest specialist since "Jack," our cellarmaster at 75 Mark Lane before the war. If I ever knew his surname I have forgotten it, he was always "Jack" as Harry was "Harry." It may be thought that bottling consists of filling a bottle, driving in the cork and labelling, but there is more to it than that. Harry's bottlings of old Madeira were outstanding; his secret was in the landing age and fining he gave to his pipes. Except for the war years Harry had spent his life in cellars. He came to Evans, Marshall from Berry Bros., whom he joined in 1946 and where he had bottled many fine Madeiras. His work with Berry Bros. entailed visiting private cellars of the nobility all over the country, where he learned much about old port and Madeira. He fined and bottled the pipe of port

Noël Cossart's father and grandfather, Charles John Cossart and Charles Blandy Cossart, descending on a sledge from the Mount by Vizetelly.

presented by the port shippers to Her Majesty the Queen and Prince Philip when they were married, and supervised its cellaring at Clarence House. When Evans, Marshall joined the Bass Charrington group he became Hedges & Butler's cellarmaster and dealt with both Blandy's and Cossart, Gordon's Madeiras. Later he ably performed the duties of majordomo at Hedges & Butler's well-known functions and receptions.

Recent legislation

The new legislation set out by the Instituto do Vinho da Madeira in 1979, brought about by Portugal's imminent entry into the EEC, has done nothing towards reviving pre-phylloxera soleras; in fact, on the contrary, it hinders their maintenance by, I may say, ridiculous legislation, in that documentary proof of the *matriz* and foundation dates are required. Even if this is available, the soleras can no longer be topped up. The regulations allow new soleras to be started, but in view of the improvement in viticulture and the return of the noble varieties in quantity, shippers would prefer to market vintages rather than found soleras. I feel that if only the new generation of shippers, and legislators, had appreciated the history of dated soleras, and understood that their *raison d'être* was to preserve the character and style of the great pre-phylloxera vintages, these magnificent wines would not have become mere legends.

CHAPTER 13

WILLIAM NEYLE HABERSHAM

William Neyle Habersham, born in 1817, was a great connoisseur, an expert on wine in general and on Madeira in particular. His family had been conspicuous in Savannah from the earliest colonial days. He was the grandson of Colonel Joseph Habersham, the first postmaster-general of the United States. After graduating from Harvard in 1836, William Neyle entered his father's firm, Robert Habersham & Co., founded in 1744. This house owned a fleet of vessels and continued a successful business for nearly 150 years, sending its ships with Georgia pine and rice to European ports, to return with Spanish and Madeira wines in ballast. William Neyle built up an almost priceless collection of Madeira, based on stocks inherited from several generations of his family.

A great palate

There is no doubt that William Neyle Habersham had one of the greatest palates of his day or perhaps of all times. Ward McAllister, also a Savannahian, describes in his book, *Society as I Have Found It* (New York 1890), how the expert, on tasting a mixture his host had thrown together, said, "if he could believe his host capable of mixing a wine he would say it was half Catherine Banks and half Rapid" (the names of the two ships which had brought the Madeiras) – which it was. Mr. George DeRenne, a Madeira expert himself and whose collection has already been mentioned, noted in his diary how he had tested Habersham's ability to taste wines at his Wormsloe plantation. Custom forbade table cloths when Madeira was served and on the polished boards of his table Mr. DeRenne had arranged nine unlabelled decanters. Habersham tasted and called the names of each: Trinity Sherry, Hurricane Madeira, Painted Pipe Madeira, Chillingsworth Madeira, Leacock Sercial, Margade Madeira. He hesitated at the next saying "I can identify this wine, except that I know DeRenne had none," and went on to name the remaining wines. When he returned to the decanter which had puzzled him he said: "This wine is Molyneux Sherry and it has been away from Savannah for some years, and only recently returned." He was absolutely correct. The wine had been brought to Wormsloe that day by General A. R. Lawton, who was present at the gathering.

Considering the accuracy and fine tuning of William Neyle Habersham's palate, it is not surprising that he could work wonders on the wines he imported, which were often exposed to rough handling during long sea voyages and to adulteration by the crews. There is no doubt that he liked the Rainwater-type Madeiras and perfected them but, as mentioned in Chapter 10, he did not invent them; in fact he may not have even known of the name. So Habersham's Rainwater may have referred to an exceptionally bright light type, as suggested by the late F. Gray Griswold in his book, *Madeira*, published in 1929. He says the "so called Habersham Rainwater wines had been treated in an artificial manner by a secret method by which the wines not only became lighter in colour, but also in body yet preserving their full flavour and bouquet." He adds, "some judges preferred them to all other wines but this, I believe, was not universal and they were considered an acquired taste."

At first William Neyle kept his wines in the business establishment on the bay, but later they were moved to the Habersham mansion, now pulled down, on the corner of Harris and Barnard Streets in Savannah. There he had built himself a solarium over the ballroom, referred to in his journal as the cupola. It was so private that it was only accessible from his dressing room. Here he treated the Madeiras he imported, making them "lighter and brighter" than other Madeiras. The Atlanta *Constitution*, describing this solarium, wrote: "There are casks and kegs and carboys and flasks and bottles of wine of almost priceless kinds. The entire store will aggregate possibly 3,000 quarts and contains old Madeiras and Sherries that for half a century have been the delight of epicures in every part of the country." It was in fact quite normal in the south to keep Madeira in attics rather than in cellars, just as it is in Funchal, which is precisely on the same latitude as Savannah and where all the wine is stored above ground.

William Neyle Habersham's house, now demolished, stood at the northwest corner of Harris and Barnard Streets in Savannah, Georgia.

Habersham's estufa

The Atlanta *Constitution* goes on to describe Habersham's solarium: "The rooms are constructed as for a conservatory, and in the early days of the old mansion it is possible that they served this purpose. There is no floor division between them other than an open framework, across which boards are lain and through which the sunlight filters freely. On every side and on the roof is glass, admitting the rays of the sun without hindrance. Mr. Habersham was accustomed to transfer his rare vintages from one part of the two rooms to another, to the end that they might imbibe from the sunlight some of its warmth and strength. His wines were the pride of his life, and he could not gain his own consent to immure them in the darkness of some underground cellar. He liked to spend his time in their company, inhaling their delicate aroma and gloating over the matchless colour." In other words William Neyle Habersham had built himself an *estufa do sol*, where he gave his Madeira a secondary *estufagem* by means of the sun's rays. This process would certainly have improved his Madeiras by ageing, but it would not have made them pale, light and elegant. On the contrary, it would have concentrated and, if anything, darkened them. Therefore, he had some process of his own of making his Madeiras light and pale yet retaining their full flavour.

Habersham's secret

We know that heat and light played a great part in treating the Habersham wines. His grand-daughters remembered the demijohns stored in the solarium, which were moved and turned frequently to get more sunlight. It is said that he sent a hogshead for a long voyage on the footplate of a railway engine but, unfortunately, for he kept no notes, or if he did they are not available, we do not know the results.

Today there are many clarifying and stabilising agents, but in Habersham's day the usual method of fining was either fish gelatine (isinglass), egg white, veal or ox blood. The following recipe used on September 28th 1787 is typical of the time:

To Fine a Pipe of Madeira with Kid's Blood

Successful recipe for fining Captain Battrap's Pipe of pleasant light wine, pale as Sherry, already drawn off fine and bottled for London.

Draw from the pipe two gallons of wine in a quartz in which desolve some pieces of ising paper. Take a pint and a half of the kid's blood and as it runs hot from the animal into a large pan pour in the other quantity of wine at the same time keep stirring with a whisk. Then add the quantity the ising paper was desolved in and let them be well incorporated together with the whisk before it is poured into the pipe. When done, let the whole remain mixed for 15 to 20 minutes, mixing well by a stick put in at the bung hole.

In 1836, the ship Waccamaw carried more than 90 casks of Newton, Gordon, Murdoch & Co. Madeira to Charleston and Savannah. This shipping manifest lists the barrel sizes and customer initials branded into the barrel heads. A bottle of Waccamaw Madeira appears in Habersham's notebook in 1883, having been traded for a bottle of his "Hurricane."

It is my theory that Habersham used Louisiana clay to make his wine *lighter* and *brighter*. Louisiana clay, known on this side of the Atlantic as Spanish earth, was the forerunner of kaolin and bentonite. The later miraculous montmorillonite clay, as its prospectus states, is "capable of absorbing ten times its weight of water forming a gelatinous paste causing a coagulation of the proteins, which increase proportionately as the acidity is greater and the tannin content smaller." Louisiana clay would have been available to Habersham and, although crude in comparison with bentonite, would have produced the effect that so puzzled his friends. It is possible that he also used some form of activated vegetable carbon, followed by filtration, to mature and decolourise raw young Madeira imported in bulk on his ships.

Civil War

Malcolm Bell Jr. has written to me as follows:

> "The Civil War shattered the good life of William Neyle Habersham. Two soldier sons were killed on the same day at the Battle of Atlanta and the aftermath of the conflict wrecked the family business that had thrived on Savannah's Bay since Colonial times. A Harvard graduate, talented musician, skilled fisherman and connoisseur of fine wines, Neyle Habersham put his knowledge to good use and by selling rare Madeiras and Sherries to a distinguished clientele was able to eke out a living for his family. A record of Mr. Habersham's transactions in these very special wines in the library of the Georgia Historical Society records many sales of wines with interesting, romantic names to Ward McAllister and to his fashionable 'Four Hundred' in New York and Newport. Generous, perhaps to a fault, the record also shows many gifts to friends, to churches, and to the sick of Savannah, as well as purchases by men whose names were well known in Savannah in the period 1860-1890. The Madeiras listed were frequently named for the ships on which they were transported. The wines also assumed the names of families, or clubs, or of particular events, and sometimes the names were as transitory as that of a wealthy young widow. The most famous of the Habersham Madeiras, 'All Saints,' was named for a quoit club

in Savannah. The name 'Rainwater,' so closely associated with Mr. Habersham, does not appear in the records.

"Ship names given to his Madeiras were *Oglethorpe*, for a famous Habersham ship; *Richmond Packet, Success, Tartar, Charming Martha, Charming Nancy* and *Charming Polly*. Family names honoured by his Madeiras were 'Gibbons,' 'DeRenne,' 'Telfair,' 'Molyneux,' 'Lawton' and of course 'Habersham's.' 'General Lee's Sercial' was used for communion at Christ Church, a gift from Mr. Habersham. Other wines frequently mentioned were *Hurricane, Earthquake, JV, Margade, Widow 1859*, and many named for their Madeira shippers. Those who bought and sold in Savannah were those for whom the wines were named, and others including J. R. Saussy, W. D. Simkins, J. R. Anderson and General G. Moxley Sorrel.

"Ward McAllister led the list of out-of-towners, but Cornelius Vanderbilt, W. R. Travers, August Belmont, C. H. Arnold, J. A. Burden, Eldridge Gerry, G. B. DeForest, and the Waterburys, Schermerhorns, Fearings, Ostranders, Baruchs, Lorillards were frequently there. Mr. Habersham gave Chauncey DePew a dozen bottles. General 'Fighting Joe' Johnston, Elsie Huger (for her wedding), Mamie Dent, and Eliza, a sick sewing woman, were given wines as were many of his faithful customers.

"Death on 20th September, 1899 brought forth column after column of tribute in the Savannah newspapers, yet William Neyle Habersham's great knowledge and interesting traffic in fine wines was not mentioned."

Sale of Habersham's wine

A list of the Madeiras which formed part of the estate of the late William Neyle Habersham and which were auctioned by Arnold & Co. of New York in 1900 by order of his grandson and executor Mr. G. Noble Jones, is given in Appendix 16. The Madeiras were sold in original demijohns holding five and three gallons each, and there is no mention of Rainwater, although practically all the wines would answer the description. The darkest is "amber," even Canteiro No. 1, which would normally be dark, having been matured in wood, is described as "pale," and the medium dark Donaldson Bual and Newton Gordon Malmsey are described as "amber" and "pale amber" respectively. I had the good fortune, through the kindness of Russell Codman, to see a specimen of the Malmsey. Compared with specimens of the same wine which we had in the island, Mr. Codman's sample was two shades paler, with wonderful nose and great delicacy.

Sercial and Rainwater

There is one curious item on the list of Madeiras belonging to the estate, which is identified as "Sweet, Pale Newton Gordon Sercial" and described as "very round and smooth, rich." There is no such thing as a sweet Sercial and Newton & Gordon would not have shipped such a Madeira. I can only presume this to be one of Habersham's Rain-water-type blends.

The margin between a Sercial and a dry Rainwater is narrow. The former is from a specific grape variety and the latter a blend. This is shown in the case of the Madeiras imported in the brig *Bramin*. Whereas Judge William Douglas, circa 1900, listed his *Bramin* wines as Rainwater, Mr. Charles Bellows, who owned a number of five gallon demijohns of Bramin Madeira, identifies his as "Sercial and a splendid specimen." Personally, I think it likely that the judgement of Mr. Bellows, a wine scholar, was correct. He had his own Rainwaters (rich and dry) and writes on the subject as follows: "I do not know what causes Madeira to be Rainwater if it has ever been scientifically explained, but it is a freak condition

Ward McAllister, who acted as Habersham's agent in selling to the New York social elite in the late nineteenth century.

of wine caused by lack of colour in the grape, sudden change of temperature, starvation in the lees or other natural causes, but it is of so rare occurrence that Rainwater is highly prized as a curiosity." Bellows & Co.'s Rainwater is exquisite to this day.

From Habersham's sales journal we can see how very meticulous he was over his transactions. He sold some Painted Pipe and Hurricane Madeiras to Cornelius Vanderbilt in March 1889 through Ward McAllister. When Vanderbilt asked for the history of these

Bill of lading for wine to Savannah per famous ship "Two Sisters" 1780.

wines, Habersham invited McAllister to cancel the sale as he could not give precise historical facts, writing that his wines had been buried in the war and after the war put into a damp cellar and the marks obliterated. McAllister, reporting this to Vanderbilt, wrote:

> "By the above you see the Old Man is too honest to say anything not squarely the truth. I have the Hurricane and the Painted Pipe myself. In naming these wines Habersham relied on his own taste (which I know never fails) and the history of these wines I have been familiar with for years. Painted Pipe was imported by Thomas Gibbons in 1791 from Newton, Gordon, Murdoch & Scott,* sold to him by Gibbons. Hurricane is a South Carolina wine imported by the ship of that name by the Blake family of South

Carolina, an old Welsh family, who planted rice on the Savannah River, an officer of the Guards of Her Majesty's Household Troop who came over to America."

CHAPTER 14

SOME GREAT COLLECTIONS

Dr. Michael Grabham

Apart from my grandfather and father, I learned about *old* Madeira from my great-uncle by marriage, Dr. Michael Grabham. He seemed to appreciate the interest I took in his very fine old wines, teaching me what to look for in old Madeira, and allowing me to taste from his priceless collection.

Dr. Grabham practised medicine in Madeira to the ripe old age of 98. He was the oldest member of the Royal College of Physicians and one-time organist at St Paul's Cathedral in London, as well as being, with his brother-in-law, Lord Kelvin, one of the first men to delve into electronics. He was a prolific writer on biology, botany and other scientific subjects, including Madeira's climate, plants and fish. When as a boy I asked him how he knew so much, his prompt reply was, "What I don't know I invent." He was a great lover of wine, of which he drank a considerable amount, and at the time he probably had the finest cellar on the island. His favourite tipple, however, was pink gin, and among the decanters of rare old Madeira on his sideboard, I can remember a silver label inscribed NIG.[54]

Michael Grabham

On January 2nd 1929, *Punch* wrote of Uncle Michael, when he was 89 years old:

> There was an old man in Madeira
> Whose stories got queera and queera
> The guests gathered round
> Said the *vinum* was sound
> But his *veritas* rather too *vera*.

1792 Napoleon

Michael Grabham was son-in-law to Charles Ridpath Blandy and acquired, through his wife, the remains of the 1792 Napoleon pipe,[55] which had been bottled by his brother-in-law, John Blandy, in 1840. On his 93rd birthday, the old doctor told André Simon: "This wine was made in the year my father was born, and was bottled by my brother-in-law in 1840 which happens to be the year I was born. I happened to marry Charles' daughter, that is how it came to me, and why I give it to you today." Dr. Grabham presented a dozen bottles of this wine to the Saintsbury Club in London.[56]

Challenger Madeira

Another treasure in the Grabham collection was Challenger Madeira. This wine from the São Martinho district was taken on board HMS *Challenger* on her long voyage of scientific exploration in the year of the phylloxera, 1872. The *Challenger* was a wooden corvette of 2,306 tons which had crossed the Atlantic several times. She sailed from Madeira to Cape Town, then to Kerguelen Island and Melbourne, thence via New Zealand to the Fiji Islands, Torres Strait, Banda Sea, China Sea to Hong Kong. She then explored the western Pacific to Yokohama, crossed the ocean by Honolulu and Tahiti to Valparaiso, passed through the Magellan Straits to Montevideo and home via Ascencion, the Azores and Madeira to Sheerness. When she touched at Funchal in 1876 on her way home she landed the remains of her stock of São Martinho, which was then bottled. The age of the wine when it left the island is not known, but when it returned it was truly a *vinho da roda*, having been submitted to intense heat and cold. I do not think there is any left, but when I had the good fortune to taste it, it was perfectly sound, delicious with almost overpowering fragrance.

The 1815 Canavial "Waterloo" Madeira

Dr. Grabham's cellar also included the Canavial Waterloo Madeira: from Count Canavial, a Portuguese nobleman of the first class, a Bual vintaged in 1815. Part of this *lote* was purchased by Sir Stephen

Gaselee and brought to Cambridge. In 1960 I compared Canavial Bual 1815 with others of the same year and found that although it had lost some vinosity it was the finest. Dr. Grabham also had Verdelho 1838, placed in demijohns in 1935 and bottled at various times up to 1954. Dr. Grabham also possessed quantities of Blandy's Commemoration Solera 1811, a fine Bual solera founded to commemorate the firm's establishment. Only 475 bottles were produced; one, No. 114, recorked in 1961 but bearing its original labels, was sold in 1977 by Christie's for £175.

In 1952 Dr. Grabham's son, Walter, very properly gave his fathers's cellar to Graham and John Blandy, great-grandsons of the man who had partly collected it. There were also bottles of Bual and Sercial labelled "Old Cask." Others undated bore the names of the districts Câmara de Lobos, Campanario and Santa Cruz, all of which were certainly centenarian. The youngest wine was a pipe of Câmara de Lobos 1902 which the doctor had bought himself as must and matured as a *canteiro* in his cellar at Quinta do Val, which is now delicious. He called this wine Faraday Madeira and when asked why, he would say "because it pleases me."

Sir Stephen Gaselee

One of the great collectors of vintage Madeira in the 1940s was Sir Stephen Gaselee, KCMG, CBE, and holder of the Grand Cross of the Military Order of Christ (Portugal's highest order). He possessed in his cellar at Cambridge many of the same wines to be found in the cellar of his friend, Dr. Michael Grabham, in Madeira. Sir Stephen was an eminent scholar, librarian and keeper of the papers at the Foreign Office. He also became president of the Bibliographical Society in 1932 and honorary librarian to the Athenaeum. He subsequently presented to the Cambridge University library his collection of early printed books and rare early 16th-century books, the largest gift of its kind ever received by the University.

He was distinguished by the archaic originality of his broadcloth cutaway tail coat, his spats, red socks, and an Old Etonian bow tie, to which he added a silk hat in London or a panama abroad. To quote the *Dictionary of National Biography* 1941-1950: "As a sopra-dilettante in the best sense of the word he dispensed a distinguished hospitality in which luxurious and often experimental dining was set off only by wines chosen (and whimsically explained) with the discrimination of a connoisseur."

Sir Stephen Gaselee

When he left Cambridge he became tutor to Prince Louis Francis of Battenberg (later Lord Mountbatten), after which he travelled extensively, attaining experience of foreign countries and courts which stood him in good stead for his later duties. He also acquired great knowledge and love of fine food and wine. Madeira was his favourite and he collected possibly the largest and finest cellar of that wine in the United Kingdom, which he housed in the cellars of Magdalene College. He often imported Madeiras direct in pipes and hogsheads, bottling the contents in Cambridge. His favourite way of drinking Madeira was in, and with, turtle soup, which caused Ralph Lusty to use large quantities of Madeira in making his turtle soup for City of London banquets.

Sir Stephen's friends on the island were Mr. Harry Hinton, the Bishop of Funchal and my father, who were commissioned to hunt out parcels of vintage Madeiras and soleras for him. Besides the grand Madeiras I have already mentioned, namely the Canavial Bual 1815 and Verdelho 1838, which came from Dr. Grabham, he purchased from the Henriques and Bianchi famiies Sercial 1864, Bastardo 1870, Bual E.B.H. 1870 and Sercial 1860; and from Dr. Baltazar Gonçalves, one time mayor of Funchal, Lomelino Bual 1870. Sir Stephen acquired through my father, or Harry Hinton,

Bianchi Tintas 1865 and 1883, Malvasias 1808 and 1880, Bual 1872, Cossart's Bual 1818, and from H. M. Borges, Terrantez 1862. The Bishop of Funchal found for Sir Stephen a fine Bual 1846 from João Baptista Leal, a descendant of Robert Leal who owned extensive properties at Porta da Cruz on the north of the island.

The Carvalhal Sercial

The highlight of Sir Stephen's collection was Carvalhal's Sercial bought from T. T. da Câmara Lomelino. Vintaged in 1808 and unblended, this wine had originally come from the vineyards of Count Carvalhal, a nobleman who ruined himself gambling in Paris. His nephew sold his Quinta do Palheiro to John Blandy in the 1870s and it is now known as the Blandy Gardens and visited by thousands of tourists. The count was a flamboyant character, possessing a fine cellar. Sercial 1808 was bought for the Lomelino firm, which rebottled it in 1914. I was told by Dr. Alfredo Leal that it was the best Sercial he knew. The year 1808 is especially noted for fine Malmsey. Sercial of that year is very rare and it is only from this particular bottling that we know that there *was* a fine Sercial produced in 1808. It is a very fine example. Probably the last bottle was sold by Edward Blandy at Christie's in 1976 for £125, the highest auction price for a single bottle ever recorded up to that time. The bottle had passed from Lomelino to the Blandy cellar and had been recorked in January 1948 by Antonio Bianchi, and again in December 1975 by his son at the Madeira Wine Association.

Sir Stephen Gaselee was a very distinguished fellow of Magdalene and honorary fellow of King's. During his lifetime he was a most generous benefactor to their senior wine accounts. On his death in 1943 he bequeathed part of his pre-1834 Madeira to the fellows of both colleges.

In his will Sir Stephen was also generous to his family, friends and clubs. Because of heavy death duties his executors sold the rest of his wines to Ronald Avery, his friend of the Athenaeum, Carlton and Beafsteak Clubs. This acquisition was the foundation of Ronald's great stock of vintage and solera Madeiras and, out of a dozen straight vintage Madeiras shown at Avery's tasting in 1960, to which I have referred, eight came from Sir Stephen's collection. Although it is sad that a distinguished connoisseur's cellar should become divided, I am sure that Sir Stephen, who collected wines with such care and taste, would be happy that they should give pleasure to many who would not otherwise have had the opportunity of enjoying such great Madeiras.

Old rarities

Up to the last war it was common practice to maintain wine in big houses in sufficient quantities to enjoy drinking; but today few people can afford to keep collections of old wines except as a valuable investment. Most of these cellars included Madeiras and, being the longest lasting, old Madeira is often found at auctions today.

Apsley House cellar

Included in a recent wine sale at Christie's of pre-phylloxera Lafite, old Madeira, rare wines and liqueurs, was the property of His Grace, the Duke of Wellington, removed from the cellars of Apsley House, "No. 1 London." There was a quantity of Old India Madeira in early 19th-century bottles. The original bin label read, "Bin No. 16/MADEIRA/The Marquis of Wellesley." The Marquis of Wellesley, brother of the Iron Duke, had been governor-general of India, and it was believed by the family that this Madeira, shipped out for official entertaining, was brought back from India by the Marquis in 1844, since when it remained in the bin until the sale. In the cellar book of 1876, there is a note that there were 260 bottles. It is possible that this Madeira originated from some pipes of old London Particular shipped to Lord Mornington (later Marquis of Wellesley) by Newton, Gordon & Murdoch, and it is probable that it was bottled in India between 1798 and 1805. The bottles had wax capsules but no labels, whereas most of the bottles of old Madeira which appear at auctions are labelled but frequently have no capsules, since they have been recorked but left uncapsuled to allow the wine to breathe through the cork.

CHAPTER 15

THREE MADEIRA TASTINGS

The 1895 "Grand Tasting"

For a century prior to 1936, week-long annual tastings of Madeiras were held at Cossart, Gordon's offices, at 75 Mark Lane, London. In 1895 the event was described as a "Grand Tasting" to celebrate the firm's 150th birthday. No fewer than 36 blended Madeiras were on show, ranging from Good (Dry, Rich and Very Rich) at 17s to Crown Madeira at 50s per dozen. There were three styles of Rainwater: Dry, Medium and Rich, also old East and West India Madeiras in bottle from 4 to 56 years and in wood. There was a full range of soleras from 1808 to 1868, and straight vintages from Bual 1828 to Cama de Lobos 1862.

Fortunately, my grandfather's and great-uncle's notes have been preserved, as well as those of my father, who was then 19 years old. From other people's tasting notes one gathers, in addition to an impression of the wine, an idea of the character of the person, his likes and dislikes, and individual tastes. Some people's remarks are cryptic, others flowery. Some react more than others to acidity. For example, my grandfather and great-uncle tolerated acid, but my father, a younger man, reacted violently to the slightest imbalance in wine.

As well as their notes I have two more sets, one marked "JD" and another "Mr. Liston," who was our salesman at the time. They all agreed that Fine Rich, London Particular and Crown Madeira were the best in their classes. These wines were listed then at 18s, 26s, and 50s per dozen, respectively; today they cost £43, £48 and £103 per dozen. Opinions regarding the Rainwaters were mixed but they all placed Malmsey Solera 1808 first and Bual Soleras 1822 and 1845 next. The Malmsey was listed at 140s and the two Buals at 110s per dozen; today their cost is £37, £33 and £22 *per bottle* respectively. Solera 1862 was offered in wood at £120 per pipe (the equivalent to 65s per dozen duty paid in bottle). Some bottles of this solera, bottled by Berry Bros. between 1930 and 1943, were sold at Christie's in 1977 for £23 per bottle.

Among the vintage Madeiras it is difficult to assess which was considered to be the best, probably because there were too many, but all the notes agree that Verdelho 1838 was very fine. Great-uncle Henry, whose notes are short and to the point, just said, "The best Verdelho." This says a great deal because he did not appreciate Verdelho, describing it as "neither fish nor meat." Verdelho 1838 was still in wood in 1895 but was offered at 200s per dozen, bottled in London. The same vintage from Dr. Grabham's cellar, bottled in 1945, was recently sold in London at £42 per bottle.

'Academy of Ancient Madeira Wines'

Seventy-one years after the "Grand Tasting" just reported, I assisted John Baker and Grendon Gooch to arrange a two-day tasting in Evans, Marshall & Co.'s Water Lane cellars in May 1959. The event was entitled "Academy of Ancient Madeira Wines" and was attended by some of the great wine writers and palates in England, including André Simon, Ronald Avery, Raymond Postgate, Dermot Morrah and F. G. Cox of Harvey's. Only four of our soleras were shown but this time the prices had increased to 325s and 320s per dozen respectively for 1808 and 1815, and 310s for 1822 and 1845. The assembled company put the 1808 first, followed by 1845. Because old soleras were becoming extinct as a result of the Madeira Wine Association's policy, a 1910 vintage Verdelho was also shown. It was considered to be typical of "modern" post-phylloxera vintages, which were just appearing at the time, and I am glad to say, was met with approval.

Among the ancient vintages were the following: Terrantez 1898, which caused much discussion; Malmsey 1880 (this great wine from the best Malvasia vineyards was kept in wood for 75 years before being bottled); Bual 1882, bottled in 1938, recorked 1957; Sercial 1860 bottled from glass demijohns in 1958. The *very* ancient wines consisted of Verdelho 1844 and 1805 (the latter was in cask for over 140 years); Bual 1868 from Dr. Grabham's cellars; Bual 1846, the favourite of the late Czar of Russia; Bual 1844, Reserva Visconde Val Pariso, bottled from the cask in 1936; Terrantez 1862 put in demijohns in 1905 from the cask and bottled in standard bottles in 1936; Terrantez 1846 bottled in 1924 from the wood; the great Cama de Lobos 1789 from the Torre Bella vineyards at Torre, matured in wood until 1900 when placed in 20-litre demijohns (the specimen shown was bottled in 1950); Terrantez 1795 – this 18th-century Madeira was matured in cask until it was bottled in 1926 and recorked for the tasting in January 1959.

With such a magnificent array it was almost impossible to gather a collective opinion. Personally, having tasted them on both days, I found they were better on the second, especially those from the ullaged bottles. This was most evident in the two late 18th-century specimens, which I think were still a little bottle-sick even though the bottles had been opened two days before. Both wines were sound and vigorous, with body and fine nose, and I would say the Terrantez was generally preferred. In the "ancient" range, the Malmsey 1880 was undoubtedly preferred – a great luscious pungent wine with fine lingering sweetness. From among the "very ancient" it was really difficult to choose, and preference hovered between the Terrantez 1862 and Reserva Bual 1844. Terrantez is an acquired taste, and were I to say the 1862 was the best it would be my personal preference, so perhaps the great Bual Reserva 1844 would be my professional choice. Certainly Ronald Avery and André Simon preferred the Bual; the former bought of it heavily and offered it for sale in 1960. However, many of those present preferred the Verdelhos 1805 and 1844.

Tasting of modern Madeiras

On October 5th 1979, Cossart, Gordon & Co. presented a tasting of modern vintages and soleras at 30 Pavilion Road. The wines were selected by David Cossart, and there were only two people present besides myself who had been present at the "Academy" twenty years earlier, namely my former colleagues John Baker and Grendon Gooch. The gathering was well attended by experts but, this time, most of the company were members of the Institute of Masters of Wine, which was still in its infancy in 1959. Also there were many ladies present, showing a profound interest; very different from the earlier tastings at which there had been none. In spite of the fact that my mother was an expert taster and blender, my grandfather and father objected to ladies at tastings on the grounds that their perfume masked the aroma of the wine. I found the new generation of wine experts generally more experienced and knowledgeable than my generation at their age. I appreciated their clear cut verdicts on the wines shown; and the ladies were a distinct asset.

Most of our soleras had run out so only Malmsey 1808, Bual 1822 and Bual Centenary Solera 1845 were shown. The latter should not be confused with 1745-1945 Duo-centenary Celebration, which is a Reserve Blend. These soleras were now priced at £30, £25 and £15 per bottle respectively, as opposed to 320s, 310s and 300s per dozen in 1959. The vintage Madeiras were all modern post-phylloxera wines: Malmsey 1893, a small vintage but one of the first of note after phylloxera (this specimen was from Mr. Francisco Firminio's vineyard in the Campanario district); Malmsey 1916 (most of the Malmsey of this year had been destined for imperial Russia); Malmsey 1920 the last Malvasia Candida from Fajã dos Padres, considered to be as good as the famous 1880; Malmsey 1954, still relatively immature; Bual 1895 from Câmara de Lobos, the first good Bual vintaged after phylloxera; Verdelho 1934, which was almost up to the standard of the excellent 1907 and 1910 vintages; and Sercial 1940, from the Jardim da Serra district, considered one of the best Sercial vintages.

My palate is now becoming rather jaded and Madeira must either be very good or very bad to come through; however, all these modern vintages came through all right. Unfortunately, the Verdelho had not been allowed enough time to rest so it was not quite bright, but I found it a classic Verdelho, well-balanced, light and delicate with a characteristic bitter aftertaste. Sercial 1940 I found a really noble Madeira, fine, delicate, with a splendid nose and typical nutty finish. My preference went to the luscious Malmsey 1920 followed by Malmsey 1916, both exquisite Madeiras.

CHAPTER 16

GETTING THE MOST OUT OF YOUR MADEIRA

Collecting and drinking Madeira is not only exciting and enjoyable but can also be lucrative. It has an inflation-proof potential, as will be seen from prices of Madeiras coming under the hammer. However, great care must be taken when buying Madeiras for laying down. In fact I recommend that the experience and advice of a reputable wine merchant should be relied upon by those who are unfamiliar with these wines. However, should the reader wish to back his knowledge, I suggest that no "varietal types"[57] should be contemplated and only the heavier, full-bodied wines of high quality be put down. Varietal types are mostly Tinta and will develop and mature, but the true Verdelhos, Buals and Malmseys have a better start and will age faster.

Storing Madeira

Wine contains living organisms so it will continue to develop and age during all its life if kept under suitable conditions. Madeira is not demanding, so there is no need to have a proper cellar in which to keep it. An adapted room or cupboard is sufficient, as long as it is airy and away from bright light, hot water pipes and not subject to excessive vibration. Ideal temperatures for storing wines are between 12 and 15 degrees Centigrade (53 to 58 Fahrenheit), but in the case of Madeira, where heat features prominently in its treatment, the temperature may exceed this amount, as long as it does not go above 18 or below 9 degrees Centigrade. There are different opinions as to how Madeira should be kept. Some experts say the bottles should be standing, and others say lying on their sides. In my experience the wine benefits most from being stored in a vertical position, so that it has space to breathe through the cork.

Certainly full-bodied Buals and Malmseys should be kept upright. The lighter Rainwater, Sercial and Verdelho may, if more convenient, be stored lying down, but I advocate that if possible all Madeiras should be kept standing. Should the wine be intended for one's own consumption, wax seals or capsules ought to be removed so that it may breathe freely. But if it has been acquired for an investment, the seal should be kept intact, especially if it contains initials or a crest. Standing bottles do not need the dry surroundings required by bottles lying on their sides, in fact dampness is desirable because it will keep the corks moist. If Madeira is kept standing on shelves or tables, make quite sure these are strong and secure. Bottles must be readily accessible without moving others next to them. Remember the wine should be undisturbed, as far as possible, until it is drunk. If bins are used, they should be diamond-shaped to prevent rolling when other bottles are removed. In the same way as game books, fishing, and hunting diaries are kept, one should maintain a cellar book in which purchases and consumption are entered, as well as condition, character, preference and impressions. It is desirable to note who is present when Madeira is served and one's guest's comments on the wine. These details make history, with which Madeira is so closely associated, and are always interesting to look back on.

Corks and corkscrews

The quality of corks is important for the preservation of Madeira in good condition. Corks in bottles kept standing last longer than those in bottles lying on their sides, so recorking is normally only required every 15 to 20 years. The cork trees suffered from being stripped too often during the last war so some rather inferior cork was produced. This matter has now been corrected, but some of the island bottlings have puny corks and may require earlier recorking. Disgorging, rebottling and recorking should be done professionally. However, should the odd bottle need recorking at home, only use the best quality one-and-a-quarter inch long corks: avoid stopper corks and those horrible plastic or metal affairs. Any pith there may be at the ends should be cut out and after scalding the corks should be soaked in Madeira wine for 6 to 12 hours. The cork should go into the bottle under pressure so a corking tool or "flogger" will be necessary, obtainable from home wine-making shops.

Corkscrews with flattened and edged screws may be used. The narrow gimlet type which will pull through the core of a perished cork should be avoided. But there is nothing better than the double flat-pronged "butler's friend." The flat prongs are eased down on each side of the cork and with a twisting pull the cork will come out clean and whole. For hard dry obstinate corks the double-lever extractor is useful, and when the core has been pulled out and the cork has stuck in the neck, tongs may be needed. They should be heated until they are glowing red; the neck of the bottle is gripped just below the flange for a minute or two until the glow has faded. Remove the tongs and, gripping the neck with a cloth soaked in cold water where the tongs have been, twist, and the top of the bottle will come away cleanly. When drawing a cork it is advisable to use a hand guard, or at least a cloth round the bottle. There are splendid old-fashioned leather combined hand guards and bottle stirrups, which are placed over the bottle on the floor with one's feet on lugs on each side of the stirrup. This gives more leverage and there is no jolt to the bottle when the cork is drawn.

Handling

All fortified wines throw a deposit, but Madeira least of any. The exporter has matured it carefully on the island and most probably submitted it to refrigeration treatment before shipment. The importer has certainly allowed the necessary landing age before fining, filtering and bottling, so the wine is ready to drink when purchased from the merchant. But this does not always mean that one can shake the bottle and expect it to pour "candle-bright." If the wine has been in bottle for a long time, there may be a very fine film or crust on the sides of the bottle, which may be disturbed with movement. This should be allowed to fall to the bottom before pouring or decanting. There used to be back labels on fortified wines explaining this fact but, unfortunately, this practice is disappearing. All Madeiras require a resting period before consumption, especially the rich heavy wines.

In my opinion, wine baskets are pretentious and unnecessary because if the bottle is gently handled the wine may be poured "candle-bright" to the last half glass. I am reminded of the story John Ernest Blandy used to tell of being invited to luncheon by the directors of the Swedish Wine Monopoly before the war. A bottle of his grandfather's Cama de Lobos 1792, bottled by his father, had been opened and he was asked to serve it. With great pomp and ceremony he started to pour but only a few drops fell into the president's glass. Further tilting and gentle shaking of the bottle did not have the desired effect so he was more vigorous. To his horror a cockroach dropped into the glass with a plop. As the wine had been bottled before J. E. was born it was not held against him!

Decanting

Decanting, which passes oxygen into Madeira and brings forward the taste and perfume, is desirable even if it consists only of passing the wine into a fresh clean bottle. Decanting should be performed three to four hours before the wine is to be drunk, and it is sometimes helpful to use a silver or glass decanting funnel, but plastic funnels should be avoided as they can impart an unpleasant taste. Sheffield Plate or silver funnels with turned ends are often used. The turned end will direct the wine down the side of the bottle or decanter, thus preventing bubbling and shock when the wine hits the bottom. The decanting funnel should ideally be the same temperature as the wine which will pass through it. If there are bits of cork in the Madeira it may be strained through a fine linen handkerchief. If the linen should be old and worn, so much the better, and it must be free of soap or detergents. Decanters should never be washed with soap or detergents. They may be cleaned inside by shaking with No. 8 or 9 chilled shot in them. Fine glass should be washed in hot water only, then rinsed in cold, and polished with a leather or soft non-fluffy glass-cloth.

Pamela Vandyke Price asserts that fine glass lights up even the most perfectly appointed table, just as sparkling eyes light up a pretty face. Madeira decanters should be onion-bellied, solid broad-based or ship's type decanters, of plain uncoloured glass. The less cutting and decoration the better, to allow the light to shine through the wine. There are few things more beautiful to the wine lover than light reflected from wine in fine glass on a well set table. Decanter coasters are designed so that they slide on the polished table avoiding unnecessary movement to the wine and they also embellish the sideboard. Madeira may be left for months on ullage after the bottle has been opened, with no ill effects, except that it may eventually become a little flat. I would recommend that, if the bottle is not drunk, the remains should be rebottled and put away in half- or quarter-bottles. I keep what I call a "decanting carboy," into which I pour all the sediment. When it has settled I usually obtain a bonus bottle of fine old Madeira, and the lees are turned into aromatic vinegar. The vinegar must be kept well away from wine: I make and keep it in a garden shed.

GETTING THE MOST OUT OF YOUR MADEIRA

Old-bottled Madeira

Madeira which is very old in bottle naturally becomes bottle-sick, and requires to be left uncorked from four to eight hours before tasting. The ideal is to decant the bottle immediately after opening and leave the decanter unstoppered for several hours before drinking. Old Bastardo is especially prone to bottle-sickness and needs particularly long to breathe. In fact the period of allowing old wine to breathe cannot be overdone in the case of Madeira. When in the United States in 1960, I was asked by a Boston friend to examine some very old Madeira he had bought in London as he thought it had "gone off." The wine was of course bottle-sick. After the bottles had been left uncorked overnight it opened out and was magnificent, so he had no cause for complaint. One of the wines was a Berry Bros. 1834 vintage Bual bottled in 1891 "Same as supplied for the Royal Cruise in HMS *Ophir* in 1901." There were also specimens of our soleras 1815 and 1868, both bottled by Berry's in 1951.

Enjoying Madeira

Materialists will assert that the glass from which wine is drunk cannot change its taste, but to my mind, the aesthetic pleasures of wine savouring are not only derived from the sensations of eyes, nose, and palate, but the shape, feel and quality of the glass from which it is sipped are all important. An elegant, well-balanced glass will give more pleasure in the hand than a thick heavy one. The beauty of color can be appreciated better from a colourless glass. A large, tall, thin glass, half filled so that the bouquet can be released, is ideal for drinking Madeira. Environment also counts for a great deal. Madeira is at its best when the day's rush is over, after a good dinner, when food and flowers have been removed, candle light shines on polished silver and wood, and there is good company and intelligent conversation.

Madeira tastes thinner and lighter in cold weather and you may find that if a light dry Rainwater or Sercial is your normal choice in summer, it can well be replaced by a heavier Rainwater, or even a Verdelho, when winter draws in. The dry and semi-dry Madeiras make excellent aperitif wines and will improve by being served chilled but not iced. In the old days in Madeira, bottles of aperitif Rainwater and Verdelho to accompany the soup were wrapped in wet napkins and placed in a draught. I still think this the best way of chilling.

Madeira with food

Sercial, Rainwater and Verdelho are at their best with, and in, soup and are quite indispensable to turtle soup. But I personally think that a good nutritious kitchen soup made from boiling mixed vegetables in stock is delicious with a rich Bual, especially on a cold night when dining before the fire. If there are sufficient supplies of both wine and soup a very adequate meal can be made from this combination with toast and it is ideal for quiet winter evenings.

Sercial came into fashion in Georgian days as a late-night final stirrup cup, to clean the mouth and revive the palate after excessive drinking of rich wines. If necessary, it could be used for the same purpose today. However, a much more enjoyable use for it is with avocado pear, which seems to be a perfect complement to Sercial, bringing out the nutty flavour. The avocado should either be cut in half, flavoured with salt and pepper only, and eaten with a spoon, or mashed with salt, pepper and Madeira, and spread on toast as Midshipman's Butter. Verdelho is good with all cheeses, but with the stronger varieties such as Stilton, Bual is better.

The rich and luscious Buals and Malmseys are best accompanied by the sweet, pastry or dessert. Strawberries are especially delicious with a little Madeira poured over them and taken with a glass of Malmsey, which does not seem to smother the delicate flavour of the fruit and brings the character of the wine to its best. Rich Madeira and *gateau* are an exquisite combination and a most delicate jelly can be made from the richer Madeiras. Make the jelly in the usual way, using half each of Malmsey and water, remembering that more gelatine is required with wine than with juices. Flavour with lemon peel and cinnamon stick.

There is an old-fashioned sweet, which, no doubt, some can remember on bills of fare as Tipsy Malmsey Squire and on menus as Tipsy Squire au Malvoisie. Sometimes the Squire and Malmsey were left out and it was just Tipsy Cake. This splendid affair of tower sponge cake soaked in Malmsey, surrounded by jelly, studded with almonds and piped with whipped cream is delicious with old Verdelho. One tipsy squire is said to have sought from his doctor a prescription to reduce the colour of his brick red nose, "Drink more of your old Malmsey and it will go blue" was the medico's unsympathetic reply.

GETTING THE MOST OUT OF YOUR MADEIRA

Elevenses and five-o'clock Malmsey

André Simon tells us of the pleasure of early morning Malmsey as elevenses with savoury biscuits, and as a five-o'clock with "Madeira cake" which is purely a British invention and unknown on the island. True Madeira cake is *bolo de mel*, a very rich, spicy cake which goes beautifully with any Madeira. Some English writers have erroneously referred to it as honey cake, but it is in fact made with treacle. The Portuguese in Madeira use the word *mel* for both honey and treacle: *mel de abelhas* means honey from bees, and *mel de canna* honey from cane, or treacle. Should you wish to try this delicious spicy cake, here is my mother's recipe for making 2 kgs divided into ten cakes. Like the wine, the older it is the better.

2 kg flour
75 gm sugar
75 gm butter
50 gm lard
1.25 l black treacle
25 gm chopped candied peel
50 gm ground almonds
50 gm ground walnuts
3 gm ground cinnamon
4 gm ground aniseed
2.5 gm ground cloves
50 gm bread yeast (bakers')
3 gm soda

Mix butter, lard, treacle and sugar over gentle heat, stir well. Mix other ingredients and add yeast. Pour both together and stir well until completely mixed. Leave mixture in earthenware vessel covered with a cloth in a warm place for two days to rise. Split into about ten flat cakes and bake in a moderate oven for about 20 minutes.

Old Madeira

To quote André Simon again: "Old Madeiras may still be bought today, but of course, they are rare and very dear. There are no young Madeira wines, such as there are young Alsatian or Beaujolais wines, but there are some that are not so very old and their cost is extremely reasonable." Andre wrote that about 30 years ago, and although now there is nothing that *he* would consider to be extremely reasonable in price, there are good Rainwaters or Sercial, Verdelho, Bual and Malmsey types which should cost from £3.50 to £4 per bottle, and undated soleras and Reserves which are about 25 years old costing £9 to £12. There are fine straight vintages between 1910 and 1954 to be obtained at around £35 to £40 per bottle; a vintage 1895 would cost about £60 per bottle. To those who can afford and appreciate them the old and very old Madeiras are worth every penny of their considerable cost.

Carlo de Bianchi used to speak of old Madeira as *vinho de lenço* (handkerchief wine) because he maintained that a few drops on his handkerchief were more manly and fragrant than scent. It is of course a matter of personal taste, but in my opinion these great old wines should be savoured in dimmed light, without food; and often if you are by yourself, you are more able to concentrate on exploring the depth of the Madeira.

Madeira in the kitchen

Paula Peck and Florence Aaron provide two of my favourite dishes in an article in the American magazine, *House Beautiful*, entitled "A wine that shines from soup to nuts." They say regarding Madeira in the kitchen:

Going to a picnic in Madeira

GETTING THE MOST OUT OF YOUR MADEIRA

There are wines that are so negative, or so delicate, that their flavour disappears in cooking. There are others so aggressive that they drown out all other flavours. Madeira has the ability, more than any other wine, to blend, to add of its own characteristic flavour without over-powering others. More than this, it tends to fuse all other seasonings. Perhaps it is so at home in the kitchen because it has already been through a heating process of its own, so takes kindly to heat and can act nobly as a catalyzing agent for other food flavours.

These are two of their recipes:

Rognons de Veau, Duc de Clarence (Veal kidneys in Madeira sauce)

- 2 veal kidneys
- 2 tablespoons butter
- 1 carrot, diced
- 8 small white onions
- 1/2 cup chopped parsley
- 2 cups sliced mushrooms (canned may be used)
- salt and pepper
- 1/2 teaspoon thyme
- 1 small bayleaf
- 1 cup Rainwater Madeira
- 1/2 cup brown meat gravy

Trim fat and core from kidneys. Slice half-an-inch thick. Cover with cold water and place over a medium flame until just boiling. Remove from heat and drain. Melt butter in a heavy pot. Add carrots, onions, and a little parsley. Cook over low heat until vegetables are soft on the outside. Stir in sliced kidneys and mushrooms. Season with salt, pepper, thyme, and bay leaf. Add 3/4 cup Madeira. Cover pot tightly and place in a 350° oven for an hour-and-a-half, or until kidneys are tender. Remove lid from pot. Skim off any fat. The liquid in the pot should barely cover kidneys. If there is too much, reduce it over a high heat, after removing kidneys. Stir in meat gravy. When mixture begins to bubble again, add remaining Madeira. Arrange on serving plate, sprinkle with chopped parsley and serve. Serves four.

Celeri Zino (Celery hearts, Madeira style)

- 3 spring onions, minced
- 1 clove garlic, minced
- 2 tablespoons olive oil
- 3 cups celery hearts, cut in one-inch pieces
- 1 teaspoon chopped fresh dill
- 1/4 cup of chicken stock
- 1/4 cup of Madeira
- 2 egg yolks

Saute spring onions and garlic in olive oil until soft and golden. Add celery, salt and pepper to taste and chicken stock. Simmer covered for about 15 minutes, or until the celery is just tender. Stir egg yolks and Madeira together. Add some of liquid from saucepan to yolk mixture. Then stir yolk mixture into celery. Continue to cook over a low flame, stirring constantly but gently, until the sauce thickens. Sprinkle with chopped dill. Serves four.

Sauce Madère and *Jambon au Madère* could not be prepared without Madeira. They are made as follows:

Sauce Madere (Madeira sauce)

- 1 teaspoon meat glaze
- ½ pint of Espagnole sauce
- ½ pint Madeira wine

Add the meat glaze and the Madeira to the Espagnole sauce. Heat gently. This is particularly delicious served with ham dishes. But local housewives cheat by simply melting a soup cube in three tablespoons of boiling water and adding rich Madeira to make up to half a pint. Herbs are added to taste and the mixture heated with a teaspoon of butter stirred in before serving.

Jambon au Madère (Ham with Madeira sauce)

| Slices of cooked ham | Madeira |
| Vegetables of choice | grated cheese |

Warm slices of cooked ham in a shallow Madeira lake. Serve with a tinned or fresh *macédoine* of vegetables, over which cheese has been grated.

Veal or Chicken Cooked in Sercial

This recipe is for small pieces of veal cooked in Sercial Madeira or pieces of chicken breasts, boned and sliced into small squares and beaten flat as an alternative.

Dip the meat in seasoned flour, fry it in a heavy pan in a good lump of butter. When brown on either side add about three tablespoons of Sercial Madeira. Let it bubble. Add a tablespoon of stock. Stir. Reduce the heat, simmer a few moments, add chopped parsley, garnish with boiled potatoes.

Alternative method for Ham with Madeira Sauce

6 1/2-inch thick slices of ham   freshly ground pepper

GETTING THE MOST OUT OF YOUR MADEIRA

1/2 oz butter	8 fl oz Madeira
1/4 oz flour	5 fl oz double cream
2 teaspoons tomato paste	1/4 cup chopped parsley

Trim ham slices to uniform size. Arrange in an overlapping row in a buttered shallow baking dish. Melt the butter in a saucepan and stir in flour and tomato paste. Add pepper to taste and gradually stir in Madeira. Cook over low heat, stirring continuously, until mixture thickens. Remove from heat and stir in cream. Add parsley. Pour sauce over ham and bake in the oven Regulo 5 (375°F) for about 10 minutes or until the ham is heated through.

Chicken with Sercial

3-4 lb chicken
salt
3 oz pork fat
2 tablespoons flour
1 large cup chicken stock
1 small cup Sercial
4 oz green olives (stoned)

Wash the chicken inside and out and dry well. Cut into serving portions and season with salt. Coat each portion thoroughly with pork fat (reserving a little) and put into a saucepan with a small amount of stock. Set to cook over a slow heat. In a frying pan, heat the reserved fat and brown the flour in this. Then add the remainder of the stock and the cup of Sercial, and stir well. Pour this sauce over the chicken portions. Add half the olives and cook over a low heat until the meat is tender and the sauce has thickened. Arrange the chicken pieces on a serving dish. Cover with the sauce and garnish with the remaining olives. Serve with croutons of fried bread and a lettuce salad.

Lagosta Madeirense (Lobster Madeira)

1 lobster	2 egg yolks
1/4 pint of milk	a little butter
salt and pepper	6 tablespoons Madeira

Dice a cleaned lobster. Beat egg yolks into the milk. Set aside. Now cook the diced lobster in the butter, well seasoned with salt and pepper, simmering in a covered pan for about seven minutes. Add the Madeira to the pan at this stage and cook for a further five minutes. Over a lowered flame now add the milk and egg mixture, stirring to avoid curdling. Cook gently for another minute. Serve as soon as the sauce thickens.

Madeira Pudding (Known on the island as *Puddin Ingles*)

> 4 oz bread diced fine
> 1/2 pint of milk
> 2 eggs
> 2 oz castor sugar
> 1 teaspoon grated lemon rind
> 1 wine glass of Madeira

Mix the bread, sugar and lemon rind together in a basin. Bring the milk to the boil. Pour it on the beaten eggs, stirring meanwhile. Add the Madeira. Pour this mixture over the diced bread, sugar and lemon rind and let it soak for 15-20 minutes. Then pour into a buttered mould and steam gently for two hours. Serve with custard, wine sauce or jam syrup.

Madeira cups and warmers

There could be no better pick-me-up in winter than a cup of steaming Bovril or Oxo well laced with Malmsey. Not only will it bring a glow in winter, but it will help to assist the restoration of circulation after that invigorating dip in the icy summer sea.

For those who appreciate nogs, cups, coolers or what have you, there are the following:

Madeira Nog (or, as it is called locally, *Gemada*)

> For each person:
> 1 egg
> 1 tablespoon brandy
> cinnamon to taste
> ¼ pint iced milk
> 1 wine glass Malmsey

Pour all ingredients into blender and whisk until quite frothy. Drink cold in large tumbler.

Madeira Mist (in winter)
(for eight glasses)

> 2 tablespoons brandy
> 1 bottle sweet Madeira
> 2 cups grapefruit
> 1 cup castor sugar
> 4 tablespoons apricot brandy
> 1 cup sliced pineapple

Heat together the Madeira, sugar and apricot brandy. Then add the grapefruit and sliced pineapple. Serve hot.

Madeira Crystal (in summer)

   For 24 glasses:
   1 bottle dry white wine to every 3 glasses of dry Madeira
   1 slice lemon balm or borage
   soda water
   ice

Mix all ingredients except for the soda and allow to stand for about two hours. Sweeten to taste. Serve well iced and before serving add half a pint of soda water.

Madeira Cobbler

Half fill a tall glass with crushed ice over which pour two glasses Rainwater Madeira, and a teaspoon of syrup, or one teaspoon icing sugar dissolved in a tablespoon of water. Garnish with fresh fruit and a sliver of pineapple.

Madeira Nig

Pour one measure of gin and half a measure of Rainwater over ice; do not shake. Serve with a green olive in a cocktail glass.

Madeira Cup

   1 large piece of ice
   2 liqueur glasses brandy
   1 liqueur glass abricotine
   1 bottle Madeira
   1 liqueur glass curaçao
   1 bottle iced soda water
   fruit garnish

Place the ice in a large jug. Add the ingredients in the above order. Stir well, and decorate with fruit in season.

Madeira Party Punch

   1 quart cider
   1/2 wine glass brandy
   fruit in season
   1 sprig mint
   1 wine glass Madeira
   1 1/2 bottles iced soda water

Mix all the ingredients except the soda water and stand the bowl on ice for at least half-an-hour. Add the soda water just before serving.

Madeira Murmur

¼ gill gin
½ tumbler broken ice
¼ gill Madeira
½ teaspoon angostura bitters
¼ teaspoon lime juice
lemon peel

Stir all ingredients with the ice and strain into a glass.

VERSES

COMPOSED AT THE REQUEST OF JANE WALLAS PENFOLD,

BY WILLIAM WORDSWORTH, ESQ.

POET LAUREATE.

Fair Lady! can *I* sing of flowers
    That in Madeira bloom and fade,
I, who ne'er sate within their bowers,
    Nor through their sunny lawns have strayed?
How they in sprightly dance are worn
    By shepherd-groom and May-day Queen,
Or holy festal pomps adorn,
    These eyes have never seen.

Yet though to me the pencil's art
    No like remembrances can give,
Your portraits still may reach the heart
    And there for gentle pleasure live,
While Fancy ranging with free scope,
    Shall on some lovely Alien set
A name with us endeared to hope,
    Or peace, or fond regret.

Oft as we look with nicer care
    Will Fancy widen her embrace;
A *Heart's-Ease* will perhaps be there,
    A *Speed-well* will not want its place:
And so may we, with charmed mind,
    Beholding what your skill has wrought,
Another *Star of Bethlehem* find,
    A new *Forget-me-not*.

From earth to Heaven with motion fleet,
    From Heaven to earth our thoughts will pass,
A *Holy-thistle* here we meet,
    And there a *Shepherd's Weather-glass*;
And haply some familiar name
    Shall grace the fairest sweetest plant,
Whose presence cheers the drooping frame
    Of English Emigrant :—

Gazing she feels its power beguile
    Sad thoughts, and breathes with easier breath,
Alas! that meek, that tender smile
    Is but a harbinger of death;
And pointing with a feeble hand
    She says, in words, by faint sighs broken,
" Bear for me to my native land
    This precious flower, true love's last token ! "

Rydal Mount,
1st January, 1843.

These verses appear in Knight's "Poetical Works of William Wordsworth" with the heading "To a Lady, in answer to a request that I would write her a poem upon some drawings that she had made of flowers in the island of Madeira." The lady was Mrs. Jane Wallas Penfold, who included the poem in her book "Madeira Flowers, Fruits and Ferns" published by Reeve Brothers of London in 1845. The book contains 15 exquisite coloured drawings with a description of history of Madeira plants. Jane Penfold was the daughter of Robert Wallas and the wife of William Penfold, partner of Henry Veitch in the firm of wine shippers Penfold & Veitch (1813-1858), successors to Robert Wallas & Co., established in 1803. The Penfold family lived at Quinta da Achada, where Mr. John R. Blandy now lives.

Mountains from Pico Arrieiro.

APPENDIX I

MADEIRA VINTAGES, 1774-1956

Incorporated in the first article I ever wrote was a list of 17 of the best vintages from 1789 to 1880. This list was published in the 1958 summer issue of *Wine*. A revised and augmented list comprising 42 vintages from between 1789 and 1956 was published in *Christie's Wine Review 1977*. As a result of later experience and with the help of my grandfather's and father's notes which have come to light, I have been able to go back to vintage 1774 and add considerably to the *Christie's Review* list. A new list follows:

1774   Small, but generally very good
1775   Generally very good
1783   Small, Bual and Verdelho good
1787   Small, generally good
1788   Generally very good
1789   Cama de Lobos very fine
1790   Cama de Lobos very fine
1792   Bual especially good
1795   Generally very good

1803   Generally very good
1805   Generally very good, especially Verdelho
1806   Cama de Lobos and São Martinho good
1808   Generally very good, Malmsey best ever known. Sercial fine
1812   Bual very fine
1814   Bual very fine
1815   Waterloo vintage. Bual good
1816   Bual very fine
1817   Generally good, especially Sercial
1822   Generally excellent
1824   Generally very fine, especially Bual
1826   Generally very fine, especially Sercial

1827 Generally very fine, especially Sercial
1834 Generally very good, especially Bual
1836 Generally very good, especially Sercial
1837 Generally very good, especially Malmsey
1838 Generally very good, especially Verdelho
1839 Generally very good, especially Malmsey
1840 Generally very good, especially Sercial and Verdelho
1842 Generally very good, especially Sercial
1844 Generally very good, especially Bual
1845 Generally very fine, especially Bual
1846 Generally very fine, especially Terrantez, Bual and Verdelho
1848 Generally very good, especially Bual and Terrantez
1850 Generally very good, especially Verdelho
1851 Generally very fine, especially Sercial, Bual and Malmsey
1852 Oidium struck the vines
1854 Very small, but generally very good, especially Sercial
1857 Very small, but generally very good, especially Sercial
1858 Very small, but generally very good, especially Verdelho
1860 Very small, but generally very good, especially Sercial
1862 Small, Terrantez of this year is considered very fine, also Malmsey
1863 Small, generally very fine, especially Malmsey and Bual from Cama de Lobos
1864 Small, generally good, especially Bual and Malmsey
1865 Small, generally good, especially Tinta
1866 Small, generally good, especially Tinta
1867 Small, generally good, especially Tinta
1868 Small, generally good, especially Bual – excellent
1869 Small, generally good, especially Bual
1870 Small, generally good, especially Sercial
1872 Phylloxera. The small amount of wine was very fine
1873 Very small vintage, but some fine wine from Quinta da Paz
1874 Very small vintage, but some fine wine from Quinta da Paz
1880 Malmsey of this year was extremely fine
1882 Very small, some fine Bual
1883 Very small, some fine Sercial
1884 Very small, some fine Sercial
1885 Very small, some fine Malmsey
1891 Generally good, especially Bual
1892 Generally good, especially Sercial

MADEIRA VINTAGES

1893 Generally good, especially Malmsey
1895 Generally fine, especially Bual. The first normal vintage since 1873
1898 Generally very fine, especially Verdelho and Sercial
1900 Generally very fine
1902 Generally very fine
1903 Small, but generally fine, especially Sercial
1905 Very small, but good, especially Sercial and Verdelho
1906 Small, but good, especially Malmsey
1907 Generally fine, especially Verdelho
1910 All wine excellent, especially Sercial, Bual and Verdelho
1914 Small vintage, but Bual especially fine
1915 Generally very good, Bual especially fine
1916 Generally very good, Malmsey very fine
1918 Generally very good
1920 All wines very good, especially Malmsey, but Bual excellent
1926 Generally very good, Bual the finest this century
1934 All wines excellent, especially Verdelho, Bual and Malmsey
1936 Generally very fine, Sercial the finest this century
1940 Generally very fine, Sercial especially good
1941 Generally very fine, Bual and Malmsey especially good
1944 Generally very fine
1950 Generally very fine, Sercial especially
1951 Generally very fine
1952 All wines very fine, Verdelho and Malmsey excellent
1954 Generally very fine, Bual, Malmsey and Bastardo especially good
1956 Generally very fine, Bual and Malmsey especially good

Prospective vintages (1960-1981) are discussed in Appendix II

APPENDIX II

NOTES ON VINTAGES, 1863 TO 1981

There are three post-phylloxera and pre-1900 vintage Madeiras to be found on the market today which are worthy of note. These are Bual 1863, a magnificent specimen of a true Bual from Campanario; Malmsey 1893, a light well-balanced Madeira with a fine nose; and Bual 1895, a full-flavoured fruity "fat" wine, with marked acidity and a fine subtle nose.

I have the following comments to make regarding the post-1900 vintages, which are all very fine, and in particular:

Sercial 1905, 1910, 1940 and 1950

Both 1905 and 1910 are truly great examples of Sercial. They are fine Madeiras, delicate on the palate with a superb nutty nose. I prefer 1910, but it would be hard to find modern Sercials with such character and elegance. Both the 1940 and 1950 are fine delicate Madeiras with complex, classy noses. The 1940 is really noble with an almost salty and nutty finish. 1950 has all the qualities of its elder brother but is still comparatively young for Sercial. There are two bottlings of the 1950. The first was bottled in 1975 for Viuva Abudarham & Filhos and marketed by Corti Brothers of Sacramento, California. The second, from a vineyard higher up at Jardim da Serra, was only bottled by the Madeira Wine Association in 1981 and is now on the market. Although there is little to choose between the two, the second bottling may be rather smoother than the one bottled in 1975.

Verdelho 1902, 1905, 1907, 1910, 1934 and 1952

These are all light delicate fruity typical Verdelhos. Personally I prefer the 1907 and the 1910. The 1934 and 1952 are light, delicate well-balanced wines but not yet fully developed. They should however become splendid examples of their kind.

Bual 1914, 1915, 1920, 1926, 1934 and 1941

Bual 1915 is a splendid Bual which will become superior to its ancestor vintaged 100 years earlier. The 1914 is dryer and lighter, but very fine. Bual 1920, 1926 and 1934 are the finest this century has produced. Personally I prefer the 1920 but they are all noble wines. The 1934 is full-bodied, luscious with great elegance, and the 1941 is lighter and paler than the rest, but with a fine nose and attractive finish.

Malmsey 1906, 1916, 1920, 1952 and 1954

The first three Malmseys are very great wines, well-balanced with fine aroma. The 1916 is rather dryer than most of its type, but owing to its acidity is extremely fresh and youthful in the mouth with an interesting taste of cloves, reminiscent of the old days when Malmsey was fermented with some leaves. The 1920 is really rich, full-bodied, soft with charm and an aromatic nose. Unfortunately these splendid Malmseys are not plentiful now but the 1952 and 1954 vintages are on the market. These are both relatively immature but they are now ready to lay down: I am convinced that, in time, they will rival the great Malmsey vintages of 1808 and 1880. They are both full-flavoured and soft.

I would recommend all the above wines for laying down, in particular, Sercial 1940 and 1950, Verdelho 1934 and 1952, Bual 1915, 1920, 1926, 1934 and 1941, and Malmsey 1916 and 1920 (if obtainable) and 1952 and 1954.

In April 1982 I was able to inspect the *lotes* that João Teixeira, who was then the Madeira Wine Company's technical director, had selected and was holding in wood for observation. Should these wines develop as expected they will be declared vintages and bottled as shown:

Sercial	*Verdelho*	*Bual*	*Malvasia*	*Terrantez*
1962	1968	1960	1970	1975
1963	1969	1969	1972	1976
1967	1975	1970	1978	1978
1976	1976	1971	1979	1979
1978	1980	1972	1980	1980
1979	1981	1975	1981	1981
1980		1978		
1981		1979		
		1980		
		1981		

NOTES ON VINTAGES

I have the following remarks to make regarding these Madeiras:

Sercial

All fine typical wines with character. The 1962 has been in cask for 20 years and in my opinion is almost fully developed. Considering Sercial is slow to develop it has come on very rapidly and will soon be ready for bottling. Although the 1978, 1979, 1980 and 1981 are still harsh and undeveloped, I am sure that they will all become vintage wines and will be bottled as vintage Madeiras in due course.

Verdelho

The 1968, 1969, 1975 and 1976 are all light, elegant wines with great potential. The 1975 is maturing well, but I was most impressed by 1976. However, I consider the 1969 to be the best of the older Verdelhos. The vintages after 1976 are all too immature for me to form an opinion but I think they will develop into fine Madeiras.

Bual

The first five vintages mentioned are all fine robust examples. I think that I would say the 1969 is the best. The vintages after 1972 are maturing well but are still rather rough. However, all these wines are full-bodied and have long life ahead of them.

Malvasia

I found all these Madeiras lacked the body and richness which I would have expected, no doubt because they are of the *Malvasia Babosa* variety, *Malvasia Candida* being almost extinct. It is being revived and it is expected that in the near future there will be sufficient to declare vintages. Vintages 1978, 1979, 1980 and 1981 are still too young for me to form an opinion but I think they have capabilities. I preferred the 1970 but the 1972 should also become a very fine light Malmsey.

Terrantez

I was very pleased to see stocks of this splendid variety building up. As with Sercial, Terrantez develops slowly and so vintages 1980 and 1981 were hardly ready to taste, but the rest are developing rapidly and should become fine examples of this almost forgotten Madeira. I had not previously had the opportunity of tasting Terrantez as young as these, so I did not feel qualified to criticize but I was surprised to find them all much lighter than I expected and without the accentuated bitter finish of old Terrantez, possibly because they were not fermented with stalks, skins and some leaves as in olden times. It may be that this characteristic develops with age. I preferred the oldest wine, and could not make up my mind between 1976 and 1979 for second place. The latter is lighter than the former which is particularly full, but I am sure they will all grow into fine Madeiras to be drunk next century.

APPENDIX III

MADEIRA AT AUCTION

Emanuel Berk

Since at least 1766, when the wine figured prominently in James Christie's first sale, Madeira has been sold at auction, in both England and the United States. But the modern era for Madeira auctions can be traced back to 1966, when Christie's Wine Department was reestablished, having been disbanded during World War II.

In Appendix III of the first edition of *Madeira, The Island Vineyard*, Noël provided a very general compilation of auction records for Madeiras sold between 1966 and 1983. There was no analysis of trends and no sales were singled out, and the prices cited were not the highest achieved, but simply the most recent prices obtained. The focus was overwhelmingly on sales at Christie's in London—because that's where Madeiras were largely sold in the 1960s and 1970s. However, there were a smattering of results from Sotheby's in London, Christie's continental sales and the legendary Heublein auctions in the United States.

An Evolving Market

The 1970s received the lion's share of attention in the first edition. It was a time when Madeiras were offered only a few bottles at a time and almost always in London. The wines themselves were often quite rare and occasionally legendary. In hindsight, prices were astonishingly low, but this was a time when few buyers were competing for Madeira.

During the 1980s and 1990s, a far greater number of bottles were being sold, yet prices remained low. During the 1970s, fewer than 100 bottles of high-quality Madeira may have appeared at auction *worldwide* in a given year. During the 1980s, the yearly average was at least six times that. And in the 1990s the figure doubled again, to about 1200 bottles a year on average.

In part, this reflected an expansion of the auction market beyond London to America, with sales in New York, Chicago, Los Angeles and Las Vegas contributing to far greater activity than in previous years. But the growth was to a greater extent a reflection of the appearance of large parcels of wine, sometimes sold in single sales, but occasionally spread over a period of months or years.

The problem with these large parcels was that the market couldn't digest them. Even profoundly great Madeiras, of remarkable age—such as the Quinta do Serrado and Acciaioly Madeiras sold beginning in 1989—brought shockingly low prices when offered in too great a quantity.

However, the first decade of the 2000s brought a change of fortune for Madeira at auction. The amount of wine appearing in sales dropped dramatically, which turned out to be a good thing. The number of bottles of Madeira sold annually was little more than half the previous decade. After two decades in which large quantities characterized the most important sales, rarity returned to the sale rooms, and New York replaced London as the scene of most of the decade's most exciting sales.

Four Decades of Madeira Sales

Within months of undertaking this second edition of *Madeira, The Island Vineyard* it became clear that updating this appendix would not be easy and that we would have to begin from scratch. Existing compilations of world wine auction prices proved to be very incomplete (at least for Madeira), and it proved impossible to try to aggregate smaller databases. We were forced to rely mostly on original sources—auction catalogues and prices realized—and to laboriously compile the results lot by lot. We're sure that some lots slipped through our net. Yet, by the time we were done, we had compiled more than 6000 auction lots sold between 1971 and 2010. As catalogued by the auction houses, these lots represent 681 wines, giving us a unique view of Madeira's evolution as a collectible.

The following table summarizes Madeira sales during this 40-year period at the following venues:

Christie's *London King Street, London South Kensington, Chicago, New York, Los Angeles*
Sotheby's *London, New York, Las Vegas*
Zachy's *New York, Los Angeles, Las Vegas*

MADEIRA AT AUCTION

Hart Davis Hart *Chicago*
Davis & Co. *Chicago*
Morrell & Co. *New York*
Phillips *Bath*

The table presents, based on the results compiled, the total number of bottles sold of these 681 Madeiras, along with their high and low selling prices during each of three periods: 1971-1989, 1990-1999 and 2000-2010.

If no price is given for a particular period, we found no record of the wine being sold by any of the seven houses in either the U.S. or the U.K. Irrespective of the number of bottles sold at one time, all prices are per bottle and, where appropriate, have been converted into U.S. Dollars using the rate of exchange prevailing at the time of the sale. All prices include buyer's premium where charged.

Finally, as a benchmark, the table provides the year and location for the highest price achieved.

Madeiras at Auction 1971-2010

			High-Low Price During Period			Highest Price	
		# bts	1971-1989	1990-1999	2000-2010	Year	Location
1715	Unknown Producer Moscatel	2		2,848		1997	CL
1748	Justino Henriques Verdelho Solera	17		264-715	1763-3000	2007	CNY
1760-1780	Dutch Dry Madeira	1			891	2001	PB
1779	Unknown Producer Verdelho	2	256	158-417		1985	CL
1789	Averys Grand Cama do Lobos	3	305		1604-1686	2004	SL
1789	Rutherford & Miles Cama de Lobos	3			1763-7200	2007	CNY
1789	Rutherford & Miles Cama de Lobos Solera	4	31-33			1976	CL
1789	Texeira Sercial "RT"	8		845-2070	592-2574	2005	HDH
1789	Unknown Producer Cama de Lobos	2		516	2868	2008	HDH
1789	Unknown Producer Verdelho	5	166	1,139	1283-3055	2004	ZLA
1790	HM Borges Terrantez	14	295-1595		479-3120	2010	CNY
1790	Unknown Producer Malvasia	1			3025	2010	SNY
1790	Unknown Producer Moscatel	1			3388	2010	ZNY
1792	Blandy Bual (bottled 1840)	49	172-1654	308-1542	1522-6844	2006	ZNY
1792	Blandy Extra Reserve Solera	38	39-658	492-911	904-4541	2008	ZNY
1792	Justino Henriques Malmsey Solera	4	352	418	1195	2009	HDH
1792	Unknown Shipper (Goelet Collection)	1		1,150		1999	MOR
1795	Abudarham Terrantez (bottled 1942)	1			4560	2007	CNY

MADEIRA THE ISLAND VINEYARD

Year	Name	# bts	1971-1989	1990-1999	2000-2010	Highest Price Year	Location
1795	Barbeito Terrantez	125	498-606	297-1495	1058-6463	2004	ZLA
1795	Barbeito Terrantez Garrafeira Particular	45		368-534		1994	CL
1795	CVM Terrantez	45	276-591	295-2103	870-5200	2007	CNY
1795	F.F. Ferraz Terrantez	22	757	805	1719-2866	2008	CL
1795	Southside Madeira Assoc. Terrantez	2		847-864		1996	CL
1795	Unknown Producer Terrantez	19	247-315	495-2415	3286-3385	2010	ZNY
1800	"CG" Bual	2		1254-1955		1999	SNY
1800	Unknown Producer (Believed Thos. Jefferson)	1		23,000		1997	SNY
1801	T. Buchanan (Goelet Collection)	1		460		1999	MOR
1802	Acciaioly Terrantez	132	167-267	179-690	1410-2700	2007	CNY
1802	Barbeito Verdelho	2		172		1986	CL
1802	Bual (Believed Blandy)	1			1560	2007	CNY
1802	Unknown Producer Bual	3		275		1994	CL
1804	Principe Bual Solera	1	22			1976	CL
1805	Lomelino Grand Reserve	3		151	1355	2005	CL
1805	Newton, Gordon & Lewis Catherine Banks	2		713	1920	2007	CNY
1805	Unknown Producer Terrantez	3		372	2280	2007	CNY
1806	Brig Twins (Goelet Collection)	24		268-422	912	2007	CNY
1806	Frances (Goelet Collection)	18		345-403	1080	2008	ZNY
1806	Unknown Producer Sercial (Goelet Collection)	1			960	2010	CNY
1807	T. Buchanan (Goelet Collection)	9		268-391		1999	MOR
1808	"SS" Sercial (Kassab)	4	214-238			1987	CL
1808	Blandy (Luscious) Malmsey Solera	41	57-191	328-513	288-1673	2008	ZNY
1808	Cossart, Gordon Malmsey Solera	7	108-193	440	528-1920	2007	CNY
1808	Lomelino Choice Malmsey Solera	1		537		1999	SL
1808	Extra Malmsey Solera	3			600	2007	CNY
1808	Leacock Malmsey Solera	38			545-1793	2008	ZNY
1808	Lomelino Sercial Carvalhal	5	234	387	600-1810	2008	CL
1808	Rutherford & Miles Malmsey Solera	2			1043	2006	SL
1808	Unknown Producer Malmsey	3			653	2000	CL
1810	"JS" de Freitas	1			960	2008	ZNY
1811	"PW" Malvazia Candida	2		340-375		1997	CL
1811	Blandy Commemoration Bual Solera	16	65-171	368-555	576-968	2010	ZNY
1811	Unknown Producer (ex-Henry Cabot Lodge)	2		195		1991	SL
1812	Lomelino Malmsey Solera	4		343	900	2007	CNY
1812	Mayflower (Fearing)	6	77			1984	CCHI
1814	Rutherford & Miles Boal Solera	9		139-286	589-900	2007	CNY
1814	Rutherford & Miles Verdelho Solera	31	31-160	176	461-1089	2010	CNY
1814	Unk. Producer Verdelho Solera	8	25-55			1986	CL
1815	Berry Bros. Waterloo Solera	5			239-255	2000	CL
1815	Cossart, Gordon Bual Solera	60	39-81	154-896	691-1645	2003	SNY
1815	Grabham Waterloo Boal	7	131-262			1977	CL
1815	Harvey's Bual Solera	2		154-495		1992	CCHI

MADEIRA AT AUCTION

		# bts	High-Low Price During Period 1971-1989	1990-1999	2000-2010	Highest Price Year	Location
1815	Lomelino Bual	3		474	1016	2008	ZNY
1815	Lomelino Bual Solera	5	25-73	194	343	2007	CSK
1815	Monteiro Old Boal Reserve	1		396		1992	CCHI
1815	Newton, Gordon & Lewis "Violet" (Goelet Collection)	6		288-489	1020	2007	CNY
1815	Saccone & Speed (Malmsey) Solera	22	30-108		277-657	2008	ZNY
1815	Teixeira Sercial	1			1020	2010	CNY
1815	Unknown Producer "S" Sercial	3		294	900	2008	ZNY
1815	Unknown Producer Boal	19	205	95-319	1195-2040	2007	CNY
1817	"Juno" (Goelet)	6		288-307	900	2008	ZNY
1818	Blandy Grabham Sercial Solera	3	176	187	1560	2007	CNY
1818	Newton, Gordon "Southern Cross" (Goelet Collection)	3		460-598		1999	MOR
1818	Rutherford & Miles Malmsey Solera	15		197	430-1029	2010	ZNY
1820	Barbosa Boal Câmara de Lobos	1			956	2009	HDH
1820	Berry Bros. Bual	5	81	176	710	2006	CSK
1820	Justerini & Brooks Very Old Bual	4		87-111		1993	CL
1820	Lomelino Boal Solera	102	23-91	58-397	178-944	2006	ZNY
1820	Shortridge Lawton Bual	1		313		1997	CL
1820	Unknown Producer Verdelho	2		555	576	2006	CSK
1820	Unknown Producer Verdelho (Kassab)	2	176-197			1987	CL
1822	Averys Verdelho Solera	93	31-121	110-151	365-1200	2010	CNY
1822	Blandy Grabham Verdelho Solera	7	46-165			1989	CLA
1822	Cossart, Gordon Bual Solera	11	20-105	99-220	717	2008	ZNY
1822	Cossart, Gordon Malmsey Solera	1			500	2007	CL
1822	Cossart, Gordon Verdelho Solera	2		100		1993	CL
1822	CVM Grabham Verdelho Solera	1			1140	2007	CNY
1822	Grabham Verdelho Solera	3		143-248		1992	CCHI
1823	Blandy Bual Solera	2		176	600	2007	CNY
1824	Rutherford & Miles Malmsey Solera	5		79		1986	SL
1824	Unknown Producer Terrantez	1	161			1985	SL
1825	Freitas & Irmao Reserva	1			840	2008	ZNY
1825	Leacock Seco (rebottled 1932)	66			158-224	2008	CL
1825	Lomelino Boal Solera	12	58	154-159	303-708	2006	ZNY
1825	Unknown Producer Boal	1		555		1996	CL
1825	Unknown Producer Sercial "S" (Kassab)	9	160-230	430	780	2008	ZNY
1826	Averys Bual Solera	1			403	2006	CSK
1826	Barbeito Sercial Garrafeira Particular	19		146-394	657-710	2007	CNY
1826	Blandy Bual Solera	51	33-242	92-287	235-1320	2007	CNY
1826	Madeira Wine Association Old Bual Solera	1			837	2008	ZNY
1826	Rutherford & Miles Selected Bual Solera	2		197		1999	SL
1826	Torre Bella Boal	1	184			1988	CL
1827	Quinta do Serrado Boal	1321	55-252	114-385	411-2585	2004	ZLA
1828	Blandy Bual Solera	6	94-154		600-653	2000	CL
1828	Unknown Producer Boal (Kassab)	2		537		1999	SL

MADEIRA THE ISLAND VINEYARD

			High-Low Price During Period			Highest Price	
		# bts	1971-1989	1990-1999	2000-2010	Year	Location
1830	Barbeito Malmsey	24			249-306	2003	SL
1830	Cunha "APC" Tinta Velha	1			384	2006	CSK
1830	Justino Henriques Sercial Solera	3	165		353	2004	ZNY
1830	Lomelino Sercial Solera	10	32-44		269-598	2008	ZNY
1830	Quinta do Serrado Malmsey	1228	92-163	109-537	235-1400	2007	CNY
1830	Unk. Producer Malmsey (Kassab)	1	230			1988	CL
1832	Acciaioly Terrantez	353	81-154	121-430	303-1111	2008	ZLV
1834	Barbeito Malvasia	86		394-633	222-1778	2006	ZNY
1834	Barbeito Terrantez	18		227-880	819-1521	2005	HDH
1835	Averys Sercial Solera	1			192	2006	CSK
1835	Blandy Sercial Solera	44	20-29	83-310	192-600	2007	CNY
1835	Leacock Sercial Solera	1		169		1999	SL
1835	Quinta do Serrado Boal	12			516-720	2007	ZNY
1836	Acciaioly Malmsey	254	139-201	77-716	470-1600	2007	CNY
1836	Cossart, Gordon Solera	21		83-118	833	2010	SL
1836	Harvey R.S. Solera	14	56-59		230	2006	CSK
1836	Lomelino Bastardo	30			459-802	2008	CL
1837	Acciaioli Bual	202	67-167	132-575	468-826	2007	CL
1838	Averys Verdelho	6	28-73	277	896	2008	ZNY
1839	Acciaioli Verdelho	171	70-114	138-150	353-702	2005	HDH
1839	Blandy Malvasia Fajã dos Padres	2	87-108			1982	CL
1839	Unknown Producer Malvasia Fajã dos Padres	5	138	125		1987	CL
1840	Borges "B"	6	93-108		518-557	2006	CSK
1840	Justerini & Brooks Cama do Lobos	6		101		1993	CL
1840	Newton, Gordon, Cossart & Co. "The Rebel" (Goelet Collection)	58		219-489	777-1200	2007	CNY
1840	Newton, Gordon, Cossart & Co. The Rebel	12	79			1984	CCHI
1840	Perestrello Terrantez	3	171-286	441		1996	CL
1840	Rutherford & Miles Bual	3	28-33		660	2008	ZNY
1840	Unknown Producer Boal Raro Velho do Campanario	14	48-193		422-600	2008	ZNY
1842	Unknown Producer Terrantez	45	39-264	198-440	806	2006	CSK
1845	Berry Bros. Bual Solera	36	29-143	49-264	239-645	2010	ZNY
1845	Cossart, Gordon Bual Solera	350	28-95	47-645	67-847	2010	SNY
1845	Lomelino Quinta da Paz	37	172-180		430-745	2008	CL
1846	Averys Terrantez	20	178-372	440	508-2032	2008	ZNY
1846	Blandy's Campanario	31	70-150	207-396	274-650	2000	CNY
1846	Cossart, Gordon Verdelho Reserve Velhissima	6	78-91			1977	CL
1846	HM Borges Malvasia	2			896	2008	ZNY
1846	HM Borges Terrantez	42	31-216	187-609	636-2700	2007	CNY
1846	Leacock Terrantez	9			2178	2008	CL
1846	Unknown Producer Terrantez	3	87-130	462	2149-2640	2007	CNY
1846	Unknown Producer Tinto	6	19		589	2006	SL
1846	Unknown Producer/Varietal	3	26		518	2008	CNY
1847	Shortridge Lawton Boal	5			496-900	2007	CNY
1847	Unknown Producer Moscatel	1		143		1990	CCHI
1848	Blandy Bual	1			428	2001	PB
1848	Christopher & Co. Bual	7	25			1982	CL
1848	Ratcliff & Dawe Madeira	1	32			1976	CL

MADEIRA AT AUCTION

		# bts	High-Low Price During Period			Highest Price	
			1971-1989	1990-1999	2000-2010	Year	Location
1849	Miles Verdelho	2	52	466		1999	SL
1849	Shortridge Lawton Boal	2	26-117			1985	SL
1850	Blandy Malmsey Solera	1			499	2006	SL
1850	Blandy Sercial Solera	2			222	2005	HDH
1850	CVM Verdelho	47	79-176	93-537	260-1140	2007	CNY
1850	D'Oliveira Verdelho	24	49	193-394	237-893	2007	ZNY
1850	Unknown Producer Malvazia	1	79			1984	CL
1850	Unknown Producer Sercial	13	19	99		1990	CCHI
1851	Averys Solera	1			359	2008	ZLA
1851	Berry Bros. Verdelho Solera	60	30-121	49-132	219-524	2010	ZNY
1851	Blandy Boal Solera	6	13		330-780	2007	CNY
1851	Leacock Bual Solera	6		121	161-968	2010	ZNY
1851	Wardrop's	1	202			1988	CL
1853	Lomelino Malmsey Solera	92	12-29	54-279	198-900	2007	CNY
1856	Barbeito Bual	8	57	100-124	188-720	2010	CNY
1856	Blandy Grabham Boal Solera	4		83	720	2007	CNY
1856	Leacock Boal	2		165-242		1992	CCHI
1858	Henriques & Henriques Verdelho	2			655	2008	ZNY
1859	Sercial Imported for Goelet (Goelet Collection) demijohn	2		2530-2760		1999	MOR
1860	Averys Sercial	2	117			1986	CL
1860	Blandy Bual	3			777-1210	2010	CNY
1860	Blandy Sercial Solera	4			212-257	2007	CNY
1860	Cossart, Gordon Sercial Solera	267	34-107	52-518	143-538	2008	HDH
1860	CREVM Boal	3	72-209			1989	CL
1860	Henriques & Henriques Old Bual	2		242	295	2006	ZLA
1860	Leacock Sercial Solera	7	22-35		121-294	2004	ZNY
1860	Torre Bella Terrantez	1	236			1988	SL
1860	Unknown Producer Boal	4			322	2003	ZNY
1860	Unknown Producer Terrantez	1	134			1984	CL
1860	Unknown Shipper Sercial bottled 1957 (Dr. Balthazar Gonçalves)	4	84-92			1977	CL
1860	Yate's Sercial Finest Old Solera	2			144	2006	CSK
1861	Shortridge Lawton Boal	7			378-900	2007	CNY
1862	Averys Verdelho Reserva Velha	2	86-143			1977	CL
1862	Barbeito Bual	22	172	33-128		1986	CL
1862	Berry Bros. Finest Solera bottled 1930-43	7	20			1977	CL
1862	Berry Bros. Finest Solera	30	12	132	359	2008	ZNY
1862	Berry Bros. Malmsey Solera	2			515	2010	ZNY
1862	Blandy Malmsey	1	130			1985	CL
1862	Blandy Malvasia Velha	25	57	206-501	343-518	2006	CSK
1862	Blandy Terrantez	6			1610	2006	CL
1862	Blandy Verdelho	2	138			1980	CL
1862	D'Oliveira Sercial	12			478	2010	HDH
1862	EBH Terrantez	1	194			1985	CL
1862	HM Borges Terrantez	19	85-197	748-770	1200-4800	2007	CNY
1862	HMB Terrantez bottled 1936 ex-João A. Santos	4	91-108			1977	CL
1862	Lomelino Rare Old Malmsey Solera	37	35	88-121	454-571	2008	ZNY
1862	Lomelino Verdelho	1			461	2006	CSK
1862	Madeira Wine Assoc. Terrantez	1		254		1994	CL

MADEIRA THE ISLAND VINEYARD

			High-Low Price During Period			Highest Price	
		# bts	1971-1989	1990-1999	2000-2010	Year	Location
1862	Rutherford & Miles Terrantez	3		231-606		1999	SL
1862	Terrantez (bottled by CJZ, 1977)	1			3167	2008	CL
1862	Unknown Producer Terrantez	2		219		1996	CL
1863	Barbeito Bual	48		259-518	115-780	2007	CNY
1863	Berry Bros. Malmsey Solera	30	24-39	49-322	448-645	2010	ZNY
1863	Blandy Boal	2			448-1080	2007	CNY
1863	Blandy Boal Velho	12	68-85	133-154	392-557	2006	CSK
1863	Blandy Malmsey Solera	316	31-147	95-345	198-1020	2007	CNY
1863	Cossart, Gordon Bual	6		206-239	640	2007	CNY
1863	João Romão Teixeira Boal	45		154-287	176-357	2004	SL
1863	Junta Nacional Delgacio da Madeira Boal	2	116-121			1987	CCHI
1863	Leacock Boal	18	120-176	242-431	269-600	2007	CNY
1863	Leacock Malmsey Solera	131	8-31	110-176	179-717	2008	ZNY
1863	Miles Malmsey Solera	20			445-645	2010	ZNY
1863	Miles Malvasia Solera	14		110	448	2009	HDH
1863	Unknown Producer Boal "B"	1	82			1985	CL
1863	Unknown Producer Boal	12	166	165-285		1997	CL
1863	Unknown Producer Boal Velho	1	86			1986	SL
1863	Unknown Producer Malmsey Solera	1	30			1977	CL
1863	Welsh Bros. Bual	19		132-201	155-660	2007	CNY
1864	Averys Cama de Lobos Solera	14	38-56		189-339	2008	SL
1864	Averys Sercial "EIM"	1	103			1986	CL
1864	Blandy Bual	4		108		1992	CL
1864	Blandy Grand Cama do Lobos	696	31-160	52-345	196-726	2010	ZNY
1864	Blandy Sercial	4	231	99-165	382	2009	HDH
1864	Cossart, Gordon Bual	1	286			1989	CL
1864	Cossart, Gordon Verdelho	9	98-132		614	2006	CSK
1864	EBH Sercial	2	34-153			1977	CL
1864	Henriques & Henriques Sercial	3		81-176	667	2007	CNY
1864	Herdado do Francisco E. Henriques Sercial	3	159			1988	CL
1864	Lomelino Boal	1			538	2006	CSK
1864	Unknown Producer Old Bual 1864 (bottled 1885)	1	93			1986	CL
1865	Harvey's Malmsey Solera	38	41-72		192	2006	CSK
1865	Lomelino Verdelho Solera	45	14-47	55-154	208	2002	CL
1865	Shortridge Lawton Bual	4		123	666	2010	ZNY
1865	Unknown Producer Malmsey	7			321-726	2010	ZNY
1866	Verdelho ex-Visconde Val Pariso	1	91			1977	CL
1868	Berry Bros. & Rudd Finest Solera	10	63		164-230	2006	CSK
1868	Blandy Boal Velho	1			406	2006	CL
1868	Blandy Bual	31		230-244	518-956	2008	ZNY
1868	Blandy Bual "ABS"	1			529	2006	CL
1868	Blandy Malmsey	7	108	312-394	374-714	2007	ZNY
1868	Cossart, Gordon Bual "EBH"	3			1275	2008	ZNY
1868	Cossart, Gordon Solera	3			218	2006	CSK
1868	Cossart, Gordon Very Old Boal "EBH"	4			3600	2007	CNY

MADEIRA AT AUCTION

		# bts	High-Low Price During Period 1971-1989	1990-1999	2000-2010	Highest Price Year	Location
1868	EBH Boal	3	164-173			1987	CL
1868	EBH Very Old Boal	30	73-203	768	545-594	1999	CL
1869	Blandy Boal	28		203-340	780	2007	CNY
1869	Leacock Malvazia	12			516-688	2008	CL
1869	Lomelino Boal	3			499-557	2006	CSK
1869	Miles Verdelho	1			557	2006	CSK
1869	Monteiro Sercial Reserva	1			652	2007	CNY
1869	The Badminton House Malmsey	17	58-60		432	2007	CNY
1869	Unknown Producer Boal				288	2006	CSK
1870	Adegas do Torreão Terrantez	1	149			1985	CL
1870	AEVM Rare Rich Malmsey	3	209-275	220		1985	CCHI
1870	Averys Bastardo	3	131-140	499		1999	SL
1870	Averys Sercial "MJ"	1			422	2006	CSK
1870	Barbeito Malmsey	19	20		163-285	2001	PB
1870	Barbeito Rare Rich Malmsey	18	68	349-356	357-780	2010	CNY
1870	Blandy Bastardo	9	115-163	386-499	749	2006	CSK
1870	Blandy Boal "EBH"	1			634	2006	CSK
1870	Blandy Malmsey	13		259-299	147-412	2003	CNY
1870	Blandy São Martinho	3	104		657	2008	HDH
1870	Blandy Sercial	3			637	2008	ZNY
1870	Blandy Terrantez	13	265	143-428	531-657	2008	HDH
1870	Blandy Verdelho Solera	9		155	140-294	2004	CNY
1870	CVM Malmsey	21		110-132		1992	CCHI
1870	João Romão Teixeira Boal	39		243-322	133-294	1999	SL
1870	Justinho Henriques Rare Fine Malmsey	1			900	2007	CNY
1870	Leacock Sercial	36			401-917	2008	CL
1870	Lomelino Bual Solera	33	38-63	95-167	302-515	2010	ZNY
1870	Lomelino Sercial	4	96-97		438	2008	ZNY
1870	Lomelino Sercial Solera	112	21-72	59-170	36-907	2010	ZNY
1870	Lomelino Sercial Solera Magnum	3		202		1990	CCHI
1870	Longitude USS Guard	7	286	234-546	1440	2007	CNY
1870	Madeira Wine Association San Martinho	2	153-168			1980	CL
1870	Rutherford & Miles Sercial Verdelho	5	16-20	88		1993	CCHI
1870	Shortridge Sercial	2			600	2007	CNY
1870	Taylor Fladgate Sercial	1		2,007		1998	CNY
1870	Unknown Producer Boal	15		208-285	400	2010	CNY
1870	Unknown Producer Bual Solera	2			191-199	2000	CL
1870	Unknown Producer Old East India Solera	1	59			1978	CL
1870	Unknown Producer San Martinho	2	88-114			1986	CL
1870	Unknown Producer Sercial	6		30-259		1996	CL
1870	Unknown Producer Sercial Solera	1	63			1986	SL
1870	Unknown Producer Terrantez	7	155-315			1989	CL
1871	Blandy Sercial	1		121		1991	CCHI
1871	Cossart, Gordon Sercial	2	77	297		1997	CL
1871	Harvey's Malmsey Solera	25	27-29	55-58	218	2006	CSK
1871	Loeb Malmsey	2			374-393	2005	ZLA

MADEIRA THE ISLAND VINEYARD

Year	Name	# bts	1971-1989	1990-1999	2000-2010	Highest Price Year	Location
1871	Unknown Producer Malmsey Solera	1		121		1992	CCHI
1872	Justino Henriques Rare Rainwater Solera	8	209	110-143	192-1020	2007	CNY
1872	Leacock Verdelho Solera	5		105	220	2004	ZNY
1874	Faial Sercial	2		121	283	2006	ZLA
1874	Wine Society Malvasia	1		289		1995	CL
1875	Abudarham Rainwater Solera	24		46-51		1990	CCHI
1875	Barbeito Malvasia	87	41-315	165-322	151-660	2010	CNY
1875	Barbeito Sercial	1			382	2002	SNY
1875	Blandy Bastardo	12		431	867-1200	2007	CL
1875	Blandy Malvasia	1		230		1998	CNY
1875	Blandy Sercial	52	72-193	158	184-550	2000	CNY
1875	Cossart, Gordon Bastardo	22		193-369	695-1179	2006	SL
1875	D'Oliveira Malvasia	1			660	2010	CNY
1875	D'Oliveira Moscatel	36		316-645	418-1031	2007	ZNY
1875	D'Oliveira Sercial	1			307	2006	ZNY
1875	D'Oliveira Verdelho	1		92		1995	DAV
1875	Henriques & Henriques Malvasia Special Reserve (bottled 1957)	2	193			1988	CCHI
1875	Leacock Malvasia	1			194	2001	CL
1875	Leacock Sercial	22	37-41	67-287	233-960	2007	CNY
1875	Rutherford & Miles Sercial	1			320	2000	CNY
1875	Unknown Producer Grand Cama de Lobos Solera	9	32			1985	CL
1875	Unknown Producer Malvasia Garrafeira Particular	2			600	2007	CNY
1875	Unknown Producer Moscatel Reserva	1			346	2006	CSk
1875	Unk. Producer Rainwater Solera	1			235	2004	SNY
1875	Veiga França Boal	1			211	2003	SL
1876	Unknown Producer Verdelho	1		339		1999	SL
1877	Borges Terrantez	11		131-271	900	2007	CNY
1877	Torre Bella Verdelho	12	134		241-324	2001	CL
1877	Torre Bella Verdelho Caldeira	24	98-151			1988	CL
1877	Torre Bella Verdelho Torre	63	110-156		241-324	2001	CL
1878	Christopher's Bual Solera	55	12-17	77-110	284	2003	CL
1878	Rutherford & Miles Bual Solera	8	17-110		272	2006	SL
1878	Torre Bella Verdelho	12	124		199	2001	CL
1878	Wine Society Bual Solera	2			454	2010	ZNY
1879	Justino Henriques Rare Sercial Solera	1			345	2001	CNY
1879	Torre Bella Verdelho S. Antonio	13			345-1093	2002	SNY
1879	Torre Bella Verdelho Torre	18	73-95			1988	CL
1880	Avery & Esquin Malvazia Frasqueira Particular	4			248-570	2007	CNY
1880	Blandy Malmsey	69	53-128	72-458	585-1029	2010	ZNY
1880	Blandy Sercial Solera	2	50			1986	CL
1880	Blandy Verdelho Solera	163	17-209	30-230	120-520	2010	CNY
1880	Cossart, Gordon Reserva	1	275			1986	CCHI
1880	CVM Malmsey	18	95-275	112-130	478-649	2006	HDH
1880	D'Oliveira Terrantez	40		156-287	256-1058	2005	ZNY

MADEIRA AT AUCTION

		# bts	High-Low Price During Period			Highest Price	
			1971-1989	1990-1999	2000-2010	Year	Location
1880	"FJD" Verdelho	1		284		1998	CL
1880	HM Borges Verdelho	1	87			1985	SL
1880	Rutherford & Miles Sercial	2	47			1984	CL
1880	Torre Bella Verdelho	8			165	2001	CL
1880	Unknown Producer Bual	1			288	2006	CSK
1880	Unknown Producer Malvasia	3		195	1999	2000	CL
1880	Unknown Producer Mavasia "FC"	1	54			1984	CL
1881	CVM Malmsey	2	94			1986	SL
1881	Leacock Terrantez	31			287-473	2008	CL
1881	Rutherford & Miles Bual	2			416-461	2006	CSK
1882	Blandy Bual				600	2007	CNY
1882	Blandy Verdelho	7	86	95	230-295	2005	ZLA
1882	Cossart, Gordon Campanario Reserva	1			144	2000	SNY
1882	Cossart, Gordon Verdelho	4		165-322	259-336	2004	SL
1882	Cossart, Gordon Verdelho "AO-SM"	1			454	2009	HDH
1882	Leacock Verdelho	15	132-176	117	320-328	2005	HDH
1882	Lomelino Boal	5			365-418	2008	ZNY
1882	Unknown Producer Boal	1	65			1982	CL
1883	Acciaioli Bual	14	86	117-145	205	2001	PB
1883	Averys Tinta Porto Moniz "Visconde Val Pariso"	2	69-169			1977	CL
1883	Blandy Malmsey	8		105		1995	CL
1883	Unknown Producer Tinta	1	126			1989	CL
1884	Blandy Sercial	2		176		1997	DAV
1884	Blandy Sercial "BG"	4			1050	2007	CNY
1884	Campanario ex-Luis Policarpo	1	113			1977	CL
1885	ABS Malmsey	2		80		1993	CL
1885	Barbeito Malvasia	1			454	2009	HDH
1885	Barbeito Verdelho	38		89-197	162-900	2010	CNY
1885	Blandy Malmsey "ABS"	6			360-960	2007	CNY
1885	Blandy Sercial	19	37-60		236-346	2006	CSK
1885	Lomelino Verdelho	2			288	2006	CSK
1885	Unknown Producer Terrantez	1	93			1985	CL
1885	Unknown Producer Verdelho	1			233	2004	CL
1886	Blandy Malmsey	24	76-138	86-392		1999	SL
1886	Unknown Producer Malmsey	10	50	40-66		1994	CL
1886/7	Blandy Terrantrez (bottled 1900)	3	100		720-1244	2008	CL
1887	Lomelino Old Malmsey	1			333	2006	CSK
1887	Quinta do Serrado Boal	2			403	2001	CLA
1887	Torre Bella Verdelho	4			165	2001	CL
1887	Torre Bella Verdelho São Felipe	17	135-147	264-308	351-353	2005	CNY
1888	Justino Henriques Rare Bual	1			595	2008	ZNY
1888	Unknown Producer Verdelho	12		42		1999	SL
1889	Justino Henriques Rare Malmsey	7		132	288-476	2008	ZNY
1890	Averys Malmsey	4	79-80		660	2007	CNY
1890	Barbeito Malmsey	5		100-102		1995	CL
1890	Blandy Malmsey	4			388-476	2008	ZLV
1890	Dr. Manuel José Vieira Malvasia	2	63	304		1999	SL
1890	Henriques & Henriques Bual	1		220		1997	DAV
1890	Justino Henriques Boal	1	121			1984	CCHI

MADEIRA THE ISLAND VINEYARD

			High-Low Price During Period			Highest Price	
		# bts	1971-1989	1990-1999	2000-2010	Year	Location
1890	Justino Henriques Malmsey Solera	1		116		1990	CCHI
1890	Leacock Sercial	48			172-244	2008	CL
1890	Lomelino Sercial	4	75		288	2006	CSK
1890	Monteiro Bual	3			220	2007	CNY
1890	Unknown Producer Ponta da Pargo Sercial	1			250	2006	CSK
1891	Unknown Producer Cama do Lobos (bottled 1897)	1	114			1986	CL
1892	Barbeito Sercial	2			360	2007	CNY
1892	Cossart, Gordon Sercial	18	41-48	83-96	307	2006	ZLA
1892	Leacock Sercial	1	40			1976	CL
1892	Unknown Producer Sercial	1	68			1984	CL
1893	Averys Malmsey	1		361		1999	SL
1893	Blandy Verdelho	1			777	2008	ZNY
1893	Cossart, Gordon Malmsey	8	79	173	502-600	2007	CNY
1893	EBH (bottled 1946)	2	150		1067	2007	CNY
1893	EBH Very Old Boal	1	157			1988	CL
1893	Leacock Sercial	1			201	2006	ZNY
1893	Rutherford & Miles "EBH" (bottled 1946)	2	142		614	2006	CSK
1893	Unknown Producer Malmsey	13	54-242	466	336	1999	SL
1894	Henriques & Henriques Bual Solera	2	29			1985	CL
1894	Henriques & Henriques Extra Choice Founder's Malmsey Solera	129	17-40	31-187	107-379	2006	HDH
1894	Henriques & Henriques Verdelho Solera	3	32			1987	CL
1894	Unknown Producer Bual	1	80			1977	CL
1895	Aalholm Slots Madeira	16	42-64			1989	CL
1895	Barbeito Boal	1		241		1999	SL
1895	Blandy Verdelho	1	86			1986	CL
1895	Cossart, Gordon Bual	92	84-198	88-284	225-450	2007	CNY
1895	D'Oliveira Malvasia	15		198-233	382-600	2007	CNY
1895	Krohn Bros.	1			317	2008	CL
1895	Leacock HFS "JPW"	11			201-206	2008	CL
1895	Unknown Producer Terrantez	1			1320	2007	CNY
1896	Blandy Bual	1		176		1997	DAV
1896	Leacock HFS "E"	35			172-201	2008	CL
1897	Lomelino Boal	1		201		1999	CL
1897	Lomelino Malmsey	18		81-241		1991	SL
1897	Quinta do Serrado Bual	2			510	2007	CNY
1897	Unknown Producer Malmsey	14	42-66			1980	CL
1898	Antonio Henriques Verdelho Solera	2			135	2003	CL
1898	Barbeito Verdelho	17		110-198	206-476	2008	ZLV
1898	Blandy Sercial	5	34-165		113	1985	CCHI
1898	Blandy Terrantez Reserva	7			1500	2007	CNY
1898	Blandy Verdelho	4			480	2007	CNY
1898	Henriques & Henriques Bual Solera	82	18-88	43-143	79-351	2005	HDH
1898	Henriques & Henriques Sercial Solera	71	11-44	44-269	66-510	2007	CNY

MADEIRA AT AUCTION

		# bts	High-Low Price During Period			Highest Price	
			1971-1989	1990-1999	2000-2010	Year	Location
1898	Henriques & Henriques Verdelho Solera	75	16-37	138-165	87-420	2010	CNY
1898	Unknown Producer Cama de Lobos (bottled 1921)	3	144	99-263		1996	CL
1899	AO-SM Terrantez	1		677		1999	CL
1899	Blandy Terrantez	17		154-330	460-1200	2007	CNY
1899	Blandy Terrantez "AO-SM"	2			896	2009	HDH
1899	Cossart, Gordon Terrantez	2		593-759		1994	CL
1899	Leacock Terrantez	1	187			1987	CCHI
1899	Welsh Bros. Terrantez	3		176-264		1998	DAV
1900	Adegas do Torreão Boal	13	102-125	229-392		1999	SL
1900	AEVM Malmsey	2	99			1984	CCHI
1900	Averys Moscatel Reserve	3		165	247	2003	CL
1900	Barbeito Bual "MBV"	8		288-633	470	1999	SNY
1900	Barbeito Boal	6			235	2002	SL
1900	Barbeito Malvasia	76		244-404	159-800	2010	CNY
1900	Barbeito Sercial	3			116	2000	CL
1900	Barbeito Verdelho	25			114	2000	CL
1900	Blandy Verdelho	39	31	169-421		1999	CL
1900	Cossart, Gordon Boal	1			326	2006	CSk
1900	Cossart, Gordon Boal "LPR"	2	176-198			1988	CCHI
1900	Cossart, Gordon Moscatel	6		173-230		1999	SNY
1900	de Sousa Boal	1059		114-681	87-950	2010	CNY
1900	D'Oliveira Malvasia	50	63	192-537	329-660	2010	CNY
1900	D'Oliveira Moscatel	390	11-104	117-805	221-560	1998	CNY
1900	D'Oliveira Verdelho	59		244-537	186-441	1999	SL
1900	Ferraz Boal	2	143	288		1998	CNY
1900	Henriques & Henriques Century Malmsey Solera	118	27	37-412		1999	CL
1900	Justino Henriques Bual Solera	6	88	88-384	230	1999	CL
1900	Justino Henriques Malmsey	1	130			1988	CCHI
1900	Justino Henriques Sercial Solera	1			303	2010	ZNY
1900	Leacock Malvazia	14		421	229-258	1999	CL
1900	Leacock Moscatel	11		124-125		1993	SL
1900	Rutherford & Miles Malmsey	5			284-326	2006	CSK
1900	Unknown Producer "M"	1			653	2006	CSK
1900	Unknown Producer Boal	28	91-112	114-122	69-186	2000	CL
1900	Unknown Producer Moscatel	4	48-161			1988	SL
1900	Unknown Producer Moscatel Velhissimo	1		165		1999	CL
1900	Unknown Producer Verdelho	1			159	2000	CL
1901	Adegas do Torreão Malvasia	8	97-164	161-174		1998	CL
1901	Barbeito Malvasia	41	136	121-215	234-403	2002	CNY
1901	Unknown Producer Cama de Lobos (bottled 1928)	2	72			1987	CL
1901	Unknown Producer Malmsey	12	158-184			1988	CL
1901	Unknown Producer Malvasia	8	137			1989	CL
1902	Barbeito Verdelho Pico dos Barcelos	4			270	2008	ZNY
1902	Blandy Terrantez Reserve	24		134-144		1995	SNY
1902	Cossart, Gordon Verdelho	40	36-53	156-182	165-575	2010	ZNY
1902	de Sousa Boal	3			125	2002	CL
1903	D'Oliveira Bual	50		215	219-353	2005	ZNY

MADEIRA THE ISLAND VINEYARD

Year	Name	# bts	High-Low Price During Period 1971-1989	1990-1999	2000-2010	Highest Price Year	Location
1904	Blandy Sercial	2			622	2008	CL
1904	Supreme Court Brand Old Reserve Solera	1	132			1989	CCHI
1904	Torre Bella Verdelho Torre	6	83			1988	CL
1905	Blandy Terrantez	2	253		500	2008	ZNY
1905	Cossart, Gordon Sercial	22	39	103-187	253	2002	CNY
1905	D'Oliveira Verdelho	359	16-64	77-197	134-472	2005	ZNY
1905	Leacock Sercial	1			304	2005	HDH
1905	Madeira Wine Associ. Sercial	10	83-132	132	115	1992	CCHI
1905	Torre Bella Verdelho Câmara de Lobos	3			257-263	2005	HDH
1905	Torre Bella Verdelho Nogueira	44	87-95	220	234-316	2006	HDH
1905	Torre Bella Verdelho Torre	24	86-92			1988	CL
1906	Abudarham Malmsey	2		105		1992	CCHI
1906	Blandy Malvazia	2			236	2006	HDH
1906	Cossart Malmsey/Malvazia	25		101-288	237-411	2005	SNY
1906	Leacock Malvazia	19	73	66-188	499-511	2007	CL
1906	Lomelino Malmsey/Malvazia	27	100	95-124	195-388	2008	ZNY
1906	Welsh Bros. Malmsey/Malvazia	10		132-276	137	1996	CNY
1907	Blandy Bual	259	34-143	83-561	171-657	2008	HDH
1907	D'Oliveira Malvasia	12			219	2010	HDH
1908	Blandy Bual	1			176	2005	HDH
1908	Blandy Malvazia	1		110		1991	CLA
1908	D'Oliveira Bual	14		139	259-298	2009	HDH
1908	Leacock Bual	3		95		1992	CCHI
1910	Barbeito Bual	20		164	79-262	2010	ZNY
1910	Barbeito Sercial	45	79	86-102	97-332	2006	HDH
1910	Blandy Boal	3		95		1992	CCHI
1910	Blandy Malmsey/Malvazia	7		110-141	176-358	2009	HDH
1910	Blandy Sercial	1		110		1994	DAV
1910	Blandy Verdelho	1		176		1997	DAV
1910	Cossart, Gordon Bual	1		81		1994	DAV
1910	Cossart, Gordon Malmsey	5		66-92		1994	DAV
1910	Cossart, Gordon Sercial	11		127-141	212	2006	CL
1910	Cossart, Gordon Sercial	6			176-418	2009	HDH
1910	D'Oliveira Malvasia	24	17			1981	CL
1910	D'Oliveira Sercial	215	17-45	184	202-221	2006	CSK
1910	Leacock Bual	5		53		1993	CCHI
1910	Leacock Malmsey/Malvazia	9		70	117-176	2005	HDH
1910	Leacock Sercial	42		62-117	186-241	2008	CL
1910	Lomelino Sercial	1			478	2008	HDH
1910	Rutherford & Miles Sercial	6	45			1985	SL
1910	Unknown Producer Sercial	1	44			1985	CL
1910	Unknown Producer Verdelho	2			359	2008	ZNY
1910	Welsh Bros. Bual	1		66		1992	CCHI
1910	Welsh Bros. Malvasia	7		55-70		1992	CCHI
1910	Welsh Bros. Sercial	3		154-158		1998	SNY
1911	Blandy Bual	66	33-130	59-176	293-307	2006	CSK
1911	Torre Bella Malvasia Câmara de Lobos	4			149	2001	CL
1912	Blandy Malmsey	1			286	2007	ZNY
1912	da Silva Verdelho Solera	3			124	2004	CL

MADEIRA AT AUCTION

		# bts	High-Low Price During Period			Highest Price	
			1971-1989	1990-1999	2000-2010	Year	Location
1912	D'Oliveira Verdelho	21			239-260	2006	SNY
1912	Shortridge Lawton Boal	1	132			1987	CCHI
1912	Vinhos da Madeira Verdelho Solera	2			167	2006	CL
1914	Abudarham Bual	5		165	165-196	2006	CLA
1914	Barbeito Malvasia Quinta Piedade	12			219	2010	HDH
1914	Cossart, Gordon Bual	12	209	113-175	346	2006	CSK
1914	Leacock Bual	19	107-231	77-84	316	2003	SL
1914	Madeira Wine Association Boal	1	220			1988	CCHI
1914	Rutherford & Miles Bual	4		110	205-211	2005	HDH
1914	Unknown Producer Malvasia Fajã dos Padres	1	63			1986	SL
1914	Welsh Bros. Bual	28		63-115	129-165	2004	ZNY
1915	Cossart, Gordon Bual "LMR"	136	47-150	39-239	160-265	2007	CL
1915	LMR Bual	19		125-167	154-311	2007	CL
1915	Lomelino Bual	2		114		1996	CL
1915	Lomelino Malmsey	15		78-152		1996	CL
1915	Rutherford & Miles Bual "LMR"	63		47-73		1994	CL
1915	Shortridge Lawton Malmsey	8		151		1990	CLA
1915	Unknown Producer Bual	13	56		382	2008	ZNY
1916	Barbeito Malvasia	1			288	2002	CNY
1916	Cossart, Gordon Malmsey	52	65-240	83-155	326-578	2007	CL
1916	Rutherford & Miles Sercial	2	43-58			1985	SL
1917	Balthazar	5	86-108		475-499	2006	SL
1917	Blandy Verdelho	2		74		1994	SL
1919	Unknown Producer Boal	5	74		240	2006	CSK
1920	Blandy Bual	15		121-163	403-700	2010	CNY
1920	Cossart, Gordon Bual	54	60	93-158	187-418	2008	ZNY
1920	Cossart, Gordon Malmsey	248	51-100	66-462	105-950	2010	CNY
1920	de Sousa	1		76		1990	CL
1920	Duque de Sant'ana Malmsey	2			717	2009	HDH
1920	Favilla Vieira Malvasia	20			180-259	2010	HDH
1920	Leacock Bual	6		77		1992	CCHI
1920	Rutherford & Miles Bual	2			218	2006	CSK
1920	Welsh Bros. Bual	4		93		1998	SNY
1922	D'Oliveira Bual	42		64-134	228-258	2007	ZNY
1925	Barbeito Sercial	1			169	2001	PB
1926	Cossart, Gordon Bual Campanario Francisco Firmino (bottled 1976)	12	93-119			1986	CL
1926	Cossart, Gordon Malmsey Solera	33		72-138	115-354	2006	HDH
1926	Cossart, Gordon Solar do Val Formoso ex-Noël Cossart	12	27			1976	CL
1926	Francisco Firmino Bual Campanario (bottled 1976)	45	25-107			1987	CL
1927	de Freitas Boal	1	82			1988	SL
1927	D'Oliveira Bastardo	20			279-480	2010	CNY
1927	Leacock Bastardo	28		20	215-489	2007	CL
1927	Leacock Sercial SJ (St. John Vyd.)	48			149-172	2008	CL
1928	da Silva Verdelho	1		109		1997	CL
1928	Leacock Verdelho "EEL"	104			79-86	2008	CL
1929	Barbeito Verdelho	42			157-199	2010	HDH
1930	Veiga França Bual Solera	4		107		1999	SL

MADEIRA THE ISLAND VINEYARD

Year	Wine	# bts	1971-1989	1990-1999	2000-2010	Highest Year	Location
1931	Blandy Verdelho	12	45-52			1986	CL
1932	Blandy Verdelho	16		85-316	176	1999	SNY
1932	HM Borges Malvasia/Malmsey	14		104-131	156-467	2007	CL
1933	Blandy Bual	42			113-489	2007	CL
1933	Blandy Malmsey	1			81	2001	CLA
1933	Cossart, Gordon Malmsey	19		57-67	242	2010	ZNY
1933	Justino Henriques Malmsey	1298		72-159	53-144	1997	CL
1933	Leacock Malmsey/Malvazia	37		64	211	2005	HDH
1933	Shortridge Lawton Malvasia	2		157		1997	CL
1934	Barros & Sousa Malmsey Fajã	4	51			1987	CL
1934	Blandy Bual	3			162-246	2005	HDH
1934	Blandy Verdelho	1			293	2005	HDH
1934	Cossart, Gordon Bual	133		63-105	90-422	2007	CL
1934	Cossart, Gordon Verdelho	18		74-211	151-222	2005	HDH
1934	Henriques & Henriques Malmsey	9		126	400	2010	CNY
1934	Henriques & Henriques Verdelho	27	28-42		176-339	2007	HDH
1934	Henriques Boal	3		153		1998	CNY
1934	Justino Henriques Verdelho	983		22-125	36-237	2006	ZNY
1931	Leacock Bual	20		68-94	218	2005	CL
1934	Rutherford & Miles Bual	12	42-51	110	249-359	2008	ZNY
1934	Rutherford & Miles Verdelho	11	43-51		295-319	2008	ZNY
1934	Unknown Producer Fajã Malmsey/Malvasia	8	43-57		192	2006	CSK
1934	Welsh Bros. Bual	5			110-173	2002	CNY
1935	HM Borges Boal	2		114		1994	SL
1936	Cossart, Gordon Sercial (bottled 1947) (Cossart Family)	11	119-365	176-268		1985	CL
1937	D'Oliveira Sercial	13		47-99		1996	DAV
1939	Adegas de Torreão Terrantez	1		394		1999	SL
1939	Barbeito Unknown Grape Variety	1			211	2003	ZNY
1939	Blandy Calheta	29			215-294	2008	CL
1940	Blandy Sercial	8		86	222-236	2006	HDH
1940	Cossart, Gordon Sercial	20	34	69-96	134	2006	CSK
1940	de Sousa Boal	4		93		1995	CL
1940	HM Borges Verdelho	4		50		1993	CCHI
1940	Justino Henriques Sercial	730		30-46	24-97	2004	CL
1940	Welsh Bros. Sercial	5			104	2002	CNY
1941	Cossart, Gordon Bual	12			520	2010	CNY
1941	Cossart, Gordon Bual "CDGC"	105	31-50	62-171	508-700	2010	CNY
1944	Henriques & Henriques Sercial Reserva	4	32			1986	CL
1947	Malvasia Candida (bottled 1957 to commemorate Elizabeth II's visit to Madeira)	1		95		1994	CL
1948	Barbeito Malvasia	13			68-107	2006	ZLA
1948	Henriques & Henriques Boal Special Reserve	1	286			1988	CCHI
1949	Barbeito Malvasia	15			133-199	2010	HDH
1950	Blandy Sercial	4			180	2008	ZNY
1950	Cossart, Gordon Sercial	71		21-58	118	2006	CL
1950	Leacock Sercial	14			63-140	2005	HDH
1950	Rutherford & Miles Sercial	32	17-56	90	42	1999	SL

MADEIRA AT AUCTION

		# bts	High-Low Price During Period 1971-1989	1990-1999	2000-2010	Highest Price Year	Location
1950	Torre Bella Tinta Negra Mole	7			102	2006	CSK
1950	Torre Bella Tinta Negra Mole "Torre"	26	35-43			1988	CL
1951	Unknown Producer Terrantez	2	71			1988	CL
1952	Averys Bual Silver Jubilee	6	23			1983	CL
1952	Cossart, Gordon Bual Silver Jubilee	18		88	400	2010	CNY
1952	Ellis Son & Vidler Bual Silver Jubilee	54		21-146		1999	CL
1952	Leacock Malmsey (Jubilee Selection)	49	26-65	46-99		1994	DAV
1952	Leacock Verdelho (Jubilee Selection)	7			141-222	2005	HDH
1954	Abudarham Boal	1	132			1989	CCHI
1954	Blandy Bastardo	1			160	2001	PB
1954	Blandy Bual	30		41-77	173-179	2006	CL
1954	Blandy Terrantez	4		100	205-234	2005	HDH
1954	Casa dos Vinhos Boal	12			93	2010	CL
1954	Cossart, Gordon Malmsey	1		116		1990	CCHI
1954	Henriques & Henriques Bual	64	37-48	29-93		1997	CL
1954	Henriques & Henriques Malmsey	33		32-68	199	2010	HDH
1954	Justino Henriques Boal	36		30-33		1996	CL
1954	Justino Henriques Verdelho	754		30-72	24-121	2006	CL
1954	Leacock Terrantez	40		49-70	42-550	2010	CNY
1954	Leacock Verdelho	6			128	2006	CL
1954	Rutherford & Miles Verdelho	6		41		1994	SL
1957	Barbeito Bual	12		60		1994	CL
1957	D'Oliveira Reserva	1		143		1998	DAV
1959	Berry Brothers & Rudd Very Old East India	12			77	2000	SL
1960	Barbeito Bual	56	23-24	44-62		1995	CL
1963	Leacock Sercial	2		41		1994	SL
1963	Unknown Producer Bual	1		33		1998	DAV
1964	Blandy Malmsey	27		36-46	54	2005	SL
1964	Justino Henriques Bual	1033		29-81	24-138	2007	CNY
1964	Justino Henriques Malmsey	350		36-86	59-151	2010	ZNY
1968	D'Oliveira Bual	36		58	200	2008	ZNY
1969	Christopher's Rare Verdelho	24			22-23	2002	CL
1969	D'Oliveira Sercial	23			55-71	2008	ZNY
1969	Leacock Malmsey	2		61		1994	SL
1969	Miles Sercial	42		48-50		1995	CL
1971	Blandy Bual	2			45	2001	PB
	A.G. Pacheco (bottled 1927)	37	172		79	1986	CL
	Acciaioli Especial Old Malmsey for private entertaining	18	84-89			1989	CL
	Antonio Caetano Aragão Terrantez pre-1900	6	23			1975	CL
	Augusta c. 1820 (Goelet Collection)	12		244-273		1999	MOR
	Averys Verdelho Reserva Velhissima c. 1846	4		331	787	2006	CSK
	Black Warrior Imported 1840 (Goelet)	11		219-402	1900	2007	CNY
	Coffin bottled from demijohn #9 (Goelet Collection)	19		230-391		1999	MOR

MADEIRA THE ISLAND VINEYARD

		High-Low Price During Period			Highest Price	
	# bts	1971-1989	1990-1999	2000-2010	Year	Location
Commodore Perry Imported 1829 (Goelet Collection)	3		517-546		1999	MOR
Henriques & Henriques Boal Velho Reserva (bottled 1906)	27			176-219	2010	HDH
Henriques & Henriques Malvasia Reserva	2			529-646	2005	ZNY
Henriques & Henriques "WS" Boal	4	80			1988	CL
Hurricane c. 1820 (Goelet Collection)	14		211-345		1999	MOR
John Harvey East India Loeb	1			287	2008	ZLA
Krohn Bros. probably pre-1917	3	37			1986	CL
Krohn Imperial Reserve No. 1 (blend of soleras 1808-1826)	12	63			1988	CL
Krohn pre-1917 (rebottled 1982) (Mrs. Raleigh Krohn)	1	10			1982	CL
Leacock "A"	70			77-100	2008	CL
Leacock Malvasia "VMA" (Velhissima)	44			47-76	2008	CL
Leacock Reserve (bottled in Madeira in 1879)	2	286			1986	CCHI
Leacock Velho Verdelho (bottled 1920s)	99			53-73	2008	CL
Lewis date unknown (decanted 1880) (Goelet Collection)	2		173		1999	MOR
March & Benson "Victoria Wine" (imported 1841) (Goelet Collection)	3		368-460		1999	MOR
Murdock, Yuille, Wardrup & Co. (imported 1825) (Goelet Collection)	42		238-307	900	2008	ZNY
Old India Madeira Bin 16 Marquis of Wellesley	20	61-92			1977	CL
Paxton's East India Madeira (Early 19th Century)	1	230			1984	CL
Penfold & Veitch (decanted 1909)	1	132			1987	CL
Rogers & Gracie via India (Imported 1823) (Goelet Collection)	1		276		1999	MOR
The Mexican (imported 1841) (Goelet Collection)	9		199-345	1320	2007	CNY
Torre Bella Verdelho Mistura 1877-1905 "Casa Torre Bella"	54	58-61			1988	CL
Watts Early 19th Century Bin 18 (bottled 1835)	1	198			1971	CL

Key

CL – Christie's – London; CNY – Christie's New York; CCHI – Christie's Chicago; CSK – Christie's South Kensington; CLA – Christie's Los Angeles; DAV – Davis & Co. Chicago; HDH – Hart Davis Hart Chicago; MOR – Morrell & Co. New York; SL – Sotheby's London; SNY – Sotheby's New York; SLV – Sotheby's Las Vegas; PB – Phillips Bath; ZNY – Zachy's New York; ZLA – Zachy's Los Angeles; ZLV – Zachy's Las Vegas

APPENDIX IV

IMPORTANT AUCTIONS OF MADEIRA

Emanuel Berk

Harry Johnson's Madeiras

Arguably the finest collection to come to auction during the 1970s belonged to Harry Johnson, a Floridian who was Avery's biggest Madeira buyer during the 1950s and 1960s. This was the time when the firm was the world's finest source of rare old Madeiras, including such painfully rare wines as the 1789 Cama de Lobos, the Visconde Val Pariso's Verdelho Velhissima c. 1846, and a number of iconic wines that had belonged to Stephen Gaselee.

Johnson appears to have bought heavily of these wines; it is said that he purchased about 25 cases of the 1789 Cama de Lobos. Johnson was said to be Avery's best customer, even marrying Ronald Avery's secretary.

Befitting this period of small, select auctions of Madeira, the Johnson wines were always sold in small amounts. Apparently the largest single auction of his wines was on September 29, 1977, when a total of 58 bottles, generally with Averys provenance, were offered. This included single bottles of 1789 Cama do Lobos and 1883 Tinta, 2 bottles each of 1862 Verdelho Reserva Velhissima and 1864 Sercial, 3 bottles each of 1838 Verdelho and 1846 Terrantez, 4 bottles each of 1860 Sercial and 1862 Terrantez, 6 bottles of Verdelho Reserve Velhissima (believed 1846) and 7 bottles of 1815 Grabham Waterloo Boal. Also from Johnson were an impressive 6 bottles of 1792 Blandy (bottled 1840), which he purchased from Averys.

The Quinta do Serrado Sale, 1989

Quinta do Serrado was the ancient estate of the Henriques family, situated in the heart of Camara do Lobos. Wine was produced there for centuries, and on December 7, 1989, two of Serrado's greatest wines were offered at Christie's in London: an 1830 Malvasia and an 1827 Bual, each of which was said to have been demijohned in 1935 and bottled in 1988 for shipment to London. The number of bottles was dizzying: nearly 1,000 of each. Most of it sold that day, but the amount of wine was so great that a few dozen bottles lingered in a London warehouse for another seven years before finally being sold.

Because of both the large amount of wine offered and the poor state of the old Madeira market at that time, the wines sold at low prices. Five and ten-case lots of 1827 Bual went for 600GBP (including buyer's premium), while the 1830 went for 770GBP. These Sterling prices equated to $87 and $101 per bottle, respectively. It is a testament to the strength of the Madeira market in 2010 that both wines have current market values approaching $1,500 *per bottle*.

The Acciaioly Sale, 1989

Oscar Acciaioly represented the last generation on the island of one of Madeira's oldest families. Descended from the Dukes of Burgundy with an illustrious history in Florence, Italy, the Acciaiolys arrived in Madeira in the early 1500s and by legend were responsible for bringing the Malvasia Babosa grape to the island.

When Acciaioly died in 1979, his remaining wines were divided into two parts. One part went to his second wife, who in turn sold them to Mario Barbeito. The second part went to his sons Michael and David, who consigned them, in their original state with original labels, capsules and corks, to Christie's in London.

The sons' wines were offered at several sales, but principally on July 15, 1989, when 135 lots of old Acciaioly Madeiras kicked off the morning session at Christie's on King Street. The sale encompassed the following vintages: 1802 Terrantez (more than nine dozen bottles); 1832 Terrantez (more than 21 dozen bottles); 1836 Malmsey (more than 15 dozen bottles); 1837 Bual (more than 14 dozen bottles); 1839 Verdelho (more than 14 dozen bottles), and 1883 Bual (about 2 dozen bottles).

Because of the volume of wine, prices, especially for the larger lots, were low, with 1802 Terrantez selling for $229 a bottle and 1832 Terrantez for just $100. Today, the 1802 Terrantez has become one of the world's most sought-after Madeiras, regularly fetching prices of about $3000 a bottle.

Justino's and de Sousa's Long Runs

In the 1990s, when a less venerable Madeira appeared in sale after sale, the market soon became weary, resulting in ever-diminishing prices. The best examples of this phenomenon were the large quantities of Justino Henriques vintages—1933, 1934, 1940, 1954, 1964—that appeared beginning in 1996. By the time these wines had run their course nearly a decade later, prices were no higher than they were ten years earlier, despite a general strengthening of the vintage Madeira market in the interim.

De Sousa's 1900 Boal tells a similar story. As it approached its 100th birthday, it began to appear in 1994, in small 2- to 3-bottle lots at Christie's. Over the next nine and a half years hardly a Christie's-London sale went by without a few lots of 1900 de Sousa. Prices initially rose, but then they stalled, and the lowest price per bottle, $87, was recorded in the very final sale in February 2003.

Other Highlights from the 1980s and '90s

In November 1988, a few months before the Quinta do Serrado and Acciaioly sales, Christie's London tested the Madeira waters by selling 243 bottles of wine from the island's Torre Bella estate. This property, the island's largest, was created when Madeira was first settled and João Afonso Correia received vast tracts of land from the Portuguese crown. In 1812, Correia's male descendents were given the title of Visconde de Torre Bella.

However, Correia's descendents had difficulty procreating and by the 1980s, just two family members remained: the Condessa de Torre Bella, and the widower of her late sister, Captain David Ogilvie Fairlie, who owned a few hundred bottles of Madeira made on the estate between the 1870s and 1950. The Fairlie-owned bottles sold at Christie's in 1988 came in a variety of shapes, many resembling old Burgundy or Champagne bottles. But they had in common a front label reading "Torre Bella – Madeira" and an explanatory Christie's Wine Department back label.

This large sale produced modest prices, ranging from $35 for a 1950 Tinta Negra Mole to $184 for a single bottle of 1826 Torre Bella Boal.

Mills B. Lane & More Quinta do Serrado, 1990

The sale of the Mills B. Lane Madeiras in 1990 was a reminder of the Madeira culture that once flourished in the American South. Lane was born to wealth in Savannah, Georgia, in 1912, and like any well-born Savannian, he was taught that Madeira was his heritage. Until his death in 1989, he was one of this country's last great Madeira connoisseurs.

Within months of his death, nearly 600 bottles of his Madeiras were sold at two Christie's sales: 260 bottles in London, on June 28, 1990, and 339 bottles in Chicago on February 3, 1990. The wines were mostly Blandy's, Cossart Gordon, Leacock and Lomelino, purchased through his contacts at the Madeira Wine Assocation.

The June 28, 1990, Christie's London sale also saw more Quinta do Serrado go on the block, less than seven months after the first sale. The results were disastrous in a saturated market: a further combined 960 bottles of 1827 Bual and 1830 Malmsey were offered for sale, but only 258 found buyers. More than 700 bottles were unsold.

The "Thomas Jefferson Madeiras," 1997

In its May 16, 1997, New York wine auction, Sotheby's in partnership with Sherry-Lehmann offered three lots with ties to Thomas Jefferson. Each lot was a bottle that purportedly once belonged to the President. One bottle contained an 1800 Madeira filled to mid- to low-shoulder, another was half full with the same wine, and the third was empty.

All three bottles bore similar handwritten labels chronicling ownership from Jefferson to Douglas Thomas in 1890. According to the labels, the bottles had originally been purchased in 1843 at a sale of Jefferson's effects by Philip Evans Thomas, the first President of the Baltimore and Ohio Railroad.

The bottle with the best level brought $23,000, a record for any Madeira, while the remaining two bottles went for $6037 and $2300 respectively.

There can be little doubt that the bottles contained a Madeira of appropriate age. Douglas Thomas, a Baltimore banker, was arguably the most knowledgeable Madeira connoisseur in America; the labels themselves appear to be contemporary to Thomas' ownership and an 1896 Baltimore newspaper article echoes

Thomas' belief in the wine's authenticity. However, the Jefferson ownership has been questioned (*The Billionaire's Vinegar* by Benjamin Thomas, 2008), because scholars at Jefferson's home of Monticello have no record of a sale of his effects in 1843. And so we may never know if this was in fact a Jefferson Madeira.

Two Collections at Sotheby's, 1999

On March 17, 1999, Sotheby's in London had the privilege of offering Madeiras from two private collections, which combined to produced 114 lots. A number of wines set new records, of which some still stand today.

The Goelet Collection, 1999

The last truly important Madeira auction of the twentieth century was the Goelet sale at Morrell & Company in New York. In the nineteenth century, the Goelet family had been second only to the Astors in the extent of their real estate holdings—as well as the size of their wealth. And like other wealthy New York families, they were serious about their Madeiras.

Peter P. Goelet (1764-1828) was a particular connoisseur of Madeira who passed his collection on to his son Robert, who in turn left it to his sons Robert III and Ogden. On September 18, 1999, a portion of this collection was sold by Morrell & Company in New York.

The collection was extraordinary because it represented the buying and connoisseurship of at least four generations of Goelets. Also, most of the bottles have original labels, of the type used in the United States in the nineteenth century. Some of the labels appear to date from the early part of that century, making them among the earliest printed paper wine labels (of *any* type) still in existence.

Also, a number of the wines came from William Neyle Habersham, the Savannah Madeira connoisseur who traded heavily with the New York elite after the Civil War. From 1878 until his death in 1899, Habersham regularly transacted business with William H. Fearing, a New York society wine merchant who seems to have had a near-monopoly on the Madeira business of Peter Goelet's grandson, Robert III. Most of the bottles in the collection have a Fearing label on them, either because Fearing sold Robert the wine, or because Fearing bottled Madeiras that Robert had inherited in demijohn.

Finally, the Goelet wines are rare examples of the glass-aged Madeiras popular in the United States in the nineteenth century. The old Madeiras available today typically have spent most of their lives in barrel—enhancing their color, sweetness and fullness of flavor. The Goelet wines were in wood a relatively short time and are superb examples of old, pale, glass-aged Madeira.

The Lenoir Josey Sale, 2000

The collection of Lenoir Josey occupied an entire sale at Zachy's Christie's in late 2000, of which just 20 lots were Madeira. However, like the rest of the wines in the sale, they were of very high quality: 1792 Blandy's, 1862 HM Borges Terrantez, 1846 Blandy's Campanario, and 1875 Cossart Gordon Bastardo were among the highlights. Prices were more typical of the 1990s than the 2000s, with the 1792 bringing $2200 and the 1862 Borges just $1200.

Christie's South Kensington, 2006

Historically, Christie's best Madeira sales have been at King Street, but in February 2006 an outstanding sale was held in South Kensington. The wines belonged to a Birmingham, England, collector, raising money to add a conservatory to his house. Though the prices he received seem modest just four years later, they far exceeded the consignor's expectations at the time.

Highlights of the sale included 1846 Averys Verdelho Reserva Velhissima (2 bottles each at $787), 1811 Blandy's Commemoration Bual Solera ($576), 1815 Cossart Gordon Waterloo Bual Solera ($691), 1846 H.M. Borges Terrantez ($1152) and three bottles of 1842 Terrantez with no shipper's name ($806).

A total of 349 bottles of 95 different Madeiras were sold, in 163 lots, with an average per bottle sale price of $292.

Christie's New York, 2007

In late 2007, a long-time New York-area Madeira collector anonymously consigned part of his large, well-chosen collection to Christie's in New York. Ninety-eight lots were sold, representing only 298 bottles, with a gross of $345,093. This sale can be seen as a turning point in the Madeira auction market, with an average bottle price of over $1150. The 98 lots generated an incredible 72 records that have yet to be broken. Today, this sale stands as the high-water mark for Madeira prices at auction.

Highlights of the collection were a bottle of 1789 Rutherford & Miles Cama do Lobos which sold for $7200; 1795 Abudarham Terrantez, bottled 1942 ($4560), 1862 HM Borges Terrantez ($4800), and 1868 Cossart Gordon Very Old Boal "EBH" ($3600). A case of 1795 Barbeito Terrantez brought $36,000.

More Madeiras from this important collection achieved high prices at Christie's New York on November, 12, 2010.

The Graham Lyons Sale, 2008

Graham Lyons, a British wine collector who was a frequent buyer at London sales in the 1970s, consigned part of his massive collection to Zachy's for a sale in New York in April 2008. The collection, which spanned all the world's wine regions, included 111 bottles of fifty different Madeiras, of which eleven sold for more than $1000 a bottle.

Despite the small number of bottles of Madeira in the sale, it was a stellar group, including 1846 Averys Terrantez ($2032), 1792 Blandy's Extra Reserve Solera ($2988), 1846 Averys Verdelho Reserva Velhissima ($1195), 1862 HM Borges Terrantez ($2788), 1815 Lomelino Bual ($1016), the rare 1838 Averys Verdelho ($896) and the very rare 1789 Rutherford & Miles Cama de Lobos ($4900).

A subsequent single-owner sale of Lyons' wines, including many Madeiras, was held by Zachy's on December 3, 2010.

The William Leacock Collection, 2008

On December 11, 2008, William Leacock, the last of the Madeira Leacocks, sold his wine collection at Christie's in London. Other former members of the Madeira trade have sold wine at auction, but since records have been kept, there's never been a sale even remotely like this one.

His collection represented virtually everything still belonging to the Leacocks, major players in the Madeira trade for 250 years. William was the only son of Edmund Leacock, who had bought out his brother Julian's interest in the business in 1953. So, the wines ended up with William.

Yet there's much more to the importance of this collection. It was the crème de la crème—the result of a consolidation in the Madeira trade that left the Leacocks and Blandys in control of the Madeira Wine Association and its stocks of old wine. With an eye to the future, both families pulled out a few bottles of all the greatest wines for their own collections.

There has never been a major auction of Blandy family-owned wines. The Blandys had more offspring than the Leacocks, which led to more dividing of the family jewels over the generations. No Blandy descendent has ever sold more than a few bottles at a time, but on one day, William Leacock sold most of the Madeira he inherited: twenty-five unique and irreplaceable wines, of which two-thirds were from the eighteenth or nineteenth centuries. And though the most important wines generally numbered under three or four dozen bottles, such quantities are unprecedented in at least the past half century. A total of 1,236 bottles, in 182 lots, were offered for sale, including:

1795 F.F. Ferraz Terrantez (20 bottles)
1808 Leacock Madeira Solera (36 bottles)
1836 Lomelino Bastardo (24 bottles)
1845 Lomelino Quinta da Paz (34 bottles)
1846 Leacock Terrantez (9 bottles)
Undated HM Borges Terrantez—believed 1862 (48 bottles)
1868 EBH Very Old Bual (23 bottles)

Although a few lots achieved very high prices, the large quantities in the sale resulted in many of the wines selling below what they were worth. For example, the 23 bottles of 1868 EBH Very Old Bual sold for an average price of $568. A bottle of the same wine bearing a Cossart Gordon label sold for $3600 in New York in December 2007.

Another terribly undervalued wine in the sale was the undated HMB Terrantez, which is believed to be the famous 1862. The 48 bottles sold for an average of $566 a bottle. In contrast, at three U.S. sales during 2007 and 2008, 1862 HM Borges Terrantez sold for $2788, $3824, $4200 and $4800.

Finally, the 34 bottles of 1845 Lomelino Quinta da Paz sold for a modest $627 a bottle. The last time this legendary wine had been seen at auction was 1987. As for the 1836 Lomelino Bastardo—whose final 12-bottle lot sold for a mere $459 a bottle—this great Madeira has not only never before been seen at auction, but at 172 years old, it could well be the oldest Bastardo ever auctioned.

Now that the Leacock wines have been dispersed, it seems unlikely that a Madeira collection of such magnitude, rarity, importance and exceptional provenance will ever again come onto the market.

APPENDIX V

COSSART, GORDON PRINCIPALS 1745 TO 1990

Dates	Title of firm	Names of partners	Dates
1745-1748	Francis Newton	Francis Newton George Spence	1745-1805 1748-1758
1748-1758	Newton & Spence	Thomas Gordon Thomas Newton	1758-1802 1758-1763
1758-1775	Newton & Gordon	William Johnston Thomas Murdoch	1775-1790 1791-1839
1775-1791	Newton, Gordon & Johnston	William Gordon Sr. J.D. Webster Gordon	1798-1809 1802-1850
1791-1802	Newton, Gordon & Murdoch	Robert Scott William Cossart Sr.	1805-1827 1809-1823
1802-1805	Newton, Gordon, Murdoch & Co.	H.S. Wilbraham E.W. Reilly	1823-1823 1826-1834
1805-1834	Newton, Gordon, Murdoch & Scott	Peter Cossart William Cossart Jr.	1831-1870 1840-1887
1834-1839	Newton, Gordon, Murdoch & Co.	William Gordon Jr. Charles S. Marsh	1840-1859 1848-1855
1839-1861	Newton, Gordon, Cossart & Co.	Russell Manners Gordon Leland Crosthwait Cossart	1850-1857 1867-1898.
1861-1907	Cossart, Gordon & Co	Webster Gordon Cossart Charles J. Cossart	1872-1921 1874-1929
		London	Madeira
1907-1990	Cossart, Gordon & Co. Ltd. London	Henry Peter Cossart 1880-1935 Sidney Gordon Cossart 1915-1952	Charles John Cossart 1874-1929 Charles Blandy Cossart 1904-1922
1953-1990	Cossart, Gordon & Cia. Lda. Madeira	Noël Cossart 1952-1976 Charles David Gradidge Cossart 1976-1990	Arthur R. Blandy Cossart 1930-1936 Noël Cossart 1936-1976

APPENDIX VI

MADEIRA WINE SHIPPERS

Lists of British firms 1722-1880, compiled by Charles J. Cossart from his scrapbooks dated from 1880 to 1898.

1722
At a meeting of the British Factory held on October 26th, 1722, the following factors were present, all shippers except as otherwise noted:

William Rider HM Consul	Alexander French
Joseph Hayward	Augustus Lynch
John Miller	John Bissett
Daniel Noyer	Benjamin Bartlett
P. Vallette	William Goddard
Richard Miles	George Lawrence
James Pope	

1748
In a letter dated December 6th 1748 Francis Newton mentions shippers besides himself: Mr. Richard Hill, Mr. Chambers, Mr. Rider, Mr. Gordon, Stevens & Partner, and Mr. Catanach. In the above list of factors HM Consul is Mr. Rider, but Newton also mentions a Mr. Rider. This may be the same man as mentioned in 1722.

1754
A Consular Certificate issued by HM Consul at Funchal, in the "Archives" of "The Navy and Overseas," in the National Library, Lisbon, declares that the following British residents were trading in Funchal on January 31st, 1754; all shippers except as otherwise noted:

John Catanach	John Searle
William Murdoch	Francis Newton
Richard Hill	William Nash Shipper & HM Consul
Thomas Lamar	John Scott
Richard Hill Jr.	Sam Sills Shipper & HM Vice Consul
Matthew Hiscox	John Pringle
James Gordon	Charles Chambers

1786-1790

Scott & Co.	Moore
Charles Alder	Robert Linton
Allen Aravia & Co.	Denyer
Brush	Denyer & Blackburn
Condell	Wm. Foster & Sons

MADEIRA THE ISLAND VINEYARD

Lamar & Lynch
Lamar, H. B. & Co.
Allen & Co.
Nowlan & Leacock
L. H. Bissett & Co.
Lynch
A. Ahmuty
J. D. S. Duff
Johnston & Co.
George Sealy
Lamar
J. L. Banger
Phelps & Morrissey
Fleming
Duff
Searle
Foster
Murdoch, Fearns & Co.
Newton, Gordon & Johnston
Allen, A. & Co.
J. Searle & Co.
Phelps & Co.
Condell & Co.

C. & Wm. Lynch
Widow Foster & Son
Lamar, H. B. & Lynch
Robert Cock
Condell Innes & Co.
J. & W. Phelps
E. More
Denier B. & Co.
S. Banger & Co.
S. Towns & Co.
Foster & Co.
Linton & Sealy
Murdoch & Co.
Bissett
Towns
Dubisson
Newton, Gordon, Johnston
Selby Towns
William Alder & Co.
Brush Selby & Co.
Lynch & Co.
Duff & Co.
Leacock & Co.

1790-1799

Wm. Foster & Sons
Banger & Co.
S. Weston & Co.
I. M. Pintard
Scott & Co.
Gordon Duff & Co.
J. C. Smith
Magrath & Higgins
C. & W. Lynch & Co.
Dunn
James Ayres Dunn
James Moore
Condell Innes & Co.
Ahmuty Masterton & Co.
J. & W. Phelps
Linton & Co.
J. J. & W. Leacock
Charles Alder
Allen & Co.
Sheffield & Co.
Goodall

Reilly
Selby
Cock
Linton
Allen
Casey
Murdoch Fearns & Co.
Newton, Gordon & Murdoch
Newton, Gordon & Co.
Silas Twiner
Hills Bissett & Co.
Linton & Bell
C. Alder & Co.
Leacock
James Sheffield
Lynch & Co.
M. Masterston & Co.
Phelps & Co.
Forbes White & Co.
T. Hayward

1800-1804

J. C. Smith
Newton, Gordon & Murdoch
C. & Wm. Lynch & Co.
Bellringer

Magrath & Higgins
James Ayres & Co.
J. White & Co.
Banger & Co.

MADEIRA WINE SHIPPERS

C. Alder &. Co.
Sheffield (James)?
Condell Innes & Co.
M. Masterton & Co.
Gordon Duff & Co.
J. & W. Phelps & Co.
Scott & Co.
Forster & Sons
Joseph Selby
J. Blackburn & Son
I. F. Smith
J. Horne
Henry Young
Allen & Co.
Young & Lamar
Hill Bissett & Co.
Magrath & Co.
Bissett & Co.
Forbes & Co.
James Sheffield & Co.
Leacock
Banger
Allen
Phelps
Selby & Ayres
Wardrop & Co.
Lamar
J. R. Setuval
Reilly

Bissett
Phelps & Co.
Lynch & Co.
J. Horne & Co.
James Gordon
J. & Wm. Leacock
Condell
Bissett & Phelps
Murdoch Yuille Wardrop & Co.
W. Phelps & Co.
Condell & Co.
Charles Alder & Co.
Leacock & Co.
Robert Linton
John Anglin
Newton, Gordon, Murdoch & Co.
Murdoch, M. & Co.
William & H. Young
R. Symonds
Forbes Crawford & Co.
J. & W. Leacock & Co.
Riggs
Robert Cock
J. W. Phelps
Martin Bicker
Fleming & Co.
Forbes & Co.
Duff & Co.
Fitzgerald

1805-1809

Gordon Duff & Co.
Newton, Gordon & Murdoch
Smith & Robinson
Leacock & Co.
Murdoch, M. & Co.
Phelps & Page & Co.
G. & R. Blackburn
Sheffield & Young
Haywards & Co.
Joseph Selby
C. & W. Lynch & Co.
Scott & Co.
Lynch & Co.
Ayres
Murdoch Yuille Wardrop & Co.
Consul Pringle
Francis K. Smith
W. S. Shaw
S. Anglin & Co.
Colson Smith & Co.

C. Alder & Co.
W. S. Shaw
J. & W. Leacock
Widow Foster & Co.
Blackburn & Co.
M. Dougall
J. Phillips
J. Karrick
W. Harwood
J. Beasly
W. S. Shaw
Linton & Co.
J. Herald
S. Clement
J. Morris
J. & W. Leacock & Co.
James Carey
Wardrop & Co.
Cathcart & Co.
James Reilly

MADEIRA THE ISLAND VINEYARD

J. Welsh Consul
James Ayres Consul
Hicklin & Anglin
Charles Alder
Foster & Co.
Colson Smith & Robinson
Sheffield & Yuille
Lamar
Martin Bicker
W. Foster & Sons
R. Linton
Hayward & Co.
Leacock (J.)
John Anglin
Condell & Co.
Henry Crawford
Newton, Gordon,
   Murdoch & Scott
Condell
Leacock & Co.
Condell Innes & Co.
Magrath & Co.
Magrath & Higgins
R. & P. Symonds
R. Foster
Maitland & Co.

Newton, Gordon & Co.
John Bellringer
Houghton & Co.
Mr. Young
Cathcart Foster & Co.
C. McCabe
J. Gould
J. Haughton
William Hunter
Linton & Gough
Agent (Hart)
John Bennet
G. D. Welch
I. Ray
J. Cameron
Magrath & Co.

Beasly
J. M. Douglap
H. Crawford & Co.
Beiker
Briken
Keir & Co.
Manly & Heart
Maneby

1810-1811 (April)

Gordon Duff & Co.
Wardrop & Co.
Newton, Gordon,
   Murdoch & Scott
D. Maitland
J. Robinson & Co.
Manly & Co.
J. Anglin
S. & C. Smith
Phelps & Page & Co.
Lynch & Co.
G. Gould & Co.
John Searle
R. & R. Symonds
S. Youngs
Scott & Co.
Linton & Co.
M. Stocks
G. Gould
H. Crawford & Co.
Blackburn & Co.
S. T. Alder & Co.
Keirs & Co.
James Carey
S. Houghton

M. Stokes
Sheffield & Young

J. Cathcart
M. Beiker & Co.
Crawford & Co.
J. & R. Blackburn & Co.
Leacock & Harris
J. Robinson & Oliveira
J. Bellringer
M. Wallace
Shaw
McCabe
A. Doran
T. Edwards
Beikens
Smith & Co.
J. D. Lewis & Co.
Begbie
S. Bennet
Scott
J. Stanley
C. W. Lynch & Co.
Innes & Co.

MADEIRA WINE SHIPPERS

December 1823 - May 1824

Gould Roupe & Co.
Scott Loughman & Co.
J. Blandy & Co.
Murdoch Yuille Wardrop
Symonds Ruffy & Co.
James Selby
J. B. Bocage
John Searle & Co.
W. Findly
Murdoch Yuille & Co.
Keirs & Co.
J. H. March & Co.
J. C. T. Uzel
John Anglin
J. R. Blackburn & Co.
Minett & Sons
James Houghton
Newton, Gordon, Murdoch & Scott
Gordon Duff & Co.
J. E. Reilly
Phelps & Page & Co.
Alex Hally
R. Brousce
P. Wallace
Murdoch Wardrop & Co.

October 1828 - December 1828

Gordon Duff & Co.
Staner
Symonds & Co.
T. Edwards & Co.
March & Co.
Thomas Dunn & Co.
Lewis & Co.
Kruger
Newton, Gordon, Murdoch & Co.
Keirs & Co.
John Blandy
Murdoch Yuille & Co.
G. & R. Blackburn
Blandy & Co.
Gordon Duff
Leacock Harris & Co.
Scott Loughan & Co.

By December 1828 the number of British shippers in the island increased to 71. In 1855 these were reduced to:

Newton, Gordon, Cossart & Co.
Leacock Harris & Co.
Welsh Brothers
R. Donaldson
Henry Dru Drury
Shortridge Lawton & Co.
Gordon Duff & Co.
T. Edwards & Co.
Blandy Brothers
Rutherford, Browne & Miles
Krohn Brothers & Co.
Henriques Lawton
John Hutchins
T. S. & J. W. Selbey
G. & R. Blackburn

During the phylloxera period in the 1870s the above were reduced to:

British
Cossart, Gordon & Co.
Blandy Brothers & Co.
Leacock & Co.
Rutherford, Browne & Miles
Welsh Brothers
Krohn Brothers
Henry Dru Dury
Shortridge Lawton & Co.
T. S. & J. W. Selbey (incorporated in Cossart, Gordon)
T. Edwards & Co. Barão da Conçeicão

Other nationalities
T. T. da Camara Lomelino
Viuva Abudarham & Filhos
F. F. Ferraz & Cia.
Luiz Gomes da Conçeicão & Cia.
A. P. Cunha
Henriques & Henriques
Camara & Freitas
Luis Soares Henriques
Meyrelles Sobrinho & Co.
H. M. Borges
Roberto Leal

1880

The principal shippers, with total quantities of wine cleared for export from the island at the Madeira Custom House during the year 1880, compiled from official sources, were:

Firm	Total (pipes)
Cossart, Gordon & Co.	1,073
Krohn Bros & Co.	608
Henriques & Lawton	247
Blandy Brothers & Co.	176
Leacock & Co.	153
H. Dru Drury	140
A. P. Cunha	117
Barâo da Conceição	105
Luis Soares de S. Henriques	100
Camara & Freitas	65
Viuva Abudarham & Filhos	61
John Hutchison	59
Tarquinio T. da Camara Lomelino	43
Welsh Brothers	42
Robert Wilkinson	37
Meyrelles Sobrinho & Co.	31
Robert Donaldson	30
T. S. & J. W. Selby	25
Frank Wilkinson	22
168 shippers of less than 20 pipes each	557
Total	3691

The total shipments for the last three years were:
1878: 2125 pipes; 1879: 2923 pipes; and 1880: 3691 pipes

APPENDIX VII

SHIPPERS AND IMPORTERS, 1984

Shipper, Funchal	United Kingdom	United States
Belem's Madeira Wine Lda.	Not represented	Portuguese Importers, Inc., 975 Reed Rd., Stamford, CT
Blandy's Madeira Lda. M. W. Co.	Hedges & Butler Ltd., Three Mill Lane, Bromley-by-Bow, London E3 3DU	House of Burgundy, Inc., 534 West 58th Street, New York, NY 10019
H. M. Borges, Sucrs. Lda.	Amverdiffe Ltd., Liverpool	Classic Wine Imports, Inc., 1356 Commonwealth Ave, Boston, MA
Carma Vinhos Lda.	John Harvey & Sons, Harvey House, Whitchurch, Bristol BS99 7SE	Not represented
Cossart, Gordon & Co. Lda. M. W. Co.	Cossart, Gordon & Co. Ltd, 57 Cambridge St., London SWIV 4PS	Almaden Vineyards, Inc., 1530 Blossom Hill Road, San José, CA 95118
Henriques & Henriques Lda.	Atkinson, Baldwin & Co. Ltd., Saint Mary's House, 42 Vicarage Crescent, London SW11 3LB	Robert & Philip, Inc., Willwood Rd, Stamford, CT *and* Merchant du Vin, 214 University St., Seattle, WA
Leacock & Co. (Wine) Lda. M. W. Co.	Direct Wines (Windsor) Ltd., New Aquitaine House, Paddock Road, Reading, Berks RG4 OJY	World Shippers & Importers, 1616 Walnut Street, Philadelphia, PA 19103
Rutherford & Miles Lda. M. W. Co.	Rutherford, Osborne & Perkin Ltd., Martini Terrace, 80 Haymarket, London SW1	National Distillers Products Co. 99 Park Avenue, New York, NY
Shortridge Lawton & Co. M. W. Co.	Prospero Wines Ltd., 2 Warrington Crescent, London W91ER	To be appointed
Miles Madeiras Lda. M. W. Co.	Not represented	Wines & Spirits Inc., 4400 East 14th Street, Des Moines, IA 50516
T. T. da Camara Lomelino Lda. M. W. Co.	Russell & McIver Ltd., The Rectory, St Mary-at-Hill, London EC3R 8EE	To be appointed
Vinhos Viuva Abudarham & Fos. Lda. M. W. Co.	Not represented	Corti Bros., 5760 Freeport Boulevard, Sacramento, CA 95822
Vinhos Barbeito (Madeira) Lda.	Deinhard & Co. Ltd., 29 Addington St., London SEI 7XT	Park, Benziger & Co. Inc., Scarsdale, NY 10583
Welsh Bros (Vinhos) Lda. M. W. Co.	Not represented	Bonsal Seggerman & Co. Inc., 27 The Plaza, Locust Valley, NY

Note: The initials M. W. Co. indicate membership of the Madeira Wine Company Limitada.

MADEIRA THE ISLAND VINEYARD
SHIPPERS, 2010

At the end of 2009, eight companies are registered with the Instituto do Vinho, do Bordado e do Artesanato da Madeira (IVBAM) as exporters:

        H. M. Borges, Sucrs, Lda.
        Henriques & Henriques – Vinhos S.A.
        Madeira Wine Company, S.A.
        Pereira D'Oliveira (Vinhos), Lda.
        Vinhos Barbeito (Madeira), Lda.
        Vinhos Justino Henriques, Filhos, Lda.
        J. Faria & Filhos, Lda.
        P. E. Gonçalves, Lda.

Of these, only the first six are actively involved in the exportation of quality Madeira. A seventh company, Artur de Barros e Sousa, also produces quality wines, but they are not registered for export. They are a partidista—in business to make and mature wine for sales to exporters and other traders. However, they do sell wine locally to visitors.

APPENDIX VIII

EARLY SETTLERS

Most of these names exist at present, in one form or another, and are the leading family names in Madeira. This list was compiled by Charles J. Cossart from Dr. Azevedo's edition of Gaspar Fructuoso's *As Saudades da Terra* for Miss Ellen M. Taylor's work, *Madeira – Its Scenery & How to See It*, published by Edward Stodart, London 1882, and was used by Mr. A. J. Drexel Biddle, FRGS, PGSA, FRMS, in his comprehensive treatise in two volumes on *Madeira, Land of Wine*, published in Philadelphia and San Francisco in 1901.

Distinguished Madeiran colonists

ABREU This family, from Portugal, settled in Madeira and had grants at the Arco da Calheta. It became a margado (entail) in 1545.

ACHIOLI, or ACCIAIOLI Simon Achioli, from a distinguished Florentine family, settled in 1515.

AGRELLA Fernão Alvaro d' Agrella, in 1480.

AGUIAR One of the first settlers was Diogo Alfonso d'Aguiar, early in the fifteenth century.

ALBUQUERQUE First mentioned in 1570.

ALDROMAR Bissayan, in 1500.

ALLEMÃO Henrique Allemäo, or German Henry, a Polish prince to whom large tracts of land at Magdalena do Mar were given by Prince Henry in recognition of services at arms. Supposed to have been Ladislas VI King of Poland and Hungary who, according to legend, having been defeated by the Turks at Varna in 1444, wandered about the world in shame. The story is that after the battle of Varna Ladislas joined the Infante Dom Henrique against the Moors, and in recognition of valour he was given the district of Magdalena in Madeira, where he built a palace; and was called King. The grant of lands and title of Lord of Magdalena were confirmed by King Alfonso of Portugal in 1457. Henrique Allemão married in Madeira and had a son, who was drowned when his boat was sunk by a fall of rock at Cabo Girão. There are no direct descendants left in the islands.

ALMADA Pedro de Almada settled about the beginning of the sixteenth century. He was a nephew of the celebrated Conde de Abranches. In recognition of good service rendered, the King of England conferred on him the Order of the Garter in 1501.

ALMEIDA Constança Rodrigues de Almeida was wife of João Gonçalves Zarco. Amador de Almeida was given a grant of arms in 1538.

ALVARES Luiz Alvares da Costa founded the monastery of St. Francis in Funchal in 1473.

AMARAL Francisco d' Amaral, Machico, 1557.

AMIL Settled early in the fifteenth century. In Dam Manoel's time João Fernandes de Amil was entrusted with the building of the hospital in Funchal in 1561.

ANDRADE Early in the fifteenth century.

ANNES Early in the fifteenth century. Founded the chapel of São Bartholomeu in Funchal, now demolished.

ARAGÃO From Dam Pedro de Aragão, brother of Isabel of Castille.

ARANHA From one of this family Becco dos Aranhas was named.

ARAUJO About the end of the fifteenth century.

ARCO From João Fernandez de Andrade, a Galician, who took the name of Arco after founding the chapel of São Braz at Arco de Calheta.

ARNÂO From William Arnold, who accompanied Phìllippa, Queen of John I, to Portugal.

ATAIDE His daughter married the third captain of Funchal.

ATHOUGUIA One of the first settlers. The parish of Athouguia at Calheta retains his name.

AYRES Gonçallo Ayres Ferreira, one of the companions of Zarco, was father of Adão Gonçalves, the first Madeira-born boy, who built the original Mount Church.

AZEVEDO From Manoel Faria de Azevedo, who was wrecked at Madeira on his voyage to India from Portugal.

AZINHAL From Estevão do Azinhal in 1471.

BAPTISTA From Messer Baptista, a Genoese settler in 1480.

BARBOZA Pedro Barboza married Dona Helena de Menezes, heiress of Garcia Moniz, Morgado of Caniço.

BARRADAS In 1573 Antonio Barradas was the notary of the hospital of Funchal.

BARRETO Two soldiers in this family distinguished themselves in Tangier.

BARROS One of the earliest colonists.

BAYÃO From Dam Arnalda Bayão, Belchior Bayão, among the first settlers.

EARLY SETTLERS

BERINGUER From Pedro Beringuer de Lemilhana, of Valencia, a noble of the Spanish court, came to Madeira in 1480.

BETTENCOURT From Henrique and Gaspar de Bettencourt, French cavaliers, who in 1450 came to Madeira with their uncle Maciot de Bettencourt, after he sold his possessions, the Canary Islands, to Prince Henry.

BORGES From Duarte Borges, a noble, in 1538.

BOTELHO From a gentleman of the bed-chamber of the Infante Dam Luiz-Francisco Botelho de Andrade, one of whose sons perished at Tangier with Dom Sebastian.

BRAGA João de Braga was one of the first colonists.

BRANCO Diogo Branco, great benefactor to the hospital.

BRANDÃO Duarte Brandão, in the reign of Dom John II.

BRAZ Fernão Braz, a member of the town council in 1471.

BRITO From Pedro de Brito de Oliveira Pestana, who came to Madeira in 1470.

BRUM From Paulo Brum, a Frenchman.

CABRAL From a noble of Prince Henry's household in the beginning of the fifteenth century.

CAHUS From Jean Cahus, a Frenchman, in 1580.

CAIRES, or CAIROS An old and noble name. Constantino de Cairos of Madeira is mentioned in old records as having been a valiant soldier in India.

CALDEIRA One of the first colonists. Settled at Camara de Lobos.

CAMARA Joáo Gonçalves Zarco took the additional surname of da Camara, which, as well as the arms granted by Prince Henry, was confirmed by King Alfonso V in 1460.

CAMELLO Settled in Madeira in 1471.

CANHA From Ruy Pires de Canha, one of the earliest colonists. The parish of Canhas derives its name from him. He built the first church there.

CARDOZO An old Portuguese name. Nuno Fernandez Cardozo was Morgado of Gaula.

CARVALHAL From Lopo de Carvalhal.

CARVALHO From Antão Alvarez de Carvalho, one of the first settlers.

CASTEL-BRANCO From Dom Guiomar de Castel-Branco, who died in 1629, leaving a large estate to the church at Ribeira Brava.

CASTELLO-BRANCO A. D. Joáo de Noronha Castello-Branco

distinguished himself against the Moors.

CASTRO From Diogo Fernandez de Castro, in the reign of Dom João II.

CATANHO From Kyrio and Raphael Catanho, Genoese; the former had been captain of the body-guard of Francis I of France.

CEZAR From a Genoese, brother to André Cezar, celebrated in history.

CHAVES Martin de Chaves, an early settler in 1471.

CIDRÃO From Joáo Cidrão, a citizen in 1448. One of the town bridges bears his name.

CISNEIRO From Dom Francisco Cisneiro, of Toledo, captain of one of the companies of Spanish troops who took possession of Madeira in 1584.

COELHO One of the first colonists.

CORREIA From Alvaro Alfonso Correia, gentleman of the bed-chamber of the first Duke of Bragança. He built the church of Nossa Senhora do Calhau, and died in 1490.

CORTEZ From Manoel Cortez, of Oporto, in 1615.

COSTA From Luiz Alvarez da Costa. He founded the convent of São Francisco in Funchal.

COUTO Founder of the chapel at Santo Amaro.

CUNHA One of the first settlers.

D'EÇA or DE SÁ Dona Joanna d'Eça was first lady of the bed-chamber to Queen Catherine of Bragança, wife of Charles II of England.

DORIA From Estevão Annes Cinta Doria, a Genoese noble, in 1480.

DRUMMOND From John Drummond, son of Sir John Drummond, Lord of Stobhall, brother of Annabella, Queen of Robert III of Scotland. Authentic documents prove that this John Drummond came to Madeira in 1425, evidently as a refugee, as it was not until on his deathbed that he revealed his real name. Up to that time he went by the name of "João Escocio," or John the Scot. He married Branca Alfonso, sister of the first vicar of Santa Cruz. His descendants are numerous at present in Madeira. The present head of the family is the Morgado d'Aragão.

DURO From Manoel Mendes de Duro.

ESCOBAR From Pedro de Escobar, a Spaniard, who settled in Madeira in 1500.

ESMERALDA From Jean d'Esmenaut, a Fleming, in 1480, who built the great mansion where Columbus stayed in Rua do Esmeralda.

ESPINOLA From Leonardo and Antonio Spinola, Genoese, of the family of Spinola, celebrated in history.

EARLY SETTLERS

FARIA From Braz Gil de Faria, an early settler near Camara de Lobos.

FAVILLA From Fernão Favilla, a noble of the court of Dom Manoel, early in the sixteenth century.

FERNANDEZ One of the first names in lists of colonists.

FERREIRA From Braz Ferreira, who died in 1493.

FIGUEIRA From Gonçallo Figueira, who came from Galicia in the reign of King Fernando. Alvaro Figueira was the first of the name who came to Madeira.

FIGUEIROA From Pedro de Figueiroa, settled at Machico and Santa Cruz early in the sixteenth century.

FLORENÇA From João Salvati, a Florentine who, concerned in the conspiracy against the Médicis, fled to Madeira in 1478, where his descendants are known by the name of Florença.

FRANÇA From André de França, a Polish gentleman, who came to Madeira in 1450. His ã son, João de França, built the church of Nossa Senhora da Graça at the Estreito da Calheta.

FRAZÃO From Pedro Frazão. who was settled in Madeira in 1532.

FREITAS From Gonçallo de Freitas, one of Dom Fernando's court; also from João Rodriguez de Freitas of Algarve, who married the widow of Henrique Allemáo, the Polish prince, Morgado of Magdalena.

FRIAS From Romeu de Frias, an Italian, whose lands retain his name.

GALHARDO From a Frenchman named Gaillard.

GAMA From Lourenço Vaz Perreira de Gama.

GIL From Vasco Gil, a man of some note in Funchal in 1472. His lands retain his name.

GIRALDES From Pietro Giraldes, a Florentine, who founded a hospital at Calheta in 1535.

GOËS From Dom Anião da Astrada, Senhor de Goës in Asturia.

GOMES From João Gomes, one of Prince Henry's pages.

GONÇALVES From João Gonçalves Zarco, the discoverer of Madeira, and also from other colonists of the name of Gonçalvez.

GRAMACHO From Ruy Gramacho, a noble.

HENRIQUES From Dom João Henriques, third son of the Senhor d' Alcaçovas, chief huntsman of Dom Alfonso, Dom João II, and Dom Manoel, kings of Portugal in the fifteenth and sixteenth centuries.

HENRIQUES DE NORONHA From Dom Garça Henriques of Seville.

HEREDIA From Dom Antonio de Heredia, captain of the Spanish force sent to Madeira when Portugal was subject to Spain, in 1582.

HOMEM From Garcia Homem de Sousa, who married Catherina Gonçalves da Camara, daughter of Zarco. He was a noble of the household of Dom Manoel.

JAQUES From Raphael Jaques, an English merchant, who settled in Funchal in 1570.

JERVIS From Richard Jervis, an Englishman, who settled in Funchal in 1660. The present representative of this family is the Morgado Jervis.

LEAL One of the more ancient names of Madeira, especially at Porto da Cruz, where, on their property, the Lombo dos Leães, is the chapel of São João Nepumuceno.

LEME From Martim Leme, a Flemish cavalier, who had been gentleman of the bed-chamber to the Emperor Maximilian, and came to Madeira in 1483.

LIMOGES From the Frenchman Philippe Gentil de Limoges.

LOBO From Pedro Lobo, a cavalier in Prince Henry's court. It was he who brought the letter from Dona Beatrix and the Vicar of Thamar, forbidding the Madeirense to obey the Bishop of Tangier.

LOMELINO From two illustrious Genoese, Urbano and Baptista Lomelino, in 1470.

MACEDO From Martim Gonçalves de Macedo, one of King John I's captains, at the battle of Aljubarrota.

MATTOS An ancient name – begins with Luis Fernandes de Mattos Coutinho, who came to Madeira in 1580. He was descended from the kings of Leon.

MEDINAS From an ancient Spanish family.

MELLO This family is connected with the da Camaras and the Noronhas through Dona Branca de Mello.

MENDES From Martim Mendes de Vasconcellos, who was one of the four nobles sent by King John I to marry Zarco's four daughters.

MIALHEIRO, now MALHEIRO From Pedro Gonçalves Mialheiro, a Portuguese of noble family, in the fifteenth century.

MIRANDA From João Lourenço de Miranda, one of Zarco's companions on his first voyage to Madeira, and after whom the Ponta de São Lourenço is named.

MONDRAGÃO From João Rodrigues Mondragão, a Biscayan of noble family, who came in 1500.

MONIZ One of the first settlers in Madeira was Vasco Martim Moniz de Menezes.

EARLY SETTLERS

MONTEIRO Settled in Madeira during the reign of Dom Sancho I.

NETTO From João Rodrigues Netto, a nobleman from Salamanca. He lived in Funchal, and had a street made that the procession of Corpus Christi might pass his house. The street is named Rua dos Nettos.

NORONHA Dona Maria de Noronha was wife to the second captain of Funchal. The Quinta dos Padres at Campanario was the property of this family.

ORNELLAS From Alvaro de Ornellas, a noble of Prince Henry's court, one of the first colonists.

PERESTRELLO From Bartholomeu Perestrello, the first captain of Porto Santo.

PERRY From Joseph Perry, an English merchant, who settled in 1650.

PIMENTEL From Pedro Pimentel, a noble of the royal household. Came to Madeira in 1470, and married Dona Isabel Drummond.

PINTO From Lapo Fernandes Pinto, of noble descent. Came in 1500; had grants of the best lands at Santa Anna and the Ilha.

POLANCO SALAMANCA From Francisco de Salamanca Polanco, a native of Burgos, and one of the Spanish captains sent to Madeira in 1582.

QUINTAL From Diogo da Costa do Quintal, who built the chapel of Nossa Senhora das Angustias on his estate.

REGO From João de Regar a noble of Algarve.

RUA From Alvaro Annes da Rua, one of the first colonists, who died in 1471.

SANHA From Manoel Alfonso de Sanha, who had large grants of land from Ponta Delgada to the Lambada das Vaccas. He built the church at Ponta Delgada.

SAUVAIRE, now SAUVAYRE From Honorato Sauvaire of Marseilles, who came to Madeira in 1660 as French consul.

SCHOMBERG Extinct. Their lands were at Ponta do Sol.

SPRANGER From Adrian Spranger, a German, in 1600.

TEIVE From Diogo de Teive, Prince Henry's squire, who built the first sugar-mill in Madeira.

TEIXEIRA From Branca Teixeira, who married Tristam Vaz, first captain of Machico. Her husband took the name of Teixeira, or Teixeyra, as it was originally spelled.

UZEL From Ruy Vaz Uzel a Frenchman who settled at Atabua.

VARGAS From Christovão Vargas, a Spaniard of noble family.

VASCONCELLOS One of the oldest colonists.

VIZOVI From Robert Willoughby, an Englishman, whose name was changed to Vizovi. He came to Madeira from Portugal with his wife, Dona Antonia Coibem, in 1590. He was a knight of the Order of Christ in Portugal.

First Settlements

The first two settlements were at Funchal and Machico, and the next town built was Santa Cruz. Ponta do Sol was also an early settlement, and during the first years of its history acquired a good local reputation for the enterprise of its inhabitants.

APPENDIX IX
MUNICIPAL DISTRICTS OF MADEIRA AND PORTO SANTO

Municipal districts (*Concelhos*)	Parishes of
Funchal	Sé, Nossa Senhora da Monte, Santa Luzia, São Gonçalo, Santa Maria Maior, São Pedro, São Roque, Santo Antonio, São Martinho, Sagrado Coracão.
Camara de Lobos	Camara de Lobos, Campanàrio, Quinta Grande, Curral das Freiras, Estreito de Camara de Lobos.
Ponta do Sol	Canhas, Magdalena, Ponta do Sol, Ribeira Brava, Serra d' Agua, Atabua.
Calheta	Arco da Calheta, Calheta, Estreito da Calheta, Prazeres, Fajã da Ouvelha, Jardim do Mar, Paul da Mar, Ponta da Pargo.
Porto Moniz	Porto Moniz, Achadas da Cruz, Ribeira da Janella, Seixal.
São Vicente	Ponta Delgada, Bóa Ventura, São Vicente.
Santa Anna	Santa Anna, Fayal, São Roque, São Jorge, Arco de São Jorge.
Machico	Machico, Agua de Pena, Santo Antonio da Serra, Caniçal, Porto da Cruz.
Santa Cruz	Camacha, Caniço, Santa Cruz, Gaula.
Porto Santo	Nossa Senhora da Piedade.
Selvagens & Desertas	(Concelho of Funchal) Sé.

MADEIRA THE ISLAND VINEYARD

Altitudes of principal mountains, stations, or localities in Madeira

	Meters		Meters
Pico Ruivo	1,950	Pico da Arrebentão	1,171
Pico das Torrinhas (or Torres) do Poizo	1,823	Pico dos Bodes	1,135
		Pico da Cruz Campanàrio	936
Pico das Torrinhas de Boa Ventura	1,794	Levada in Ribeira Frio and Ribeira da Metade	c. 915
Pico Arrieiro	1,796	Torreiro da Luta	850
Pico Grande	1,643	Ribeiro Frio	750
Pica Ruivo on the Paul da Serra	1,626	Quinta Veitch, Jardim da Serra	750
Pico da Lagoa	1,451	Church at Carnacha and Santo Antonio da Serra	c. 701
Paisa Pass	1,390		
Eucumiada de Sao Vicente	c. 1,200	Church in the Curral das Freiras	613
Mount Church	599		
Cabo Girão (Brazen Head)	589	Santa Anna Hotel	c. 330
Penha d' Agua	583	São Jorge	325
Palheiro	548	Levada de Santa Luzia	170
Portella Pass	548	Quinta da Val	c. 106
Mirante Vista do Machico	538	Deanery	c. 90
Estreito de Camara de Labos	493	Quinta do Val Pariso	71
São Roque Church	344	Santa Luzia	70
		Madeira Wine Company	59

Altitudes of principal mountains on Porto Santo

Porto Santo	Meters	Desertas	Meters
Pico do Facho	507	Deserta Grande	highest 488
Pico da Gandia	492	Bugia Island	highest 411
Pico Juliana	455	Chão Island	highest 98
Pico Castelo	441		
Pico Branco	423	*Selvagen Island*	highest 150
Pico Ana Ferreira	278		
Pico Malhada	265		

APPENDIX X

QUINTAS AND HOUSES

from Charles J. Cossart's notes on old houses and quintas

Quintas built and laid out by Englishmen, 1760-1860

Quinta or house	Place	Owner
Bello Monte & wall round prazer (summer house)	Monte	Charles Murray HM Consul General

This was the first quinta built by an Englishman. It was passed over by Consul Murray to the Bishop and priests in 1788. The house was demolished and rebuilt as a hotel by Captain Sottero in 1915-16. It is now a school.

Quinta or house	Place	Owner
Quinta da Monte *also known as Quinta do Gordon Gordon and Quinta do Cossart*	Monte	J. D. Webster Gordon, 1802. Rebuilt by Peter Cossart in 1831 and extended by Leland Cossart in 1860
Quinta Cava	Monte	A. Wardrop. Extended by Charles Cossart in 1864
Quinta Valpariso	Valpariso	J. Holloway
Small *quinta*, M. da Camara's *quinta*	Valpariso	James Bean
Quinta da Achada	Camacha	William Penfold
Quinta Seicheiros	Santo da Serra	R. Ellicote
Quinta da Serra	Santo da Serra	J. Burnett
Quinta da Junta	Santo da Serra	John Blandy
Quinta Revoredo	Santa Cruz	John Blandy
Quinta do Pico do Infante	Pica do Infante	Robert Bayman
Quinta do Porto da Cruz	Porto da Cruz	Robert Donaldson
Quinta St Anna	Caminho do Monte	R. Davies
Quinta Palmeira	Caminho da Torrinha	H. Blackburn. Extended by H. Hinton
Quinta Magnolia	Ribeiro Seco	T. H. March
Quinta Pico São João	Pico S. João	T. Edwards. Repaired by T. Leacock
Quinta Holloway	C. do Meio	J. Holloway
Quinta Jesus, Maria, José	Estreito de Cama de Lobos	T. H. Edwards
Quinta Vigia	Funchal	R. Davies

MADEIRA THE ISLAND VINEYARD

Quinta or house	Place	Owner
Quinta Sta. Luzia	S. Luzia	John Blandy
Quinta da Levada	S. Luzia	A. Wardrop. Extended by Charles Cossart
Quinta Santa Cruz	Sta. Cruz	William Grant
The Deanery	Funchal	G. Stodart. Extended by C. Power
The Hermitage	S. Cruz	William Grant
Quinta Cama de Lobos	Cama de Lobos	Henry Veitch
Quinta Gorgulho	São Martinho	Henry Veitch
Quinta dos Pillares	São Martinho	Henry Veitch
Quinta Jardim da Serra (small *quinta*)	Jardim da Serra	Henry Veitch
Quinta Veitch (large *quinta* and tomb)	Jardim da Serra	Henry Veitch
Quinta St. Amaro	St. Amaro	William Telling
Quinta Levada de Santa Luzia	Sta. Luzia	John Anglin
Quinta St. Andre	Sta. Luzia	William Casey
Quinta da Pontinha	Funchal	William Grant
Quinta do Val	Val Formoso	James Murdoch

There was a small house here before, used as "Bachelor's Hall" until it passed to Quinta dos Pinheiros in 1771, when J. Murdoch bought the Val and laid out his quinta, practically rebuilding the house. Dr Renton lived at the Val between 1830 and 1839. He committed suicide there. H. Winbourne mentions staying at the Val on his way to the West Indies in January 1802.

Quintas bought or occupied by English families, 1760-1860

Quinta	Place	Owner
Maravilas	Funchal	The Hon. Caroline Norton
Achada	Funchal	Richard Hill, and later William Penfold
Pinheiros	Torrinha	Bachelor's Hall
Paz	Caminho do Monte	J. Lewis
Achadas	Camacha	James Gordon, and then William Hinton
Til	Funchal	James Gordon, and then William Hinton
Cava	Torrinha	Robert Wallace, and then William Cossart
Fayas	Camacha	H. Harris and later T. Taylor
Camacha Achada	Camacha	Park
Ameixeiras	Santo da Serra	T. H. March

QUINTAS AND HOUSES
Houses in Funchal occupied by British firms and consulates, 1760-1870

Address	Purpose	Owners
154 Rua dos Ferreiros	Stores & residence	Newton, Gordon/Newton, Gordon, Murdoch/Newton Gordon, Murdoch, Scott/ Newton, Gordon, Cossart & Co., and Cossart, Gordon & Co.
72 Rua dos Ferreiros	Stores & residence	Scott Penfold & Co.
94 Rua dos Ferreiros	Stores & residence	Keirs & Co.
94 Rua dos Ferreiros	British Consulate	Consul George Stodart, 1836-1858
8-10 Rua São Francisco	Stores & residence	John Blandy & Sons
16 Rua São Francisco	British Consulate	Consul Captain Erskine, 1858-1868
22 Rua da Alfandega	British Consulate	Consul George Hayward, 1868-1885
24 Rua da Alfandega	Stores & residence	Blackburn & Co.
22 Rua da Alfandega	British Consulate	Consul B. Penfold, 1885-1888
27 Rua dos Netos	Stores & residence	Joseph Selby & Sons
24-32 Rua das Merces	Stores & residence	Scott Penfold & Co.
25 Rua das Merces	Stores & residence	William Grant
Rua do Carma, now Largo do Phelps	Stores & residence	Phelps & Page & Co.
81 Rua da Carreira	Stores & residence	T. H. Edwards & Co.
12 Rua da Carreira	Stores & residence	John Searle & Co.
155 Rua da Carreira	Stores & residence	John Lewis & Co.
3 Rua da Bispo	Stores & residence	Leacock & Co.
3 Calçada de S Loreneo	Stores	Leacock & Co.
41 Rua dos Murcas	Stores & residence	Ellicott Roope & Co.
Jardim Piqueno	Stores & residence	John Hayward & March
29 Rua de João Tavira	Stores & residence	Burnett Houghton & Co.
2-5 Rua das Queimadas de Baixo	British Consulate	Consul H. Veitch, 1809-1836
78 Rua S de Outubro through to Rua dos Ferreiros	Stores & residence	H. Veitch, then Scott, Penfold & Veitch, and later Cossart, Gordon & Co.
28 Rua da Esmeralda	Stores & residence	Gordon Duff & Co.

Alexander Gordon, the founder of Gordon Duff & Co., and his brother James were implicated in the Scottish rebellions of 1745, with Francis and Andrew Newton. No 28 Rua do Esmeralda was the house occupied by Christopher Columbus during his stay in Madeira. Built by Jean d'Esmenaut (João Esmeralda), a Flemish merchant, in 1494, it was one of the only two-storied buildings of the time. Originally gothic, it was added to in the Portuguese Manuelino style, as is shown by a window in the garden of Quinta Palmeira. When

MADEIRA THE ISLAND VINEYARD

Gordon Duff left the island during the oidium, the building was used as a granary by the town council, who unfortunately demolished it in 1892. Gaspar Fructuoso refers to the building as a "great mansion." In his novel Theodor Hook, who stayed in it in 1813 as a guest of Gordon Duff, calls it a palace. There is a drawing of the House of Columbus by John A. Dix in A Winter in Madeira and a Summer in Spain, published in New York in 1850.

APPENDIX XI

ROBERT ALLSTON'S MADEIRAS

In his work *The South Carolina Rice Plantation*, compiled from the papers of the late Mr Robert F. Allston, Professor J. H. Easterby of Charleston College reveals the contents of the "Wine Room" at Chicora Wood Plantation as follows:

Number mark'd	Description	When Imported	When bottled	When finished
No 1.	1/4 Pipe = 11 4/12 Dozen Newton, Gordon, Murdock and Co's Madeira 10 yrs. old	In 1830 with Ward, Magill and Heriot—$36	May 1831	4 Bottles on floor
No 2.	1/4 Pipe Madeira—same brand and character—in closet over the Piazza	in 1831, with Ward and Magill $90	May 1832	done
No 3.	1/2 Pipe *Sercial* Madeira, same brand—22 Dozen	In 1833 by myself, cost and charges $200 in the wood	July 1834	74 Btl 11 Shelf B
No 4.	8 *Dozen* Madeira of various quality—all good—some superior.	In and previous to 1830 a present from *Mrs. B. Huger*		18 Bottle Shelf B
No 5.	1/8 Pipe = dozen Madeira rich N. G. M. and Co's *Reserve* 1817?	Bo't by Ward and me of A. W. Campbell the 1/4 Pipe @ *$150*	Summer 1836	31 Btles Shelf G
No 6.	1/4 Pipe = 11 dozen *Tinta* Madeira N. G. M. and Co. 2 Doz in box /62	In 1835 by me $112.50	1836	68 Bottles Shelf F
No 7.	1/4 Pipe = 10 4/12 dozen *Burgundy*—Madeira N. G. M and Co.	In 1835 by me $70	"	
No 8.	1/4 Pipe = *11 dozen* fine nutty Madeira N. G. M. and Scott—*Gov'r's Wine*	In 1837 for Govr. Butler, W. Hampton, Ward and me the Pipe $580	May 1838	Shelf G

No 9.	1/4 Pipe *Sercial Madeira* old as reputed but I think 'fined = 7 dozen and 7 N. G. M. and Scott	In 1838 in the name of Govr. Butler for Ward, A Robertson J H Allston and me $120	Summer 1839	12 Bottles on floor
No 10.	1/8 Pipe *Golden Sherry* in Demijohns	In 1838, Gourdin and Math. order'd by A. J. White		29 Bottles Shelf R
No 11.	1 Demijohn *old Madeira* from my good Aunt Mrs. E. F. Blyth (Brown paper tied over the cork)	bottled into Hock bottles and placed on Shelf in Wine room	1840	1 Bottle on floor
No 12.	15 Gall. Demijohn Amontillardo Sherry Wine 1840 bot at J. Vaughn's sale exposed to the Sun in its box till bottled—the box and straw about the Demi-john entirely decay'd at bottom.		1844	
No 13.	1 Do. Do. pale Sherry exposed to the Sun and weather till bottled—In attic N. E. side	1842 McNeil and and Blair	1844	Shelf S
No 14.	1/2 Pipe O. P. Madeira *Leacock*—1842 in name of Govr. *Butler* (1/4 pipe same for Hon A. P. Butler) This Cask was exposed to the weather and turn'd over every day or two until bottled. Cost $210.04 = 22 8/12 Doz Bottles (School House up in Attic)		May 14th 1844	
L. 1832	Leacock Wine from Dr North's Est.	1832 3 Doz. = $44.50		In boxes
	Brown Sherry Do	3 Doz.—$44.50		" "
No 15.	1/2 Pipe—20 4/12 Dozen bottles of all sorts & sizes V. P. Leacock's Madeira. In School House Attic north of No 14. In Cask it has been 6 months exposed to Sun and weather agitated ocasionally and [illegible]	Imported for me in 1845	July 28th 1846	

ROBERT ALLSTON'S MADEIRAS

1/4 Cask Golden Sherry Cork leak'd and I got from it but a few Dozen placed in Wine room on Sherry shelf	imported same time	Shelf P
Brandy Larronde 1 Qr. Cask—8 Demijohns	Decr. 1846	Basement
Claret " 10 Cases	" "	"

No. 16. "Mansanilla" 1/4 Pipe— 12 Doz | March 1847. East attic. | Apl. 1847 | Shelf R

2 Doz of this wine sent to Mr. J. H. Tucker

Brandy 2 Doz. in the Basement	Selected by J. H. Tucker in 1849	Mark'd 1805——

No 17. Madeira 1/2 of a 1/2 Pipe 2 Dozen sent as present to J. D. E. | Imported from J. D. Edwards taken with J. J. Ward. East Attic S. side | 1849 | Shelf D

No 18. Tinta 1 Qr Cask | Do. Do. Do. | 1849 | " C

No 19. Sherry 1/4 Cask "Pale Curious"—14 2/12 Dozen —$250 | 1851 G and M. E Attic N. side | 1851 Septr. | Shelf Q L & M

1856
Oct 31st Wine from the sale of R M Allan's Estate
Lot   Bottles
No 2. Leacock Madeira   20 on Shelf I
No 3.   "   "   52 on Shelf H
No 4.   "   "   65 on   "   A 2 Doz box'd /62
No 6. Pale Sherry   42 "   "   O 20 bot in box /62
No 7. Borodino Sherry   48 "   "   V 27 bot in boxes   "
1 Demijohn and 8 bottles of Pale Sherry Imported in 1845, on floor.

The reference to Newton, Gordon, Murdoch's "Burgundy Madeira" in No. 7 is interesting. The name was used before Madeira was fortified and since this lot was imported in 1835, it must have referred to a type, probably a "Tinta" Madeira, which is referred to in No. 6.

APPENDIX XII

ELIZABETH DAVID AND "THE NAPOLEON MADEIRA"

Elizabeth David was arguably the most important British food writer of the twentieth century, responsible for revolutionizing how the British ate. When she began writing just after World War II, the British were arguably the world's most sophisticated wine connoisseurs, but they were hopelessly parochial when it came to food, mired in a cuisine of roasted meat and boiled vegetables. Drawing on the cuisines of France, Italy, Greece and north Africa, she introduced Britons to a world of tastes and smells they didn't know existed, and became a culinary icon in the process.

Having written such classic books as *Mediterranean Food* (1950), *French Country Cooking* (1951), and *French Provincial Cooking* (1960), Ms. David suffered a stroke in 1963, at age 49. From then on, most of her writing was in the form of magazine articles, including a piece on Madeira for *Tatler* magazine. In researching the article, she initially focused on the legend of the 1792 Madeira given to the exiled Napoleon on his way to St. Helena, but she eventually chose to write about Noël Cossart's recently published book.

Ms. David's findings on the Napoleon Madeira were contained in letters written to David and Noël Cossart in the spring of 1985. Noël apparently wrote Ms. David about her research twice, but only one letter survived as a carbon copy in Noël's files, which is the source of all the correspondence that follows—reprinted with the permission of the Elizabeth David Estate.

The Correspondence

26.2.85

Dear David,

So many thanks for putting the Madeira info through my letter box. The list of your vintage Madeiras will be very useful. And what a lovely notice by your Doctor Elliott Burrows.

At the London Library recently I unearthed a journal kept by Baron Gourgaud, one of the friends who accompanied Napoleon into exile and stayed with him on St. Helena on until the end. He recorded how Northumberland stopped off Funchal and how Consul Veitch came on board and in fact dined with Napoleon and his companions. He also recorded that some magnificent peaches were sent out to the ship, and a lot of live chickens and so on.

My notes are already packed so I can't say exactly what else Gourgaud noted, but he didn't actually mention a pipe of Madeira being brought aboard. But that doesn't prove anything. The ship only stayed twelve hours so Veitch would have needed to work pretty fast – which after all he easily could have done. (I expect your father knows the Gourgaud journal).

Napoleon certainly had some Madeira in his cellar on St. Helena because in an article by André Simon in the Wine and Food Quarterly ALS mentions 30 bottles of Madeira as among the wines charged to N's account for 1816—

Anyway, I'm sure your father has all this, and if he says the story is true he must have a good reason and I don't question it. I just thought it would be fun to be able to produce the evidence. If it isn't forthcoming never mind.

Love to you
Elizabeth

15 rue Jean-Jaurès, Uzès, Gard, 3070 France
March 6th 1985

Dear Mr. Cossart

Thank you so much for your letter and for taking so much trouble to send me more information concerning the Veitch-Napoleon-Madeira episode. It's all very interesting.

While I disagree entirely with Rupert Croft-Cooke's summary dismissal of the story, I do see that there are some curious discrepancies to be taken into account. R.C-C doesn't mention them, but for one thing it seems a trifle odd that Veitch, himself a Madeira shipper, should have chosen to sell Napoleon a wine which he, Veitch, must have known wouldn't be drinkable for twenty years or more.

Next, in 1822, when the pipe of 1792 came back to Madeira from St. Helena, Veitch is supposed to have sold it to Charles Blandy. But, according to your dates, Charles Blandy was born in 1812 and so would only have been ten years old at the time Veitch sold the pipe in question.

I can't find any date for the birth of Charles's son John but I see in my notes from R.C-C that he died in 1912, although at what age is not revealed. But that he was old enough in 1840 to have bottled the wine seems unlikely, particularly as you mention that your paternal grandmother Anna Mary Blandy married your grandfather in 1874, and in your letter you say that she was John Blandy's twin.

Of course these are minor confusions, and are probably perfectly easily explained, they do not in any way invalidate the crucial point of the story.

I expect that David has told you of or sent you the notes I wrote him in great haste just before I left for France. At the time I couldn't get at those I had made from the journal kept by General Gourgaud who accompanied Napoleon to St. Helena because they were packed.

I came across General Gourgaud's Journal when I was looking for something quite different – concerning Napoleon's life on St. Helena, but if you don't know the book I think the passage relevant to Madeira may be of interest to you. When I get back to London I'll get the pages photocopied and send them to you.

The book is in the London Library. Its full title is General Baron Gourgaud. Sainte-Hélène, Journal Inédit de 1815 à 1818. Paris 1899.

Here are the main points: Vol.1

August 23 Fair weather, a good wine. We are making two knots an hour. At midday we sight Porto-Santo; at 2 o'clock Madeira.

August 24 We can pick out all of the buildings of Funchal and the vines. A strong Sirocco wind is blowing. The English consul comes aboard to greet the Admiral... The first grade of wines is for private customers in London; the second for the merchants; the third for... (illegible to the editors of the journal); the fourth for its merchants. The pipe of 40 dozen bottles sells for 63 pounds sterling ... we have been brought some peaches with firm yellow flesh, some figs and grapes. The English consul, M. Wilch who gave me these details dines with us and his Majesty. 84° Fahrenheit.

August 25 A great number of beasts, chickens and fruit are brought on board. At 8 o'clock in the evening we resume our voyage, at a speed of 8 to 10 knots an hour...

I found nothing further relevant to the Veitch story, and no mention of a pipe of wine being brought on board Northumberland. That doesn't say there wasn't one. Clearly General Gourgaud was interested in the subject of Madeira wines, even if Napoleon wasn't, and Veitch could easily have arranged with someone at dinner that afternoon with the generals and Napoleon to have a pipe of wine put on board next day, and without Gourgaud nothing in his journal. With the temperature at 84° F, a Sirocco blowing and all the livestock and fruit being brought aboard, he wouldn't have made notes of everything...

Do you have a copy of the Wine and Food Society's anthology published some while after André's death? The articles and other bits and pieces were chosen by Claud Moiny, who called the collection *The Bedside Book* (1972).

In it there's an article by André about Napoleon's food and drink on St. Helena. Most of it is a straight translation of Carême's introduction – or part of it – to his 5 volume *L'Art de la Cuisine Française au XIX Siècle*, but André added on a little list of wines which he says were in Napoleon's cellar at Longwood in June 1816. He doesn't say where he got the information from, but as he was always buying odd wine accounts and suchlike at auction (as of course you know) it may have been from something in his own collection.

Anyway he quoted 240 bottles of Bordeaux, 60 of Graves, 30 of Madeira, 150 of Teneriffe, 15 of Champagne, 15 of Constantia, 630 of Cape, 180 of beer. (No burgundy. No reference to a pipe of Madeira.)

Now I won't bother you any more with this longhand screed, for which I apologise. (No typewriter here).

I'll make what I can of the story without going into too much detail or speculation, which the *Tatler* readers wouldn't take in anyway. In fact I'm wondering whether it wouldn't be better if I kept it for another publication more suitable, and write something from a different angle for the *Tatler.* Your book is so packed with wonderful and fascinating information – the chapter about India for example – and the whole tradition and history of Madeira and its glorious wines that there is no need for me to make more than a brief résumé of the Napoleon story, and let people buy the book and find out for themselves.

David sent me a copy of the *Decanter* review by Dr. Elliott Burrows. I agree with everything he says. Of course I am abysmally ignorant of the whole subject, but I love the book and I love such

Madeira as I've ever drunk, and I hope I may be able to communicate my enthusiasm to readers.

With all good wishes and thanks
Yours sincerely
Elizabeth David

25th March 1985,

Dear Mrs. David,
    Please forgive me for not having thanked you for your very interesting letter of March 6th but I have not been too well, I think that you must soon be comming (sic) home so I will send this to your London home!
    I am rather disturbed regarding the discrepancies in the Blandy dates and will go into them. My Blandy Pedigree is in Madeira to have the new additions added and as soon as Adam returns it I will go further into the matter. In the mean time I would be most greatful (sic) to you if you could get me the pages of General Gourgaud's journal about this stay in Madeira. I have not the journal in my library, although I have Padre Francisco Augusto da Silva's account of Napoleon's passage, in Portuguese, which is based on General Bourgaud's journal. I have in my library a volume of Napoleon's Last Voyages being accounts of his voyages to Elba from the diaries of Admiral Sir Thomas Ussher in the "Undaunted," and to St Helena from the journal of John R. Glover, Secretary to rear Admiral Cockburn in "Northumberland." The latter gives a full description of the passage by Funchal. I have also notes taken from the diary of Sir George Bingham, commander of the troops which garrisoned St Helina (sic) and who also was in H.M.S. Northumberland. All the accounts seem to tally, of course the Northumberland and her escort did not anchour, they stood off Funchal while the troop ships and supply ship went into the bay to load, so any bulk wine would have been shipped in the supply ship "Weymouth." Loading was made very hazardus (sic) by the strong east wind blowing (Leste wind described on page II of my book) in fact, inspite (sic) of the fact that there is a "leste" wind nearly every August, the superstitious inhabitants attributed this destructive wind to Bonaparte being off the island, and were extremely apprehensive that their grapes, which were nearly ripe, would be

more than destroyed by the "leste" that this Atila had brought! A great deal of wine was loaded my own firm shipped over 10 pipes. If you wouls (sic) be interested I will ask David to photocopy my notes and send them to you. The amount of wine and food Napoleon consumed, as well as all his party in (sic) interesting, his normal breakfast, according to Mr. Glover was soup, roasted meat, a haricot marmalade, with porter and claret as a beverage. He never used a knife or fork eating everything with his hands. I think he must have developed the gastric complaint on St. Helina (sic). As soon as he boarded "Northumberland" he requested Admiral Cockburn to send a Brig to france (sic) for wine, and the "Peruvian" was sent to Guernsey on 8th August to procure French wines and to rejoin the convoy at Madeira where the French wine was put on "Northumberland."

All the narrators mention the wine, books and fruit Mr Veitch brought on board. Admiral Cockburn and Sir George Bingham expected Mr Veitch's visit and tried to keep him from meeting Napoleon, who was skulking in his cabin ever since they entered the bay of Funchal. When the "Northumberland" was passing the Deserta Islands the surgeon mentioned to Count Las Casas that these baren (sic) rocks resembled St. Helina (sic). Count Las Casas mentioned this to Napoleon which put him in a bad temper so he stayed below. By chance he looked on deck and saw Mr. Veitch who called him "Your Majesty" which delighted the Corsican corporal, who walked with him on deck and invited him to dine. Mr. Glover mentions going ashore to buy wine for Admiral Cockburn, Napoleon and the Mess. I do not have the article by Andre about the food and wine on St. Helina (sic) but I have seen it, and have often wondered why so much more Teneriffe than Madeira. I can only presume that the Madeira was more popular.

I am sure you will write an excellent piece for the Tatler without going too much into dates. If you chose to write from a different angle why not the pipe of Gunner Madeira given to the R.A.Mess? There are still officers alive who remember the Madeira wine, and who would be interested. However it may bring forth some correspondence.

Please excuse this too long and badly written letter.

Yours sincerely,
Noël Cossart.

APPENDIX XIII

MADEIRA'S FLYING BOAT ERA, 1949-1958

For two centuries, Madeira, with its spectacular scenery and subtropical climate, has been a major tourist destination, particularly for the British. It was also long considered a perfect place to avoid, or recover from, diseases like tuberculosis. However, because of the island's location 1300 miles south of England and 500 miles west of Africa, getting there was not always easy. There was no airport on the island before 1961, and travel by boat, even in the twentieth century, took more than three days. Yet, between 1949 and 1958, there was another option: flying boats.

In May, 1949, Barry Aikman's Aquila Airways began regular flying boat service between Southampton and Funchal, cutting the travel time to nine hours. The service was considered "luxury" for its time, with hot meals served in flight and a cocktail bar from which the "flying barman" kept passengers relaxed. Aquila described its service as "the last word in air comfort."

The planes were designed to take off from and land on water and were of types used by the British military in World War II. Two types of flying boats were used on the Southampton-Funchal route: Sunderland "Hythes," designed to carry 27 passengers, and Short "Solents," equipped for 42 passengers.

Throughout its brief history, which ended on September 30, 1958, Aquila's low-flying, unpressurized aircraft offered a luxury alternative to British vacationers. But despite their comforts, and the quick journey, they were not for everyone. (Noël Cossart, for example, preferred to travel by sea.) The cabins were not pressurized and the planes had more than their share of mechanical problems and far too many crashes. The most tragic accident was the one that sealed Aquila's fate: the November 15, 1957, crash of a Madeira-bound flight, killing thirty-five of the fifty passengers and all eight of the crew.

Emanuel Berk

The Journey

Elizabeth Nicholas

In 1951 and 1952, a travel writer for The Times of London, Elizabeth Nicholas, visited Madeira on at least three occasions to research her book, Madeira and the Canaries (published 1953). As he did for other visiting writers, Noël Cossart volunteered to be her guide, teaching her about not only about Madeira's wines but the history of the British on the island. Full of charm and insights, and superbly written, Nicholas' book is an often overlooked gem in the Madeira bibliography. And she begins her story with her first flight from Southampton to Funchal in one of the early small Aquila flying boats.

It has long been my opinion that the best way to approach a new country, and especially a new island, is by sea. Yet the first time I visited Madeira I came by air, and in that I find nothing to regret. The swift transition from the cold, wet, lonely misery of Southampton Water in February to the blue, sun-splintered Bay of Funchal was in itself compensation; it was achieved overnight, in a matter of nine hours.

At 11 p.m. we were in the office at Aquila Airways at Southampton, muffled in furs and great coats, red of nose, cold of

The flying boat "Hampshire" in Funchal's harbor in 1949.

feet. We viewed each other with distaste, marking out those of our travelling companions who, if God were kind, would be booked for another hotel from that we had ourselves selected. We sat on stuffed leather benches, in the brilliance of a singularly cruel flourescent light, and waited until our names were called. One by one we rose and entered the inner chamber, clutching passports, tickets, traveller's cheques, foreign currency; it was somewhat like the end of term. I expected to be told whether, or not, I had done well in my examinations and indeed English immigration officials do carry with them the faint aura of the headmistress whose duty it is, for our own good, to deal dispassionately with all our little failings.

I passed my examination. I showed my passport, I showed my ticket, I said I had £10 in English banknotes and £50 in traveller's cheques. I said I expected to be away about three weeks and that I was travelling on business. What business? I was a journalist, and going to Madeira to write articles for my paper. What paper? *The Sunday Times*; this, I might add, I said with a certain smug satisfaction. An unexceptionable paper, not likely to employ an incipient Pontecorvo or Fuchs; it guaranteed, rather, my respectability. So far so good; but why, I asked myself, this curiosity.

"You have a very nice job," the official remarked politely, handing me back my passport.

"Yes, indeed," I replied with equal courtesy. "I often think so myself."

I had passed. Others were not so fortunate. One couple, and I shall remember them always for the poignant horror of their misfortune, were rejected. Their visa was not in order; they could not go. Consternation, discussion, pleading, not passionate, but of despair and grief, a dull, hopeless, dry eyed pleading, all to no avail. A car would be summoned, they could go to the awful majesty of the X hotel, return to London on the morrow. . . . There, the visa would be put in order, and the company took no responsibility (rightly in this case) but in view of the grievousness of their circumstance, every effort would be made to fit them in the next plane although it was, in fact, fully booked. It was Friday night and the next plane left on Tuesday. . .

It might be worth adding here that curiosity led me to inquire what, precisely, was wrong with the passports and I discovered that though man and wife were travelling on one passport, one visa was not enough. They should have had two. A timely warning; I hope, to other married couples who travel on one passport.

Out to the customs; no musk rats in my luggage, nor parrots, nor industrial goods. Parrots, however, are no longer contraband. The other day, returned from Paris, I saw that Parrots had been overscored from the list of forbidden imports; part of the process of setting the people free, no doubt.

From customs shed out onto the slipway; here there was beauty and loveliness and silver sleekness. The great hull of the flying boat floating lightly on the water, the great wings sweeping out over the dark sea, the great tail rising sheer and powerful into the night sky.

We crept into the huge interior; the inside of a flying boat is rather like a small hotel; upstairs and downstairs, first and second floor, no lift, but all other modern conveniences. A bar to relieve the monotony of flight, a promenade deck, ladies' retiring room; thoughtfully equipped with a fine selection of Miss Arden's preparations with which the ladies can, in cheerful experiment, while away an hour or two.

As I sat down I cast a gloomy eye around the cabin wondering, as I always do in such circumstances, if these were the people with whom fate had ordained I should die. I mentioned this once, light-heartedly, to a fellow traveller as we sat waiting in the lounge at Northolt, and, recoiling from me nervously, she said it was a perfectly morbid idea and now I had put it into her head she would always think of it too as she sat expectant . . . She then picked up her mink and withdrew, as from a spot blighted with plague.

There is, in connection with the flying boat to Madeira, one slightly sinister operation, that of a steward closing, before take off, the watertight doors which separate each compartment, and tightening them up by aid of a wheel. Buoyancy, I said to myself; if we hit something on the water, and are holed, only one compartment will thus be flooded. Let us hope not my compartment. If this thing must be, let it be the compartment where sits that singularly unattractive couple who were so disagreeable to the stewardess. As Saki said, some people would be immeasurably improved by death.

We were towed out, into the dark and oily passages of Southampton Water. The great docks at night; in this a flying boat has all the romance of the liner, the freighter and the tramp. At the beginning is a port, the cranes and the wharves and the derricks, the railway sidings, the water-reflected lights, the huge Cunard pier and the great liners, floodlit, outlined against the fierce sky, vast and wonderful things, imperious, noble, of infinite majesty. Ships at night, all the way through the docks, lying silent and splendid, names pin pointed, *Queen Mary* or *Queen Elizabeth*, *Mauretania* or *Caronia*, grey hulls, red funnels, and with them the supreme mystery which belongs to all ships immobile and at rest.

The bows which have cut water in the Hudson and the St. Lawrence, the Plate and the Yellow River, the Delta or the Swan River; indifferent and yet animate, carrying always with them something of home. Steel and rivets, forged together on Tyne or Clyde, in Barrow or Belfast, and sent out to know all the seas and oceans of the world and yet be of us always. There is in this great pride and great emotion; never, I think, have I felt stronger emotion, a thicker tightening of the throat than when I saw, seven days out from Aden, in the vast and terrifying compass of the Indian Ocean a lighted ship move towards us at night. She passed within half a mile, a sister ship, homeward bound, passengers crowding the rail, and we saluted each other as we passed. In this there was something which was profoundly moving; perhaps because the war was over barely a year and there was still something brave and magnificent in safe seaways, in lighted ships moving openly at night about their lawful occasions.

This was, perhaps, a tangible proof of peace and of a world once more pacific; and yet, always, I think, it would have been moving. For ships at night carry with them the magic of the unknown; and of our mastery over the devious and changing oceans which ring the known world.

All this in Southampton Water as we were towed down to the open sea, to the light-pricked runway; twinkling red and green, and the moon sloping on the dark water surface and the plane speeding and throbbing and skimming swift and irrevocable towards the mystery of flight, the strange moment when we are no longer earthbound but light in the air, the great plane throwing off the clutching grasp of the waves and rising powerful and free at last in the night sky.

Beneath us the lights of Southampton wheeled a moment and were gone; only the dark sea and the clouds and the path of the moon, wrinkled and gold on the world surface. This surely is a moment similar to that which the bull fighter calls a moment of truth; liberated from earth and lonely in the sky, moving towards the point whence no return is possible: the point of departure disappeared in the black obscurity of night, the point of arrival far over the globe's horizon and between the two the long passages of the sky, featureless and without warmth, and no guide but that set in a small circle of glass out in the cockpit, the stars and the messages which rode towards us on invisible waves of sound. Flying the night sky is a wonderful and terrible thing.

And we flew, straight out across the English Channel, over the little islands which lie near the French coast and are yet of us; the only British earth to be occupied and afflicted by the Germans, Guernsey and Jersey, Alderney and Sark, now free and at peace, black patches on the moon, golden stretches of the sea. Across the Breton Peninsula, Ushant, and Finisterre-but the true Finisterre is far to the south, the outstretched finger of Portugal where lie Cape St. Vincent and Sagres, where Prince Henry the Navigator taught his seamen and the huge, menacing Atlantic waves break angrily on the first rock they have encountered in close on four thousand miles.

Nobly, Nobly Cape St. Vincent to the North West died away ... this was the end of the world to the ancients who set out to find that which was new; this surely was the last faint speck of reality for Zarco when he sailed in the year 1419, and carried upon the Atlantic Isles and claimed them for his sovereign and for Portugal...

Here, in the north, the French too have their Finisterre. We flew over it, over the Bay of Biscay, over the northern tip of Spain, the cold and Atlantic Spain, the margin of grey rocks and green-fringed mountains and sandy caverns where the grey sea swirls in bearing a white spume on its broken surface. Over Corunna, the city of balconies which glisten and gleam in the strong sun; over Sir John Moore and his massive tomb around which I had seen small children play and scuffle and laugh. We carved not a line, and we raised not a stone wrote Wolfe, and this was indeed true, for the English had time only to scoop a narrow grave in the inhospitable soil and thus take leave of their general. But time has redressed that and now Moore has all the elegant trappings of immortality; over Corunna then, and across the sea again, beneath an immensity of stars.

We dozed in the plane; it was cold; I fortified myself with coffee liberally braced with Courvoisier. Sacrilege, no doubt, but what can one do when it is cold? Brandy cost 1s.3d. for a very liberal nip indeed. Once, on the horizon I saw the black outline of land and a great fire burning on its surface. A huge fire; surely, that it was visible so many miles away, licking a wood and friendly substance,

THE FLYING BOAT ERA

glaring angrily at the night. The moon rose and was still. Inside our fragile shell passengers slept and snored and turned. Beside me was an old woman of eighty-four, making her first flight. She had eaten six sandwiches and poured a nice cup of tea down her ancient throat and now she slept, her hat tipped forward rakishly over her forehead, her hands clasped as in prayer. She woke at 6 a.m. bright as a button, and professed herself much interested in her experience; flying is so different, she said, apologetically.

I did not sleep; I envy with bitterness and sometimes hatred those who can sleep in trains, in buses, in cars or aeroplanes. I cannot sleep unless I am in my bed; or completely, utterly exhausted. I slept once on a sack of mails on the freezing floor of a Dakota plying between Naples and Bari, but then I was exhausted. I was not exhausted on the way to Madeira and I did not sleep.

I watched the night, the stars and the rippled sea and the moon. It is a simple snobbism in travel-writing to reel off a long list of memorable sights, ending BUT never have I seen anything to equal.

I will nevertheless say that I have made several memorable night flights; over the Western Desert from Cairo West to the Gulf of Sidra and seen Benghazi peer through the faint dawn; over the Australian desert between Perth and Melbourne; I have left Launceston at dusk and flown across the Tasman Sea, the sun setting with all the colour and flame of a parrot's plume, and Sydney Harbour at the end, blazing with light. I have flown from New York to Washington and New Orleans; from New Orleans over the Caribbean and landed at Merida in the soft, warm, sweet darkness of the Mexican night; I have flown over the mountains of Guatemala and come upon Guatemala City at dawn where the scent of flowers seemed to rise into the skies and meet us. And I have flown into London, sprawling, vast, practical, grey and cold and felt in me the good, strong, happy knowledge that I was home. All splendid and wonderful flights; BUT I would not match them with the night flight to Madeira, across the margins of Europe and into the Atlantic, watching the shadow of the plane rush smoothly over the distant sea, and dawn come up sharp and swift and then the distant jag of land; the rocky outline of Porto Santo, the crags of the Desertas, the miraculous landfall after eight hours of flight and, suddenly, brushing almost against our wing tip, the hilly coastline of Madeira and the blue water of the bay.

We flew down the coast, and all the hillside dotted with tidy little white houses, the sea breaking into smooth white foam, and we roared over Funchal, turning out to sea, back again, and gently, gently, settled once more on the fluid, restless, known surface of our world.

That was how I first came to Madeira, the plane settling down between rising curtains of white-lashed water, speed once more to be estimated against a still background of solid earth, slowing gently, the anger going out of our motion, till we were stopped and restful, lying once more on a swelling sea. But this time it was not the black sea of Southampton; it was the brilliant sea of Madeira.

APPENDIX XIV

ROY BRADY

Wine has produced its share of characters, but few have been more colorful, nor more devoted to the beverage, than Roy Brady. Trained as a mathematician, Brady moved from Chicago to Los Angeles in the early 1950s to work in the aircraft industry. But wine had already become his true passion and he immersed himself in it as a drinker, collector, scholar, writer and iconoclast for more than fifty years. He had an insatiable thirst for knowledge about all aspects and all types of wine, and he amassed a remarkable collection of tasting notes, books, wine labels, merchants' catalogues, and scraps of information collected through correspondence. And since Madeira was perhaps his favorite wine—it was certainly the wine that he admired most—it is not surprising that Brady corresponded with Noël Cossart.

Roy Brady's first experiences with Madeira were during the 1940s in Chicago. However, the wines available to him were mediocre, and Brady thought some of them fraudulent, leading him to the conclusion that great old Madeiras—like those in the books of George Saintsbury and H. Warner Allen—no longer existed.

Then in May, 1952, he visited a wine shop in Washington D.C. where he saw two intriguing old Madeiras for sale: a Rainwater and a Malmsey, both demijohned in 1832 in Baltimore. His suspicions being what they were, he passed on them, later writing that "I came close to missing two of the greatest wines I have ever tasted."

It was not until he visited Boston the next year that he finally lowered his guard. There, at S.S. Pierce he was confronted with a wine described as an 1846 Terrantez for $11.75 a bottle. According to a mimeographed sheet he was given, Pierce's chief buyer, Charlie Codman, had persuaded Cossart Gordon to part with a small quantity of this wine recently bottled from cask. Despite the high reputations of both S.S. Pierce and Cossart Gordon, Brady again balked, but over the next three days he allowed himself to imagine that the wine might be genuine. Finally, on his last day in Boston, on his way to the airport, he returned to the store and bought a bottle.

This bottle of 1846 Terrantez lay in his cellar untasted for more than five years, but it fanned the flames of passion. In 1954, he was back in the Washington, D.C., wine shop where he had seen the two old Baltimore Madeiras. The store's proprietor Fred Burka told Brady that he had purchased the wines in demijohn and had them bottled in 1949, and gave him a taste of both wines. Brady later declared the Madeiras "so unlike anything I had ever tasted that I did not know quite what to make of them." He bought a bottle of each.

Brady's Madeira collecting went into high gear when, in 1956, he discovered that Averys in Bristol, England, was offering a range of old Madeiras. Reassured by Ronald Avery's reputation (Brady called him "the wine merchant beneath whom all others are ranged at various distances"), he bought dozens of bottles from Averys over the next several years, shipping them through San Francisco's Esquin Imports.

Brady was to make himself his generation's most avid, and knowledgeable, American connoisseur of Madeira. He was educated, first and foremost, through the wines he experienced, which he bought largely from Averys. He also read voraciously, acquiring every book or article he could find on Madeira. However, given how little had been written, his thirst for knowledge was far from satisfied. To find answers to his many questions, he went to the two men he regarded as the world's leading experts: Noël Cossart and Ronald Avery.

His correspondence with Ronald Avery began first, on May 23, 1956, and lasted more than seven years. At least 22 letters were exchanged between the two men, involving not only wine orders, but also a wide-ranging discussion of Madeira. His letter-writing to Cossart began later, on September 16, 1958, when he sought more information about the bottle of 1846 Terrantez he had bought in Boston in 1952. However, because his first letters were sent in care of the Madeira Wine Association, the replies came from someone other than Noël. In fact, it is testament to the muddle of brands at the MWA that the first reply was written not on Cossart, Gordon letterhead but on that of Leacock & Co., with an indecipherable signature. Soon, Brady was receiving letters on Blandy's letterheads as well—each signed by the MWA's managing director Horace Zino—but nothing from Cossart, Gordon.

It was not until April 1962 that Brady finally made contact with Noël Cossart, when Noël wrote him at the suggestion of a mutual friend in London, Warner Everett. For the next year, Brady wrote increasingly detailed letters to Noël, probing for background not only on specific wines, but on the state of Madeira production and sales. Noël responded with a wealth of information, providing historical details where needed, recommending wines available in the US market, and even books that could help satisfy Brady's curiosity. During this correspondence, Brady wrote "Old Madeira," which appeared in *Wine and Food*, in Spring 1963. He included a draft of the article with his September 25, 1962 letter to Noël, asking for criticism and for permission to use a quote from one of his letters. Noël pointed out several errors that were corrected when the article was published.

Their letter writing ceased in May, 1963, not to resume for twenty-two years. The publication of *Madeira, The Island Vineyard*, reconnected them, if only briefly. On February 23, 1985, Brady wrote to his old mentor, probably for the last time, complementing him on his book, and Noël replied in kind.

Emanuel Berk

The Correspondence

23 February 1985

ROY BRADY

Noël Cossart
c/o Michael Broadbent

Dear Mr. Cossart:

I am delighted with your book. I read it straight through as soon as it arrived and have been rereading parts constantly since then. It is fortunate that you managed to put le sport aside long enough to finish it. If only it had been available thirty years ago! My doubts would have been laid aside sooner and I would own a great deal more old Madeira than I do.

When I began reading about wine in the late forties I discovered Sir Stephen Gaselee in Simon's books and in his Wine and Food. Old Madeira seemed the most enchanting of wines—and the most mysterious and unattainable. It seemed impossible that I would ever taste one, and most certainly not one from Sir Stephen's collection. Now your book makes the stunning revelation that I have been drinking Gaselee Madeiras for twenty-some years. How exciting it would have been to have known it. I bought many Madeiras (sic) from Ronald Avery. I knew him, first by correspondence in trying to learn something about the Madeiras I was buying, then in person when he made his first visit to California and came down to dinner here. Later we stayed in his flat in Bristol, and I went to the Hospices de Beaune auction with him. Yet, in spite of all the talk he never mentioned that he had any Gaselee Madeiras. I knew Reg Gunyon too, and he didn't mention it either. There seems almost to have been a conspiracy of silence about Madeira.

I still don't know exactly which were the Gaselee wines. I gather that the Verdelho 1838 and Bual 1815 were, but both, unfortunately, are gone. I usually bought one dozen of a wine and occasionally two or three, but I was too generous with the wines before I had full confidence in them. Once I let the Southern California Wine and Food Society have eight bottles of Sercial 1860. At times Ronald was more reluctant. He let me have only one bottle of Muscatel 1909 and no 1792 Solera. I bought many odd bottles elsewhere including all the Blandys that Sherry-Lehmann had in New York. In all I had at least sixty vintages and half as many dated soleras. That does not include the many doubtful or clearly fraudulent wines, some, regrettably, with apparently reputable names.

This looks like a good season for Madeira around here. In April David Pamment and Darrell Corti are conducting a tasting here, haven't seen a list but I think there will be some not so very old vintages. A friend is planning a vintage Madeira dinner and asked me to help choose the wines. He got several hundred bottles of vintage Madeira by a fluke. Around 1970 he bought a large cellar, mostly French, which included the Madeira. Apart from that I doubt it would ever have occurred to him to buy a bottle of Madeira. And then I am going to give my last Madeira tasting which will include the 1779 Verdelho you cite on p.162. I wonder if that could be the Gaselee 1779 that Simon described in Vintagewise. Broadbent doesn't know. Will also have a Madeira Bronco 1790, Blandy which I bought from Sherry-Lehmann over 25 years ago at the then enormous price of $27.50. We will end with the two 1900 Muscatels, the Avery and one I bought recently with a customarily unsatisfactory label, or neck-tag actually. The stencil says, "Reserva Moscatel 1900." The tag says, "Over 70 years matured in oak cask." Why couldn't it have given the date of bottling and let us figure it out? It is from Pereira de Oliveira (sic) from whom I have never had a wine and know nothing beyond your mention on p.120. I did get one bottle of that Rainwater, demijohned 1832, you mention on p. 71. We will have it. And, by the way, I was never so surprised in my life as in finding my name prominently displayed in your book. I haven't decided on the other Madeiras yet, but I hope to make the combined events comparable if not equal to your "Academy of Ancient Madeira Wines."

Madeira is the last great wine in the world. Over the last forty years I have watched the others decline. Burgundy is far gone though no one but Anthony Hanson has dared say so. Recent vintages of the Dom. de la R.C. are a disgrace. Serena Sutcliff (sic) did cast some doubts on them a year or so ago. California wines, despite all their self-congratulations, have declined in recent years. The French were shocked by the quality of California wines but quickly recovered and took the line, "Ah, yes, California wines are powerful and impressive, but they lack French delicacy and elegance, and they overpower food." Most California winemakers fell for it and began vying with one another to make wines that wouldn't overpower a cup of weak tea. I was thinking about abandoning wine and drinking malt whisky. Then a couple of months ago a new shipment of my favorite Glenfarclas 12 year arrived with a new label and a new lightness. I hunted up a bottle of the old stuff and made a blind comparison to be sure. So whisky is going too. Some attribute this view to senility, but old Madeira remains as good as ever. I have just been drinking a bottle of Terrantez 1862, H.M.B. In recent years I have mostly been drinking my old Madeiras myself. I open a bottle and have a glass every day or so. Happily my wife doesn't like them.

The three tastings noted above will be written up in an article for the new *Journal of Gastronomy* of the American Institute of Food and Wine.

Congratulations on the book. I hope you find another one in your library and the Cossart, Gordon archives. Also glad that you made suitable provision for the archives, hope also for the library. In spite of much talk André Simon never made disposition of his library, and it is now scattered all over the world. I am gratified that

I was able to get a dozen volumes, but I would much rather have seen it kept intact in an institutional library.

Sincerely,
(signed) Roy Brady

P.S. I'm glad to see that some "recent" Madeiras are still good. Last year I had CDGC Boal 1941 and Solar do Val Formoso Bual 1926. Enclosed is an article I wrote after visiting Madeira in 1976. The somewhat irreverent and telegraphic style was dictated by the nature of the publication and the very small number of words I was allowed.

19th March 1985.

Mr. Roy Brady.
9218 Shoshone Avenue.
Northridge.
California 91325
U.S.A.

Dear Mr. Brady,

I was very pleased to hear from you by your letter of 23rd February, and I thank you for your kind words regarding my book. I am very glad you enjoyed it although its writing caused me to smoke some five million "gaspers" and to give them up after a stroke, heart failure and gout. It seems to be a success and has received the "What Wine book award." I think that we are both 15 years older since we first started to correspond.

Ronald Avery and Reg Gunion (sic) asked me to research the history of their Madeiras for their American customers, but it was difficult to find out which had been Sir Stephen Gaselee's at the time for lack of documentation. Ronald had stuck his label on all the bottles. Lady Gaselee is still alive. She is 90 and we still correspond. The Verdelho 1838 and Bual 1815 were certainly Gaselee Madeiras. I sold the Sercial 1860 to Ronald in 1959 for 450/s per dozen as I did Malvasia 1880, Bual 1882, Terrantez 1898, 1846, 1862, and 1795, also Cama de Lobos 1789 and Reserva V.V.P. 1844. I also sold to Ronald some of our Muscatel 1900, which was the first transported by motor transport. Gaselee did have some of the 1779 Verdelho but it was gone before he died so it did not go to Ronald. The Pereira de Oliveira Muscatel should be good but light, as it was produced before the old man died, but recently they have blended up some of his wine, which although master blends are not the real thing, like a Pereira de Oliveira Terrantez 1880 I have recently tasted in Norwich. A fine Madeira but obviously blended with old Verdelho.

You certainly seem to have an interesting tasting programe. Young David Pamment is a new commer (sic) to Madeira, but to hear him talk one would think he invented it, he calls himself an "engineiro!" Darral (sic) Corti has very fine Madeira Wine. His Sercial Abuderham 1950 is very fine and I wonder if he still has the wines David and I sold him which you mention in your P.S. The Solar do Val Formoso 1926 was from a pipe my great uncle put down for me the year I joined the firm and wine trade. The CDGC (Charles David Gradidge Cossart) was from a pipe I put down when my son (now in charge of the business) was born.

Noël Cossart

APPENDIX XV

JOHN DELAFORCE

Born in 1908, John Delaforce joined his family's Port house, Delaforce Sons & Co., in 1931. When he retired, he devoted himself to historical research about Port and the British community in Portugal in the eighteenth and nineteenth centuries. He had three books to his credit: *The Factory House at Oporto* (1983), *Anglicans Abroad, the History of the Chaplaincy & Church of St. James, Oporto* (1982) and *Joseph James Forester, Baron of Portugal* (1992).

Delaforce wrote to Noël just after his book was published, exploring some historical points, including the possible existence of a British Factory building in Madeira.

The Correspondence

Quinta dos Girassols
4470 Maia
Portugal
30th October 1984

Dear Noël,

It is a very long time since we last met, so I hope you will remember me.

I have been reading your book on Madeira with the greatest interest and admiration. It is excellent and so well produced and illustrated. As you may know, Christie's published my book on the Factory House at Oporto, so we are both as it were in the same "stable".

I have learnt much from your book, as sadly I and also I think most of the Port shippers have never had the knowledge we should about Madeira, and perhaps the reverse is the case with the Madeira shippers.

I had realized that America was a far larger and earlier market for Madeira than for Port, but not to the extent you relate. Some of my wife's ancestors on her mother's side, by name Waldo, went from Bristol to New England about 1650 and the first, Cornelius, was a wine merchant at Chelmsford, Mass. His grandson, also Cornelius, was a wine merchant at Boston and he placed the following advertisement in the Boston News-Letter of September 5th 1734:

"Best London Market Madera (sic) wine, lately imported hither via St. Kitts: to be sold by the Pipe, Hogshead or Quarter Cask by Messr. Samuel and Cornelius Waldo."

I do not know if that is an early reference to Madeira in New England, but perhaps it is of interest for your records.

As regards the Factories, may I correct you with regard to the Portuguese feitorias, reference your page 27, last para.

In fact they established feitorias in West & East Africa some years before those in India and the first was at Arguim, in what is now Mauretania, in about 1443. Subsequently also in Senegal and Gambia and on the Gold Coast, and then following the rounding of the Cape in 1488 at Sofala. All these were earlier than their Factories in India.

You mention on page 28, para 3, an actual Factory House at Madeira. But was this really a house owned collectively by the Factors, or was it one belonging to one of them or to the Consul and used for their meetings, as was the case in Lisbon?

In my research I never found any definite evidence of a Factory House in Funchal, and this tends to be confirmed by the records of the old Factory, published from the papers of C.J. Cossart, in which there is never any mention of a House in the accounts or elsewhere. If there had been one, surely the accounts would have included expenses in connection with it? I corresponded with John Farrow after seeing his publication "Impressions of Madeira," because they had incorrectly marked "British Factory" in Rua da Carreira and he said that "as far as we know the British Factory did not have its own building but normally met in the British Consulate". I would welcome any definite evidence you have on the subject, so I could mention it in any future edition of my book.

Madeira was first imported here for the Factory House in 1818 in hogsheads and was very popular. The types bought were "Most Superior East India" and Sercial.

It is interesting that there were comparisons between Madeira and Burgundy in the days before fortification. The same was the case here and in 1802 there was a reference to "The Burgundy Grape" and an offer was noted of "Curious Old Port of high Burgundy flavours". The description "curious" was popular it seems. In the same connection a shipper wrote to a customer in 1807, "Respecting Burgundy grape, we know of none grown in this country by that denomination and we conceive it merely a finesse of a certain house with a view to amusing their correspondents with novel names for their superior wines".

As late as 1821 a customer asked for his wines "to be with no more Brandy than is sufficient to preserve them". I do not believe that Port was fully fortified to the full strength we have now much before the middle of the 19th century.

I wish I had such extensive records here to work with as you have had.

Forgive such a long letter, but on these subjects my pen seems to run away with me!

Wishing your book every success,

Yours sincerely,
John Delaforce.

From "White House"
Upper Olland Street.
BUNGAY. SUFFOLK.
NR35 1BH.

John Delaforce.Esq.
Quinta dos Girassois
4470 Maia.
PORTUGAL.
23rd November 1984.

Dear John,

I was delighted to get your letter of 30th October, after not having seen you for such a long time. I certainly do remember you and your kindness to me when I visited Oporto after the war.

I am glad my book interested you and thank you for your kind words. It was certainly the American market which gave impetus to the Madeira trade, and in fact it was brought to the U.K. from the U.S. This is reflected by the amount of elegant Madeira clubs still going strong in the southern states.

I am indebted to you for the correction regarding "feitorias" on page 27 and have made a note of it in case the book is reprinted.

Although the house mentioned on page 27 at 78 Ribeira de Santa Luzia has always been called "the Factory House" locally there is no confirmation that it ever belonged to the Factors collectively, either in the Factory papers as they are, or my grandfather's notes.

There is evidence that rooms in the house were set aside for use by the Factors such as dining room, office etc. The Factors first met at Mr. Pringle's house (H.M.Consulate) at 5 Rua das Queimadas, until Henry Veitch built the house at R. Santa Luzia (now R. 5 de Outubro) circa 1810.

It became his residence and the consulate, and then the offices of Scott, Penfold and Veitch until Newton, Gordon & Cossart took it over in 1838.

I was interested to hear that the Oporto Factory imported East India and Sercial in 1818. I presume the Sercial was served after Port, a fashion started by the Prince Regent. I am grateful for your information regarding Cornelius Waldo. I think the advertisement must be one, if not the, earliest and I will try to verify this.

The label "Madeira Burgundy" was common practice before fortification, for wine made from the Tinta or Burgundy Grape (Pinot Noir) which was imported from the Duchy. It was also called Tinto, Tintoreto or Tent. Today the Tinta Negra Mole or Mole Preta has been developed from the Pinot Noir and Grenache. It is interesting to note that that in the list of Madeiras at Robert Allston's rice plantation on page 186 there are both "Burgundy" and "Tinta" imported after fortification.

I hope that we may meet up some time soon, I only go up to London for the Old Codgers lunch in May and November as I do not like the place now. I was in Madeira for the book launch on 23rd October and David went to launch it in Savannah.

With kind regards,

Yours sincerely,

Noël Cossart.

P.S. I have your excellent book in my library. I now have over 2000 publications on wine and Madeira.

APPENDIX XVI

THE C. H. ARNOLD SALE OF HABERSHAM MADEIRAS, 1900

LIST OF MADEIRAS
Belonging to the Estate of The Late
WILLIAM NEYLE HABERSHAM, ESQ.
OF SAVANNAH, GA.
SOLD BY
C. H. ARNOLD & CO.
27, South William Street, New York.
1st November, 1900

Demijohns	
13 of 5 gals	LEACOCK MADEIRA
	Amber, elegant, dry fine bouquet.
1 of 5 gals	LEES OF ABOVE
5 of 5 gals	NEWTON-GORDON SOLERA
1 of 3 gals	Pale, very fine, grand style.
7 of 5 gals	MADEIRA No.3
2 of 3 gals	Amber, good style, choice old.
1 of 3 gals	NEWTON-GORDON 1817 SERCIAL
	Very pale, elegant, perfect.
7 of 5 gals	NEWTON-GORDON SERCIAL
	Straw, light body, old, smooth and dry.
3 of 5 gals	NEWTON-GORDON SERCIAL
	Pale amber, full, round, good style.
8 of 5 gals	DONALDSON SERCIAL
	Pale, smooth, delicate.
1 of 5 gals	DONALDSON SERCIAl
1 of 3 gals	Amber, full bodied, nutty.
3 of 5 gals	VERY FINE OLD SERCIAL
	Pale, high flavor, round and dry.
1 of 5 gals	HURRICANE MADEIRA, 1809
	Amber, grand style, very choice.
3 of 3 gals	LEACOCK SERCIAL
	Pale, dry, high flavor, fine nose.

1 of 3 gals	SOLERA, 1827 SERCIAL
	Straw color, dry and delicate, perfect type, rare.
2 of 5 gals	CHILLINGSWORTH MADEIRA
1 of 5 gals	Amber, round, smooth, good body, medium, dry.
6 of 5 gals	NEWTON GORDON 1827 SERCIAL
	Straw color, very dry and delicate, perfect type, delicious bouquet, a gem of the collection.
1 of 5 gals	OLDEST NEWTON-GORDON SERCIAL
2 of 3 gals	Very pale, dry, smooth, good body.
2 of 5 gals	CANTEIRO MADEIRA NO.1
	Pale, medium dry, very soft.
1 of 3 gals	TELFAIR 1809, SERCIAL
	Pale straw, elegant, dry, a gem of the collection.
1 of 3 gals	OLD NEWTON-GORDON
	Straw color, very round and dry, a choice wine.
2 of 5 gals	SWEET, PALE, NEWTON-GORDON SERCIAL
	Very round and smooth, rich.
15 of 5 gals	DONALDSON SERCIAL
1 of 3 gals	Straw color, old, very round, fine bouquet. Highly recommended.
2 of 5 gals	NEWTON-GORDON SERCIAL
	Straw, dry, delicate, a choice lot.
6 of 5 gals	DONALDSON BUAL
2 of 5 gals	Amber, full-bodied, nutty, fine type.
2 of 3 gals	
1 of 5 gals	SAME, DARKER AND DRYER.
3 of 5 gals	NEWTON-GORDON FINEST SERCIAL
1 of 3 gals.	Pale, dry, very elegant.
1 of 5 gals	LEES OF DONALDSON MADEIRA
	Rather dry, full bodied, good wine.
3 of 5 gals	DONALDSON V. R. MADEIRA
2 of 3 gals	Amber, Bual type, dry, good body.
6 of 5 gals	CHILLINGSWORTH RESERVE 1812-14
2 of 5 gals	Amber, dry, good nose, fine wine.
4 of 5 gals	M. B. MADEIRA NO.1
1 of 3 gals	Full-bodied, grand wine.
3 of 5 gals	BEST, VERY CHOICEST OLD MADEIRA
1 of 3 gals	Pale, amber, high, dry flavor, rare lot.
3 of 5 gals	ALL SAINTS' MADEIRA
1 of 3 gals	Perfection, one of Mr Habersham's very oldest wines and so named by the late Ward McAllister. Imported in 1793 by W. H. Gibbons and Nat. Hayward.
4 of 5 gals	CROWN SERCIAL
	Pale, good body, dry, exquisite flavor.
1 of 3 gals	NEWTON-GORDON MALMSEY MADEIRA
	Pale amber, fine type, a very rare wine.

THE HABERSHAM SALE

5 of 5 gals	NEWTON-GORDON A. C. MADEIRA
	Amber, perfection, one of Mr. Habersham's oldest wines.
4 of 5 gals	MARGADE MADEIRA
	Pale amber, finest possible, exquisite nose, dry, great delicacy.
4 of 5 gals	COSSART, GORDON P. P. 1824 MADEIRA
	Pale amber, same type as above, fine nose, dry elegant wine.
2 of 5 gals	NEWTON-GORDON RESERVE
1 of 3 gals	Amber; good nose, dry.
5 of 5 gals	NEWTON-GORDON M. J. V. MADEIRA
	Big wine; dry and nutty.
10 of 5 gals	OGLETHORPE MADEIRA LOT A.
	Amber; dry; good body.
7 of 5 gals	OGLETHORPE MADEIRA LOT B.
	Pale amber, good nose, dry.
2 of 5 gals	NEWTON-GORDON J. J. V.
	Amber, full body, nutty, dry.
1 of 5 gals	B. M. R. CHILLINGSWORTH
1 of 3 gals	Pale amber, dry, fine nose, delicate.
1 of 5 gals	BEST NEWTON-GORDON SERCIAL
	Straw color, light, dry, elegant.
2 of 5 gals	NEWTON-GORDON BUAL
	Pale amber, very choice old Bual, rather dry.
1 of 5 gals	SERCIAL MADEIRA
1 of 3 gals	Pale, good body, dry, very pretty wine.
2 of 5 gals	MADEIRA
	Pale, very old, Sercial type, nice wine.
1 of 5 gals	MADEIRA
	Straw, dry, fine old wine.
1 of 5 gals	BLEND OF SUNDRY FINE MADEIRAS
	Pale amber, dry, Sercial type with body.
1 of 3 gals	BLEND OF FINE OLD MADEIRAS
	Straw color, dry.
1 of 5 gals	LEES OF FINE OLD MADEIRAS
	Pale amber, dry.
3 of 1 gal	LEES OF FINE OLD MADEIRAS
	Pale, dry, very choice, old.

Postscript to the Arnold & Co. Sale of William Neyle Habersham's Wines

By the 1890s, William Habersham's stocks of fine Madeira ran low, and so he was forced to rely more heavily on Sherry, a wine that had long figured prominently in his business. In fact, he was no stranger to including a little Sherry in his Madeira blends and was steadily increasing the amount that he used. He believed that with sufficient time in his solarium, he could make Sherry taste like fine old Madeira. And to prove the point, in 1897 he sent samples of seven different Sherries to C.H. Arnold, the New York merchant who would later handle the wines from his estate. The purpose of the samples, as Habersham wrote in his journal, was to show Arnold how Savannah's climate affects Sherry. At the same time, Habersham told his longtime New York agent William Fearing that if he heated a particular high-quality Sherry, "it would be more like a Madeira than [another Habersham Sherry] he bought of me which he thinks is a Madeira."

C.H. Arnold & Co.'s catalogue was published on November 1, 1900, barely a year after Habersham's death. It is impressive for the range and volume of wines, with multiple three- and five-gallon demijohns offered of most of the Madeiras. However, the wines did not all sell quickly; some lots weren't sold until 1905. Bellows & Co. of New York and Elder Harrison of Baltimore, both important Madeira merchants at the time, were among the last buyers.

What is most interesting about the wines is how few of Habersham's usual blends appear. There is only one demijohn each of Hurricane and Painted Pipe (carrying the dubious dates of 1809 and 1824, respectively) and no Earthquake, "LB," or "P," the other wines on which he had most relied for repeat business. On the other hand, a number of wines on the list – Donaldson Sercial, Donaldson Bual, Margade, Crown Sercial, Newton, Gordon "JJV" and Newton, Gordon "AC" – were put into his solarium for aging after 1890 and were never heavily used for blending.

This suggests that unlike most of the wine that Habersham sold while he was alive, a large number of wines in the Arnold Sale were original, unblended wines.

Emanuel Berk

APPENDIX XVII

HABERSHAM'S "HURRICANE"

Emanuel Berk

William Habersham's notebook at the Georgia Historical Society makes it clear that many of his most famous wines were blends, created again and again from whatever wines he had on hand, using his renowned palate to maintain a consistent character. The names may have implied some particular history to the wine—such as a special barrel ("Painted Pipe"), a cask marking ("00") or a ship ("Charming Martha," "Richmond Packet" or "Violet"). But they were really only brands.

For example, in 1889 Ward McAllister told Cornelius Vanderbilt that Habersham's "Painted Pipe" Madeira was imported by Thomas Gibbons in 1791. In fact, this was a name concocted by McAllister nearly a century later, in 1883. The wine itself was created by Habersham by blending equal parts of eight different wines from his collection. Between 1883 and 1889, Habersham sold over 700 bottles of Painted Pipe to various customers, including 120 bottles to Vanderbilt.

Hurricane was an even more famous Habersham wine, and despite what customers were told, it never had anything to do with a ship named "Hurricane." Habersham sold his first "Hurricane" Madeira in late 1875, after several months of experimentation, by blending together different Madeiras. According to his notebook, he was unhappy with his May 20, 1875, blend (he called it "a great mistake") because it was too sweet. But by August, he had a winning blend, composed of ten of his best old Madeiras plus a tiny amount of his best Sherry.

He created four more "Hurricanes" in 1878, 1881, 1887 and 1891, and of the 2000 total bottles made, about half were sold to his New York agent, William H. Fearing. As was typical for Habersham, Hurricane's recipe changed each time he made it. The

1878 blend was composed of eleven different Madeiras, including a good dose of the previous blend plus, again, a small amount of Sherry. The 1881 blend consisted of 13 Madeiras, in equal parts, plus one part of Sherry. Habersham was obviously quite pleased with this blend, writing proudly (with drawings of fingers pointing at the words) "Old 'H' Matched." Of the 14 wines that went into the 1881 blend, Habersham described 7 as "extra," 3 as "good," 2 as "fair" and 2 as "weak."

By the 1890s, Habersham still had demand for Hurricane, as it was by then well-known in New York, but his stocks of blending Madeiras were scant. So, in creating a new blend in 1891, he was forced to use 70% Sherry and only 30% Madeira. He sold less of this wine than any previous Hurricane. And as for its likeness to previous blends, Fearing chose to label the sixty bottles he bought as "Mayflower," discarding the Hurricane name for good.

From the Goelet family collection, a bottle of Habersham's Hurricane Madeira, labeled by William H. Fearing, the New York wine merchant and Habersham's largest customer from 1878 until Habersham's death in 1899.

GLOSSARY
of Portuguese Words and Technical Terms Used in Connection with Madeira

Abafado   See *Vinho abafad*.

Acetification   Formation of vinegar.

ACIF Associacao Commercial y Industrial do Funchal. Regulates, amongst other matters, exports from the island.

Adega   Building in which wine is made, matured and kept.

Aerobic fermentation   Fermentation conducted in the presence of air. Usually the first part of the fermentation process.

Alcolisado   See *Vinho Alcolisado*.

Amadurecido   Referring to a wine, "mellow."

Anaerobic fermentation   A fermentation from which air is excluded; the second part of the fermentation.

Armazem de calor   A heated wine store in which wine is matured.

Armazem   A warehouse in which wine is stored or matured.

Arrobo   Concentrated grape juice for building up wine.

Aveludado   Referring to a wine, "luscious."

Baçelo   A vine plant.

Bagaço   Skins and stalks left behind after pressing.

Barril   A barrel measuring 45 litres used at the vintage as a measure for buying must.

Baumé   The weight or sugar content in wine measured by a hydrometer. All measurements of wine are taken at a temperature of 15° C.

Bentonite   Aclarifying and stabilizing agent used for fining.

Boca do lagar   The spout out of which must runs from the *lagar* into the *tina*.

Body   The fullness of wine.

Boracho   A goat skin in which wine is transported.

Branco seco   A very pale dry wine.

Burn wine, to   To distil wine.

Casta Breed or variety of vine.

Casta boa Good variety, such as *Tinta Negra Mole* and *Verdelho*.

Casta nobre Noble variety. *Sercial, Bual, Malmsey, Terrantez, Bastardo.*

Canada An old Portuguese measure equal to 1.7 litres.

Caneco A 20-litre copper measure.

Cased A cask is said to be "cased" when covered by an outer cover with packing between to prevent pilferage.

Canteiro A scantle. See *Vinho canteiro*.

Cavalo (Literally a horse.) Root stock, e.g. *riparia, rupestris* or *labrusca* vines upon which to graft scions of *Vitis vinifera*.

Corça A sledge pulled by oxen, for transporting pipes.

Cooperage Place where coopers work to build or repair casks.

Corda do lagar Rope wound round bagaco upon which *vara do lagar* rests to press out the must after treading.

Cuba de calor A vat in which wine is heated for *estufagem*.

Cuba A large vat for storing wine.

Demijohn Large glass bottle usually holding 5, 10, 20 or 25 litres.

Dry As opposed to sweet. A wine is said to be dry when all the sugar in it has been converted to alcohol by fermentation or "fermented right out."

Encorpado Referring to wine, "full-bodied."

Enchertos Grafts or scions for grafting onto root stock.

Estagio The period of rest required by Madeira after *estufagem*.

Estufa A hot house in which madeira is matured or aged.

Estafado See *Vinho estufado*.

Estufa de sol A glass house where madeira is matured by the sun's rays.

Estufagem The process of aging madeira by heat.

Fermentation The process caused by yeast acting upon sugar to produce alcohol and carbon dioxide. See *Aerobic fermentation*.

Fining Removal of suspended solids from wine by adding wine finings, which may be organic (gelatine, isinglass, egg whites, albumen, ox blood etc), mineral (bentonite, kaolin) or vegetable (alkaline alginates).

Finish The aftertaste of a wine. Effect of sensation after swallowing and exhaling.

Fortification Increasing the strength of wine beyond that achieved by natural fermentation by adding spirit.

Funchalense Pertaining to Funchal or native of.

GLOSSARY

Garafão A wicker covered demijohn.

Garrafeira or frasqueira A bottle store or cellar.

Hogshead Half a pipe, 46 imperial gallons or 209 litres.

Hybrid vine In Madeira, European vines crossed with American vines.

Instituto do Vinho da Madeira Madeira Wine Institute, the official body regulating all matters to do with Madeira wine.

Junta Naçional do Vinho National official body governing matters to do with wine in Portugal, to which the Instituto do Vinho da Madeira is answerable.

Lagar A wine press.

Lees The sediment deposited at the bottom of the cask or bottle by maturation. Or the dead yeast and solids left behind after fermentation.

Leve Referring to wine, "light-bodied."

Lodge Shippers' wine store where wine is treated. In Madeira these are called "stores."

Lote A parcel of wine.

Louisiana clay Same as Spanish earth.

Macio Refering to wine, "soft."

Madeira de honra An old Madeira offered at an auspicious function. During the monarchy, used to toast the monarch.

Maderisation A rude word used to describe other wines which have acquired the characteristics of madeira through oxidation.

Madère d'origine, Madère de l'Ile French names for imitation madeira made in France.

Mangara Local word for the mildew *Oidium tuckeri*.

Mosto Must, unfermented grape juice.

Nose The aroma of wine.

Octave One eighth of a pipe, or half a quarter cask, 11-12 imperial gallons or 52-53 litres.

Oidium tuckeri (mangara) A member of the mushroom family. It forms patches of grey mould on the leaves and on the grapes, which split and shrivel.

Olfacto The "nose" or aroma of a wine.

Outras castas Varieties of vines which are not *Vitis vinifera*.

Palhete or **Palhetinho** The Portuguese for Rainwater Madeira. A very pale light wine. Derived from the word *palha* meaning straw.

Partidista The equivalent of the French *courtier* who sells *lotes* of wine to shippers, although not a shipper himself.

Passagem Racking or airing wine by passing it from one vessel to another.

Pé Lees.

Pé de cuba Fermenting wine put into the fermenting vessel to start fermentation.

Pipe See *Shipping pipe*.

Poio A terraced vineyard.

Phylloxera vastatrix A form of lice which originated in America, known as American vine lice. Between 1870 and 1885 it destroyed practically all then vines in Europe. There are two forms: **gallicole** which lives on the leaves, destroying them; and **radicole** which attacks the roots of the vines and destroys them. The combination of the two forms completely destroys the vine.

Quarter cask A quarter of a pipe equal to 23 gallons or 104-105 litres.

Quartilho An old Portuguese liquid measure equal to ¾ of a pint or 0.45 litres. Used today as a measure for a workman's daily ration of Madeira.

Queimar To burn or distil wine.

Quinta A large house and estate containing a farm, equivalent to a French *château*. The name is derived from *quinta parte* (fifth part) because in olden times the farmer paid a fifth part of the produce to the landlord in lieu of rent.

Racking Siphoning wine off lees to clear and stabilize it.

"Red cap"' A Cossart, Gordon & Co wine worker. After 1758 the uniform was a blue drill suit and red cap.

Repisa The second pressing of the grapes.

Rotula A label.

Scantle The wooden beams upon which scantling pipes and storage pipes rest.

Scantling pipe A large pipe mostly used for storage but when used for shipping holds one-and-a-half pipes or 138 gallons, 627 litres.

Secção de vinhos Associacão Comercial do Funchal. The Wine Section of the Funchal Commercial Association, to which all shippers belong. It takes the place of Gremio as in Oporto, but is not government controlled. Not to be confused with Madeira Wine Company to which only some shippers belong.

Selecçionado Choice or selected.

GLOSSARY

Shipping pipe Usually referred to as a pipe, is the standard shipping measure for Madeira in bulk holding 92 imperial gallons, 110 old or American gallons, 418 litres.

Spanish earth A heavy clay used for fining; see Bentonite.

Tina or **Tina do lagar** The open butt into which must pours from the *lagar*.

Tonel A heavy oak cask for storage, usually 2,500 litres but going up to 45,000 litres.

"Topping up" Replenishing soleras.

Ullage Depletion of wine from a cask due to evaporation or drawing of wine.

Vara do lagar The hinged, weighted wooden beam for pressing out the *repisa* from stalks and skins.

Velho or **velha** Old. Example: masculine *velho* as in *vinho velho*. Feminine *velha* as *reserva velha*.

Velhissimo or **velhissima** Very old.

Vindima Vintage: the picking of grapes.

Vinho abafado Wine which has had its fermentation arrested by addition of alcohol.

Vinho alcolisado Fortified wine.

Vinho de avinhar Wine used for seasoning new casks. Usually special *lotes* of young wine which finally becomes vinegar.

Vinho canteiro Wine which has been matured without *estufagem*.

Vinho claro Clear wine siphoned off lees after fermentation.

Vinho concertado Literally, mended wine. Must which has been concentrated by boiling, thinned by adding ordinary wine and was used for building up the body of wine. No longer used except for making communion wine.

Vinho cru Raw wine before *estufagem*.

Vinho estufado Wine which has been through the *estufa*.

Vinho de frasqueira or **vinho de garrafeira** A fine old vintage Madeira.

Vinho de gastos Literally, wine for wasting, used for giving to company employees.

Vinho generoso Fortified wine, same as *alcolisado*.

Vinho de lenço A very special old aromatic Madeira.

Vinho liquoroso Liqueur wine which has been *abafado*. Usually very sweet made from *Malvasia* or *Muscatel* grapes and stronger than other Madeiras.

Vinho seco Dry wine. Applied to unfortified wine which has been fermented right out for local consumption.

Vinho surdo Must which is not allowed to ferment by adding spirit. Used for sweetening.

Vinho tratado Treated fortified wine as opposed to *vinho seco*.

BIBLIOGRAPHY

Updated 2010

Adams, Dr. Joseph. *A Guide to Madeira*. London, 1801.
Albert of Monaco, Prince. *La Carrière d'Un Navigateur*. Monaco, 1966.
Albuquerque, L. de, and Vieira, A. *The Archipelago of Madeira in the XV Century*. Funchal, 1988.
Amerine, Maynard. Cossart, N. Madeira – The Island Vineyard. (Review) American Journal of Enology & Viticulture. Vol. 36, No. 1, 1985
Anon. *A Journal of a Voyage Round the World in His Majesty's Ship Endeavour in the Years 1768, 1769, 1770, and 1771*. London, 1771.
Anon. *A Collection of Voyages round the World performed by Royal Authority, Containing a Complete Historical Account of Captain Cook's First, Second, Third and Last Voyages*. 6 vols. London, 1790.
Anon. *A Guide to Madeira, containing a short account of Funchall*. London, 1801.
Anon. *An Historical Account of the Discovery of the Island of Madeira, Abridged from the Portugueze Original. To Which is Added, An Account of the present State of the Island, in a Letter to a Friend*. London, 1750.
Anon. *An Historical Sketch of the Island of Madeira*. London, 1819.
Anon. *125 Anos de Cerveja na Madeira* [by José Adriano Ribeiro]. Funchal, 1996.
Anon. *20 Anos de Autonomia e Desenvolvimento*. Funchal, 1996.
Anon. The Records of the Zodiac Club, 1868-1915. New York 1916.
Aragão, A. *A Madeira Vista por Estrangeiros*. Funchal, 1981.
Atkins, J. *A Voyage to Guinea, Brasil and the West-Indies*. 2nd. ed., London, 1737.
Arturo, Alberto. *Estufa de Banger*. Funchal, 1844.
Aubertin, J. J. *Six Months in Cape Colony and Madeira*. London, 1886.
Avery, L., ed, *Ronald Avery*. London, 1976.
Banks, Joseph. *The Endeavour Journal of Joseph Banks 1768-1771*. London, 1962.
Bannerman, David A. *Birds of the Atlantic Islands*. Vol II. London, 1963.
Barrow, John. *A Voyage to Cochin China in 1792 and 1793*. London, 1806.
Barry, Richard, *Mr. Rutlidge of South Carolina*. New York, 1942.
Bell Jr., Malcolm. "The Romantic Wines of Madeira" *Georgia Historical Quarterly*. Vol 38 (December, 1954). 322-36.
Berk, Emanuel. A Century Past: A Celebration of the Madeira Party in America. Sonoma, 1999.
Berk, Emanuel. Antebellum Nectar: Champagne & Madeira in Pre-Civil War Charleston & The United States. Sonoma, 2000.

Biddle, A. J. Drexel. *Land of Wine*, 2 vols. Philadelphia, 1901.

Bird, James. *Machin; or, the Discovery of Madeira*. London, 1821.

Bolton, W. *The Bolton Letters. The Letters of an English Merchant in Madeira 1695—1714.* Edited by A. L. Simon. London, 1928.

Bolton, W. *The Bolton Letters. The Letters of an English Merchant in Madeira.* Vol. II. 1701—1714. Produced by G. Blandy, Funchal, 1960. Reprinted 1976 and 1980.

Bowdich, T. E. *Excursions in Madeira and Porto Santo.* London, 1825.

Bowles, William Leslie. *The Spirit of Discovery.* London, 1809.

Brassey, Lady Annie. "Madeira." In *the Trades, the Tropics, and the Roaring Forties.* London, 1885.

Brazão, João do S. *Análise ao Sector Vitivinicola da Região Autonoma da Madeira.* Madeira, 1994.

Bridge, Horatio & Simpson, D. H. *Journal of an African Cruiser.* London, 1968.

Butler, Frank Hedges. *Wine and Wine Lands of the World.* London, 1926.

Burton, Sir Richard. *To the Gold Coast for Gold.* London, 1883.

Cabral do Nascimento, João. *Estampas Antigas da Madeira.* Funchal, 1935.

Cabral, Guilherme Read, *Angela Santa Clara.* Funchal, 1895.

Camara, Benedita. *A Economia da Madeira 1850-1914.* Lisbon, 2002.

Camden, C. G. Noel Viscount. *The British Chaplaincy in Madeira.* London, 1847.

Canavial, Conde de, *Os Tres Sestemas de Tratamento dos Vinhos da Madeira.* Funchal, 1900.

Candler, Allen D., ed, *Colonial Records of the State of Georgia*, Vol. IV.

Carita, Rui. *A Planta do Funchal de Mateus Fernandes.* Coimbra, 1983.

Carita, Rui. *História da Madeira.* Funchal, 1989.

Clode, Luíz Peter. *Registo Bio-bibliográphico de Madeirenses sec XIX-XX.* Funchal, 1983-1987.

Coleridge, Henry Nelson. *Six Months in the West Indies in 1825.* London, 1826.

Combe, William. *A History of Madeira.* London, 1821.

Cooper, William White. *The Invalid's Guide to Madeira.* London, 1840.

Cossart, Charles & John. *Copy of Records of the Establishment of the Chaplaincy & Notes on the Old Factory of Madeira.* London, 1959.

Cossart, N. *Madeira, The Island Vineyard.* London, 1984.

Coulter, E. Merton. *Thomas Spalding of Sapelo.* Louisiana, 1940.

Craddock, Fanny and John. *Time to Remember.* London, 1981.

Croft-Cooke, Rupert. *Madeira.* London, 1961.

Croft, J. *A Treatise on the Wines of Portugal.* York, 1787.

Croft, John. *A Treatise on the Wines of Portugal.* London, 1788.

Dillon, Frank. *Sketches in the Island of Madeira.* London, 1850.

Dix, John Adams. "A Winter in Madeira." *A Winter in Madeira and a Summer in Spain and Florence 1842-43.* New York, 1850.

Driver, John. *Letters From Madeira in 1834.* London and Liverpool, 1838.

Du Cane, Florence. *The Flowers and Gardens of Madeira.* London, 1909.

Duncan, T. B. *Atlantic Islands. Madeira . . . in Seventeenth-Century Commerce and Navigation.* Chicago and London, 1972.

BIBLIOGRAPHY

Eliot, Admiral Samuel Morison. *Admiral of the Ocean Seas. A Life of Christopher Columbus.* Boston, 1942.

Elliott, Trevor. *The Wines of Madeira.* Gosport, Hampshire, 2010.

Eckersberg, John Fredrik. *Views of Madeira.* Dusseldorf, 1840.

Embleton, Dennis. *A Visit to Madeira in Winter 1880-1881.* London, 1882.

Fairchild, David. "Madeira on the Way to Italy." *National Geographic Magazine.* Vol. 18, #12 (December, 1907). 751-771.

Forster, Georg Adam. *A Voyage Round the World.* London, 1777.

França, I. de. *Journal of a Visit to Madeira and Portugal (1853—1854).* Funchal, [1970].

Forster, G. *A Voyage Round the World in His Britannic Majesty's Sloop RESOLUTION, commanded by Capt. James Cook, during the Years 1772 ...* 2 vols. London, 1777.

Fructuoso, Dr. Gaspar, ed. *As Saudades da Terra.* A 15th Century Manuscript. Lisbon, 1870.

Fructuoso, Dr. Gaspar. *Saudades da Terra.* Funchal, 1873.

Fructuoso, Dr. Gaspar. *Livro Segundo das Saudades da Terra.* Ponta Delgado, 1968.

Fructuoso, Dr. Gaspar. *Las Islas Canarias (de "Saudades da Terra").* La Laguna de Tenerife, 1964.

Frumkin, Lionel. *The Science and Technique of Wine.* London, 1965.

Gardner, J. Starkie. *The Geology of Madeira.* London, 1888.

Gomes, Major J. Reis. *o Vinho da Madeira — Como se Prepara um Nectar.* Funchal, 1937.

Gonçalves, A. B., and Nunes, R. S. *Ilhas de Zargo. Adenda.* Parte I. Funchal, 1990.

Gourlay, William. *Observations of the Natural History, Climate and Diseases of Madeira.* London, 1812.

Grabham, Michael Comport. *Climate and Resources of Madeira.* London, 1870.

Grabham, Michael Comport. *The Climate and Resources of Madeira.* London 1889.

Grabham, Michael Comport. *Sub-Tropical Esculents.* London, 1922.

Grabham, Michael Comport. *Plants Seen in Madeira.* London, 1926.

Grabham, Michael Comport. *Plants Seen in Madeira.* London, 1934.

Grabham, Michael Comport. *Madeira Garden Sketches.* London, 1926.

Grabham, Michael Comport. *The Garden Interest of Madeira.* London, 1926.

Grant, Gordon, and Culver, Henry B. *The Book of Old Ships.* New York, 1924.

Green, George Alfred Lawrence. "Island of Diving Boys." *Islands Time Forgot.* London, 1962. 195-208.

Gregory, D. *The Beneficent Usurpers.* London and Toronto, 1988.

Griswold, Frank Gray, Old Madeiras. New York. 1929.

Griswold, Frank Gray, The Kittens. New York. 1916.

Guill, James Harold. *The Early History of Madeira 1418-1518.* Berkeley, 1951.

Hancock, David. "Commerce and Conversation in the 18th Century Atlantic: The Invention of Madeira Wine." *The Journal of Interdisciplinary History.* XXIX Autumn, 1998. 197-219.

Hancock, David. "A Revolution in the Trade." *The Early Modern Atlantic Economy.* Cambridge, 2000. 105-153.

Hancock, David. *Citizens of the World: London Merchants and the Integration of the British Atlantic Community, 1735-1785.* Cambridge, 1995.

Hancock, David. "War, Wine and Trade, 1750-1815." Lisbon, 2004.

Hancock, David. "The Emergence of an Atlantic Network Economy in the Seventeenth and Eighteenth Centuries: The Case of Madeira." Ramada Curto and Anthony Molho, eds., *Commercial Networks in the Early Modern World.* Florence, 2002.

Hancock, David. "Self-Organized Complexity and the Emergence of an Atlantic Market Economy, 1651-1815." Peter Coclanis and Jack Greene, eds., *The Atlantic Economy During the Seventeenth and Eighteenth Centuries.* Columbia, SC, 2005. 30-71.

Hancock, David. *Oceans of Wine: Madeira and the Emergence of American Trade and Taste.* New Haven, 2009.

Harcourt, Edward Vernon *A Sketch of Madeira.* London, 1851.

Harcourt, Edward Vernon, *A Sketch of Madeira.* London, 1880.

Harcourt, Susan Vernon. *Sketches in Madeira Drawn from Nature and on Stone.* London, 1851.

Hawkesworth, J. *An Account of the Voyages undertaken by the order of his Present Majesty for making Discoveries in the Southern Hemisphere.* 2 vols, the second vol. being *An Account of a Voyage Round the World in the Years 1768, 1769, 1770 and 1771 by Lieutenant James Cook, Commander of his Majesty's Bark the Endeavour.* 4th ed., Perth, 1787.

[Hawthorne, Nathaniel.] *Journal of an African Cruiser.* New York, 1848.

Henderson, Alexander. *The History of Ancient and Modern Wines.* London, 1824.

Herrick, Suzanne Hiller. *Leacocks.* San Rafael, 1994.

Hodgson, Capt. Studholme. *Truths From the West Indies.* London, 1838.

Holman, James. *Travels in Madeira.* London, 1840.

Hopkins, F. S. *An Historical Sketch of Madeira.* London, 1819.

Hurst de França, Isabella. *Journal of a Visit to Madeira and Portugal, 1853-1854.* Funchal, 1970.

Hutcheon, J. Edith. *Things Seen in Madeira.* New York, 1928.

Jeaffreson, J. C. *A Young Squire of the Seventeenth Century.* 2 vols. London, 1878.

Jeffs, J. *Sherry,* 4th ed., London, 1992.

Johnson, James Yates. *Madeira, Its Climate and Scenery.* 3rd ed., London, 1885.

Johnson, James Yates. *A Handbook for Madeira its Climate and Scenery for Invalids and Other.* London, 1885.

Jullien, A. *The Topography of All the Known Vineyards.* London, 1824.

Koebel, W. H. *Madeira Old and New.* London, 1908.

Koebel, W. H. *Madeira Old and New.* London, 1909.

Kummer, Corby. "Imperishable Wine: The Tempered Virtues of Madeira." *The Atlantic* Vol. 270, No. 6. (December, 1992). 140-2.

Lacerda, José de. *Dictionary of Portuguese and English Language (In Naval Language).* Lisbon, 1963

Layton, Tommy. Restaurant Roundabout. London, 1944.

Lee, Harold. *Madeira and the Canary Islands.* Liverpool, 1888.

BIBLIOGRAPHY

Lemps, A. H. de *Le Vin de Madère*. Grenoble, 1989.

Lethbridge, Alan. *Madeira: Impressions and Associations*. London, 1924.

Ley, Charles David, ed. *Portuguese Voyages 1493-1663*. London, 1947.

Liddell, Alex. *Madeira*. Faber & Faber. 1998

Lowe, Richard Thomas. *Manual of Flora of Madeira*. London, 1881.

Lowe, Richard Thomas. *Ferns, Flowering Plants and Land Shells*. London, 1872.

Lowe, Richard Thomas. *The Fishes of Madeira*. London, 1843.

Lyall, Alfred. *Rambles in Madeira and in Portugal in the Early Part of M.DCCC.XXVI*. London, 1827.

Lysons, Rev. Samuel. "Machin and Madeira: An Attempt to Investigate the Truth of the Romantic and Interesting Discovery of that Island". *Gloucester Illustrations No. 1*. London, 1861.

Macaulay, James. "Notes on the Physical Geography, Geology and Climate of the Island of Madeira." The Edinburgh New Philosophical Journal. Edinburgh, 1840.

MacCulloch, John. *The Art of Making Wine*. London, 1816.

Major, Richard Henry. *The Life of Prince Henry of Portugal*. London, 1868.

Manuel de Mello, Francisco. "The Discovery of Madeira." *Epanáphoras de Vária História Portugueza*. Lisbon, 1660. 537p.

March, Charles Wainwright. *Sketches in Madeira, Portugal and the Andaluzias of Spain*. New York, 1856.

Marsh, A. E. W. *Holiday Wanderings in Madeira*. London, 1892.

Mauro, F *Le Portugal, Le Bresil, et l'Atlantique au XVII Siècle (1570—1670)*. Paris, 1983.

Mayson, R. *Portugal's Wines and Wine Makers*. Chapter 17. London, 1992.

Mayson, R. "Does Anyone Know How to Make Madeira?" *Decanter*, May 1991.

McAllister, Ward. *Society as I Have Found It*. New York, 1890.

Mello, Francisco Manuel de. *Epanaforia de Varia Historia Portuguesa*. Lisbon, 1660.

Menezes, Charles Azevedo de, and Fr Silva, Francisco A. da. *Elucidario Madeirense*, 2 vols. Funchal, 1922.

Metcalfe, Jesse. Wandering Among Forgotten Isles. New York 1927.

Miles, Cecil H. *Dona Maria*. Funchal, 1955.

Miles, Cecil H. *A Glimpse of Madeira*. London, 1949.

Miles, Cecil H. "Once Upon a Time." *Revista Islenha*. #15 (July-Dec 1943). 83-109.

Miller, Barry. "The American Madeira Tradition." Unpublished dissertation. London, 1990.

Minchinton, Walter. "Britain and Madeira to 1914." *Actas I Colóquio Internacional de História da Madeira*. Funchal, 1989. 498-521.

Mitchell, S. Weir. *A Madeira Party*. New York 1895, 1897, 1902, 1910 and 1922.

Mitchell, S. Weir. A Madeira Party. Privately Printed 1958.

Montefiore, Joshua. A Commercial Dictionary containing the Present State of Mercantile Law, Practice and Custom. Philadelphia, 1804. 115-125.

Monteiro, Jose Leite. *Estampas Antigas de paisagem e Costumes da Madeira*. Funchal, 1951.

Nash, Roy. *Scandal in Madeira: The Story of Richard Thomas Lowe.* Sussex, 1990.
Newell, Colonel Herbert Andrews. *The English Church in Madeira.* Oxford, 1931.
Nicholas, Elizabeth. *Madeira and the Canaries.* London, 1953.
Nunes, Adão. *Peixes da Madeira.* Funchal, 1953.
Ordish, G. *The Great Wine Blight.* London, 1972. New ed., London, 1987.
Ovington, John. *A Voyage to Suratt In the Year, 1689.* London, 1696.
Ovington, John. *A Voyage to Suratt in the Year 1689.* London, 1929.
Pamment, D. "An Intricate Art." *Decanter Magazine's Guide to Madeira,* 2nd ed., 1987.
Parkinson, C.N. *Trade in the Eastern Seas.* Cambridge, 1937.
Penning-Rowsell, E. "Christie's Wine Auctions in the 18th Century." *Christie's Wine Review* 1972. London, 1972.
Penning-Rowsell, E. "Auctioning Wine in the18th Century." *Country Life,* 6 October 1966.
Penzer, N. M. *The Book of the Wine-Label.* London, 1947.
Pestana, E. A. *Ilha da Madeira.* 2 vols. Funchal, 1965, 1970.
Pereira, Eduardo Clemente Nunes. *Ilhas de Zargo.* Funchal, 1989.
Pereira, Fernando Jasmins. *Estudos Sobre História da Madeira.* Funchal, 1991.
Peres, Damião. *A Madeira Sob os Donatarios.* Funchal, 1914.
Phillips, James Duncan. *Salem and the Indies.* Boston, 1947.
Picken, Andrew. *Madeira Illustrated.* Funchal, 1840.
Pitta, M.D., Nicolau Caetano Bettencourt. *Account of the Island of Madeira.* London, 1812.
Pocock, Nicholas. "Logbooks of the Minerva (Snow) Archive/Manuscript 1772-1776." *Collections of the Mariner's Museum Newport News.* VA, (30 & 31), Vol. 1. 246-262.
Redding, Cyrus. *A History and Description of Modern Wines.* London, 1833.
Redding, Cyrus. *A History and Description of Modern Wines.* London, 1836.
Reid, William and Alfred. *Madeira a Guidebook of Useful Information.* London, 1891.
Ribeiro, Orlando. *Ilha da Madeira Até Meados do Século XX.* Lisbon, 1985.
Riddell, Maria. *Voyage to Madeira, Leeward and Caribbean.* Edinburgh, 1792.
Robertson, G. *Port.* London, 1978.
Robinson, J. *Vines, Grapes and Wines,* London, 1986.
Robinson, J. ed. *The Oxford Companion to Wine.* Oxford and New York, 1994.
Roessler, E. B., and Amenne, M. A. *The Age of Madeira.* California, 1973.
Rose, J. Holland. *Napoleon's Last Voyage.* London, 1814.
Rutledge, Anna Wells. "After the Cloth Was Removed." *Winterthur Portfolio,* Vol. 4., 1968, pp. 47-62.
Saintsbury, G. *Notes on a Cellar-Book.* London and Basingstoke, 1978.
Sanceau, Elaine. *Henry the Navigator.* London and New York, 1940.
Sanches de Baêna, Visconde de, ed. *Resenha das Familias Titulares e Grandes de Portugal,* 2 vols. Lisbon, 1890.
Santos, Rui. "A Família Abudarham do Funchal." *Revista Islenha* Vol. #12 (Jan-Jun, 1993). 106-140.
Sarmento, Colonel Alberto. *Vertabrados da Madeira.* Funchal, 1948.

BIBLIOGRAPHY

Shore, Emily. *Journals of Emily Shore 1831-1839*. London, 1891.
Shryock, Richard H., ed,. *Letters of Richard D. Arnold M.D. 1808—1876.* Durham, 1929.
Silva, F. A. da, and Meneses, C. A. de *Elucidário Madeirense*. 3 vols. Funchal, 1922. Reprinted 1940 and also in facsimile, Funchal, 1984.
Simon, Andre L. *The History of the Wine Trade in England*. 3 vols. London, 1964.
Simon, André L. *The Blood of the Grape*. London, 1920.
Simon, André L. *Madeira*. London, 1951.
Simon, André L. *A Wine Primer*. London, 1946.
Simon, André L. *Wine and the Wine trade in England*. London, 1933.
Simon, André L. *Tables of Content*. London, 1929.
Simon, André L. *Vintagewise*. London, 1945.
Simon, André L. *The Saintsbury Club*. London, 1943.
Simon, André L. and Craig, Elizabeth. *Madeira Wine, Cakes and Sauces*. London, 1933.
Singleton, Vernon L., and Esau, Paul. *The Significance of Phenolic Substances in Grapes and Wine*. New York, 1969.
Sitwell, Sacheverell. "Madeira." *Portugal and Madeira*. London, 1954.
Sloane, H. *A Voyage to the Islands Madera . . . and Jamaica*. 2 vols. London, 1707.
Smith, F. Hopkinson. *Kennedy Square*. New York, 1915.
Smith, John Jay. *Letters of Dr. Richard Hill and His Children*. Philadelphia, 1854.
Smyth, C. Piazzi. *Madeira Meteorologic*. Edinburgh, 1882.
Sousa, J. J. A. de. "O Porto do Funchal e a Economia da Madeira no Século XVIII." *Das Artes e da História da Madeira*, Vol. VII, No. 37, 1967.
Staunton, G. *An Authentic Account of An Embassy from the King of Great Britain to the Emperor of China . . .* London, 1797.
Stowsand, C. S., and Robinson, W. B. *American Journal of Enology and Viticulture*, Vol. XXIII. California, 1972.
Stowsand, C. S., and Robinson, W. B. *New York Food and Life Bulletin*. New York, 1971.
Stuart-Wortley, Emmeline. *A Visit to Portugal and Madeira*. London, 1854.
Sunderman, William. *Our Madeira Heritage*. Philadelphia, 1979.
Tavares, J. *Subsídios para o Estudo da Vinha e do Vinho na Região da Madeira*. Funchal, 1953.
Taylor, Ellen M. *Madeira, Its Scenery and How to See It*. London, 1882.
Thomas, Charles W. *Adventures and Observations in the West Coast of Africa*. New York, 1860.
Thomas-Stanford, Charles. *Leaves From a Madeira Garden*. London, 1909.
Thudichum, J. L. W., and Dupré, A. *A Treatise on the Origin, Nature and Varieties of Wine*. London, 1872.
A Treaatise on the Climate and Meteorology of Madeira by the Late J.A.Mason, M.D. (Review), in The Edinburgh Medical and Surgical Journal, Volume 74. Edinburgh, 1850. 148-180
Tremoço de Carvalho, Michael. *Gaspar Frutuoso: O Historiador das Ilhas*. Funchal, 2001.
Trigo, Adriano A. and Anibal A., *Guide and Plan of Funchal*. Funchal, 1910.

Turnbull, John. *A Voyage Round the World*. London, 1813.
Various. *Decanter Magazine's Guide to Madeira*, 2nd ed., 1987.
Viala, P., and Vermorel, V. *Ampélographie*. 7 vols. Paris, 1901-10.
Vieira, Alberto. *História do Vinho da Madeira*. Funchal, 1993.
Vieira, Alberto. *História do Vinho da Madeira*. Funchal, 2001.
Vieira, Alberto. *A Vinha e O Vinho na História da Madeira Século XV a XX*. Funchal, 2003.
Vieira, Alberto. *Breviário da Vinha e do Vinho na Madeira*. Ponta Delgado (Azores), 1990.
Vieira, Alberto. *A Rota do Açúcar na Madeira / The Sugar Route in Madeira*. Funchal, 1996.
Vizetelly, Henry. *Facts about Port and Madeira*. London, 1880.
Vizetelly, Henry. *Facts about Port and Madeira*. London and New York, 1880. Reprinted in facsimile, Baltimore, n.d.
Weaver, H. J. *Reid's Hotel Jewel of the Atlantic*. London, 1991.
Wells, Edward Watkinson. *Journal of a Trip to Madeira*. Funchal, 1971.
White, R. *Madeira Its Climate and Scenery*. London and Madeira, 1851. 2nd ed., rewritten with the addition of much new matter by J. Y. Johnson. Edinburgh, 1857.
Wilde, William Robert Wills. *Narrative of a Voyage to Madeira and Along the Mediterranean Islands*. Dublin, 1852.
Wildes, Henry Emerson. *Anthony Wayne*. New York, 1941.
Wood, Frances Anne Burney. *Great Niece's Journal: Being Extracts from Journals of Fanny Anne Burney*. Boston, 1926.
Wortley, E. S. *A Visit to Portugal and Madeira*. London, 1854.
Wright, John. *An Essay on Wines, Especially on Port Wine*. London, 1795. 42-43.

NOTES

1. In *Madeira* (Faber & Faber, 1998), Alex Liddell provides the most detailed weighing of the evidence, both pro and con. While he allows for the possibility that the story is true, his view "inclines sharply towards skepticism," and towards the idea that Michael Grabham, Noël's uncle and the son-in-law of Charles Ridpath Blandy, had concocted the Napoleon connection in 1933. That was the year when, at age 93, Grabham told the story to André Simon who in turn published it later the same year in *Madeira Wine, Cakes and Sauce*. Liddell also attempts to clear the air about the wine itself. Is it, as has been suggested at various times, a Bual or a Malvasia or a Sercial? Liddell concludes that, like most 18th century Madeiras, the wine was from unknown grape varieties and that "the wine may well have originated in Câmara do Lobos" as asserted by Henry Vizetelly 1880, but we are likely to never know that with any certainty. *Emanuel Berk*

2. A 14th-century fully decked ship about 90ft long, beam 24ft. Propelled by sweeps and single masted, with a square mainsail containing one reef point. A cog is carved on the front of Winchester Cathedral.

3. The Merchant Venturers still survives; it is now an elegant club in Bristol.

4. The Rev. Samuel Lysons, MA., FSA., Rector of Rodmarton and Permanent Curate of St. Luke's, Gloucester, in his work, Machin and Madeira, an Investigation into the Truth of the Romantic Discovery of the Island, published in London 1861, states the date of Machin's departure from Bristol as 1344. He also gives Anna's father's name as Walter Darbey, who lived in St. Augustine's Back, Bristol.

5. From Porto Santo, a poem by James D. Burns.

6. Ballast keels.

7. Zarco's two-handed sword is now in the Municipal Museum in Funchal. It is 5ft. 6in. long and used to hang in the hall at Quinta da Levada, which belonged to my grandfather.

8. Noël Cossart's mother was descended from Perestrello.

9. It was later occupied by Messrs. Gordon, Duff and Co., wine shippers, from 1790 until the firm left the island in 1810. Only a wall and one window remain.

10. These levada paths afford fascinating walking and are a good way to see the island. Pat and John Underwood describe levada walking in their book *Landscapes of Madeira*, a countryside guide for ramblers and picnickers, with drawings by Katharina Kelly. John and Pat revise the book every year, keeping it up to date, and it is a splendid guide for visitors. The book is published by Sunflower Books, PO Box 115, Exeter EX2 6YU, UK.

11. A waterspout is a weather phenomenon occurring when a column of water is drawn up from the sea to meet a whirling cloud, resulting in torrential rain.

12. A two-masted ketch-type boat also known as a dogger. In southern Europe it was a three-masted lateen schooner-type boat. Both are vessels of burden.

13. Madeira is laid down in the charts in longitude 17° but because of the difficulty of calculating longitude in the period before the development of the chronometer Lord Anson places the island "from 18°½ to 19°½ West:, an error of calculation later to place Anson's ships n deadly peril.

14. The Loo Rock, at one time a fortified island in the Bay of Funchal, is now in the centre of the mole.

15. His book *Madeira Wine, Cakes and Sauce* was published by Constable in 1933.

16. This very imposing building now houses the Maderia Wine Institute (see chapter 7, page 114).

17. It was the youngest daughter, Bella, who founded the embroidery business referred to in chapter 8.

18. John Milburn Leacock was the first resident of Madeira to own a motor car.

19. Raleigh Krohn's widow, Heather, is still living in Porto Santo.

20. Cossart, Gordon's membership of the Association ended a familiar sight in Funchal — that of the "red caps." This was the uniform of the Cossart workers, who wore blue drill suits with a bright red cap so that they could be spotted if they should stray and sit about in wine shops.

21. Among these letters is one written from New York in 1811 "per the Sumatra." It has been slit and disinfected (to let out the pestilential air). Apparently letters were punctured or slit, then placed in hot ovens and smoked to disinfect them.

22. This means the cask is gauged for payment after the voyage, so ullage is for account of the shipper.

23. The counter of Blandy's shipping office in Funchal was made from teak from the wreck of this fine clipper after she was washed ashore and broken up in a storm in 1965.

24. In the case of a cool summer, the additional yeast cells on the leaves would produce a much more vigorous fermentation and the practice is often recommended as a cure for slow or stopped fermentations. The leaves also used to be added in the belief that they gave a fragrant acidic taste to the wine following *estufagem*, but this practice is no longer carried out.

25. Old Madeira usually contains from 0.80 to 1.20 grammes of volatile acidity per litre, whereas a Muscatel of the same age would contain only 0.40 to 0.60 grammes per litre.

26. French for musty or mouldy flavoured, sometimes described in English as mousy.

27. The English word for malvina — anthocyanin diglucoside.

28. The European Members of Parliament have had the idea of turning the

NOTES

Common Market's wine lake into ethyl alcohol to mix with motor-car petrol, thus consuming the surplus wine and saving petrol; so grape growers may be producing four-start appellation contrôlée petrol.

29. Dr. Konstantin Frank, the doyen of New York State wine makers, has always been a vociferous opponent of hybrids, stating that the wine makes women sterile. Curiously, whilst in Madeira recently, the waiter in a country inn refused to serve the wide of a friend of mine with wine made locally from the concord grape. He said that in 18 years he had never been asked to serve this wine to a female customer.

30. Banana bark makes excellent washers to place between the heading boards of casks.

31. Cama or Câmara de Lobos. *Lobos* means wolves, in this case "sea wolves" or seals. *Cama* means bed and *câmara* means a chamber (room) or sheltered place. When Zarco sailed into the bay there were many seals basking on the beach. Both forms are correct. Being old fashioned, I prefer *Cama*, because I think that Zarco would have named the place 'bed of seals' rather than "chamber of seals."

32. The vintage pipe contains 12 goatskins or *barrils* of 35 litres each. Its capacity is therefore 540 litres.

33. The work of the IVM (now known as the IVBAM) covers the following: the allocation, purchase and distribution of alcohol to shippers; regulation and control of vintage; certification of grapes from specific areas, vinification methods and final inspection and approval of wine before shipment; control and budget for generic promotion; and responsibility, with committee of experts from shippers (ACIF) for legislation.

34. This is amply borne out by a study of Christie's catalogues. From 1766 until the mid-19th century Madeira appeared in most sales of wine from the cellars of gentlemen "gone abroad", "deceas'd" and so forth.

35. There is no longer an official date. At a meeting of representatives of the Instituto do Vinho da Madeira, the shippers and the growers, prices and quantities to be purchased are discussed and a commencement date for the harvest is usually set. Even so some farmers with vineyards at lower levels may pick a week or two earlier.

36. The Estrada Monumental which passes Reid's Hotel and goes on to Câmara de Lobos was called the New Road when it was first constructed.

37. All the shippers have their own methods of vinification, ranging from fermentation in individual oak casks of 630-650 litres, known as scantling pipes, up to fermentation in huge oak vessels called cubas, of 25,000 litres capacity.

38. Only a very limited amount may be made by law and it is used in small quantities in the final blending of very rich Malmsey and Bual.

39. Christie's archives reveal much evidence of this desirable practice. See illustration on page 72.

40. Due to protein, or some other material, having precipitated.

41. It would also be possible for any remaining sugar to be fermented, if yeast cells were accidentally introduced at this stage.

42. Some shippers, particularly those who heat the wine in large concrete tanks, have installed refrigerators to cool the wine very gently with a counter-current of water. As the water temperature is usually no more than 14-16 degrees Centigrade and the flow very small, the wine is cooled very gently to about 20-22 degrees. This process would never be used for the noble varieties or canteiro wines.

43. This is because loss through evaporation in wood is calculated at 0.5 degrees Gay Lussac of alcohol and five per cent of the total volume per annum.

44. King George IV.

45. Verdelho.

46. Another version of the story is attributed to President Jefferson.

47. A bottle labelled by grape variety today must by law contain 85 per cent of that variety.

48. Many shippers have called their Verdelho types Rainwater owing to the difficulty in pronouncing the word Verdelho.

49. Henry Veitch was discharged from his post of consul-general for disobeying Whitehall's instructions.

50. Apart from whether the connection to Napoleon is true (see note 1 above), there are some obvious problems with the story. The first is that Charles Blandy was only ten years when he is said to have bought the pipe. Second, Charles' son John could not have bottled the wine in 1840 as he was not born until 1841. It is more likely that Charles' *father* John both acquired the pipe and bottled it. The source of these inaccuracies appears to have been André Simon's writings, beginning with *Madeira Wine, Cakes and Sauce* (1933).

51. It should be noted that on these old labels the word "Cama" and not "Câmara" de Lobos is used.

52. *Frasqueira* means literally a box or case for bottles or flagons, implying a rare collection of old bottles of wine. The Madeira Wine Institute uses the word *frasqueira* to denote the highest classification of Madeiras. *Frasqueira* Particular Avery may be translated as Averys "Private Stock", "Collection" or "Cellar."

53. Evans, Marshall & Co. were then Cossart, Gordon's London agents.

54. A common disguise for the gin decanter in early Victorian days.

55. Rupert Croft-Cooke suggests that the 1792 vintage had no connection with Napoleon, and that its naming was only one of Dr. Grabham's pleasures. He was rather a wicked old man, fond of leg pulling, but I can guarantee the story he told about his 1792 Madeira was no leg pull and is fact.

56. Michael Grabham's brother-in-law, John Blandy, could not have bottled the 1792 Madeira in 1840 as he was not born until 1841. It is more likely that it was bottled by John Blandy's grandfather. Also see notes 1 and 49 above.

57. See chapter 10, pp. 148, 149.

ILLUSTRATION CREDITS

Noël Cossart: Noël and David Cossart, xvi; Noël Cossart as a Child (three photos), xxxviii; Cossarts and Friends at Quinta do Monte, 1892, xl; Charles Blandy Cossart, xlii; Noël Cossart as a Young Man (two photos), xlv; Graf Zeppelin I over Funchal, 1934, xlvi; Cossart, Gordon 1984 Advertisement, lv; Program for 1984 Book Launching in Savannah, lviii; Prince Henry the Navigator, 9; Zarco's Statue in Funchal, 10; Columbus' House, 14; Looking Inland from near Faial, 16; Agricultural Instruments, 19; Levada near Santo da Serra, 21; View from Cape Girão, 22; Funchal, 27; Banana Plantations near Funchal, 28; Francis Newton, 31; Thomas Murdoch, 31; Charles John Cossart, 55; Russell Manners Gordon, 55; Peter Cossart, 56; Carlo de Bianchi with Noël Cossart, 64; The Cossarts at Quinta do Monte, 1888, 66; Christie's Auction, 1828, 72; Cossart, Gordon Publicity, early 20th century, 74; 1763 New York Bill of Lading, 80; The Madeira Club of Savannah, 1976, 90; Wine Cellars in the Owens-Thomas House, 91; Opening the Able Madeira, 93; Terraced Vineyards at Cama do Lobos, 105; Câmara de Lobos, 118; Bella Phelps' Embroidery Designs, 120; Joseph and Elizabeth Phelps, 121; A Lagar, 129; Armazem de Calor, 133; Cossart, Gordon Price List, 1895, 145; The Famous 1808 Solera Pipe, 152; Vintage and Solera Madeiras, Madeira Wine Company, 159; A Typical Solera Store, 169; William Neyle Habersham's house, Savannah, Georgia, 177; Bill of Lading per Two Sisters, 1780, 183; Going to a Picnic in Madeira, 202; Mountains from Pico Arieiro, 210; The Medici Map (portion), 1351, 7; Madeira's Geographical Position, 8; Map of Madeira, 1984, from the 1st Edition, 98

Emanuel Berk: Ellis Son & Vidler Silver Jubilee Madeira, liv; Alcaforado's Discovery of Madeira, 4; Cabin Plan for the Madeira Packet Eclipse, 29; Dr. Richard Hill's Quinta Achada, 52; Boston's Club Gastronomique Menu, 82; United States Hotel, New York, Madeira bill, 1831, 85; S. Weir Mitchell's A Madeira Party, 86; Borracheiros in Funchal, 128; Torre Bella Wine Label, 157; Esquin & Co. Catalogue, 1968, 160; Cossart, Gordon's 1846 Terrantez, 162; Cossart, Gordon Solera, Bottled 1940, 170; Noël Cossart's Father and Grandfather by Vizetelly, 173; Shipping Manifest, The Waccamaw, 1836, 179; Ward McAllister, 182; Sir Stephen Gaselee, 188; Mid-19th Century Map of Madeira, xxii; Coronelli's Map of Madeira & the Canaries, c. 1690, 50; Bowen's Map of Madeira, 1752, 50

Museu Photographia Vicentes, Funchal: The Cossart, Gordon Lodge, xliii; Princess Maria Pia de Saboia's arrival in Madeira, 30; Entrance to St. John's Vineyard, 45; Henry Veitch's house, Jardim da Serra, 47; Quinta do Monte, 57;

MADEIRA THE ISLAND VINEYARD

John Blandy, 59; Charles Ridpath Blandy, 60; Hugo Krohn, 63; The Madeira Wine Association's Lodge, 1925, 67; H.M. Borges' Lodge, 69; Grapes Await Pressing at Cossart, Gordon, 103; Barrels at H.M. Borges, 124; Loading Borges Barrels on Ship, 125; Leacock's Cooperage, 137; Madeira Wine Association's Barrels, 1932, 142; Cossart, Gordon's Oxen, 149; Winston Churchill Painting in Câmara de Lobos, 1950, 156; The Palacio de Torre Bella, Funchal, 158; Michael Grabham, 185

Casa-Museu Frederico de Freitas, Funchal: Château Cossart, xxxix; The Burying Ground by Henry Veitch, 38; Funchal from the Bay by Andrew Picken, 1840, 39

Anthony Miles: Henry P. Miles, 62

Leacock Family: John Leacock's 1741 Indenture, 41

Reflections *www.20thcenturyimages.co.uk*: Ellis Son & Vidler's Cellars, liii

INDEX

Note: Page numbers in italics indicate illustrations and captions. The initials "NC" refer to Noël Cossart. The following information is not indexed: Individual wines and firms in Appendices III, VI, VII, XI, and XVI; early settlers listed in Appendix VIII; geographic information in Appendix IX; individual quintas and their owners in Appendix X; and glossary terms.

Aaron, Florence, 202–3
Able (ship), 92
Able Madeira, 91, 92–94
Abudarham. *See* Viuva Abudarham & Filhos
Academy of Ancient Madeira Wines, xlviii–xlix, 163, 192–93
Acciaioly, Michael, 238
Acciaioly, Oscar, 238
Accioli, Simon, 101
An Account of the island of Madeira (Pitta), 106
acetic acid, 136
Achada do Gramacho, 112–13
Achadas da Cruz, 110
adegas, 142
Africa, exports to, 77–78
African slaves, 11, 28, 88
aging. *See* maturation
agriculture, 11, 17–22, 23, 26, 27, 32. *See also* bananas; Madeira vines and vineyards; sugar cane
   agricultural implements, 18–19
   crops other than grapes, 18, 22–23, 27, 109
   Desertas, 24
   irrigation, 19–20
   land tenure, xxxiv, li, 20–21
   livestock, 21–22, 24
   soils, 12, 18
agua pé, 129
aguardente, 111, 130, 139
Aikman, Barry, 279
air travel, vi, 23, 29–30, 279, 280–86
Alabama (ship), 88
Albert of Monaco, 25
Albuquerque, Alfonso d,' 20, 71
Alcaforado, Franciso, 3–5, 33
alcohol content, xxix, 133, 136, 138, 140
Alfonso V of Portugal, 10, 71
Alicante, 102
Allemão, Henrique, 255
Allen, H. Warner, xlviii–xlix, 287
Allen, Phillip, xx
All Saints Madeira, 180–81
Allston, Robert, 269, 298

Almaden, liv
Almeida, Constança Rodrigues de, 256
American auctions, 220–21, 240–43
   Habersham sale (1900), 181–82, 299–302
   sales figures, 1971—2009, 221–36
American connoisseurs and devotees, 79–80, 86–87, 237, 241, 242. *See also* Habersham, William Neyle
   Brady, lix–lx, 96–97, 287–93
   Savannah Madeira Club, 89–92, 240
American grapes and hybrids, xxxii–xxxiii, 103–6, 110–11, 117, 119, 321n29
American Institute of Food and Wine, 291
American Madeira, 81, 145–46. *See also* Rainwater Madeiras
American markets and trade, 31. *See also* North American market and trade; West Indies
   Brazil, 32, 78
Anson, Lord, 35–36, 320n13
anthocyanin diglucoside. *See* malvina
ants, 17
aqueducts *(levadas)*, xxx, 19–20, *21*, 319n10
Aquila Airways, vi, 279, 280–86
Arco da Calheta, 158
Arfet, Anna d,' 4–5, 12, 319n4
Argentine ant, 17
Argentine Madeira, 83
armazens de calor, *133*, 135, 136, 140
Arnold, C. H., 302
Arnold & Co., 181
   Habersham sale (1900), 181–82, 299–302
Articles on Madeira (Bellows), 86
Arujo, Alberto de, 110
Ashley, Iris, 22
Aspidiotus hederae (lapa), 109
Associacão Comercial, 52
Atkins, Mr., 162
Atlantic Crossing Guide (Allen), xx
auctions, 190, 219–46
   Christie's sales, 1970s, 160, 161, 163, 165, 187, 189
   Gordon collection, 157–58
   Habersham estate, 181–82, 299–302

325

notable sales, 1970s—2008, 237–44
recent developments, 219–20
sales figures, 1971—2009, 221–36
Sotheby's 1982, 163
Avery, Ronald, 161, 288, 290
   at Academy of Ancient Madeiras tasting, xlviii, 192, 193
   and Cossart, Gordon wines, 144, 163, 193
   and Gaselee Madeiras, 165, 189, 292
Averys, 163, 164, 171, 237, 288. *See also* Avery, Ronald
   as Cossart, Gordon's UK agent, lv
   Gaselee Madeiras, 189–90
   1960 Madeira tasting, xlix, 160–61, 164, 189
avocado, Madeira with, 200

bacelos, 103
Baker, John, 172, 192, 193
The Ballad of East and West (Kipling), 71
Baltimore, Madeira in, 87, 97, 240, 302
Bamboo cocktail, 73
bananas, xxxiv–xxxv, 18, 27, 110, 111
Banks, Joseph, 37
Bannerman, David, 25–26
Barbeito Lda., 70, 254
Barbeito Vasconcelos, Mario, 70, 238
barrels. *See* casks
Barrete de Padre, 102
Barros e Sousa (Artur de), 254
Barter Madeira, 81
Barton & Mayhew, lvi
basketry, 23
Bass Charrington, xlviii, 173
Bastardo (Bastardinho) grape, 99
   characteristics, 102, 127, 164
   current status, xxxii, xxxiii, xxxiv, 164, 171
Bastardo Madeiras, 32, 102, 171, 199
   notable wines and vintages, 164–65, 171, 188, 244
Batista, Fulgencio, 29
beans, 109
The Bedside Book (Moiny), 276
Belem's Madeira Lda., 68
Bell, Malcolm, 80, 88, 90, 134, 180–81
Bellows, Charles, 83, 86, 87, 182–83
Bellows & Co., 183, 302
Benbow, Admiral, 35
bentonite, 180
Beresford, William Carr, 45–46
Berry Bros., 157, 171, 172, 173, 192, 199
Bianchi, Anna Lomelino de, 65, 161
Bianchi, Antonio, 65, 161, 189
Bianchi, Carlo de, *64*, 65–66, 161
Bianchi, Eugenia (later Henriques), 161–62
Bianchi, Ferdinando, 161
Bianchi, Ferdinando (younger), 161
Bianchi, Gabriel, 65, 161
Bianchi, Giovanni de, 162
Bianchi, John, 162
Bianchi, Maria Anna de (later Cossart; NC's mother), xliii, xlix, 65, 193, 319*n*8

Bianchi family, 65–66, 147, 161–62, 163
   notable wines, xlix, 160–61, 189
Bidwell, Hugh, liv–lv
Bingham, George, 277, 278
birds, 25–26, 109
Birkenhead, Frederick Smith, Earl of, 29
Bissett, Richard, 51
Blackburn (G. & R.), 97
Blackburn Madeiras, 96, 97
Black Pearle, 104
Blake family, 183–84
Blandy, Adam, 61
Blandy, Anna Mary (later Cossart), 60, *66*, 275
Blandy, C. F. Raleigh, xl
Blandy, Charles Ridpath, 60, 88, 168–69, 186
   and Napoleon Madeira, lix, 155, 156, 169, 275, 322*n*50
Blandy, Edward, 189
Blandy, Graham, xlii, 40, 61, 187
Blandy, John (1782-1855), 59, 155, 322*n*50, 322*n*56
Blandy, John Burden, 60, 186, 189, 275, 322*n*50, 322*n*56
Blandy, John Ernest, xli, 60–61, 67, 197–98
Blandy, John R., li, 61, 187, 209
Blandy, Richard, li, liv, lvi–lvii, 61, 67
Blandy & Sons, 59–60, 61, 67, 88. *See also* Napoleon Madeira
   Long as cellarmaster, 173
   notable wines, 155–56, 159–60, 168–69, 187
   soleras, 168–69, 170
   vintage Madeiras, 165–66
Blandy Brothers & Co. Ltd., xlviii, 59, 61, 84
   and MWA/MWC, xli–xlii, xliv, xlvii, lvi–lvii
Blandy family, 243
Blandy Gardens, 189
Blandy's Madeiras Lda., 60–61
Blandy's Malmsey Solera, 90, 91
blends and blending, 141, 143–44, 147, 321*n*38. *See also* Rainwater Madeira; Solera Madeiras; solera system
   grape varieties for, 99, 100, 104, 147
   Habersham's blends, 303–4
   labelling regulations, 151–52
   notable wines, 163–64
   soleras, 168, 171
Boal. *See* Bual grape; Bual Madeiras
Boal do Porto Santo grape, 99
Boal Solera (Cossart), 91
Bolger, Dermot, 158
bolo de mel, 201
Bolton, William, 40, 73, 138
Bordeaux, xxxiii
Bordeaux mixture, 109, 117
Borges (H. M.) Sucrs. Lda., 69, 254
Borges, Henrique de Menèzes, 69, 163
borracheiros, 127–28, 131
bottles and bottling, xliv, 144–45, 148, 197
Brady, Roy, 96, 287–93
Braganza, Luisa de, 33
Bramin Madeiras, 83–84, 182

INDEX

brandy, 138–39. *See also* fortification
Brazil, exports to, 32, 78
breathing, 94–95, 190, 195, 199
  shipwreck wines, 93, 94
Britain, Madeira in, xxx–xxxi
  before 1900, xxxi, 32, 48–49, 122, 146, 164
  fraudulent wines and, xxxi
  importers as of 1984, 253
  London bottlings, xliv, 145, 173
  soleras, 171–72
  twentieth century, xxxii, 121–22, 148
British Army messes, 75–77, 150
British East India Company, 71, 73, 74, 122
British Factory
  Madeira, 37–40, 46, 155, 296, 298
  Oporto, 296–97, 298
British interests in Madeira, xxxvii, xxxix, 43–46, 123
British Madeira firms. *See* Madeira merchants; *specific firms*
Brito, Francisco d'Almeida e, 103, 117, 119
Broadbent, Michael, vi, xix, l, 65, 91–92, 290
  at book launch parties, lvii–lviii
Brooks, Van Wyck, 34
Brook's Club, 75
Bual grape, xxxiii, 99, 101, 127
Bual Madeiras, 39, 110, 147, 195, 202, 321n38
  in blends, 143
  characteristics, 148, 150
  Cossart, Gordon Duo-centenary Celebration, 144, 170–71, 194
  with food, 122, 200
  fortification, 133
  Gunner Madeira, 76–77
  in India, 73
  notable post-phylloxera wines, 158, 161, 189, 194
  notable pre-phylloxera wines, xlix, 157, 159–61, 162, 170–71, 186–87, 188, 189, 191, 193, 238
  sales records, 1971—2009, 221–36
  storage, 195
  tastings, 82, 90, 191, 193, 194
  vintage notes, 211–13, 215, 216, 217
Bugio, 24
Burden, Janet (later Blandy), 59
Burgess, Mr., 139
Burgundy, 291, 296–97
Burgundy Madeira, 271. *See also* Madeira Burgundy
Burka, Fred, 96, 288
Burrows, Elliott, 274, 276–77
Butler, Pierce, 87
Butler Madeiras, 87

Cabo Girão, 110
Cabot, John, 71
Cabral, Diogo, 71
Cabral, Pedro Alvares, 71, 78
Cachudo, 101. *See also* Bual grape
Cadwalader, Lambert, 86

Cadwalader Madeiras, 86–87
California wines and viticulture, 36, 119, 125, 291
Cama (Câmara) de Lobos Madeiras, 83, 147
  in American tastings, 82, 90
  Bastardos, 165, 171
  notable post-phylloxera wines, 187, 194
  notable pre-phylloxera wines, 97, 157–58, 165, 171, 237
  notable vintages, 211–12
  Torre Bella wines, xxiii, 157–58, 163, 192–93, 239
Câmara, João José da, 42
Câmara, Jose Manoel da, 44
Câmara, Paulo Perestrello da, 31, 135
Câmara de Lobos, 118, *156*, 321n31
Câmara de Lobos vineyards, 70, *105*, 108, 110, 111
  Bianchi vineyards, 161
  Henriques vineyards, 68, 238
  phylloxera in, 116, 118
Campanario, 110, 147, 194, 215
Canada, exports to, xix, 68
Canavial, Count, 78, 135, 186
Canica, 104
Canning, George, 75
Canteiro Madeiras, xxix, 134, 147, 153, 187
capsules, 190, 196
Carãa de moça grape, 102
caramujo de dama, 109
Carême, Marie-Antonin, 276
Carl (Charles) I of Austria, 29, 57
Carma Vinhos Lda., 68
Carolina Jockey Club, 89
Carvalhal, Count, 189
Carvalhal Sercial, 189
Casa dos Vinhos da Madeira Lda., 68
cascalho soils, 18, 106
casks, 88, 132, 134, 136, 141–42, 321n37
  photographs, *124*, *137*, *142*
  pipe capacity, 73, 77, 321n32
  for soleras, 168, *169*
castas autorizadas, 99
castas boas, 99
castas nobres, 99, 154
Castelão grape, 100
Castello Melhor, Marquez de, 25
Catanach, John, 37
Catanach & Murdoch, 41, 53
Catherine (infanta of Portugal), 33
cattle, 21–22, 24
Cautley, Reverend, 46
cavalos, 103
celery hearts, Madeira style, 203–4
cellar books, 196
Cerçal. *See* Sercial grape
Cervantes, Miguel de, 135
Ceuta, 8
Challenger Madeira, 186
Chambers, Charles, 37
Chão, 24
Charles (Carl) I of Austria, 29, 57

Charles II of England, 33, 34
Château Cossart, *xxxix*, 47
cheeses, Madeira with, 200
chestnut canker, 17
chestnut trees, 107
chicken, recipes for, 204, 205
Chicora Wood Plantation wine cellar, 269–71, 298
China, exports to, 77
Choice Madeiras, 151
"A Choice Malmsey Nose" (Cossart), lvii
Christie, James (cellarman at St. James's Palace), 48–49
Christie, James (of Christie's), 48
Christie's, *72*, 75
Christie's sales, 48, 219
   1970s, 160, 161, 163, 165, 187, 189
   1980s—1990s, 238–42
   sales figures, 1971—2009, 221–36
   2006—2008, 242, 243–44
Christie's Wine Review, NC's article for, lvii
Churchill, Winston, 29, 144, 156
cigars, 79
Civil War (U.S.), xxxii, 88
Clarence, George, Duke of, 90
clay, for fining, 180
clay soils, 106
climate, 16–17, 58, 109
Clinton, Henry, 44, 46
Club Gastronomique (Boston), *82*
Coates, Patricia (NC's wife), xxiii, xxiv, xlviii, liii
Cockburn (firm), 148
Cockburn, George, 277, 278
cockroach story, 197–98
cocktails and punches, 73, 77–78, 206–8
Codman, Mrs. Russell, 83
Codman, Russell, 82, 83, 182
collections, 175, 185–90, 287–89
   Gaselee collection, xlix, 161, 165, 186–87, 188–90, 237, 289–90, 292–93
   notable sales, 1970s—2008, 237–46
Colón, Bartolomeu, 14
Colón, Cristobal. *See* Columbus, Christopher
Colón, Cristobal, Duque de Veragua, 70
Colson, Smith & Co., 46
Colson, Smith & Robinson, 46
Columbus, Christopher, 13, 14, 15, 70, 258, 267
Common Madeira, 145
Companhia Vinicola da Madeira Lda., 69
Complexa, 99
Conceição & Filhos, 67
Concord grape, 106, 321*n*29
Constitution (ship), 84
Cook, James, 36–37, 73
cooking wine, Madeira as, 111, 202–6
cooling Madeira, 136–37, 140, 144, 322*n*42
corks, 95, 190, 196
corkscrews, 196–97
corredors, 107–8
Correia, João Alfonso, 239
Corti, Darrell, 90, 290, 293

Corti Brothers, 215
Côrvo, João Andrade, 115
Cossart, Anna (NC's daugher), xlviii, li
Cossart, Anna Mary (née Blandy), 60, *66*, 275
Cossart, Arthur Blandy, xlii, xliii, xliv, 76, 245
Cossart, Charles Blandy (NC's father), xlii, *173*, 188, 191, 193, 245
Cossart, Charles David Gradidge (David; NC's son), v–vii, lvi, lvii, 93
   birth Bual, xxiii, xlvi, 130, 154, 293
   correspondence with Elizabeth David, 273–74, 275, 276
   at Cossart, Gordon, xix, li–lv, 193, 245
   photographs, *xvi*, *93*
Cossart, Charles John (NC's grandfather), 55, 60, *66*, *173*, 193
   as Cossart, Gordon director, xl, xli, 54, 56, 245
   Desertas purchase, 25
   writings on the British Factory, 37, 296
Cossart, Eustace, xlvii
Cossart, Gordon & Co., v, 40, 53–57, 60, 63
   archives, xvii, 37, 48, 80, 291, 320*n*21
   bills of lading, 80, *179*, *183*
   David Cossart's career at, xix, li–lv, 193, 245
   final sale of, lvi–lvii, lx
   firm names and principals, 1745-1990, 245
   history to 1900, xxxvii, xxxix–xl, 41–43, 52–56
   India trade, 73, *74*, 75–77
   and Madeira Wine Association, xxxviii, xliv, xlvii–xlviii, lii, liii, 68
   and Madeira Wine Company, xxxviii, liv, lvi–lvii
   NC's career at, xxxvii–xxxviii, xlii–xlv, liii, 165, 171
   North American trade, xl–xli, xlvi, liv, 80–81, 81–82, 148
   photographs, *xliii*, *103*, *149*
   price lists and advertisements, *lv*, *74*, *145*
   sea-voyage conditioning, 134
   trade in other wines and commodities, xl–xli, 54
   twentieth-century overview and directors, xli–xlix, 56–57, 62, 245
   and varietal-name labelling, 148–49
   vintage wines, 160, 163–64, 165–66
   workers' uniform, 320*n*20
Cossart, Gordon & Co. Lda., 68, 245
Cossart, Gordon & Co. Ltd. (London office), xl, xliii–xlvii, li–lv, 173, 191
   destruction of, xlv–xlvi
Cossart, Gordon soleras, xxiii, xlvii, 169, 199
   1808 Solera pipe, *152*
   exhaustion of, xlvi, 171–72, 193
   labels, *162*, *170*
   notable wines, 143–44, 164, 168, 170–71
   prices, 172, 191–92, 194
   tastings, xlviii-xlvix, lii–liii, 191–92, 193–94
Cossart, Henry, xl, xliii, 55, 56, 192, 245
Cossart, Jane, *66*
Cossart, John, 55
Cossart, John de Bianchi, vi, xxiii, xxxvii, lvi
Cossart, Kathleen Gradidge, xliv, xlviii

INDEX

Cossart, Leland, xl, 55, 56, *66*, 245
Cossart, Margaret (Margie; later Miles), xxxvii, xliv, xlix, lii
Cossart, Maria Anna de Bianchi (NC's mother), xliii, xlix, 65, 193, 319n8
Cossart, Mildred Blandy, *66*
Cossart, Noël, xvii, 61, 279, 280. *See also* Madeira, the Island Vineyard
    correspondence with Elizabeth David, lix, 274–78
    correspondence with John Delaforce, lviii–lix, 295–98
    correspondence with Roy Brady, lix–lx, 288–93
    at Cossart, Gordon, xxxvii–xxxviii, xlii–li, liii, 165, 171, 245
    death of, lvi, lx
    estate wines, xxiii
    at Evans Marshall, xlviii–l, li
    photographs, *xvi, xxxviii, xlv, 64, 93*
    retirement, vi, xix–xx, li–liv
    vintage Madeiras stolen from, 154
Cossart, Patricia. *See* Coates, Patricia
Cossart, Peter (1807-1870), xxxvii, xl, 39, 53, 55–56, 170, 245
Cossart, Peter (brother of Noël), xxiv, xxxvii, xlv, lii, lvi, 68
Cossart, Sidney, xliv, xlv, xlvii, 149, 245
Cossart, Webster Gordon, xl, 54, 55, 56, 245
Cossart, William, Jr., 76–77, 245
Cossart, William, Sr., xxxvii, xxxix, 53, 97, 245
Cossart, William Carlton, xl, 55, 56
Cossart family, xxxvii, xxxix, 53, 55–56
Cossart-Miles, Anthony. *See* Miles, Anthony
Coulson, Sam, lvi
Coward, Noël, 47
Cox, F. G., 164, 192
Craddock, Fanny, 29
Craddock, John, 29
Cretan vines, 11
Croft-Cooke, Rupert, xviii, 143, 153, 155, 274, 322n55
Crown Madeiras, 96, 148, 167, 191
cubas de calor, 136, 140
Cunningham grape, xxxii, 104, 107, 146
Cutty Sark (ship), 84

D. L. Madeiras, 86
Darwin, Charles, 24
David, Elizabeth, xxxviii–xxxix, lix, 273–78
Davis, Jefferson, 88
Davis & Co. sales, 1971—2009, 221–36
Decanter, lvii, 277
decanting, 198, 199
Delaforce, John, lviii–lix, 295–98
Delmonico's, 89
Denmark, exports to, 125–26. *See also* Scandinavia
deposits, 197
DeRenne, George, 89, 175
Deserta Grande, 24
Desertas, 6, 16, 24–26, 278
de Sousa Madeiras, 239

Dickens, Charles, 145
Dickson, Elizabeth (later Phelps), 57, 58, *121*
disgorging, 196
distilled spirits, 111. *See also* brandy
    Madeira brandy, 138–39
Dix, John A., 268
Domaine de la Romanée-Conti, 291
Donaldsons, 67
Doria family, 165
Douglas, William W., 83–84, 85, 182
drinking Madeiras. *See* enjoying Madeiras
Drummond, John, 11, 258
Drury, Dru, 61, 64
Drury, Henry, 64
Drury & Co., 64
Duo-centenary Celebration Madeira, 144, 170–71, 194
du Pont, Eleuthère, 97
du Pont, Harry, xlix, 97
du Pont, Irénée, Jr., 97
Durban, Mrs. (later Leacock), 61
Durrell & Morgan, 138
Dutch East India Company, 73
dye exports, 24

Easterby, J. H., 269
East India Company, British, 71, 73, 74, 122
East India Company, Dutch, 73
East India Madeira, 75, 81–82, 134, 145, 147, 190
Edwards (T.) (firm), 55–56
Edwards, Jane, 55
Edwards, Thomas, 55
EEC. *See* European Economic Community
Eighth Amendment, 124. *See also* Prohibition
Elder Harrison, 302
Elizabeth II of Britain, 169, 173
Ellis Son & Vidler, lii–lv
embroidery industry, 119–20, 320n17
England, Madeira in. *See* Britain
English Rooms, 39
enjoying Madeiras, 188, 195–208
    bottle-sickness and breathing, 199
    bottle storage and handling, 195–96, 197
    corks and corkscrews, 196–97
    decanting, 198, 199
    glasses and environmental factors, 144, 146, 199
    Madeira as cooking wine, 111, 202–6
    Madeira cups and warmers, 206–8
    Madeira with food, 122, 188, 199, 200–201
    old wines, 201–2
    recipes, 200, 201, 203–8
    storing leftovers, 198
    temperature, 146, 199
Environs of Funchal vineyards, 110
Escocio, João, 11, 258
Esgana (Esganinho, Esganiso), 102. *See also* Sercial grape; Sercial Madeiras
Esmeralda, João (Jean d'Esmenaut), 14, 258, 267
espalmado training, 108
Esquin Imports, 288

estagio, 137, 140
Estreito agriculture museum, 70
Estreito da Calheta, 111
Estreito de Câmara de Lobos, 110
estufagem, xxix, 63, 133–34, 135–36, 140. *See also* heat treatment
EU (European Union), xxxii, 320–21n28
European Economic Community, European Union, 320–21n28
   wine regulations, xxxii, 104–5, 111, 114, 150–51, 174
Evans, Marshall & Co., xlviii–l, li, liv, 172, 173, 322n53
   Academy of Ancient Madeira Wines tasting, xlviii–xlix, 163, 192–93
Everett, Warner, 96, 289
experimental stations, 111–12
exports. *See* Madeira wine exports; specific markets
Extra Reserve Madeiras, 151

Facts about Port and Madeira (Vizetelly), 118, 142, 153, 168–69
Fairlie, David Ogilvie, 239
Fajã dos Padres, 110, 170, 194
family-name Madeiras, American, 86–87, 181
family names, early Madeira settlers, 255–62
Faraday Madeira, 187
Faria (J.) & Filhos Lda., 254
Farlie, Ann Ogilvy, 158
Fearing, William H., 241, 303
Feral grape, 102
Ferdinand of Aragon, 5
fermentation, 132–33, 321n37, 322n41
Fernandes, Pantaleão, 135
Ferreira, Gonçallo Ayres, 11
fertilizers, 108–9, 129
filtration, 137, 140, 144, 197
Fine Rich, 148, 191
Finest Madeiras, 151, 167
fining, 137, 140, 173, 178, 180, 197
Finland, Finnish market, 64, 125. *See also* Scandinavia
Firminio, Francisco, 194
The First Discovery of the Island of Madeira, 3, 4
fishing, in the Desertas, 25, 26
flood of 1803, 58, 155
The Flowering of New England (Brooks), 34
flying boats, vi, 30, 279, 280–86
food, Madeiras with, 122, 188, 199, 200–201
forests
   burning of, 12
   reforestation efforts, 17, 58–59
fortification, xxxi, 78, 133–34, 136, 137–40
   with cane brandy, 66, 139
   controversy about, 138, 139
   to halt fermentation, 132
   origins of, 72, 137–38
   Port, 297
   regulation of, 139–40
França, Jorge da Veiga, 70
França, Solomão, 70

France
   French in Portugal, 13, 78
   as Madeira market, xxxii, 31, 122
   oidium in, 115
François I of France, 31
Frank, Konstantin, 321n29
Franklin, Benjamin, 80
frasqueira, 322n52
Frasqueira Particular Avery, 161, 164, 322n52
fraudulent wines, xxxi, 95–96, 172, 290
Fructuoso, Gaspar, 3, 23, 268
fruit, Madeiras with, 200
Funchal (city), 12–13, 27, 262
   addresses of British firms and consulates (1760—1870), 267
   British Factory house, 38, 296, 298
   cruise ship traffic, 172–73
   early descriptions of, 36
   English Rooms club, 39
   First World War and, 123–24
Funchal vineyards, 39, 110, 116
fungus pests, 17, 100, 117. *See also* oidium

Galvão, Antonio, 33–34
Gama, Vasco da, 71
Gaselee, Stephen, 187–90
   Madeira collection, xlix, 161, 165, 186–87, 188–90, 237, 289–90, 292–93
Gaston Bazile, 104
gemada, 206
geography of the Madeira islands, xxviii, 15–17, 23, 264
George IV of Britain, 122, 146
Georgia, Madeira in, 87–92. *See also* Habersham, William Neyle; Savannah, Georgia
Georgia Historical Society, 303
Germany
   Madeira development effort, 123
   as Madeira market, xxxii, xli, 122
Gibbons, Thomas, 183, 303
Gibraltar, Bishop of, 163
Gignilliat, Thomas, 90
Glover, John R., 277, 278
goats, wild, 24, 25
Goelet, Ogden, 241
Goelet, Peter P., 241
Goelet, Robert, 241
Goelet, Robert III, 241
Goelet collection, 241
Gomes, J. Reis, 130
Gomes, Luis, lvii
Gonçalves (P. E.) Lda., 254
Gonçalves, Baltazar, 188
Gooch, Grendon, 192, 193
Good Company Madeiras, 143–44, 148
good varieties, 99
Gordon, Alexander, 45, 46, 267
Gordon, Duff & Co., 38, 267–68, 319n9
Gordon, J. D. Webster, 53, 245
Gordon, James, 37, 267
Gordon, James Murray Kenmure, 55

INDEX

Gordon, Russell Manners, xl, 53, 55, 118, 157, 245
Gordon, Thomas, xxxix, 52, 245
Gordon, William, Jr., 52, 245
Gourgaud, Baron, lix, 274, 275–76
Gouveiro, 72, 100. *See also* Verdelho grape
Grabham, Michael, xlix, 185–87, 192, 319n1, 322n55
Grabham, Walter, 187
Gradidge, Kathleen Florence (later Cossart), xliv, xlviii
grafting, 103, 108
Grant, Elizabeth (later Krohn), 62
Grant, John, 75
Grant, Wilhelmina (later Krohn), 62
Grant, William, Sr., 62, 245
grape harvest, 127–28, 321n35
grape prices, 113
grape varieties, xxviii–xxix, xxx, 11. *See also* Madeira vines and vineyards; *specific varieties*
   American species and hybrids, xxxii–xxxiii, 103–6, 110–11, 117, 119, 321n29
   EEC regulations, 104–5, 111
   harvest timing, 127, 321n35
   overview of traditional varieties, 99–102
   phylloxera and traditional varieties, xxxii, 32, 102, 117
   replanting of traditional varieties, 111–14
   varietal-named Madeiras, 148–50, 322n47
Great Britain. *See* Britain
Great Piton, 26
Grenache, 100, 298
Griswold, F. Gray, 176
guano, 108–9
gum disease, 17
Gunner Madeira, 76–77
Gunyon, Reg, 161, 290
Gustav VI of Sweden, 52

Habersham (Robert) & Co., 175, 180
Habersham, Joseph, 175
Habersham, William Neyle, 89, 175–84, 241, 299–304
   estate auction, 181–82, 299–302
   Hurricane Madeiras, 183–84, 302, 303–4
   names and origins of Habersham Madeiras, xxiv, 183–84
   palate, 175–76
   post-Civil War business, 180–81
   and Rainwater name, 146, 181
   wine treatment and storage, 176–78
Halley, Edmund, 35
ham with Madeira sauce, 204–5
Hancock, David, xxiv
Hancock, John, 85
Hansell, Haywood, 90
Hanson, Anthony, 291
Hapsburg, Charles, 29, 57
Hart Davis Hart sales, 1971—2009, 221–36
Harvey's, 164
Haysham, Robert, 40

health
   labrusca hybrids and, 106, 321n29
   Madeira as healthful place to live, 123, 279
   Madeira wine for medicinal purposes, 83–84
   wine and, xxvii
heat treatment, xxix, 63, 72, 132, 140, 203
   estufa process, xxix, 133–34, 135–36
   Habersham's *estufa do sol*, 176–78
   Madeira's longevity and, 153
   Roman wines, 135, 153
Hedges & Butler, xxiii, xlviii, 173
Henrique of Portugal. *See* Henry the Navigator
Henriques (A. E.) Sucrs Lda., 68, 69
Henriques (Justino) Filhos Lda., 69, 91, 239
Henriques, Antonio Eduardo, 69
Henriques, Eugenia Bianchi, 161–62
Henriques, Francisco Eduardo, 68
Henriques, João Joaquim, xlv, 68
Henriques, João Joaquim Gonçalves, 68, 69
Henriques, Padre, 165
Henriques & Câmara, xli
Henriques & Henriques, xxxvii, xlv, lvi, 68, 69, 254
   notable wines, 158–59, 238, 240
Henriques Filhos Lda., 69
Henry the Navigator, Prince, 5, 6, 7–9, 10, 14, 255
   and clearing of forests, 12
   and Madeira agriculture, 11
Henry VIII of England, 31
Herbemont, xxxii, 104
Hill, Richard, 37, 51
Hinton (William) & Sons, xli, 66
Hinton, Charles, xl
Hinton, Harry, xl, 25, 66, 67, 163, 188
Hinton, William, 23, 66
Hiscox, Matthew, 37
History of Portugal (Silva), 31
A History of Wine (Allen), xlviii–xlix
Hohenlohe, Frederick Karl, 123
Hood, Samuel, 45
Hook, Theodor, 268
House Beautiful, 202
houses. *See also* quintas
   Funchal houses of British merchants and consuls, xxxix, 38, 267–68, 296, 298
Houston, William, 87
How to Prepare Nectar (Gomes), 130
hunting, on the Desertas, 25
Hurricane Madeiras, 183–84, 302, 303–4

India
   Madeira in, 31, 43, 48, 71–78, 122, 150
   Portuguese trade and settlement, 37, 71
India Market Madeira, 74
industry, 12, 23, 24, 40
Institute of Masters of Wine, 193
Instituto do Vinho da Madeira (IVM). *See* Madeira Wine Institute
International Exhibition Cooperative Wine Society, xliii
irrigation, 19–20, 107, 117
Isabela grape, xxxii, xxxiii, 104, 117

Isabella of Spain, 14, 15
IVM (Instituto do Vinho da Madeira). *See* Madeira Wine Institute

Jack (cellarmaster at Cossart, Gordon), xliv, 173
Jacquet, xxxii, xxxiii, 104
Japan, exports to, 70
Japan Madeira, 83, 97
Jardim, Albert N., 68
Jardim da Serra, 47, 110
   notable wines, 141, 194, 215
Jay, William, 91
Jefferson, Christopher, 34–35
Jefferson, Thomas, xxxi, 79–80, 322n46
   Jefferson Madeiras, 240–41
Jellicoe, Lady, 29
Jesuits, 11, 36
John Blandy & Sons, 59
John III of Portugal, 78
John IV of Portugal, 32, 78
Johnson, Harry, 237
Johnston, William, 53, 245
John VI of Portugal, 58
Jones, G. Noble, 181
Josey, Lenoir, 242
"The Journey" (Nicholas), 280–86
Jubilee Solera, 143–44
Juno (ship), 86
Junta Nacional do Vinho, 139–40, 172
Justino Henriques Filhos Lda., 69, 91, 239, 254

kaolin, 180
Kelvin, Lord, 185
Kemble, Fanny, 87
Kennedy, John P., 83, 97
Key, Francis Scott, 80
Kinsey, William, 91, 92
Kipling, Rudyard, 71
Knights Templars, 9
Krohn, Edmund, 63
Krohn, Ester, 63
Krohn, Heather, 320n19
Krohn, Helen, 63
Krohn, Hugo, 63–64
Krohn, John, 62
Krohn, Nicholas, 62
Krohn, Raleigh, 63
Krohn, Ronald, 63
Krohn, William, 63
Krohn Brothers & Co., 62–64, 67, 153, 170

labels and labelling, 114, 150–52, 190, 322n47. *See also* Madeira wine names
   false dating, 95–96, 172
Lacerta dugesii, 109
Ladislas VI of Poland, 255
lagares, 129–30
Lamar, Thomas, 37
Lancaster, Joseph, 58
Lancastrian school, 58
landing age, 144–45, 173, 197

Landscapes of Madeira (Underwood and Underwood), 319n10
land tenure, xxxiv, li, 20–21
Lane, Mills, 90, 91, 92–93, 240
lapa, 109
Las Casas, Count, 278
Lauretta (ship), 88
Lawton, A. R., 176
lazy malmsey, 101
Leacock (John, John, & William) (firm), 61
Leacock, Edmund, li, 61, 243
Leacock, John, 41, 52, 61, 139
Leacock, John (Jackie), 61
Leacock, John Milburn, 61, 320n18
Leacock, Julian, 243
Leacock, Thomas Slapp, 61, 103, 117, 118
   São João vineyard, 45, 61, 110, 117, 118, 147
Leacock, William (son of Leacock founder), 61
Leacock, William (twentieth-century head of firm), li, 110, 117, 243–44
Leacock & Co., xli, xlvii, 41, 61, 67
   soleras, 170
Leacock family, lvi, 243
Leal, Alfredo, 189
Leal, Anna (later de Bianchi), 161
Leal, João Baptista, 189
Leal, Robert, 65, 161, 189
Legname, 6–7
Lennox, Robert, 44
Leonardo da Vinci, 135
leste winds, 17, 277–78
levadas (aqueducts), xxx, 19–20, 21, 319n10
Liberty incident, 85
lichen, 24
Liddell, Alex, xxiv, 319n1
The Life of Prince Henry of Portugal (Major), 34
Lightning (ship), 84
Listrão, 102
Little Piton, 26
Littorina striata, 109
liver health, 106
livestock, 21–22, 24
lizards, 109
lobster Madeira, 205–6
lodges, 142–43
Lomelino, Anna (later de Bianchi), 65, 161
Lomelino, T. T. da Câmara (firm), lvii, 65, 67, 147
   Gaselee collection wines, 188, 189
   notable wines, 161, 244
Lomelino, Tarquinio Torquato da Câmara, 65
Lomelino, Virginia, 159
London Market, 74, 145
London Particular, 74, 89, 145, 191
   prices, 47–48, 121–22, 148, 191
London sparrow, 109
Long, Harry, 173
Lopes, Diego, 31
lotes, 141–43, 167. *See also* Solera Madeiras; solera system
Louisiana clay, 180
Louis XVIII of France, 94

INDEX

Low Countries, exports to, 31
lupins, 109
Lusty, Ralph, 188
Lynch, Dominic, 86
Lyons, Graham, 243
Lysons, Samuel, 34, 319n4

machete, 130
Machico, 65, 262
   Milagres chapel, 12, 58
Machin, Robert à, xxiv, 3–5, 12, 33–34, 58, 319n2, 319n4
Machin and Madeira (Lysons), 319n4
Madeira (Croft-Cooke), xviii, 143, 153, 155, 274, 322n55
Madeira (Griswold), 176
Madeira (island), v–vi, 10–14, 16–23, 26–30
   British in, xxxvii, xxxix, 43–46, 123
   Cook's visit, 36–37
   economic impacts of oidium and phylloxera, 115–16
   geography and climate, xxviii, 15–17, 58, 264
   German development effort, 123
   maps, *xxii,* 6–7, *50, 98*
   the people, 26, 27–29
   storms of 2010, vi
   towns and parishes, 12–13, 262, 263
   as upper-class playground, 28–29
   Zarco's clearing of, 12
Madeira (Liddell), xxiv, 319n1
Madeira, the Island Vineyard (Cossart), v–vii, xvii–xx, liv, lvii–lx
   Cossart's correspondence about, lviii–lx, 289–93, 295–98
   Decanter review, 277
   Elizabeth David article, xxxviii–xxxix, 273–78
   new edition, xxiii–xxv
Madeira Actien Gesellschaft (MAG), 123
Madeira and the Canaries (Nicholas), xviii, 280
Madeira Burgundy, 100, 137–38, 298. *See also* Burgundy Madeira
Madeira cake, 201
Madeira clubs, 80, 87, 89–92
"The Madeira Era" (David), xxxviii–xxxix, 273–78
Madeira Flowers, Fruits and Ferns (Penfold), 209
Madeira islands, 6, 15–30. *See also* Desertas; Madeira (island); Porto Santo; Selvagens
   agriculture, 11–12, 17–22, 23, 26, 27
   airports and air travel, vi, 23, 29–30, 279, 280–86
   early settlers, 11, 23–24, 255–62
   European rediscovery and settlement, xxiv, xxxix, 4–6, 9, 10–13, 33–34, 284
   industry and commerce, 12, 23, 24, 26–27, 40, 119–20
   on maps, *xxii,* 6–7, *50, 98*
   mix of cultures, 11, 27–28
   plants, 22–23, 24, 25, 37, 59
   slavery, 11, 28
   tourism, 26, 29–30, 123, 279
Madeira — Its Climate and Scenery (White), 115

Madeira jelly, 200
Madeira merchants, xxx, xxxiv, 51–70. *See also* Madeira wine trade; *specific individuals and firms*
   British Factory, 37–40, 46, 155, 296, 298
   British firms, xxxvii, 40–43, 51–68, 247–52
   earliest foreign merchants, 35
   eighteenth and nineteenth centuries, 37–43
   family connections, 161–62
   First World War and, xli, 123
   Funchal addresses of British firms, 267
   good works by, 38, 46, 58–59
   levies paid by, 38, 46
   oidium and, xxxiv, 60, 97, 116, 121, 167, 267–68
   partidistas, 125–26, 254
   phylloxera and, 119, 121, 167
   Portuguese firms, 68–70
   preservation of old wines, 154
   shippers (2010), 254
   shippers and importers (1984), 253
Madeira parties, xxxi, 79, 83, 85, 122
A Madeira Party (Mitchell), 34, 79, *86*
Madeira prices, 47–48, 89, 195, 201–2. *See also* auctions
   eighteenth century, 48, 75, 79, 88
   nineteenth century, 48, 75, 79, 82, 83, *145,* 191–92
   1900—1970, 77, 96, 121–22, 125–26, 148, *160,* 164, 172
   1970—present, 113, 148, 172, 219, 220, 221–36
   soleras, 148, 172, 194
Madeira pudding, 206
Madeira sauces, 203–6
Madeira vinegar, 198
Madeira vines and vineyards, xxx, 11–12, 17, 18, 99–114. *See also* grape varieties; oidium; phylloxera
   extent of, xxx, xxxiii, 116, 121
   future of, xxxiv–xxxv
   irrigation, xxx, 19–20, 107, 117
   Madeira cuttings in Georgia, 87, 104
   notable vineyards, 109–10, 157–58
   overview of traditional grape varieties, 99–102
   pests and diseases, 17, 115–19
   Porto Santo, 23
   quality regulation, 104–5, 111, 114
   soils, xxviii, 103, 106, 117, 153
   traditional varieties today, xxxiii–xxxiv, 111–14
   viticultural techniques, 107–9, 116
   yields, 51, 106, 107
Madeira wine. *See also* enjoying Madeiras; *specific types*
   alcohol content, xxix, 133, 136, 138, 140
   color in, 100
   for cooking, 111, 202–6
   early descriptions and reputation, 34, 35, 72
   longevity, xxviii, 153–54
   overview, xxviii–xxxv
   quality regulation, xxix, 104–5, 111, 114, 132–33, 135, 136, 139–40
   for ship rations, 36–37, 73, 94
   vintage notes, 211–17

"Madeira Wine" (Cossart), lvii
Madeira Wine, Cakes and Sauce (Simon), 319n1, 320n15, 322n50
Madeira Wine Antiga, lvii
Madeira Wine Association, 38, 67, 161
   after 1970, l, li, 68
   André Simon and, 40
   Brady correspondence, 288
   Cossart, Gordon and, xxxviii, xliv, xlvii–xlviii, lii, liii, 68
   founding and early history, xxxviii, xli, xliv, 67–68
   member firms, xli, xlvii, 61, 62, 63, 65, 67, 68
   shipping firm consolidation and, xxxiv, xli, xliv, 243
   solera policy, 171, 192
Madeira Wine Company, 52, 60, 108, 159, 254
   Achada do Gramacho vineyard, 112–13
   Cossart, Gordon and, xxxviii, liv, lvi–lvii
   formation, 68
   1970s-1980s consolidations, lvi–lvii
   principals and staff, liv, lvii, 61, 62, 216
Madeira wine exports, 27. *See also* Madeira wine trade; *specific markets*
   early twentieth century, 121, 122–24, 125
   1982, 113–14
   nineteenth century, 121
   shortages, 43, 111, 115–16
Madeira Wine Institute, 114, 132–33, 136, 139, 140, 321n33
   labelling regulations, 150–51
   solera regulations, 174
Madeira winemaking, v, 127–40. *See also* blends and blending; fortification; heat treatment; solera system
   before 1700, 11, 72
   bottling, 144–45, 148, 197
   cooling, 136–37, 140, 144, 322n42
   crushing and pressing, 128, 129–32
   fermentation, 132
   harvesting, 127–28, 321n35
   oversight and quality regulation, xxix, 104–5, 111, 114, 132–33, 135, 136, 139–40
   production quantities, xxxiv, 111, 113–14, 115, 121, 123
   rest, fining and racking, 137, 140
   sea-voyage conditioning, 75, 81, 134, 153
   storage, 137, 141–43, 144, 154
   summary, 140
   sweetening, 132–33, 140, 321n38
Madeira wine names, xxxi, 83, 145–52
   family-name Madeiras, 86–87, 181
   labelling regulations, 150–52, 322n47
   ship names, 83, 84, 134, 181, 183–84, 303–4
Madeira wine trade. *See also* auctions; Madeira merchants; Madeira wine exports; *specific markets, merchants and firms*
   before 1700, xxx, 31–35, 40, 72, 73
   current state of, xxxii–xxxv
   eighteenth century, xxx–xxxi, 35–38, 40, 41–43, 75, 138–39
   fraudulent wines, xxxi, 95–96, 172, 290
   Indian market, 71–74, 75–77
   levies on shipments, 38, 46
   Napoleonic wars and, 47–48
   nineteenth century, 38–40, 47–49, 73–74
   oidium's impacts, xxxii, 48, 88, 115–16, 167
   overview, xxx–xxxv
   phylloxera's impacts, 88, 96, 118, 119, 167
   production and demand, xxxi–xxxii, xxxiv, 111, 113–14, 115, 121, 123
   shipping and bottling, xliv, 144–45, 148, 173
   soleras and, 172, 174
   twentieth century, 40, 172
Madeirense, 27–28
MAG (Madeira Actien Gesellschaft), 123
Magdalena, 110
Major, Richard Henry, 34
Malaga grape, 102
Malmsey grape. *See* Malvasia grape
Malmsey Madeiras, xxxiv, 32, 110, 122, 146. *See also* Malvasia Madeiras
   in American tastings, 82, 90, 91, 92
   in blends, 143
   bottle storage, 195
   characteristics, 101, 148, 150, 195
   fortification, 133
   notable post-phylloxera wines, 121, 192, 193, 194
   notable pre-phylloxera wines, 121, 170, 172, 181–82, 189, 191, 192, 193
   prices, 202
   serving and enjoying, 200, 201, 206
   vinho quinado, 77–78
   vintage notes, 211–13, 215, 216, 217
   winemaking, 101, 320n24, 321n38
malolactic fermentation, 132
Malvasia Candida, xxx, xxxii, 127, 150
   characteristics, 100–101, 150
   current status, xxxiv, xxxv, 150, 217
   notable wines, 170, 194
Malvasia grape, xxxiii, 11, 99, 100–101, 110. *See also* Malvasia Candida
   Malvasia Babosa, 100, 127, 150, 217, 238
   Malvasia Roxa, 99
   Malvasia São Jorge, xxxiv
Malvasia Madeiras, xxxiv, 72, 189. *See also* Malmsey Madeiras
   notable wines and vintages, 164, 189, 216, 217, 238
Malvasia Seca, 150
malvidin 3,5-diglucoside. *See* malvina
malvina (malvisa), 105, 106
Malvoisie, 11, 101
mangara. *See* oidium
manure, 109
maps, xxii, 6–7, 50, 98
marc, 129
Maroto, 100
Marsala, xxxi, 122
Marsh, Charles S., 245
Marshall, John, 80

INDEX

Martial, 153
Martines, João Freitas, lvii
massapes soils, 18, 106
Matthews, Patrick, xx, lvii
maturation, 135, 141, 195. *See also* heat treatment; sea-voyage conditioning; solera system
   aging characteristics of specific grapes, 149–50
   casks and storage, 94–95, 137, 141–43, 154, 176
   glass vs. wood aging, 241
   landing age before bottling, 144–45, 173, 197
   Madeira's longevity, xxviii, 153–54
   shipwreck wines, 93, 94
Maximilian, Emperor of Mexico, 66
Mayflower Madeira, 304
McAllister, Ward, 175, 180, 181, *182*, 183–84, 303
McNally, Alexander, 92
Medici Map, 6–7
medicinal purposes, Madeira for, 83–84
Mediterranean fly, 17
Medium Rich Bual, 77
Mello, Francisco de, 33
ménage à trois Madeira, 144
Menèzes, Pedro Fagundes Bacelar de Antunes e, 45
Merchant Venturers, 3, 319*n*3
Milagres chapel, 12, 58
mildew, 100, 117. *See also* oidium
Miles, Anthony, xix, li, liii, lvi, 62
Miles, Cecil, xliv, xlvii, liii
Miles, Charles, 62
Miles, Henry, 62
Miles, Henry Price, 61–62
Miles, Margaret (Margie) Cossart, xxxvii, xliv, xlix, lii
Miles & Co., xlvii, lvii, 61–62
Mitchell, Langdon, 79
Mitchell, S. Weir, 34, 79, 86
Mole Preta. *See* Tinta Negra Mole
Monemvasia, 11
Montluc, Payrot de, 13
montmorillonite, 180
moon phases, 108
Moore, John, 284
Moors, 5, 6, 8, 11, 28
Morales, Juan de, 5, 6
Morrah, Dermot, 192
Morrell & Co.
   Goelet sale, 241
   sales figures, 1971—2009, 221–36
Moscatel. *See* Muscatel
Mosto, Alves da, 11–12
Mountbatten, Louis Mountbatten, Earl, 188
Mullins, Thomas, xli, lvii, 60, 67
Murdoch, Thomas, *31*, 39, 44, 48, 53, 61, 245
Murdoch, William, 37
Muscatel grape, xxxiii, 99, 102, 127
   Muscatel de Quintal, 102
   Muscatel de Santa Maria, 102
   Muscatel de Setúbal, 102

Muscatel wines, 94, 102, 290–91, 292, 293, 320*n*25
MWA. *See* Madeira Wine Association

names. *See* Madeira wine names
Napoleon, lix, 155, 274, 275, 276, 277–78
Napoleonic Wars, 43–46
   impact on wine trade, 47–48
   Waterloo Madeiras, 92, 156–57, 170, 172, 186
Napoleon Madeira, xxiv, *lv*, 155–56, 169, 186
   doubts about, 319*n*1, 322*n*50, 322*n*55, 322*n*56
   Elizabeth David's interest in, lix, 273–78
Nash, William, 37
National Fund, 46
Negra grape, 100
Negra Mole. *See* Tinta Negra Mole
Nelson, Horatio, 37
Newton, Andrew, 41, 42, 43, 139, 146, 267
Newton, Francis, *31*, 138, 245, 267
   arrival in Madeira, xxxix, 35, 41–42
   on British Factory committee, 37
   early wine trade, xxxix, 42–43
   and fortification, 139
   letters in Cossart, Gordon archives, xvii
   on Malmseys, 101
   and Rainwater Madeira, 146–47
   retirement and death, 53
   and Richard Hill, 51
Newton, Gordon, Cossart & Co., 38, 53–54, 245, 298
Newton, Gordon, Murdoch & Co., 43, 44, 53, 74, 190, 245
   shipping manifest, *179*
Newton, Gordon, Murdoch & Scott, xxxvii, 53, 183
Newton, Gordon & Johnston, xxxix, 53, 88, 245
Newton, Gordon & Murdoch, xxxix, 245
Newton, Thomas, 52, 245
Newton & Gordon, 52, 86, 182, 245
Newton & Spence, 245
New World, Madeira exports to, 31, 32, 78. *See also* North American market and trade; West Indies
New York, Madeira trade in, 51, 79, *80*, 83–87, 89, 241
   Habersham's trade, 180, 181, 183
Nicholas, Elizabeth, xviii
   "The Journey," 280–86
Nicholas II of Russia, 192
noble varieties, 99
nog, Madeira, 20–26
Noronha, Filomena Henriques de, 55
North American market and trade, xxx–xxxii, xxxix, 79–97, 296, 297–98. *See also* American auctions; American connoisseurs and devotees
   Able Madeira, 91, 92–94
   before 1900, 34, 40–43, 48, 79–89, 139
   British demand and, 122, 146
   Canada, xix, 68

Chicora Wood Plantation wine cellar, 269–71, 298
Cossart, Gordon's North American trade, xl–xli, xlvi, liv, 80–82, 148
Habersham's Madeiras, 175, 176–80, 241
importers as of 1984, 253
Liberty incident, 85
Madeira clubs, 80, 87, 89–92
Madeira parties and tastings, xxxi, 79, 82–83, 85, 90–92, 290–91
Madeira plantings in Georgia, 87
notable Madeira ships, 83, 84–86
Prohibition, xli, 88, 89, 124–25
Rainwater Madeira, 96, 97, 104, 122, 146–47
shippers, 41–43, 51, 86, 88
soleras, 169
the South, xxxii, 87–92, 240
twentieth century, xlvi, 81–82, 88, 95, 124
U.S. ban on Portuguese bottled wines, xlvi, 148
wine quality and integrity, 81–82, 95–96
Northumberland (ship), 155, 277–78
Norway, Norwegian market, 63, *124*, 125, 126. *See also* Scandinavia
Notes on a Cellarbook (Saintsbury), xxvii
Nowlan, Michael, 61, 139
Nowlan & Leacock, 61
Nunes, Fernando, 23–24

oak, for casks, 141–42
oidium (*Oidium tuckeri*), 17, 96, 109, 115–16, 121, 212
  British shippers and, xxxii, xxxiv, 60, 97, 116, 267–68
  embroidery industry and, 119–20
  impact on wine production and trade, xxxii, xxxiv, 48, 88, 115–16, 121, 167
Old Gordon's Madeira, xxiii, 158
"Old Madeira" (Brady), 289
Old Reserve Madeiras, 151
Oliveira, João Pereira de, 160
Ophir (ship), 199
Oporto Factory, 296–97, 298
Order of Christ and St. James, 9
Ornelas, Baron de, 116
Owens-Thomas House, 90–91
oxidation, 135, 136

Page, Robert, 12, 58
Painted Pipe Madeiras, 183, 302, 303
Palma, Constantino, 114
Pamment, David, 290, 293
partidistas, 125–26, 254
passagem, 137, 140, 168
Passer domesticus, 109
Peck, Paula, 202–3
pedra mole, 18, 106, 107
Pedro V of Portugal, 55
Pedro Ximenez, 100
Penfold, Jane Wallas, 209
Penfold, William, 209
Penfold & Veitch, 209

Pereira, Carlos M. Nunes, 68
Pereira, Marcelino, 110
Pereira D'Oliveira, 254, 291, 293
Perestrello, Bartolomeu, 5–6, 6–7, 13, 319n8
Perestrello, Garcia, 13
Perestrello e Moniz, Filipa, 13
Perkins, Al, xviii–xix
Perry, Matthew, 83
pests and diseases, 17, 100, 109, 115–19. *See also* oidium; phylloxera
petrels, 25–26
Petrodroma mollis, 25–26
Phelps (J. & W.), 57–58
Phelps, Elizabeth (Bella), 57–58, 120, 320n17
Phelps, Elizabeth Dickson, 57, 58, *121*
Phelps, Joseph, 57, 58, *121*, 147
Phelps & Page, 58–59
Philadelphia, Madeira in, 51, 79, 80–81, 86, 87
Phillip II of Castille, 32
Phillips sales, 1971—2009, 221–36
phylloxera (*Phylloxera vastatrix*), xxxii, 17, 109, 116–19, 121, 212
  in California, 119
  control methods, 117, 118, 119
  government response, 103, 117, 119
  impact on wine production and trade, 88, 96, 118, 119, 121, 167
  resistant rootstocks and varieties, xxxii, 87, 103–5, 119
  traditional grape varieties and, xxxii, 32, 102, 117
  Vizetelly's visit to the Leacock vineyard, 61, 118
Picken, Andrew, *39*
Pierce (S. S.), 82, 96, *162*, 287
Pierce, Norman, Mr. and Mrs., 83
Pilsudski, Józef, 29
pines, 17, 59
Pinot Noir, 100, 298. *See also* Burgundy
Pinus maritimus, 59
Pinus pinaster, 17
pipes. *See also* casks
  capacity, 73, 77, 321n32
Pitta, N. C., 106
plants, native and naturalized, 22–23, 24, 25, 37, 59
Pliny, 135
Pombal, Marquis of, 28
Pommery & Greno, 40
poncha, 130
Ponta Delgada, 112
Ponta do Pargo, 110, 111
Ponta do Sol, 110
Port, xxviii, 122, 140, 148, 173, 295
  Oporto Factory, 296–97, 298
Porto Moniz, 110, 162
Porto Santo, 13, 16, 23–24, 29, 264
  phylloxera on, 117
  rediscovery and settlement, 5–6, 9
  vines and vineyards, 100, 109
Portugal, Portuguese government
  EEC entry, 104, 111–12, 150, 174

INDEX

and German interests on Madeira, 123
1974 revolution, li
Portuguese exploration and settlement
   Africa, 77–78, 296
   India, 37, 71, 296
   Madeira, xxxix, 5–9
Portuguese Madeira firms, xxxiv, 68–70, 253, 254. *See also specific firms by name*
Postgate, Raymond, xviii, xlviii, 192
Potter, Patricia. *See* Coates, Patricia
Power, Charles le P., 65
Power, Charles O. L., 65
Power, Drury & Co., xliv, lvii, 65
Power's Guide to Madeira, 65
pressing, 128, 129–32
Price, Pamela Vandyke, 198
Price, William, 89
Prince of Wales Island, 77
Pringle, John, 37
Pringle, Joseph, 44, 46, 298
profetas, 23–24
Prohibition, xli, 88, 89, 124–25
pruning, 108
pudding, Madeira (*puddin ingles*), 206
punch, 207–8

quinine, 77–78
Quinta da Achada, 51, *52*, 209
Quinta da Paz, 58, 147, 212, 244
Quinta Deão, 65
Quinta do Monte (Quinta Gordon, Quinta Cossart), 56, *57*, *66*
Quinta do Palheiro, 60–61, 189
Quinta do Salão, 165
Quinta do Serrado, 238, 240
Quinta dos Pinheiros, xlix
quintas, xlix–l
   listed with owners, 1760—1860, 265–66

rabbits, 13, 24
racking, 133, 137, 140
Raguse, Baron de, 94
Rainwater Madeiras, 146–47, 151, 182–83, 191, 322*n*48
   Blackburn Rainwater, 96, 97
   bottle storage, 195–96
   Cunningham grape in, 104, 146
   Habersham's Rainwaters, 176, 181, 182
   prices, 202
   recipes using, 203, 207
   serving, 122, 146, 199, 200
rebottling, 196, 198
recipes, 200, 201, 203–8
recorking, 190, 196
red caps, 320*n*20
Red Jacket (ship), 84, 320*n*23
refrigeration, 136–37, 144
Reid, W. A., 154
Reilly, E. W., 245
Relation Historique de la Découverte de l'Isle de Madère, 3
reserve *lotes*, 141, 153–54

Reserve Madeiras, 82, 133, 151, 202
Ribeira Brava, 111
Ribeira da Janella, 110
Ribeiro, Antonio Manuel Pereiro (Bishop of Funchal), 188, 189
Ribeiro Real, 158–59
Rider, William, 37
Riesling, 101
Rio Grande grape, 99
"Romantic Wines of Madeira" (Bell), 80, 88, 90, 134
Roman viticulture and wines, 108, 135, 153
Ross, Betsy, 80
Rothschild, Baron de, 94
Russia, Russian market, xxxii, xli, 52, 64, 122–23, 124, 194
   Krohn family, 62, 63–64
Rutherford, Browne & Miles, 61
Rutherford, David, 62
Rutherford, Jack, 62
Rutherford, James, 61
Rutherford, Osborne & Perkin, 62
Rutherford & Co., 62
Rutherford & Drury, 61
Rutherford & Grant, 61, 62
Rutherford & Miles, xliv, 62

saibro soils, 18, 106
Sail Rock, 24
Saintsbury, George, xxvii, 95–96, 287
Saintsbury Club, 186
Salvati, João, 259
Santos, João Alexandrino dos, 163
São Antonio, 109–10
São João Madeira, 117, 147
São João vineyards, 109, 110
   Leacock vineyard, *45*, 61, 117, 118, 147
São Jorge, 112
São Martinho, 51, 83, 109, 110, 128, 147
   notable vintage, 211
   notable wines, 159–60, 186
São Roque, 110
São Vicente, 110, 112
sauces, 203–6
As Saudades da Terra (Fructuoso), 3
Savannah, Georgia, 240. *See also* Habersham, William Neyle
   Cossart book launch party, lvii
   Habersham mansion, 176–78
   Madeira Club, 80, 89–92
scale insects, 17
Scandinavia, Scandinavian market, xliii, 68, 117, *124*, 147, 148
   drink laws, 63–64
   Madeira names in, 146, 147
   market growth, xxxii, 125–26
Scotch whisky, 291
Scott, John, 37
Scott, Penfold & Veitch, 298
Scott, Robert, 53, 245
scurvy, 36–37

Searle, John, 37
Seaton, Daniel, 75
sea-voyage conditioning, xxix, 75, 81, 134, 153
   notable ships, 83, 134
Seco, 72
Seixal, 110, 112
Selbey & Co., 55–56
Seldon, Susan Gale, 158
Selected Madeiras, 151
Selvagens, 16, 25, 26, 264
Sercial grape, xxxiii, 99, 103, 110
   characteristics, xxix, 101–2, 127
   winemaking, 132, 133, 140
Sercial Madeiras, 82, 83, 96, 122, 160, 188
   in blends, 143
   bottle storage, 195–96
   characteristics, 101–2, 141, 148, 149, 217
   Habersham's "Sweet, Pale Newton Gordon Sercial," 182
   notable post-phylloxera wines, 158, 194, 215, 293
   notable pre-phylloxera wines, 91–92, 157, 189
   notable vineyards, 110
   prices, 202
   recipes using, 204, 205
   serving, 122, 199, 200
   vintage notes, 211–13, 215, 216, 217
serving Madeiras. *See* enjoying Madeiras
Shakespeare, William, 32
Shand, Bruce, v, lii, liii, liv
Shand, P. Morton, v, lii
Shaw (Munson G.) Co., 148
Shaw, George Bernard, 29
shearwaters, 25, 26
Sherry, xxviii, 122, 167, 302
   in Habersham's blends, 303, 304
Sherry-Lehmann, 240, 290
shippers. *See* Madeira merchants; *specific individuals and firms*
ships
   Madeira rations, 36–37, 73, 94
   Madeiras named after, 83–84, 134, 181, 182, 183–84, 303–4
   sea-voyage conditioning, xxix, 75, 81, 134, 153
   shipboard wine sales, 172–73
shipwreck Madeiras, 91, 92–94
Shoolbred, John, 88
Shortridge, John, 52
Shortridge Lawton & Co., 52
Sills, Sam, 37
Silva, Francisco Augusto da, 277
Silva, João Vicente da, 116
Silva, Rebelo da, 31
silvado, 103
Simon, André, 40, 320n15
   article on Napoleon's food and drink, 274, 276, 278
   and Bolton letters, 40
   on enjoying Madeiras, 201
   on Gaselee wines, 289, 290
   library disposition, 291–92
   on Madeira in America, 94, 95
   at Madeira tastings, xlviii, 144, 164, 192, 193
   and MWA promotion efforts, 40
   and Napoleon Madeira, 186, 319n1, 322n50
   NC's article in *Wines of the World*, xx
Simons, William, 74
Skinner, Louis C., Jr., 159
slaves, 11, 28, 88
smoking, 79
snails, 109
Sobral, Antonio Braamcamp, 25
Society as I Have Found It (McAllister), 175
soft-plumaged petrel, 25–26
soils, xxviii, 12, 18, 103, 106, 117, 153
Solander, Daniel, 37
Solar do Vale Formoso, xlix–l
soleira, 168. *See also* Solera Madeiras; solera system
Solera Madeiras, 147, 167–74. *See also* Cossart, Gordon soleras
   auction prices 1971-2009, 221–28, 230–33, 236
   dates on, 167–68
   disreputable soleras, 172–73
   labelling regulations, 151–52
   London bottlings, 173
   notable wines, *152*, 168–72, 191–92
   prices, 148, 172, 202
   regulations, 174
   tastings, xlviii, 191–92, 193–94
solera system, 137, 140, 167, 168, *169*
   decline of, 171, 174, 192
   fortification, 133
   topping up, 141, 143, 151–52, 167–68, 174
Sotheby's sales, 1971—2009, 221–36, 240–41
soup, Madeiras with, 188, 199, 200
South America, Brazil exports, 32, 78
The South Carolina Rice Plantation (Easterby), 269
South Side Madeiras, 83, 147
Spanish earth, 180
Spanish occupation of Portugal (1580—1665), 32
sparrows, 109
special growths, 141, 143, 147. *See also specific grape varieties*
Special Reserve Madeiras, 151
Spence, George, 42, 52, 61, 139, 245
Spence, John Russel, 61
spiders, 25
St. Helena, Napoleon's voyage to, 155, 274–78
St. John Madeira, 117, 147
St. John's vineyard, *45*, 61, 110, 117, 118, 147. *See also* São João vineyards
St. Martin's Day, 90, 128
Stamp Act, 85
Stanley, Edward, 77
stock *lotes*, 141, 154
storage, 94–95, 137, 141–43, 144, 154, 176
   bottled Madeiras, 195–96
   corks and breathing, 94–95, 190, 195, 196, 199
Stuart, Gilbert, 80
Suez Canal, 122
sugar cane, 11, 18, 32, 59–60, 118
   cane brandy fortification, 66, 139
sugar merchants, 66

INDEX

sulphur dusting, 108, 109, 116
Sutcliffe, Serena, xx, 291
Sutherland, Douglas, xviii, xix
Sweden, Swedish market, 63, 125, 126. *See also* Scandinavia
sweets, Madeira and, 200
Symington, Ian, lvii
Symington family, lvi–lvii

T. T. da Câmara Lomelino. *See* Lomelino
tar, against phylloxera, 117
Tarragona, 93
tartrates, 144
tasting. *See also* enjoying Madeiras
  influences on, 144, 146, 199
tasting notes, 91–92, 191
  cellar books, 196
tasting panels, 114
tastings
  Academy of Ancient Madeira Wines (1959), xlviii–xlix, 163, 192–93
  American tastings, 82, 90–92, 290–91
  Averys (1960), xlix, 160–61, 164, 189
  Grand Tasting (1895), 191–92
  Habersham's skill at, 175–76
  1970s tastings of Cossart, Gordon wines, lii–liii, 193–94
Tatler, xxxviii–xxxix, lix, 273, 276
Taylor, James, 23
Teixeira, João, 216
Teixeyra, Tristão Vaz, 5–6, 10, 11, 261
temperance, Madeira and, 83–84
temperature
  ambient temperature when drinking Madeira, 146, 199
  for storage and serving, 146, 195, 199
Templer, C. R., 76, 77
Tent Madeiras, 100, 138, 290
Terrantez grape, xxxii, xxxiii–xxxiv, 99, 102, 104, 127
Terrantez Madeiras, 90, 91, 92, 96, 143, 287–88
  characteristics, 102, 162–63, 171, 217
  notable wines, 161, 162–64, 192, 193, 244, 293
  vintage notes, 212, 216, 217–18
Thomas, Douglas, 240–41
Thomas, Philip Evans, 240
Tierney, Edward, 49
Tierney Bart, Matthew, 49
Tinta da Madeira grape, 99
Tinta Madeiras, 93–94, 195, 212, 271, 298
  auction prices, 237, 239
  Bianchi wines, 161, 189
Tinta Molar grape, 100
Tinta Negra Mole grape, 110, 138, 147, 151
  in blends, 146, 147
  characteristics, xxxiii, 100, 127
  origins, 99–100, 298
Tinto Madeiras, 100, 138, 290
Tintoreto Madeiras, 138, 290
Tipsy Cake, 200
Tomaz, Sr., 154

tools, agricultural, 18–19
Torre Bella, Russell Manners Gordon, Viscount of, xl, 53, 55, 118, 157, 245
Torre Bella family, 55, 239
Torre Bella Madeiras, xxiii, 157–58, 163, 192–93, 239
Torre Bella vineyards, 55, 157, 239
tourism, 26, 29–30, 123, 279
  Nicholas travel piece, 280–86
  shipboard wine sales, 172–73
Trafalgar, Battle of, 44
Treatise on the Discoveries of the World (Galvão), 33–34
trellising, 107–8
Trevelyan, Walter Calverley, 155
Triunfo, 99
Truck Madeira, 81
tufa soils, 18, 106
tuna fishing, 25, 26
turpentine, against phylloxera, 117
turtle soup, 188, 200

U.S. market. *See* North American market and trade
ukulele, 130
Underwood, John, 319n10
Underwood, Pat, 319n10
Ussher, Thomas, 277

Valero, Marquis de, 36
Val Pariso, Visconde, 162
Vanderbilt, Cornelius, 181, 183, 303
Vaz Teixeyra, Tristão, 5–6, 10, 11, 261
veal cooked in Sercial, 204
veal kidneys in Madeira sauce, 203
Veiga França Lda., 70
Veitch, Henry, 38, 46–47, 209, 298, 322n49
  Funchal house of, *xxxix*, 47
  and Napoleon Madeira, lix, 155, 274, 275–76, 278
Verdelho grape, xxxiii, 72, 99, 110, 153
  in blended Madeiras, 146, 147
  characteristics, 100, 127
  winemaking, 132, 133
Verdelho Madeiras, 39, 82, 122, 146, 147, 322n48. *See also* Rainwater Madeira
  bottle storage, 195–96
  characteristics, 148, 149, 171, 195
  notable post-phylloxera wines, 160, 192, 194
  notable pre-phylloxera wines, 157, 158, 162, 170, 187, 192, 193
  prices, 202
  serving, 122, 199, 200
  vintage notes, 211–13, 215, 216, 217
Verdelho Tinto grape, 99
Verdia, 100
"Verses composed at the request of Jane Wallas Penfold" (Wordsworth), 208–9
Vespucci, Amerigo, 71
Vidal, Francisco Perry, 111
Vidonia, 100. *See also* Verdelho grape
Vieira, Alberto, xxiv

Vila, 110
vinegar, 198
vines and vineyards. *See* Madeira vines and vineyards; viticulture and winemaking
vinho abafado, 132
vinho americana, 104
vinho canteiro, xxix, 134, 147, 153, 187
vinho claro, 107, 132, 133, 140
vinho da corda, 129, 131
vinho da roda, xxix, 75, 134, 153. *See also* East India Madeira; sea-voyage conditioning; West India Madeira
vinho de lenço, 92, 202
vinho estufado. *See estufagem*
vinho generoso, 140, 141
vinho madre, vinho matriz, 167
vinho quinado, 77–78
vinho seco, 111
vinho surdo, 132, 133
viniculture. *See* winemaking
vintage Madeiras, 133, 141, 147, 153–66. *See also* Solera Madeiras; tastings; *specific types of Madeira*
  auction prices, 1971—2009, 221–35
  conversion to soleras, 167–68
  at Grand Tasting of 1895, 192
  labelling rules, 150–51
  Madeira's longevity, xxviii, 153–54
  notable collections, 185–90
  notable sales, 1970s—2008, 237–44
  preservation of old wines, 154
  prices, 202
  vintage notes, 211–18
vintages, 38–39, 92, 102
  false dating, 95–96, 172
  full list with notes (1774-1956), 211–13
  oidium, phylloxera and, 121
  tasting notes (1863-1981), 215–18
viticulture and winemaking, xxvii–xxviii. *See also* Madeira vines and vineyards; Madeira winemaking
  ancient Rome, 108, 135, 153
  California, 36, 119, 125, 291
Vitis clinton, 103
Vitis labrusca, 87, 104, 111, 117, 119
  hybrids, 104–6, 110–11
Vitis riparia, 103, 119
Vitis rupestris, 103, 119
Vitis solanis, 103
Vitis taylor, 103
Vitis vinifera, 119. *See also specific varieties*
  American hybrids, 104–6, 110–11
Viuva Abudarham & Filhos, lvii, 61, 67, 215, 293
Vizetelly, Henry, 61, 118, 142, 153, 164, 168–69, 319*n*1
  and Napoleon Madeira, 319*n*1
Vogué, Marquis de, 25
volatile acidity, 136
Volstead Act, 124. *See also* Prohibition

Waldo, Cornelius (older), 296
Waldo, Cornelius (younger), 296
Wallas (Robert) & Co., 209
Wallas, Robert, 66
Walters (T. W.) & Co., 87
Washington, George, 80
water, 19–20, 23, 24. *See also* irrigation
Waterloo Madeiras, 92, 156–57, 170, 172, 186
Watney, Dr., 84
wax seals, 190, 196
Wayne, Anthony, 89
weaving, 12
Webster, Daniel, 80, 87
Webster, Gordon, Cossart and Co., xl
Wellington, Arthur Wellesley, Duke of, 190
Welsh, George, 25
Welsh & Cunha, xli, 52, 67
Welsh Brothers, 52, 67
West India Madeira, xxix, 81–82, 134, 145, 147
West Indies, Madeira exports to, 34–35, 40
White, Robert, 115
wicker work, 23
Wilbraham, H. S., 245
Wildes, Harry Emerson, 89
Wilhelm II of Germany, 123
Wilkinson, Frank, 120
Wilkinson, Robert, 120
Williams, Stanley, xlviii
willows, 23
Wilmington and Northern Railway, 97
winds, 17, 277–78
Wine and Food (quarterly), 289
Wine and Food (Simon), 289
Wine and Food Society, 40, 276
winemaking, xxvii–xxviii. *See also* Madeira winemaking
wine merchants. *See* Madeira merchants; *specific firms and individuals*
A Wine Primer (Simon), 94, 95
Wines of the World (Simon), xx
"A wine that shines from soup to nuts" (Peck and Aaron), 202–3
Wine Trade Annual, 54
Wordsworth, William, 208–9
World War I, xli, 123–24
World War II, xlv–xlvi

Yates, Jasper, 86
York Madeira grape, 87, 104

Zachy's sales, 221–36, 242, 243
Zarco, João Gonçalves, 71, 256, 257, 284, 319*n*7
  as governor, 10–11
  rediscovery of Madeiras, 5–6, 9, 12, 321*n*31
Zino, Horace, 288
Zita (empress of Austria), 57